W9-CIA-881

The Fractured Marketplace for Standardized Testing

Evaluation in Education and Human Services

Editors:

George F. Madaus, Boston College,
  Chestnut Hill, Massachusetts, U.S.A.

Daniel L. Stufflebeam, Western Michigan
  University, Kalamazoo, Michigan, U.S.A.

**National Commission on Testing
and Public Policy**

Gifford, B.; *Test Policy and the Politics of
  Opportunity Allocation: The Workplace and
  the Law*

Gifford, B.; *Test Policy and Test Performance:
  Education, Language, and Culture*

Gifford, B., and Wing, L.; *Test Policy in
  Defense*

Gifford, B., and O'Connor, M.; *Changing
  Assessments, Alternative Views of Aptitude,
  Achievement, and Instruction*

Gifford, B.; *Policy Perspectives on
  Educational Testing*

The Fractured Marketplace for Standardized Testing

Walter M. Haney
Boston College

George F. Madaus
Boston College

Robert Lyons
University of California at Berkeley

Kluwer Academic Publishers
Boston/ Dordrecht/ London

Distributors for North America:
Kluwer Academic Publishers
101 Philip Drive
Assinippi Park
Norwell, Massachusetts 02061 USA

Distributors for all other countries:
Kluwer Academic Publishers Group
Distribution Centre
Post Office Box 322
3300 AH Dordrecht, THE NETHERLANDS

Library of Congress Cataloging-in-Publication Data

Haney, Walt.
    The fractured marketplace for standardized testing / Walter M. Haney,
George F. Madaus, Robert Lyons.
       p.   cm. -- (Evaluation in education and human services)
    Includes bibliographical references and index.
    ISBN 0-7923-9338-4
    1. Employment tests--Standards--United States. 2. Employment
tests--Economic aspects--United States. 3. Educational tests and
measurements--Standards--United States. 4. Educational tests and
measurements--Economic aspects--United States. 5. Ability--Testing-
-Government policy. 6. Ability--Testing--Economic aspects.
I. Madaus, George F. II. Lyons, Roberts, 1965- . III. Title.
IV. Series.
HF5549.5.E5H36   1993
658.3'1125--dc20   93-21880
                                                                              CIP

Printed on acid-free paper.

Printed in the United States of America

Contents

Preface   xi

1 INTRODUCTION   1

2 THE TESTING INDUSTRY   7

The Major Companies   11
The Medium-Sized Companies   27
Small Publishers   36
The Secondary Industry   37
Military Testing   40
Other Players   47
The Fractured Market   52

3 THE EXTENT OF THE MARKETPLACE
  FOR TESTS   57

Direct Indicators of Growth in Educational
    Testing   59
Indirect Indicators of Growth in
    Educational Testing   66
The Extent of Standardized Testing
    in the Employment Sector   79
The Expanding Marketplace for Testing   92

4 SOCIAL INVESTMENT IN
  EDUCATIONAL TESTING   93

Costs and Benefits: What Are We Talking About?   96
The Cost Structure of Educational Testing   98
An Estimated Testing Cost Function   109
Comparing Costs and Benefits at the Margin   119
The Benefits of Testing   120

5 FORCES BEHIND THE TESTING
  MARKETPLACE   125

Dissatisfaction and Reform   126
Legislation   133
The Focus on Outcomes of Schooling   149
Bureaucratization of Education   152
New Forces   155

6 SPIN-OFFS FROM THE TESTING
   INDUSTRY   159
      The Computer Connection   159
      Test Preparation and Coaching   174
      Honesty Testing   184

7 TEST QUALITY AND THE FRACTURED
   MARKETPLACE FOR TESTING   189
      Quality in Testing   189
      The Lake Wobegon Phenomenon   190
      The Marketing of Tests and Related Services   193
      The RFP Process   204
      Computer-Based Test Interpretation   216
      Test Preparation and Coaching   221
      Minor Mold or Major Blight?   230

8 MENDING THE FRACTURED
   MARKETPLACE   247
      Fractures in the Testing Marketplace   247
      Recent Proposals for New National Tests   255
      Strategies for Mending the Fractured
             Marketplace   271
      Conclusion   292

References   295

Appendices
      1 Estimation of Number of Students Tested in   319
             State-Mandated Testing Programs
      2 Consumer Price Index Adjustments   325
             for Inflation
      3 Calculation of Standardized Growth   327
             Expectations (SGEs)

Index   331

LIST OF FIGURES AND TABLES

LIST OF FIGURES

Figure No.	Title	Page
Figure 3.1:	Numbers of States Authorizing Minimum Competency Testing and Assessment Programs	68
Figure 3.2:	Standardized Test Sales, 1955-1990, in millions of 1988 dollars	69
Figure 3.3:	Revenues of Four Testing Companies	72
Figure 3.4:	Price Per Test Booklet in 1988 Dollars	73
Figure 3.5:	Answer Sheet and Scoring Costs in 1988 Dollars	74
Figure 3.6:	Education Index Listings Under Testing and Curriculum	75
Figure 3.7:	Business Periodicals Index Listings Under Testing	92
Figure 4.1:	Hypothetical Benefit Function for District Testing	121
Figure 4.2:	Relationship Between Total and Marginal Functions	123
Figure 6.1:	Revenue Growth for Stanley H. Kaplan Educational Centers and Princeton Review	184
Figure 7.1:	Average Standardized Growth Expectations, Total Reading and Total Math	235

LIST OF TABLES

Table No.	Title	Page
Table 1.1:	Initial Set of Results of Computerized Search of ERIC	3
Table 1.2:	Second Set of Results of Computerized Search of ERIC	4
Table 2.1:	Major Companies in the Testing Marketplace	12-13
Table 2.2:	Number of Tests for Publishers with Ten or More Tests Listed in Tests in Print (TIP)	30-31
Table 2.3:	Content Areas Tested by the ASVAB	44
Table 2.4:	AFQT Mental Category Ranges	45
Table 2.5:	Kinds of Tests in Print	53
Table 3.1:	Numbers of Tests Given Annually in Late 1980s in Education Sector	61
Table 3.2:	Extent of Testing in Military Public Sector	80
Table 3.3:	Workload Report for Federal Examinations: Number of Applications, Selections, and Veterans Selected	82
Table 3.4:	Number of Persons Tested in State and Local Civilian Public Sector	83
Table 3.5:	International Personnel Management Association Survey Results on Testing Methods	84
Table 3.6:	Number of Employment Tests in Private Sector	87
Table 3.7:	American Management Association 1990 Survey on Workplace Testing	90
Table 4.1:	The Cost Structure of the Texas Examination of Current Administrators and Teachers	101
Table 4.2:	Cost of State Assessment Programs, 1984	111

Table 4.3:   Price Data for Four Major   112-113
             Achievement Test Batteries

Table 4.4:   How We Estimate the Direct Costs   114
             of State and Local Testing Programs
             Per Student Per Test Hour

Table 4.5:   How We Estimate Per Hour   115-116
             Per Student Indirect Costs of Testing

Table 4.6:   Breakdown of Direct and Indirect Marginal   117
             Costs for State and Local Testing Programs

Table 4.7:   Total National Cost Estimates for State and   118
             District Testing Programs (millions of 1988 dollars)

Table 6.1:   Kinds of Psychware Products   168

Table 7.1:   Standardized Growth Expectations   234
             for Six Achievement Test Series

Table 7.2:   Percentages of Students Scoring Above National 236
             Median for Selected Grade Levels

Table 7.3:   Magnitude of Distortion in   244
             High-Stakes Test Results

PREFACE

This volume has had an extended gestation. Work on several aspects of what became this volume began in 1987 when Bernard Gifford asked Walt Haney and George Madaus, independently, to prepare papers for the National Commission on Testing and Public Policy of which Gifford was then Executive Director. Established with support from the Ford Foundation in 1987, the Commission was organized to conduct an analysis of the roles that standardized tests play in the allocation of educational, training and employment opportunities in the United States and to make recommendations regarding the future public policy roles of testing. However, after Gifford took leave from University of California at Berkeley to assume a position with Apple Computer, George Madaus was invited to become Executive Director of the Commission. Subsequently, Walt Haney, Ceasar McDowell, Pat Butler, Max West, Bob Lyons and Susanne Hanson at the Center for the Study of Testing, Evaluation and Educational Policy at Boston College assumed the bulk of staff work for the Commission. The report of the Commission entitled *From Gatekeeper to Gateway: Transforming Testing in America* (NCTPP, 1990) was released in May of 1990.

Though preliminary manuscripts for what became this book had been completed in 1989, staff work for the Commission diverted our attention from completing the manuscript. Then, in 1991 and 1992, several proposals for new tests and assessments appeared on the national educational scene. These developments seemed sufficiently important that we felt it vital to revise the manuscript for this book so as to take into account recent developments in the testing marketplace and in national discourse concerning testing and assessment. To some extent this has proven impossible because testing remains a prominent topic in national debates about education and the future of the U.S. economy. So if this book was ever to appear in print, we finally decided to end our story of the testing marketplace roughly around the summer of 1992. This decision may make it seem that some of what we have to say about the testing marketplace is not fully up to date when this volume appears in print. But we do not worry overmuch about this possibility, for if there is a single lesson to be learned from our review of the testing marketplace, it is simply that we must be more careful than we have in the past about relying too greatly on imperfect test instruments arising from the highly fractured market surrounding testing. If the recent past is any guide, this message will be of continuing relevance, as policy makers continue to try to use fallible test instruments for increasingly diverse purposes.

Since this book has had an extended gestation, there are large numbers of people to whom we owe thanks for prenatal care and assistance. Bernard Gifford and Linda Wing, original staff of the National Commission, are owed thanks for the impetus to start work on what became this book. Boston College staff for the Commission contributed in many ways to work leading up to this book, and we owe a special debt of appreciation to the distinguished members of the Commission itself who challenged and deepened our thinking about connections between testing and public policy. These members of the Commission were:

Bernard Gifford	José Cárdenas
Julius L. Chambers	Frederick Chang
Bill Clinton	Badi Foster
George Hanford	Katherine Hanson
Antonia Hernandez	W. W. Herenton
Francis Keppel	Robert Linn
Patricia Locke	Elridge McMillan
Edward Potter	Thomas Sticht
Glenn Watts	

Apart from the work of the Commission, numerous people were helpful to us in digging out information from obscure and unpublished source materials, including: Linda Murphy of the Buros Institute; Wayne Camara of the American Psychological Association; Kevin Gonzalez of the Information Services office of the Educational Testing Service; Pat Farrant of the Public Affairs office of the American College Testing Program; Don Elkind of the

Association of American Publishers; Robert Winter, statistician for the
Association of American Publishers; Daniel Hoerl of the Scanning Systems
Division of Associated Business Products; Michael Feuer of the Office of
Technology Assessment of the Congress of the United States; Steve Ivens,
formerly with the College Board and now with TASA; Anne Jungeblut of the
Educational Testing Service; Daniel Koretz of RAND; Charles Sproule of
IPMA; Ed Roeber of the Council of Chief State School Officers; Al Kaufman of
the Mexican American Legal Defense and Education Fund; Steve Mathews of
PRO-ED; Susan Dunn Weinberg of Western Psychological Services; Gary Putka
of the *Wall Street Journal*; W.S. Sellman of the Office of Assistant Secretary of
Defense; Michael Sokal of the Worcester Polytechnic Institute; Robert Stonehill
of the U.S. Department of Education; Alexandra Wigdor of the National
Research Council; Neil Kingston of Measured Progress; Robert Brennan and
Cynthia Schmeiser of the American College Testing Program; John Katzman of
the Princeton Review; Stanley Kaplan of Stanley H. Kaplan Educational
Centers; Christina DelValle of *Business Week*; and Larry Rudner of the
American Institutes for Research. Also thanks go to three reference librarians in
the Boston College O'Neill Library; Brendan Rapple, Barbara Mento and Marilyn
Grant, who helped us on numerous occasions.

Thanks are owed also to graduate and research assistants of the Center
for the Study of Testing, Evaluation and Educational Policy over the last several
years who have helped in tracking down source materials and references. These
include Amelia Kreitzer, Ann Tan, Sunaina Maira, James Tenero and Jennifer
Greben. Special thanks are owed to Stacey Raczek who helped in production of
page proofs for the book manuscript, and to Maria Sachs who provided us with
expert editorial assistance. We express our appreciation too to John Fremer of
the Educational Testing Service, Richard Murnane of Harvard University, and
Marc Breton and Dick Levins of the University of Minnesota who reviewed
portions of earlier versions of this manuscript and provided us with helpful
suggestions.

Finally we thank the Ford Foundation, and three present and former
officials there, Peter Stanley, Lynn Walker and Barbara Hatton, who helped us
not just through funding provided for the National Commission on Testing and
Public Policy and some of our subsequent work concerning testing, but also for
their continuing encouragement to address standardized testing issues from broad
public policy perspectives.

Though we thank all of these people for help and encouragement in preparing this book, none deserves responsibility for any shortcomings of this volume. Any errors of fact or interpretation must remain, as they should, solely the responsibilities of the authors.

W.H.

G.M.

R. L.

1 INTRODUCTION

Standardized testing in the United States has been increasing at a rapid pace in the last quarter century. The market for tests has not only been expanding rapidly, but also has been changing sharply in structure — into what we call a fractured marketplace. As the market has changed, the testing industry has been altered dramatically. Yet this industry has never received much serious scrutiny. This is odd not just because testing is becoming increasingly prominent in the social life of the United States but also because, as economists have long recognized, the structures of markets and industries have clear-cut implications for the prices and quality of the goods and services those industries provide. Under monopoly market conditions, businesses are relatively free to charge higher prices and garner higher profits than would be possible under free market conditions. Whether goods and services are provided by private or publicly controlled firms also has implications for the quality and costs of those goods and services.

The standardized testing industry as a whole does not fit neatly any one market archetype. Indeed, one of the main themes of this volume is that the market for standardized tests is highly fractured. In some segments of the testing marketplace, near monopoly market conditions prevail. In others, a relatively small number of firms have oligopolistic control. And in still others, near free-market conditions exist, with few if any barriers preventing new firms from developing and marketing new tests. Moreover, though the bulk of tests in the United States currently are the products of private free enterprise, federal and state government policies since the 1950s have been dramatically altering the standardized testing business. Already we have several kinds of national — and some federal — tests shaping the lives of our nation's students and workers.

And currently there is much dispute about the extent to which government should control the construction and use of tests in the realms of both education and employment.

Later in this volume, we describe many of these developments. Here by way of introduction all we wish to point out is the general motivation that has spurred our inquiry. Our main premise has been that the structure of markets has strong implications for how those markets perform. Though this notion has been long accepted by economists, it is a perspective that has not greatly informed educational research. Sporadically over the last several decades attention has been devoted to the market structure of schools themselves, and there has been a fair amount of research into the textbook industry. In contrast, very little scholarly attention has been directed at the standardized testing industry. There have been a few previous studies on the standardized testing industry, which will be described later in this volume; but by way of illustrating our general point that the standardized testing industry has been little examined, we recount one of several different computerized literature searches that informed our inquiry.

This illustrative literature search employed the database developed by the Educational Resources Information Clearinghouse, widely known as ERIC. ERIC is a "national information system established in 1966 by the federal government to provide ready access to educational literature by and for educational practitioners and scholars" (Houston, 1986, p. x). The ERIC system catalogs a wide range of educational literature, including journal articles, research reports, and conference papers. For all documents referenced in the system, ERIC includes not just standard bibliographic information and abstracts, but also keywords or "descriptors" designed to help identify the major or minor topics treated in the documents indexed in ERIC.[1] In the last twenty-five years, ERIC has grown into the largest and best-indexed database on educational research in the United States, if not the world. In one of the searches undertaken in the process of preparing this book, we sought to identify documents indexed with the descriptors "standardized testing," "textbooks," and "industry."[2] A summary of results is shown below in Table 1.1.

---

[1] The ERIC system of controlled vocabulary descriptors is described in the *Thesaurus of ERIC Descriptors* (Houston, 1990).

[2] This search was conducted on-line via BRS/After Dark in July of 1990. Because the ERIC database is accessible via other means, for example laser disk, and via other vendors, for example, Dialog and Silver Platter,

**Table 1.1: Initial Set of Results of Computerized Search of
ERIC**

Descriptor	Number of ERIC Entries Indexed with Descriptor
"Standardized Tests"	3529
"Textbooks"	5260
"Industry"	8514

Source: On-line search of ERIC via BRS/After Dark, July of 1990

These results indicate that a large number of educational research reports and journal articles have dealt with each of these three topics over the last twenty-five years. However, when we put the first two descriptors together with the third a very different pattern emerged.

These results, shown in Table 1.2, reveal that while a fair amount has been written about the textbook industry in the United States over the last quarter century, remarkably little has been written about the standardized testing industry. Among the 145 documents on the textbook industry that were found, the following journal article titles suggest the topics addressed:

Behind Textbook Censorship

Complimentary Copies of Textbooks: A Short Trip from Publisher to Professor to Bookstore to Students

---

replications of this search by these other channels likely will yield slightly different results. It should also be noted that this one search did not identify all literature indexed in ERIC that is relevant to our topic. To use the ERIC system effectively, one must employ multiple search strategies. This one search is cited simply to illustrate how little has been written about the testing industry.

Table 1.2: Second Set of Results of Computerized Search of ERIC

Descriptor Combination	Number of ERIC Entries Indexed with Both Descriptors
"Textbooks" and "Industry"	145
"Standardized Tests" and "Industry"	7

Source: On-line search of ERIC via BRS/After Dark, July of 1990

The Culture and Commerce of the Textbook

Books and Bucks. The Economics of College Textbook Publishing

The Unacceptable Face of Publishing.

In contrast, none of the seven documents indexed under both the "standardized tests" and "industry" descriptors actually deal with the standardized testing industry in general.

This does not mean that nothing at all has been written on the standardized testing industry. Despite its size, ERIC by no means covers all educational research literature (for example, it does not cover books). In subsequent chapters we describe the literature on the testing industry as we recount our own findings, but for now we simply wish to point out that one of the chief reasons for our inquiry has been the remarkably scant previous attention given to the testing industry as a whole.

This topic — the structure of the testing industry and implications for the quality of tests and test use — is of considerable interest in and of itself. But the ramifications of standardized testing are far broader than might initially be apparent. As we will show, standardized tests have to an unprecedented degree become the coin of the educational realm, used not just to gauge the learning of individual students but also to evaluate the effectiveness of educational programs, the quality of schools and school systems and even the educational health of the nation. Thus the testing industry, though relatively small in strictly economic terms, has wide-ranging implications for our nation's educational system. Though test sales and other indicators of use of tests and related services have been increasing sharply, the direct costs of testing are only a fraction of the resources devoted to standardized testing.

The fragmentation of the growing testing marketplace raises serious questions about the quality of many tests and testing services. Of particular concern to us is one vital aspect of test quality, namely test validity. As we will show, recent developments in the testing marketplace appear to be undermining the valid interpretation and use of test results. Hence we argue that a variety of policy alternatives need to be seriously considered in order to help protect not just test takers and users, but also the broader educational and public interests of the nation.

These, in brief, are the main themes of this volume. After these introductory remarks, chapter 2 describes the testing marketplace — the large, medium and small companies that build tests and provide a variety of test-related services, as well as sponsors and users of tests. Chapter 3 recaps evidence on the extent of the marketplace for standardized tests and the recent growth in testing. Chapter 4 presents our estimates on the direct and indirect costs of standardized testing — arguing generally that the former are actually a minor portion of the total resources devoted to testing. Chapter 5 outlines some of the broad social forces behind the burgeoning market for standardized testing and auxiliary services. Chapter 6 describes some of the spin-off industries that have grown up around standardized tests. Chapter 7 discusses problems arising from the changing marketplace with regard to test quality and use. Finally, in chapter 8 we present alternative strategies that might be employed to improve the use and prevent the misuse of tests as instruments of social and educational policy. In particular, we discuss proposals that have arisen prominently in the last year to develop new national tests to be used for both educational and employment purposes.

Before turning to this itinerary, several important caveats and limitations of our study should be made clear. We use the term "standardized testing" quite broadly to refer to commercially prepared instruments designed to measure a wide range of traits (e.g. reading comprehension, problem solving skills, quantitative aptitude or personality characteristics). By "commercially prepared" we mean both tests sold for purchase by individuals and groups and tests that are constructed on contract or constructed in-house by government agencies or other large organizations, but that may not be sold commercially.

While this usage excludes locally prepared non-commercial tests, such as teacher-made tests, it does, as we will show, encompass the increasingly wide and varied uses to which commercially prepared and government sponsored tests are put in the United States.

We should point out also that the topic of standardized testing is very large and we cannot treat all aspects of it thoroughly in this one volume. For example, the history of standardized testing in the United States goes back more than a century. Similarly, topics of test development and scaling, test bias, fairness of test use, and legislation and litigation concerning tests all are important topics with respect to the current state of standardized testing in the United States. We will touch briefly on some aspects of these large topics in subsequent chapters as we analyze the testing marketplace, and we provide references to relevant literature, but we readily acknowledge that none of them is treated thoroughly here. We trust that this work may still be of interest to people concerned with these perspectives on standardized testing.

Finally, it has proven extremely difficult to find information on many aspects of the testing industry and the testing marketplace. Many companies, for example, treat data on test sales and revenues as proprietary information and will not release it. Similarly, basic descriptive data on some important government testing programs (e.g. the numbers of tests given and and how results are used) have proven unobtainable, in part because of government deregulation and cutbacks in government data gathering activities over the last decade. Thus for many aspects of the testing marketplace, we can provide only informed estimates. We will of course document our sources and methods of inquiry as thoroughly as possible, but in some cases we have been given information by industry insiders who asked that they not be quoted or cited by name. We attempt in this volume to rely on such unnamed sources sparingly, but the fact that some aspects of the testing marketplace are shrouded in such secrecy suggests the importance of our inquiry. For as standardized tests have become increasingly prominent instruments of educational and employment policies in the United States, we need to understand something of the market conditions that lead to their creation, sales and application.

2 THE TESTING INDUSTRY

A definitive analysis of the testing industry in the United States describing how standardized testing grew from a fairly obscure academic enterprise in the late 19th century into a major commercial endeavor in this century has yet to be written. Over the last fifty years there has been a variety of treatments of various segments of the testing marketplace. A few analysts have provided relatively broad accounts of the industry (e.g. Holmen & Docter, 1972; Kohn, 1977; Fremer, 1989). Several people have written sketchy accounts of the history of standardized testing in the United States in general (Cronbach, 1975; Haney, 1981, 1984), in education (Resnick 1981; Madaus & Kellaghan, 1992), in psychology (Sokal, 1987), and in employment (Hale, 1982). A number of histories have been written on particular testing programs (e.g. Ruger's 1975 history of the American College Testing Program; Peterson's 1983 history of the Iowa Testing Programs; Hazlett's 1974 and Greenbaum, Solomon & Garet's 1977 accounts of the early history of the National Assessment of Educational Progress), or on particular testing organizations (e.g. Nairn & Associates' 1980 history and critique of ETS; Sokal's 1981 account of the founding of the Psychological Corporation; Valentine's 1987 history of the College Board). Additionally, there have been a number of biographies of people important in the development of testing in the United States, such as Edward Lee Thorndike (Clifford, 1968), Lewis Terman (Chapman, 1980), G. Stanley Hall (Ross, 1972), James McKeen Cattell (Sokal, 1987b), and Walter Dill Scott (Mayrhauser, 1989).

Finally, since around 1960 there has been a steady stream of books and articles critical of standardized testing in general, and of particular testing companies (most often the Educational Testing Service). This genre of literature goes back at least to the 1920s and Walter Lippmann's criticism of some of the interpretations of results of World War I tests. Easily the most famous critical work on testing from the early 1960s was Banesh Hoffmann's (1962) *The Tyranny of Testing*. However, numerous other attacks on testing, in the popular periodical literature, in books, and in hearings before the U.S. Congress, appeared in the 1960s. (See Moughamian, 1965; Haney 1981; and Kellaghan, Madaus & Airasian, 1982, for reviews of critical literature from this period.) Since 1960, dozens of articles and books critical of educational and psychological testing have appeared, including:

- Martin Gross's *The Brain Watchers* (1962)
- Hillel Black's *They Shall Not Pass* (1964)
- Vance Packard's *The Naked Society* (1964)
- Brian Simon's *Intelligence, Psychology and Education* (1971)
- Joel Spring's *The Sorting Machine* (1976)
- Ned Block and Gerald Dworkin's *The IQ Controversy* (1976)
- Paul Hout's *The Myth of Measurability* (1977)
- J. Lawler's *IQ, Heritability and Racism* (1978)
- Allan Nairn and associates' *The Reign of ETS: The Corporation that Makes Up Minds* (1980)
- Mitch Lazarus's *Good-bye to Excellence: A Critical Look at the Minimum Competency Testing Movement* (1981)
- Stephen Jay Gould's *The Mismeasure of Man* (1981)
- Andrew Strenio's *The Testing Trap* (1981)
- David Owens' *None of the Above* (1985)
- James Crouse and Dale Trusheim's *The Case Against the SAT* (1988).

Yet even the critics of standardized testing (except for Kohn's sketchy 1977 treatment) have not undertaken a serious analysis of the testing industry. Rather they tend to share the critical approach taken by Banesh Hoffmann more than a quarter century ago. Hoffmann observed that "test-making has developed into a large, lucrative and increasingly competitive business" (Hoffmann, 1962, p. 37). He even identified the top testing companies as ETS, the Psychological Corporation, Science Research Associates, California Test Bureau, and Harcourt, Brace and World (p. 40). Yet Hoffmann aimed his critique primarily at one company and its tests, namely the Educational Testing Service. He explained:

> I have focused the main attack on the Educational Testing
> Service for a reason that is complimentary to that
> organization: one makes the strongest case by criticizing the
> best test-makers, not the worst. (p. 209)

Academics who write about educational and psychological testing
similarly have given little attention to the commercial side of testing.
Textbooks on testing by such authors as Lee Cronbach (1984) and Anne
Anastasi (1988) virtually ignore the structure of the testing industry (save for
listings of companies through which tests are made available), and even the
National Research Council, although it undertook a major study of testing in the
early 1980s and successfully compiled a two-volume report on the uses,
consequences, and controversies of testing (Wigdor & Garner, 1982), gave
absolutely no account of the commercial side of testing, or of the structure of the
industry.

There appear to be several reasons for these omissions. One is that the
industry is large and diverse. *Tests In Print III* or *TIP3* (Mitchell, 1983), for
example, listed 565 publishers of 2,672 tests. However, the TIP figures exclude
many tests developed for or by government agencies, or individual companies for
their own use, since TIP covers only "commercially published" tests. Literally
hundreds of tests exist that are not commercially published. Johnson and
Bommarito (1971), for instance, prepared a handbook on 300 unpublished tests
available for use with children and youth. When Heyneman and Mintz (1976)
reviewed 3,500 proposals for research on children and youth submitted to federal
agencies in fiscal year 1975, they identified some 1,500 different test titles, only
about a third of which could be found in standard bibliographies such as the TIP
series. Thus, it is clear that the making and distribution of tests represents a
large and diverse enterprise.

A second reason for lack of scrutiny of the testing industry is that
because some kinds of test publishing are highly competitive markets,
information on sales is often a closely guarded secret. Here, for example, is part
of Kohn's account of his effort to investigate the testing industry more than a
decade ago:

> I questioned key officials in the field's half-dozen dominant
> firms, and none was willing or able to estimate such
> elementary figures as the number of students tested annually in

the United States, the number of tests sold each year by
individual companies, or the economic boundaries of the
industry. None would even reveal how many of his firm's
tests were scored annually. (Kohn, 1977, p. 171)

Similarly, when New York Senator Kenneth LaValle introduced
hearings on a proposed bill to regulate testing in the state of New York, he
asserted that:

The testing industry has shrouded itself in a mantle of secrecy
that leaves it unaccountable to the public who should be able
to . . . independently assess the accuracy and validity of its
product. (New York Senate and Assembly Standing
Committees on Higher Education, 1979, pp. 3-4)

A third factor is that many individuals and companies involved in
testing like to view it as a scientific or academic enterprise rather than a
commercial venture. One of the clearest indicators of this tendency is the way in
which the Educational Testing Service (which, as we will show below, is the
largest testing company in the United States according to most indicators)
describes itself not as a testing business or company, but as an educational
service and research organization. For instance, when a new building was
dedicated in 1988 in honor of former ETS president William Turnbull, he was
lauded as one who "guided the organization through a period when it shifted from
a testing organization working primarily in the field of education to an
educational organization working through the medium of measurement and
assessment" (*ETS Developments*, Fall 1988, p. 12). Similarly, ETS's academic
claims can be seen in its referring to its headquarters as a campus and using the
title of "research scientists" for many of its employees.

Whatever the reasons for the notable lack of attention to the structure of
testing industry in the past, we think it is a subject vital to understanding the
current role of testing in the United States. Hence, in this chapter, we discuss
the most visible part of the testing industry, including the major, medium, and
small test producers; the secondary industry; government sponsors of tests; and
other players in this market. Later, in chapter 6, we discuss some of the spinoff
industries that have developed around testing.

It has long been recognized that a relatively small number of testing
companies account for the bulk of test sales. As previously noted, for example,

in the early 1960s Hoffmann identified the five largest testing companies as
ETS, the Psychological Corporation, Science Research Associates, California
Test Bureau, and Harcourt, Brace and World (Hoffmann, 1962, p. 40). Buros
(1974) reported that in the early 1970s just 45 publishers with ten or more tests
accounted for 65% of the tests in print (Buros, TIP2, 1974, p. xxxiii).
Similarly, Holmen and Docter in their 1972 study identified six major publishers
as accounting for three-quarters of all tests sold, and another 22 medium-size
publishers as dominating the remainder of the commercial market (pp. 27-29).
More recently Fremer (1989) identified six major testing firms with the largest
revenues (ETS, National Computer Systems, CTB/McGraw Hill, the
Psychological Corporation, American College Testing Program, and Riverside
Publishing).

In many respects these conclusions about domination of the testing
marketplace by a relatively small number of firms remain true today. Thus, our
discussion of the testing industry in this chapter offers brief descriptions of the
large, medium and small testing companies. However, in addition to the
corporate entities that make up the obvious testing industry there are a number
of other players, including firms that build tests on contract for other agencies,
and a wide range of other test sponsors and users. These too are discussed in this
chapter.

THE MAJOR COMPANIES

As mentioned, Holmen and Docter (1972) identified six companies as
the largest in the testing industry, and more recently Fremer (1989) listed the six
largest companies in terms of revenue. These two listings differ somewhat.
Holmen and Docter, for example, had listed Science Research Associates (SRA)
as a major commercial test publisher, but according to Fremer (1989), "SRA has
not kept up with the other companies" (p. 63) — and as we explain below, SRA
has recently become a subsidiary of a larger publishing conglomerate and its
tests are distributed by CTB (formerly, California Test Bureau). Our research has
led us to identify seven major testing companies, each with estimated annual
gross revenues, mainly from the testing business, of $15 million or more —
though it is often extremely difficult to ascertain how much revenue companies
derive from testing sales and services as opposed to other activities. Our listing

Table 2.1: Major Companies in the Testing Marketplace

Company	Key Historical Facts	Corporate Status	Major Testing Activities
Educational Testing Service (ETS)	Founded 1947; one of 3 founding organizations was College Board	Independent, nonprofit	College, graduate, and admissions testing; credentialing; research
National Computer Systems (NCS)	Founded 1962; went public in 1968	Public company	Test scoring and machine sales; test development contracts; psychological tests
CTB	Founded 1926; purchased by McGraw Hill in 1965. Part of joint venture in 1989	Division of Macmillan/ McGraw Hill School Publishing Company	Elementary/ secondary group tests; credentialing programs
The Psychological Corporation (PsychCorp)	Founded 1921; forerunner World Book, founded in 1905. Purchased by HBJ in 1969	Subsidary of Harcourt Brace Jovanovich Public company HBJ purchased by General Cinema, 11/91	Elementary/ secondary group tests, psychological/ individual tests; speech/language; business tests
American College Testing Program (ACT)	Founded 1959	Independent, nonprofit	College admissions testing; credentialling research
Riverside Publishing Company	Entered testing field 1916	Subsidary of Houghton Mifflin, Public company	Elementary/ secondary group tests; psychological/ individual tests
Scantron	Founded 1972; Public Co. 1983 Acquired by J. Harland 1988	Subsidiary of John H. Harland Co.	Test scoring equipment, forms, secondary achievement tests

Sources: Holmen & Docter, 1972; Fremer, 1989; *Million Dollar Directory*, 1990; *Ward's Business Directory of Private and Public Companies*, 1989; company catalogs; anonymous interviews.

Table 2.1: Major Companies (cont'd)

Company	Company Sales 1987 or '88	1972 Ranking by Holmen & Docter	1986 Ranking by Fremer (1989)
Educational Testing Service (ETS)	$226 million	1	1
National Computer Systems (NCS)	$242 million	Unranked	2
CTB	$50-$60 million	4	3.5
The Psychological Corporation (PsychCorp)	$50-$55 million	2	3.5
American College Testing Program (ACT)	$53 million	Unranked	5
Riverside Publishing Company	$15-25 million	5	6
Scantron	$35 million	Unranked	Unranked

of major testing companies is highly similar to Fremer's (1989) account, the major difference being that we have added Scantron. Table 2.1 summarizes information on theses seven firms, in terms of key historical facts, corporate status, major testing activities and revenues for 1987 or 1988. Additional data on these companies are provided in Table 2.2, discussed later in this chapter.

Data on annual revenues have been particularly hard to find for three of these companies, namely CTB, the Psychological Corporation, and Riverside. There are several reasons for this. Each of these companies is a subsidiary of a much larger firm, and annual reports for the parent companies usually do not show disaggregated data for the subsidiaries. Moreover, officials of these companies tend to view data on sales as proprietary and are generally willing to discuss them only in very general and oblique fashion. Thus our data on sales for some of the big seven testing companies are merely estimates.

1. The Educational Testing Service (ETS)

ETS is, according to most indicators, the largest testing company in the country. An independent nonprofit company, it was established less than 50 years ago.[1] The flagship test of ETS, namely the Scholastic Aptitude Test or SAT, actually has a much longer lineage than ETS itself.

At the turn of the century the college standards for admission were so diverse as to be anarchic. College-bound students had to take different exams — and sometimes pursue different courses of study — for each college to which they sought admission. These conditions gave rise to the founding of the College Entrance Examination Board in 1900. The Board's first common college entrance tests, essay in form, were administered in areas such as English, history, Greek, and Latin beginning in 1901. After widespread popular publicity given to intelligence testing with multiple-choice exams in the early 1920s (Haney, 1984), the Board appointed a committee of experts to advise it on the suitability of developing multiple-choice tests for use in college admissions. Among members of the advisory panel were Robert Yerkes and Carl Brigham, then professors of psychology at Yale and Princeton Universities respectively. Yerkes had headed the U.S. Army testing program during World War I, discussed later. Brigham, who also had worked in the WWI testing program, was named to head the Board's effort to try out the new multiple-choice tests. This resulted

---

[1] More detail on the history of ETS is provided by Nairn & Asssociates (1980), from a largely critical perspective, and by Donlon (1984) and Valentine (1987), from largely uncritical perspectives.

in the administration of the new Scholastic Aptitude Test, for the most part multiple-choice in format, to 8000 candidates in June of 1926.

Over the next few decades several innovations were introduced in the SAT, but the crucial event in the subsequent prominence of this test was the outbreak of World War II. With the onset of war and the need for accelerating college studies, the essay exams used by the College Board for more than forty years were abandoned. Initially this move was viewed as temporary, but after the war and studies showing that the multiple-choice SAT could predict college performance as well as essay exams, the latter were not reintroduced.

After WWII, as a result of a proposal to "merge the testing activities of the Board with those of the Carnegie Foundation for the Advancement of Teaching and the American Council on Education" (Valentine, 1987, p. 55), the Educational Testing Service was founded in 1947. Fueled by not just the testing operations of its parent organizations, but also acquisition of key staff (Henry Chauncey, then director of the College Board, resigned to become ETS's first president) and substantial capital, ETS has grown to become the most influential testing company in the United States. According to TIP2 (Buros, 1974), for example, ETS ranked first in the country in terms of numbers of tests published (130). Nonetheless, as Buros explained, the number of tests ETS officially published underestimated the influence of this testing giant:

> Although listed separately, Educational Testing Service includes Cooperative Tests and Services and Educational Records Bureau. Since ETS also constructs all CEEB tests, the ETS conglomerate is represented by 315 tests, 14.3 percent of the tests published in the United States. (Buros, 1974, p. xxxiv)

According to TIP3 (Mitchell, 1983), ETS published 207 tests, again leading to a No. 1 ranking for ETS; and according to a database developed to prepare the forthcoming TIP4 (Murphy, 1990), ETS now publishes 225 tests. But the number of tests ETS publishes itself or constructs for others still does not adequately reflect its influence. Some ETS tests are now distributed by other publishers (for example, the Sequential Tests of Educational Progress, created and copyrighted by ETS but distributed by CTB). Additionally, ETS creates some of the most widely taken tests in the country, including the SAT, the Graduate Record Examination, and the National Teachers Examination. Since

ETS is by far the most visible and well known of the testing companies, it has been the principal target for critics of testing (including Hoffmann, 1962; Nairn & Associates, 1980; Strenio, 1981; Owen, 1985; and Crouse & Truesheim, 1988). However, what ETS's critics sometimes lose sight of is that its tests, according to independent reviews published in the Buros and Mitchell *Mental Measurements Yearbook* (MMY) series, are among some of the better tests published and that less prominent publishers of lower-quality tests may deserve more severe criticism.

Also, though the firm is called the *Educational* Testing Service, it has very little market share in the the the pre-college elementary/high school, or Elhi, market. ETS did create the Sequential Tests of Educational Progress (STEP) tests, which were meant to compete with the widely used and older Elhi test batteries marketed by other publishers. However, ETS sold the marketing rights to the STEP series to Addison Wesley, apparently at least in part because it lacked a marketing and sales force with which to compete in the Elhi market. And more recently, as a result of corporate reorganizations and mergers in the publishing industry, CTB acquired the rights to market the STEP series.

But however small the presence of ETS in the Elhi market, it unquestionably is the one of the giants in the testing industry in this country and internationally. ETS's gross revenues have been increasing rapidly in recent years, growing from $107 million in 1980 to $226 million in 1988 and $300 million in 1990. Over the last 20 years, 85-90% of ETS total revenues have consistently come from the testing services it provides to the College Board and other clients (more detailed data of ETS revenue growth is presented in chapter 3).

ETS's prominence in testing is probably underestimated by both of these quantitative measures (numbers of tests published and revenues) because as a major research organization, ETS takes part in research on testing and education more generally. ETS researchers have, for example, made substantial contributions to the field of testing on topics ranging from theories of test validation to methods for test equating and scaling. An indication of ETS's prominence in this regard is available in Rudner, Stonehill, Childs, and Dupree's (1990) compilation of the affiliations of authors of documents accepted by the Educational Resources Information Clearinghouse on Tests, Measurement and Evaluation (ERIC/TME). They found that of documents accepted by ERIC/TME during a recent 18-month period, more came from people affiliated with ETS than with any of around 800 other organizations from which submissions to ERIC/TME came. The American College Testing Program, described below, was the only other test publisher to rank in the top 20 contributors to ERIC/TME.

Thus on three separate grounds, the Educational Testing Service of Princeton, New Jersey, is the pre-eminent testing company in the United States. It publishes more tests than any other firm. It has more revenues from testing than any other firm. Its employees contribute more to the professional literature on testing than those of any other firm. And perhaps not surprisingly, ETS has become something of a lightning rod for critics of standardized testing.

2. National Computer Systems (NCS)

NCS emerged relatively recently as one of the major players in the testing market, and illustrates several important developments in the testing marketplace, including its increasingly diverse nature. Though mentioned by Holmen and Docter (1972) as a major test scoring company, NCS is described in Fremer's (1989) analysis as a major testing company more generally. According to the *Ninth Mental Measurements Yearbook* (9MMY, Mitchell, 1985), NCS appears to be a relatively minor player, with only 11 entries in 9MMY. According to company annual reports, NCS total annual revenues grew from $35 million in 1980 to $284 million in 1990. Thus it appears that at least in terms of total revenues, NCS may have come to rival ETS in the testing marketplace — though it should be noted that not as large a portion of NCS's revenues derive directly from testing activities. More information on trends in NCS revenues will be presented in chapter 3.

NCS was founded as a corporation in Minnesota in 1962 and became a publicly held company in 1968 (it is listed over the counter, with the ticker symbol NLCS). According to Holmen and Docter (1972, p. 101), test scoring then accounted for 70% of NCS's data processing activity, and scoring of survey forms for the remaining 30%. Since then NCS's role has expanded to include test publishing and contracted test development. In addition to its work in the education and business markets, NCS also markets its scanning services and systems to the banking industry.

According to NCS's 1991 annual report, "more than 85% of the nation's 1,000 largest school districts use NCS scanning systems and forms for local test scoring" (p. 6). NCS also reports that it "scores the majority of all state assessment tests" in its Iowa City service bureau (formerly Lindquist's

MRC) and also that NCS scanning systems and services are provided to "70% of the nation's largest post-secondary institutions" (p. 9).

NCS markets the well-known and widely used *Minnesota Multiphasic Personality Inventory* (MMPI), which is one of the most frequently cited tests in the published research literature (see Mitchell, 1983, p. xxvii).[2] Other tests published by NCS include the Career Assessment Inventory, the Interest Determination, Exploration and Assessment System, and the Millon Clinical Multiaxial Inventory. Thus in terms of direct test publishing, NCS specializes in the psychological and guidance/counseling sectors as opposed to educational, college admissions or certification testing. However, NCS continues to derive its revenues not so much from its own tests as from the testing work it does for others. As an independent public company that subsumed the Measurement Research Center at the University of Iowa (where one of the first large-capacity optical test scoring machines was invented; Baker, 1971), NCS scores tests, sells test scoring machines, and does testing contract work for state agencies and others.[3] Scanning and psychological testing accounted for an estimated $136 million in NCS revenue in 1986 (Eberstadt Fleming, Inc., in Cicchetti, 1988). In 1991, as an extension of its work in OMR scanning, NCS introduced a high-speed computer imaging system.

NCS's emergence as a major player in the testing marketplace thus illustrates two major trends. Increasingly, the market appears to be fracturing so that for a given test, different organizations can be involved in the sponsorship, development, administration, scoring, interpretation and use of results. Also, NCS's recent growth indicates the increasing importance of computer technology in the testing marketplace, including the use of computers not just to score test results but also to produce reports "interpreting" test results, as will be discussed in more detail in chapter 7.

3. California Test Bureau (CTB)

The California Test Bureau has long been recognized as one of the major players in the testing marketplace. The firm was founded by Ethel Clark

---

[2] The actual "publisher" of the MMPI is the University of Minnesota.

[3] In 1968, with the impending retirement of its founder and president, E. F. Lindquist, the Measurement Research Center was sold for approximately $5 million to the Westinghouse Learning Corporation, a subsidiary of Westinghouse Electric. In 1983, Westinghouse sold its Iowa City subsidiary to NCS for approximately $10 million (Peterson, 1983; Anonymous, NCS acquired unit of Westinghouse, 1984).

in 1926. TIP1 (Buros, 1961) reported that CTB published 63 tests -- or roughly 3% of tests published in the United States at the time. The publishing giant McGraw Hill, which previously had been involved in a small way with testing, purchased CTB in 1965 (Holmen & Docter, 1972), and since then CTB has been widely known as CTB/McGraw Hill. In 1989 Maxwell Communication Corp. attempted a takeover of McGraw Hill. To forestall this attempt, an agreement was reached whereby a new company called Macmillan/McGraw-Hill School Publishing Company was formed (Maxwell had previously acquired Macmillan). As part of that agreement, the tests owned and published by Science Research Associates (a Maxwell company) were transferred to CTB (Lublin, 1989). London House, a Maxwell company that markets tests for the business field and had been identified by Fremer as a smaller testing company, was part of the agreement but remains a separate division within the new consortium, as does CTB.[4] We estimate that CTB's annual revenues were in the neighborhood of $50-60 million in 1988, though with the acquisition of the SRA tests in 1989, they may now be substantially higher.

TIP3 (Mitchell, 1983) lists 40 entries under CTB. The firm's two best-known products in the Elhi market are the California Achievement Test (CAT) and the Comprehensive Test of Basic Skills (CTBS) series. One source cites a CTB/McGraw Hill official as saying that in 1987 CTB sold 6 million achievement tests at a price of $2 (Gay, 1989, p. 2). According to surveys of test use over the last two decades, these two test series are among the most widely used not only by school districts and states, but also in program evaluation and in research on children and youth (Heyneman & Mintz, 1976; Gamel et al., 1975; Cannell, 1987, 1988). With the acquisition of SRA's tests

---

[4] The new Macmillan/McGraw-Hill School Publishing Company combines all or part of nine companies owned by Maxwell Communications and/or McGraw-Hill into four groups. The nine companies are SRA, Macmillan School Publishing, Barnell-Loft, London House, Glencoe Press, CTB/McGraw Hill, Random House, parts of McGraw-Hill Book Publishing, and Gregg Division. In the new joint venture they are organized into four groups: (1) the Macmillan/McGraw-Hill School Division; (2) the SRA Division, which will consist of the former SRA School Division, the SRA Information Systems and Education Division, Education Resources, Barnell-Loft, and London House; (3) the CTB Division, which will incorporate the SRA testing division; and (4) the Glencoe/McGraw-Hill Educational Division, which will combine the operations of Gregg and Glencoe Press, which formerly produced secondary school materials (Rudman, 1990).

and marketing rights to the STEP test series, CTB is now clearly the largest player in the Elhi market. Holmen and Docter listed SRA as one of the six largest testing companies in their 1972 book, but in 1987 SRA did not make Fremer's list of the largest companies. Nonetheless, until the spinoff of its tests to the new Macmillan/McGraw-Hill School Publishing Company in 1989, SRA still had a significant share of the Elhi market with 13 entries in 9MMY (Mitchell, 1985). With the acquisition of the SRA tests, CTB now publishes four of the seven achievement test series most widely used in school systems of the United States (CTB publishes the CTBS, the CAT, the SRA, and the STEP achievement batteries; the only major achievement batteries not published by CTB are the Iowa, the Metropolitan, and the Stanford series). CTB also publishes a number of widely used diagnostic, special education, minority language and adult education tests, and markets computer software for school administration, test scoring and reporting, and test construction. In addition, CTB also builds a number of credentialing exams for organizations like the National Council of State Boards of Nursing.

Without question, CTB is a major player in the testing market. As such it exhibits three important developments in the testing marketplace in the last several decades, namely the acquisition of lucrative for-profit testing companies by larger companies, the increasing prominence of computer technology, and the trend toward contracted test development. In regard to the first trend, here is how Rudman, coauthor of a test series of another publisher, described the consequences of corporate mergers:

> Some new inexperienced parent companies . . . have replaced experienced publishers with new managers [and] have brought an emphasis upon "efficiency" and "profit" that in some instances has been neither efficient nor, in the long run, profitable.

> These new corporate managers have come on the scene just as political pressures have increased to use standardized tests to monitor "quality" of learning, teaching and other tangential uses (teacher recertification, student eligibility for participation in athletics, merit bonuses for teachers and the like). They have responded to these pressures by rushing to produce tests that will ostensibly meet purposes for which

they were never intended. At the present time, these practices occur in a minority of publishing firms, but they represent a large share of test users. (Rudman, 1987, p. 6)

4. The Psychological Corporation (PsychCorp)

PsychCorp is another long-time player in the testing arena. It was founded in 1921 by James McKeen Cattell with support from Edward Lee Thorndike and Robert Woodworth — all three of whom had been professors at Columbia University and leaders in the testing movement early in the 20th century. What PsychCorp was to do under Cattell's plan was "to act as a sort of publicity agent, referral service and supply company for applied psychology in its largest sense" (Sokal, 1981, p. 57). Under Cattell's leadership, the PsychCorp "established branches in many cities, usually those which had universities with strong psychology departments" (Sokal, 1981, p. 57). Cattell's new scheme apparently was greeted with enthusiasm among psychologists, for about half of the 400 members of the American Psychological Association subscribed for stock in the new corporation. Nevertheless, the first years were very rocky. Cattell failed to provide clear leadership to the branch offices of the new corporation and its income in the early 1920s was paltry. According to Sokal's (1981) account, the early years of the PsychCorp represented a failure of applied psychology. In 1926 Cattell resigned as President and was replaced by Walter Bingham, a more pragmatically minded psychologist. Paul Achilles, an industrial psychologist and colleague of Bingham, became secretary of the corporation. Under Achilles' leadership the PsychCorp gradually began to prosper. Here is how Holmen and Docter summarized its early evolution:

> Originally the company was to act as a clearinghouse to render expert services involving the application of psychology to education and business. The clearinghouse plan did not work out well, so in the late 1920s, the corporation, under the leadership of Paul Achilles, became a supplier of psychological services and then of psychological tests. So that the American Psychological Association (APA) could exercise ethical control over the company's operations, it was given the perpetual right to buy all the company's stock. The need for APA monitoring evidently decreased until in 1947 the

APA waived its option rights in favor of a provision limiting
stock ownership to psychologists. In late 1969, Harcourt
Brace Jovanovich purchased the corporation's stock and made it
a subsidiary. (Holmen & Docter, 1972, p. 35)

Harcourt Brace Jovanovich (HBJ), prior to its acquisition of PsychCorp,
had been involved in testing primarily as a result of the merger of Harcourt Brace
and the World Book Company in 1962. World Book had been one of the earliest
and most successful test publishers, beginning with the publication of the
Courtis Arithmetic Test in 1914 and continuing with achievement and
intelligence tests by Arthur Otis and Lewis Terman in the 1920s and later. By
1930, yearly sales of the Otis/Terman group intelligence test by World Book
were over 750,000 and those of the Stanford Achievement tests were 1.5 million
(Chapman, 1980, pp. 111-112). With the merger of HBJ and World Book in
1962 and HBJ's acquisition of PsychCorp in 1969, the former World Book tests
became part of PsychCorp's line of products.

For 1969, the last year of its independent existence, PsychCorp had
sales of about $5 million, and for 1979 HBJ reported that its revenues in the area
of tests and test services were approximately $30 million (Sokal 1981). As
noted in Table 2.1, we estimate that PsychCorp's gross revenues were $50-55
million in 1987.[5] PsychCorp is clearly one of the largest companies in the
Elhi market, publishing both the Stanford and Metropolitan achievement test
batteries. In addition, it markets the Wechsler Intelligence Scales; the McCarthy
Scales of Children's Abilities used in special-education screening; and a host of
business tests. According to TIP3 (Mitchell, 1983), PsychCorp published 101
tests — leading to a ranking of No. 2 in terms of numbers of tests published.
The 9MMY (Mitchell, 1985) listing of tests new or revised since the 1983 TIP3
lists 47 test entries for PsychCorp, including a new Curriculum Reference Test
of Mastery for the Elhi market, and a number of tests in language,
communications, and adaptive behavior that are used for screening learning and

---

[5] One source, *Ward's Business Directory* (1989), reports estimated revenues of
$17 million in 1987 for PsychCorp. Fremer (1989) reports estimated
revenues for CTB of $50 million in 1986. We are inclined to believe that
the $50 million estimate is more accurate, because at the time he wrote the
paper cited (Fremer, 1989), Fremer was an executive with PsychCorp.
Also according to several industry observers with whom we have talked, the
$17 million estimate is much too low.

speech pathology problems. CTB and PsychCorp are the two biggest testing companies in the Elhi testing market.

Though PsychCorp rivals CTB in the education market it also remains strong in the field of psychological assessment — its 1990 catalog for education is 288 pages and its catalog for psychological assessment 160 pages. Thus, though the PsychCorp severed its formal relationships with the profession of psychologists more than forty years ago, it remains much as it was restructured under Paul Achilles in the 1920s, as a major supplier of psychological services and tests. After being a subsidiary of HBJ for almost a quarter-century, PsychCorp became a subsidiary of an even larger conglomerate, when HBJ was acquired by General Cinema in November 1991.

5.   American College Testing Program (ACT)

The ACT was begun in the late 1950s by E.F. Lindquist with help from Ted McCarrell, Lyle Spencer, and Jack Kough, and with support from Lindquist's Measurement Research Center, Science Research Associates, and the University of Iowa (Peterson, 1983; Ruger, 1975). The motives for starting a new college admissions testing program were several. According to Ruger's (1975) account of the history of ACT, the founders were concerned because, while the College Board admissions testing served relatively elite institutions on the East coast, the state of admissions testing at midwestern colleges and universities was still rather archaic. Lindquist, who had been a member of a College Board SAT advisory committee, also was clearly unhappy with what he saw to be a bureaucratic inertia associated with College Board programs. Referring to his attempts to suggest changes in those programs, Lindquist later recalled, "It was extremely difficult to introduce any innovations of any kind. You had to educate a half dozen committees before this could be done . . ." (p. 21). SRA also was obviously motivated by a desire to give ETS, which had begun to compete with SRA in guidance testing and publishing, some competition in the area of college admissions testing.

But whatever the reasons, in a very short time a new national college admissions testing program had begun. In 1959, the new ACT admissions tests were used for the first time. Unlike the SAT, which was a single test with two parts (verbal and quantitative), the ACT had four tests covering English, mathematics, social studies, and natural sciences. Ruger's account gives insight into why the content coverage of ACT was broader than that of the SAT. As a very practical matter, the new ACT instrument was based on the Iowa Tests of

Educational Development, which covered similar areas. Another apparent reason was the desire to cover a broader range of subject matter in which students might be able to demonstrate their learning. As one official involved in setting up the ACT later put it:

> A real concern [were] kids who really excelled in a given field, but were very average in other fields, and this kind of kid had no chance. . . . Now. . . he might be a very high scorer because of a tremendous motivation in a given area and that may be the very motivation that would make him extremely successful in a given area. Adults don't operate across the whole intellectual sphere. They operate in the field where they are active and interested. (Quoted in Ruger, 1975, p. 26)

Despite ACT's inclusion of tests covering four different subject areas it did offer a composite score, and stressed that its tests were not intended to assess students' learning of specific course material. A portion of a brochure sent to colleges and universities in 1960 read as follows:

> The individual test items in all areas have been designed to measure as directly as possible the student's ability to perform exactly the same complex intellectual tasks that the college student typically has to perform. That is, the test is concerned primarily with the generalized intellectual skills and abilities rather than with specific and detailed content. . . .
>
> The tests in social studies and the natural sciences are primarily tests of the student's ability to do the types of reasoning and problem solving, particularly in reading situations, that are unique to these fields. (Quoted from ACT, 1960, in Ruger, 1975, pp. 69-70)

Language in the 1960 brochure also tended to indicate that the composite score was aimed more at making scholarship awards than for use in general admissions decisions.

ACT has had considerable success in competing with ETS and the College Board in the college admissions segment of the testing market. Though ACT college admissions tests are not nearly as old as the SAT, they are administered annually to around a million students. Thus, ACT's prominence stems not so much from the number of tests it markets as from the breadth of use of its tests. TIP3 (Mitchell, 1983) lists 34 entries for ACT, including not just its college admissions test series but also instruments intended to aid in student guidance and counseling as well as proficiency tests that allow examinees to demonstrate mastery of and receive college credit for subject matter learned outside formal classroom instruction. According to its annual reports, ACT had revenues of about $47 million in 1987 and $53 million in 1988 (in 1988 $51.5 million came from testing and scoring activities and $1.7 million in interest income).[6] More detailed information on trends in ACT revenues will be presented in chapter 3.

As an independent nonprofit organization, ACT, like ETS, has also participated in research on testing and test theory more generally. Researchers affiliated with ACT have, for example, contributed to research on generalizability theory and assessment of nonacademic achievement. The study by Rudner, Stonehill, Childs, and Dupree (1990) mentioned earlier shows too that ACT has been one of the organizations contributing the largest numbers of documents to ERIC/TME over the last two years.

ACT is clearly the No. 2 company in the college admissions segment of the testing marketplace, after ETS. Reflecting its midwestern base of operations and the pragmatic bent of founder Lindquist, ACT tests tend to be used less in elite eastern colleges historically served by ETS and the College Board and more in the Midwest and West.

6. Riverside Publishing

Riverside is a subsidiary of Houghton Mifflin (HM), which began in the testing business in 1916 with the publication of the Stanford-Binet Intelligence Scale. Riverside's main business in the testing marketplace is in the Elhi segment with the Iowa Tests of Basic Skills and the Iowa Tests of Educational Development. Riverside also publishes the less well-known but still venerable Cognitive Abilities Test and Gates-MacGinitie Reading Tests. Neither Riverside nor HM was identified as one of the major test companies by Hoffmann (1962), but Holmen and Docter (1972) and Fremer (1989) both classify HM/Riverside as one of the big six test publishers. Kohn (1977, p. 167) reported that HM sales in 1974 from measurement and guidance services

---

6 Again we found that Ward's *Business Directory* (1989) appeared to provide an underestimate, with a listing of ACT gross sales for 1987 of $34 million.

totaled $5.5 million. According to TIP2, HM published 46 test titles in 1974, but since then the parent company has concentrated test publishing in its Riverside subsidiary. TIP3 (Mitchell, 1983) lists not a single title under HM, but 47 under Riverside. Mitchell (1985) in the 9MMY lists 15 entries under Riverside. The 1991 *Riverside Resource Catalog* covering tests, scoring services and guidance systems lists some 30 test titles, but it is revealing that close to half of the catalog is devoted to "scoring plans and services."

According to *Ward's Business Directory* (1989), Riverside had estimated gross sales of $15 million in 1987, but other observers have suggested a figure more like $25 million. Rudman (1990) reports that Riverside's publishing of the Iowa tests may have been less affected by corporate takeovers and reorganizations than other publishers' testing operations because "the Iowa Test of Basic Skills and the Iowa Test of Educational Development copyrights are held by the University of Iowa" (p. 18).

Whatever the exact size of Riverside in terms of annual sales, it is clear that this company is, after CTB and PsychCorp, the biggest publisher in the Elhi segment.

7.   Scantron Corporation

Scantron is a relative newcomer to the testing marketplace. The firm was not listed as one of the major testing companies by Hoffmann (1962), Holmen and Docter (1972), or Fremer (1989). Indeed, Scantron is not listed in any of the Buros-Mitchell MMY-TIP series as publishing a single test. Yet Scantron clearly has grown very rapidly to become, in terms of gross revenues, one of the major firms in the testing market.

Scantron was founded in 1972 and in the mid-1970s introduced the first desktop scanner to read and score test answer sheets via microcomputer (Baker, 1989). From net sales of about $1.5 million in 1977, the firm's sales grew to $8 million in 1982, $28.6 million in 1987, and $39 million in 1989. The company went public in 1983 and, not surprisingly given the recent spate of acquisitions in the publishing and technology industries, became a wholly owned subsidiary of John H. Harlan Co, in June of 1988 (Harlan is a leader in the check printing business). Scantron now has the largest market share of optical mark reading (OMR) school building-level equipment, with an installed base of 40,000 machines in schools and colleges in North America as of 1989 (John H. Harlan Co., 1989). Until recently NCS concentrated on larger-volume test scoring and scanning, for example for school districts, states, or companies, but now has entered the school building-level market.

Scantron has grown to become a major company in the testing market by selling optical scanners, software that allows microcomputers to read and analyze the scanners' output, and special machine-readable forms to be used with its scanners. Scantron makes its profit primarily from the scannable forms that schools must purchase when they are given a rent-free machine. As an article on Scantron in a trade magazine put it, Scantron has worked out a highly profitable twist on the old formula "Give 'em the razor, sell 'em the blade" (Lyman, 1989). In 1985, Scantron acquired American Testronics, which markets two nationally normed K-12 achievement series and offers a 10-day scoring service to schools. In 1985 American Testronics earned about $2 million in revenues (Paine-Webber, 1987, in Cicchetti, 1988). In TIP3 (Mitchell, 1983), American Testronics was listed as publishing 20 tests, mainly high school subject matter tests. Thus it is easy to see why the company was a natural acquisition for Scantron.

Scantron illustrates several significant recent trends in the testing marketplace: the increasing importance of computer technology in testing; the importance of the test scoring market, as compared with the more traditional test publishing market; and the rapid pace of corporate takeovers and reorganizations. Indeed, among the numerous corporate acquisitions of testing companies over the last twenty years, Scantron's buy-out of American Testronics in 1985 and John Harlan's acquisition of Scantron in 1988 seem symptomatic of a range of developments. Given the continuing influences of computer technology and the scoring and reporting end of the testing business, testing very frequently seems to be swallowed up in the spinoff endeavors associated with testing.

THE MEDIUM-SIZED COMPANIES

In 1972, Holmen and Docter reported that there were 22 medium-sized test publishers with annual sales of tests and related services ranging from approximately $25,000 to $1 million. They estimated that these 22 companies accounted for approximately 5% of the test sales made by the testing industry (Holmen and Docter, 1972, p. 45). More recently, Fremer estimated that there are at least 35 medium-sized test companies with annual revenues of over $1 million. Fremer listed both SRA and American Testronics in this category, but as noted above, both firms now are owned by larger companies. While we have sought information on many of the test publishers listed in TIP3 (Mitchell,

1983) from sources such as *Ward's Business Directory* and the *Million Dollar Directory*, we have not be able to find sufficient data to suggest substantial revisions in Fremer's estimate of some 30 mid-sized companies doing from $1 million to $15 million annual business in the testing marketplace. However, some of the companies that are only mid-sized contributors to the testing market are much larger players in other areas of the publishing industry. Prentice-Hall, for example, is listed in TIP2 (Buros, 1974) and in the forthcoming TIP4 (Murphy, 1990) as publishing only a single test, and thus cannot be classified as even a medium-sized force in the testing market; but Prentice-Hall is estimated to have gross annual sales of nearly $1 billion for 1987 in the broader book publishing and printing industry (*Ward's Business Directory*, 1989).

To provide some perspective on the mid-sized companies in the testing industry, Table 2.2 lists publishers referenced in TIP1 (Buros, 1961), TIP2 (Buros 1974) and TIP3 (Mitchell, 1983) as having ten or more tests in print in one or more of these volumes.[7] The last column of Table 2.2 shows partial data for the forthcoming TIP4 (Murphy, 1990). With regard to these partial data, it should be noted that the figures shown for TIP4 are drawn from a database of around 60% of the tests that may ultimately be listed in TIP4. Therefore in interpreting these data, while increases in numbers of tests published between TIP3 and the partial data for TIP4 may be significant, decreases in numbers of tests published (or the fact that no tests for some publishers are yet part of the TIP4 database) are not necessarily meaningful. They may indicate merely that some tests for some test publishers have not yet become part of the database for the new TIP4.

Table 2.2 reflects a fair amount about the major test publishers discussed earlier. In both TIP2 and TIP3, ETS ranked No. 1 in terms of

---

[7] Several points of clarification should be noted about the data shown in Table 2.2. First, the TIP series includes not just U.S. tests but all separately-published in-print tests for use with English-speaking subjects. TIP1 also listed some 800 out-of-print tests. Thus 11 of the publishers listed in Table 2.2, denoted with asterisks, are non-U.S. publishers. Additionally, from 1961 to 1983 some publishers changed their names; we have indicated such changes in brackets. Finally, some of the data in Table 2.2 do not appear to be comparable to those in a similar table in TIP2, because the latter had apparently been adjusted to take account of corporate changes that had occurred between TIP1 and TIP2. Since our purpose here is to illuminate such changes rather than helping people to locate and evaluate tests, we have gone back to the original TIP1 data in Table 2.2.

numbers of tests published, rising from 130 tests in 1974 to 207 in 1983.[8]
From the partial data available to us for TIP4, it seems clear that ETS will retain
its No. 1 ranking as the publisher of the most English language tests. Most of
the other major test companies also show up prominently in the Table 2.2 list
with many tests listed in TIP3 in 1983 — ACT with 34, CTB with 40,
PsychCorp with 101 and Riverside with 47. NCS Interpretive Scoring Systems
is listed in TIP3 as publishing only 11 tests and Scantron is not listed as
publishing even a single test — though as previously mentioned, Scantron did
acquire American Testronics in 1983, and this firm is listed as publishing 20
tests. Recall too that SRA, listed in Table 2.2 as publishing 80 tests in 1983,
has become a part of the Macmillan/McGraw Hill School Publishing Company
joint venture — though apparently it will continue to be listed separately in the
new TIP4.

Table 2.2 also indicates something about the degree of concentration in
the test publishing industry. If the totals shown in Table 2.2 are compared with
the total test entries and publishers listed in TIP1 in 1961 (2126 tests in print,
562 publishers); TIP2 in 1974 (2467 tests in print, 493 publishers); and TIP3 in
1983 (2672 tests in print, 565 publishers), it is easy to see that fewer than 70
publishers (15% of all publishers) have over the last thirty years published some
65-75% of the tests on the market. The partial data available for TIP4 do not
allow any direct comparisons with earlier versions of TIP with regard to
concentration in the test publishing market, though as we discuss below,
tendencies toward both greater concentration via mergers and acquisitions and
greater diversification via new entrants into test publishing are apparent in even
these partial data.

Table 2.2 also reveals something of the diversity of the testing industry
and shows some important trends in the testing industry over the last three
decades. A simple scan of the publishers in Table 2.2 shows that some more
general commercial publishers also publish tests, as do a number of agencies
connected with colleges and universities. Not surprisingly these include some of
the universities in the United States that historically have had strong programs
in educational and psychological testing, such as the University of Iowa,
Teachers College of Columbia University, and Kansas and Purdue Universities.

---

8   ETS would have ranked No. 1 in number of tests published in the 1961
    TIP1, as previously noted, if the ETS tests listed under Cooperative Tests
    and Services (50) and College Entrance Examination Board (37) had been
    added to ETS's 63.

Table 2.2: Number of Tests for Publishers with Ten or More Tests Listed in Tests in Print (TIP)

Name of Publisher/Firm	TIP1 1961	TIP2 1974	TIP3 1983	TIP4 1990
Academic Therapy Publications	-	6	30	44
Acorn Publishing	49	-	-	-
Addison-Wesley Publishing Co., Inc.	0	-	52	-
American College Testing Program (The)	-	7	34	32
American Guidance Service, Inc.	6	39	35	39
American Printing House for the Blind	-	19	1	-
American Testronics	-	-	20	5
Australian Council for Educational Research*	40	47	56	72
Bobbs-Merrill Co.	2	69	30	-
Bruce (Martin, PhD) Publishers	13	21	21	21
Bureau of Educ'l Measurement, KS/ Emp. State U.	125	39	41	42
Bureau of Educational Research, Univ. of Iowa	32	23	8	-
Bureau of Publications, Teachers College Press	17	9	6	10
Bureau of Tests	26	-	-	-
College Entrance Exam'n Board (College Board)	37	111	2	3
Consulting Psychologists Press, Inc.	21	51	79	19
Cooperative Tests and Services, ETS	50	64	-	-
CTB/McGraw-Hill	63	39	40	19
Department of Educational Research, Ontario*	15	-	-	-
DLM Teaching Resources				28
EdITS/Educational and Industrial Testing Service	-	20	20	19
Educational Records Bureau	9	10	3	-
Educational Test Bureau	103	-	-	-
Educational Testing Service	63	130	207	225
Educators Publishing Service, Inc.	-	9	17	23
Educators'-Employers' Test Service	2	11	11	11
Examinations Committee, Amer. Chemical Society	9	19	21	-
Family Life Publications, Inc.	6	16	19	-
Gibson (Robert) and Sons*	17	14	4	-
Ginn & Co. Ltd.*	-	28	-	-
Gough (Harrison) of U. California, Berkeley	10	1	1	-
Gregory (C.A.) (Bobbs-Merrill)	28	-	-	-
Grune & Stratton, Inc.	7	16	15	-
Guidance Centre, Univ. of Tortonto*	29	21	7	7
Harcourt Brace Jovanovich, Inc.	107	64	-	-
Harrap (George G.) Ltd.*	20	19	4	2
Hodder & Stoughton Educational*	-	-	36	37
Houghton Mifflin Co.	28	46	-	-
Human Sciences Research Council*	-	30	33	51

Table 2.2: Number of Tests for Publishers
(continued)

Name of Publisher/Firm	TIP1 1961	TIP2 1974	TIP3 1983	TIP4 1990
Industrial Relations Center	15	18	-	-
Institute for Personality and Ability Testing, Inc.	15	15	18	22
Instructional Materials Laboratory, Ohio State Univ.	-	14	-	-
Instructional Objectives Exchange (IOX)	-	-	12	13
McCann Associates, Inc.	-	11	13	21
Merrill (Charles E.) Publishing Co.	1	2	15	-
Monitor	-	10	13	13
Nat'l Occupational Competency Testing Institute	-	25	25	-
National Institute for Personnel Research*	15	31	22	-
NCS Interpretive Scoring Systems	-	7	11	6
NFER (Nelson) Publishing*	33	49	94	138
Ohio Scholarship Tests, Ohio State Dept. of Educ.	67	-	-	-
Oliver & Boyd Ltd*	13	5	3	3
Perfection Form Co.	10	14	14	14
PRO-ED	-	-	19	141
Pyschological Assessment Resources				50
Psychological Corporation (The)	116	94	101	18
Psychological Test Specialists	11	11	12	12
Psychologists and Educators Press	-	23	21	25
Psychometric Affiliates	37	101	68	68
Public School Publishing Co. (Bobbs-Merrill)	60	-	-	-
Richardson, Bellows, Henry & Co., Inc.	-	23	13	14
Riverside Publishing Co.	-	-	47	2
Scholastic Testing Service, Inc.	9	10	25	38
Science Research Associates, Inc.	73	75	80	78
Sheridan (Supply Co.) Psychological Services, Inc.	20	36	39	22
State High School Testing Service, Purdue Univ.	41	-	-	-
Steck Co. (Steck-Vaughn)	11	2	-	-
Stoelting Co.	39	24	43	62
Teaching Resources Corp.	-	1	17	-
Teleometrics International	-	-	14	16
United States Government Printing Office	3	4	5	2
University Book Store, Purdue Univ.	21	21	22	-
University of London Press Ltd.* (see Hodder)	38	33	-	-
Vocational Instr'l Materials Lab., Ohio State Univ.	-	-	39	41
Western Psychological Services	26	98	70	98
Winkler Publications	24	-	-	-
Total	698	757	875	917

* Non-U.S. publishers; see note 7.

Additionally, though it did not actually meet our criterion for inclusion in Table 2.2 (namely 10 or more tests listed in TIP1, TIP2 or TIP3), we have included the U.S. Government Printing Office simply to illustrate that even the U.S. government is a publisher of standardized tests.

The data in Table 2.2 also suggest something of the fluidity of the test publishing business. The data in the second column reveal that there were 51 firms listed in TIP1 with 10 or more test entries, but 17 of them were not listed in TIP3 as publishing a single test. Similarly some 20 firms shown as publishing 10 or more tests in 1983 did not appear at all as test publishers in 1961 in TIP1. These facts illustrate that the medium and small segments of the test publishing business are not terribly stable. Indeed, it often is extremely hard to track down the exact status of some publishers and their tests. As the current managing editor of the Buros Institute, the current publisher of the TIP and MMY series, put it, "It is extremely difficult to keep track of who publishes what tests. You practically need a scoresheet to keep track of who's who from week to week" (Linda Murphy, personal communication, August 1990).

The pattern of disappearing publishers between TIP1 (1961), TIP2 (1974) and TIP3 (1983) nevertheless does not appear to have been altogether random. For example, a number of the prominent test publishers in 1961 and 1974 with clear connections to colleges and universities or state departments of education do not appear at all in TIP3 (e.g., the State High School Publishing Service of Purdue University, and the Ohio Scholarship Tests of that state's Department of Education) or appear with greatly reduced numbers of tests published (e.g., the Bureau of Publications of Teachers College). While this pattern is not altogether clear, it does suggest that the ties between educational institutions and commercial test publishing, which historically have been very strong (as noted, for example, in our discussion of the founding of some of the major testing companies), has weakened somewhat over the last twenty years. Fewer medium-sized test publishers have explicit ties to educational institutions.

Also, a number of quite new test publishers rose to relative prominence between 1974 and the early 1980s. Academic Therapy Publications, Psychologists and Educators Press, PRO-ED, and Teaching Resources Corporation all are listed as publishing more than 15 tests in TIP3, but not one of them was even listed in TIP1. Among these firms, PRO-ED is particularly noteworthy. Based in Austin, Texas, PRO-ED was founded only in 1977, but by 1983 this firm had grown fast enough to rank, in terms of numbers of tests published, among the top three dozen firms listed in TIP3. PRO-ED was founded by Don Hamill after he was dissatisfied with prospects for having a test he had authored published with an established test publisher. Hamill is now author or co-author of more than a dozen tests published by PRO-ED and the firm also now publishes many tests authored by others and previously issued by smaller publishers. The *Wide Range Achievement Test* (WRAT)-Revised, for example, is now published by PRO-ED. Created originally in 1940, WRAT previously had been published by Jastak Associates, a publishing venture of the authors of WRAT and other tests. PRO-ED now also publishes the Slosson Intelligence Test and the Gray Oral Reading Tests, both of considerably older vintage than PRO-ED itself and both previously published by other firms (the Slosson by Slosson Educational Associates, and the Gray Oral Reading Test by Bobbs-Merrill). Indeed PRO-ED's 1990 catalog features "Selected products formerly published by Aspen Publishers, Hubbard, Interstate Printers and Publishers Inc., and Special Child Publications." In addition to tests, PRO-ED publishes curricular materials and journals, but the bulk of its business, amounting to estimated total revenues in 1990 of more than $10 million, derives from test sales (Anonymous personal communication, PRO-ED employee, 1991).

Comparing PRO-ED's catalog with those of some of the larger test publishers, two contrasts are apparent. First, unlike the trend among some of the larger publishers noted by Rudman (1990) toward corporate authorship of tests by unnamed corporate employees, PRO-ED's tests all list individual authors. Also, unlike catalogs such as those for CTB and PsychCorp, and in apparent conflict with professional standards concerning educational and psychological tests, PRO-ED's catalog makes no mention of any necessary professional qualifications for would-be purchasers of its tests.

But whatever its other merits or limitations, it is clear that PRO-ED has emerged, via acquisitions of tests previously published by others and aggressive marketing, in less than a decade to become one of the largest of the medium-sized test publishers. Specializing in the areas of language, clinical and special education testing, PRO-ED has grown to considerable prominence in the testing marketplace in a very short time. According to the partial data available for TIP4, as shown in Table 2.2, it appears that PRO-ED is now one of the top half-dozen firms in the United States in terms of numbers of tests published.

Like PRO-ED, many of the medium-sized test publishers listed in Table 2.2 specialize in particular segments of the testing marketplace. Western Psychological Services (WPS), for example, is listed in TIP3 as publishing 70 different tests, but most of these are in the areas of psychological guidance and counseling (among the tests offered by WPS, for instance, are ones concerning people's self-image, alcoholic tendencies and life goals). Founded in 1948, based in Los Angeles, and now headed by Ira Manson, son of the founder, WPS continues to be a private company, with estimated gross annual sales of $6 million (Dun's, 1989). Its catalog, like that of PRO-ED, lists individual authors for its tests, but unlike that of PRO-ED does indicate adherence to the standard of selling psychological tests only to "qualified professional users."

Another of the largest of the medium-sized publishers is Consulting Psychologists Press, with 79 tests listed in TIP3 (1983). The firm was set up in 1956 to publish the California Psychological Inventory (which probably remains the firm's most widely known test). The company's growth "was stimulated by arrangements to market tests controlled by Stanford Press" (Holmen & Docter, 1972, p. 46). Long-time president of Consulting Psychologists (and now chairman), John Black had been a professor and administrator at Stanford University for sixteeen years, and has been active in the company since its founding. Recent annual sales of Consulting Psychologists have been estimated at $7.75 million (Dun's, 1989, 1991).

Toward the smaller end of the medium-size test companies is Academic Therapy Publications. This firm, founded in 1970 and based in Novato, California, is a private company with estimated annual sales of about $2 million (Dun's, 1989). According to TIP3, Academic Therapy published 30 tests in 1983, mostly in the area of clinical psychological testing -- tests dealing with learning efficiency, learning disabilities, school phobia, and auditory and visual perception. According to the partial data available for TIP4, Academic Therapy is listed with 44 instruments.

An example of an even more specialized test publisher is the American Printing House for the Blind, listed in TIP3 as publishing only a single test, the Roughness Discrimination Test. This is a sort of reading readiness test for the blind, in that it tests kindergarten and first grade blind children's tactile ability as an indicator of their readiness for Braille reading instruction. Given such a highly specialized instrument, the American Printing House for the Blind can hardly be considered even a medium-sized publisher of tests. Nevertheless, with sales of $13 million, this firm is as large as or larger than some medium-size testing companies, presumably because of its sales of other materials for the blind (Information Access, 1990).

In addition to such highly specialized niches in the testing marketplace, the two relatively large segments targeted by many of the medium-sized companies are educational and occupational or employment testing. In the education sector, for example, the Examinations Committee of the American Chemical Society (publisher of 21 tests according to TIP3) issues a variety of specialized chemistry tests, intended for use in connection with high school, college or graduate coursework in chemistry. Another example is American Guidance Service of Circle Pines, Minnesota. This company publishes tests for educational levels ranging from preschool (with a preschool attainment record and a first grade readiness test) to high school (with achievement tests in subjects such as social studies and math).

Examples of firms specializing in employment-occupational testing are the National Occupational Competency Testing Institute (NOCTI) (with 25 exams listed in TIP3 dealing with specific occupations such as carpentry, cosmetology and engine repair), Teleometrics International (with 14 instruments listed in TIP3, dealing, for example, with conflict management and management relations survey) and McCann Associates (with 13 tests in TIP3, for, among other occupations, clerical workers, firefighters, police and municipal employees).

While many of the medium-sized firms clearly do specialize in one part of the testing marketplace, others span two or more segments. Two examples of companies spanning the education and employment sectors, as even their names suggest, are Educators'-Employers' Test Service and EdITS, the Educational Industrial Testing Service. EdITS, based in San Diego, California, had 20 test entries in TIP3, and according to partial data available for TIP4 continues to publish about the same number. Among these are the Eysenck Personality Questionnaire (U.S. edition), several other personality scales and a school environment preference survey. The Educators'-Employers' Test Service is somewhat smaller, with 11 entries in TIP3 and the same number in the partial TIP4 database. Among this firm's tests are a teacher rating scale clearly oriented to the education market and a sales aptitude test oriented more toward the employment market.

Later, in chapter 7, we return to discuss one relatively new segment of the employment testing market, namely that of "honesty" or "integrity" testing, which is served by a number of medium-sized publishers.

SMALL PUBLISHERS

Since the large and middle-range publishers of tests only account for about 50 companies, and TIP3 (Mitchell, 1983) lists 565 companies selling tests (and as of 1990, the partial TIP4 database listed even more), there appear to be 500 or more "publishers" each marketing fewer than 10 tests and, according to Fremer's estimate, making less than $1 million in annual test revenues (though it should be recalled that approximately 10% of the publishers listed in TIP are not based in the U.S). Also, it should be noted that we have identified numerous companies advertising tests for sale that are not listed in TIP3 and not, at least as of 1990, included in the database for TIP4. And as we will explain shortly, there are other firms in the market that do not publish or market tests but sponsor tests or build them on contract for others.

The small-publisher category encompasses considerable diversity: very small companies that publish a very limited number of tests; larger companies, such as Prentice Hall, whose main business is not testing, but who nevertheless publish a small number of tests; individuals who distribute tests they have developed for their own purposes, and a variety of specialized institutions such as professional, research and educational organizations that market only a few tests.

Firms falling into the small-test publisher category may be small in terms of overall revenue but play a significant role in highly specialized markets. An example is Silver Burdett, which markets a single test, the Music Competency Test — one of less than two dozen commercially published standardized music tests. Similarly, the American Association of Teachers of German publishes just one test, the National German Examination for High School Students, one of just a handful of standardized German tests intended for secondary school students of the United States.

Other "publishers" in the small-publisher category are individuals who have authored tests and want to make them available to others. The partial data base for TIP4, for example, lists 40 such author-publishers, the vast majority of whom distribute only one test. An example of such a publisher is one Millard Bienvenu of Natchitoches, Louisiana, who authored and "publishes" the Interpersonal Communication Inventory, an instrument listed in TIP2, TIP3, TIP4 and 8MMY.[9] This test has been mentioned a half-dozen times in the

---

[9] Dr. Bienvenu is listed in the database for TIP4 as now publishing three tests. To his Interpersonal Communication Inventory, he has added inventories concerning premarital communications and anger communications.

published literature (Mitchell, TIP3, 1988, p. 188), and apparently has been used primarily for research purposes. The author-publisher's motives hardly seem financial, since he sold it, according to 8MMY, for a mere 20 cents per test. At the same time, however, the "norms" for the instrument only "consist of means and standard deviations of students in the author's communication course" (Buros, 1978, 8MMY, p. 886). Holmen and Docter described the likely motivation behind such shoe-string test "publishing":

> Many test instruments sold by individuals and organizations in this [small-publisher] group were originally developed in connection with research projects such as doctoral dissertations or research on mental health. Once a test has been developed for a research project, publication of information about the research often leads to requests for the test. If the test author does not make his material available, then his research or development work has been largely wasted; most professionals consider this an undesirable situation. Thus, the test author begins to produce copies of the instrument and to give them away or sell them, generally at minimal cost, to interested research workers. (Holmen & Docter, 1972, p. 52)

Holmen and Docter also pointed out that though there are exceptions, such tests are often "published" without adequate validity or reliability data or manuals. Nevertheless it is worth pointing out that in some instances, author-publishers are eminent scholars in their fields. For example, Harrison Gough of the University of California, a well-known psychologist, is listed in 8MMY as distributing "for research only" an instrument he authored called the Home-Index. Gough is also author of several instruments commercially published by Consulting Psychologists Press, probably the best-known of which is the California Psychological Inventory.

THE SECONDARY INDUSTRY

Though the organizations and people who publish or otherwise distribute tests are, as we have described, extremely diverse, this diversity alone does not convey the complexity of the testing industry; there is also a wide range of organizations intimately involved with the building, sponsorship and use of tests. In addition to "publishers" of tests, from the giants such as ETS, with annual revenues in the $100's of millions, to individuals such as Dr. Bienvenu, who probably are doing well if they cover the costs of test distribution, the test industry has grown to attract numerous secondary players. These include organizations and individuals who do not publish tests at all, but who build them for others, sponsor tests or provide other test-related services. This category of the industry also includes contract companies and university-based research and development centers.

Contract Companies

An increasingly important component of the testing industry is represented by companies that do not own or publish tests, but build them under contract for governmental or private agencies. This pattern — of an organization, individual or group of individuals building a test for some other group or organization to use without formally publishing the test — goes back at least to World War I when, as discussed in more detail below, psychologists built the Army Alpha and Beta tests for use in screening military candidates. During World War II the College Entrance Examination Board provided its test-building services to the U.S. military, and at least since the 1920s psychologists have provided test-building services to businesses to help them in the screening and selection of potential employees.

The market for contracted testing began to grow more rapidly in the educational realm in the late 1960s when entrepreneurs formed small companies to conduct evaluations that schools were required to perform as a condition for receiving federal funds under the Elementary and Secondary Education Act (ESEA) of 1965. A discussion of the impact of ESEA on educational testing in the United States will be provided in chapter 5, so here we merely note that in the 1970s some of the companies doing ESEA evaluations expanded their services to answer requests for proposals (RFPs) from states to develop tests for mandated testing programs.

Small companies in the test-building category of the market include Advanced Systems in Measurement and Evaluation, which has built basic skills tests for a number of states; Assessment Systems Corporation, which offers customized tests development services; Instructional Objectives Exchange (IOX), which built, among others, a statewide test for teachers and administrators in Texas; National Evaluation Systems (NES), which has built teacher certification exams in several states; and Scholastic Testing Service, which offers item development, administration, scoring and reporting services to states. As noted in Table 2.2, some of these firms actually do market a small number of ready-built tests, but what they all have in common is that they illustrate a clear trend toward customized test development.

There are also a number of smaller companies competing in the RFP market, including Edwards Brothers; Horizon Research and Evaluation Affiliates; Beta Inc.; Education Computer Software Inc; Institute for Behavior Research and Creativity; Institute of Educational Research; Measurement Dimensions; MESA Inc.; METRI/TECH Inc.; New England Evaluation Designs; Resource Management Corporation (RMC); R & R Evaluations; and U-SAIL.[10]

Some contract companies specialize in the scoring segment of an RFP, often under subcontract with the company that wins the RFP competition to develop and administer the tests. For example, Measurement Inc. scores written essays associated with large state testing programs. By far the largest of the scoring companies is NCS, as mentioned above. In the late 1980s NCS had a contract in Texas for $9.25 million, which was probably one of the largest testing contracts awarded at the state level. NCS also has contracts totaling more than $2 million in Arizona, Connecticut, Maryland, Michigan, New Jersey, and Wisconsin. (NCS subcontracts the test development component of some of its contracts to other contract test companies.) New England Scoring Services and Delta Recognition Corp. also provide machine scoring services for the RFP market (Roeber, personal communication, 1988).

Firms specializing in customized test building do not have the RFP market to themselves. The large publishers — such as PsychCorp, CTB, ETS, and Riverside — often compete aggressively for large-scale RFP business. The RFP market for tests is one to which we will return in chapter 7 in discussing problems in the fractured marketplace for tests.

Universities and Research Centers

Another group of players in the state-level RFP testing market consists of university-based research or testing centers. The list of such organizations and the amounts of their 1987-88 contracts follow (Roeber, personal communication):

- University of Kansas Center for Educational Testing and
  Evaluation, $216,000

---

[10] Some of this information was provided by Dr. Edward Roeber, formerly with the Michigan State Department of Education, in a phone conversion (July, 1988). Dr. Roeber is now Director of the State Alternative Assessment Exchange of the Council of Chief State School Officers.

- Georgia State University, $1.2 million
- University of Rhode Island Center for Evaluation Research, $169,000
- University of Alabama, $300,000
- University of Georgia Testing Scoring, $800,000.

Additionally, we should point out that the Center for the Study of Testing Evaluation and Educational Policy at Boston College (with which the authors are affiliated) has done testing-related work for a number of school districts, and has evaluated the testing programs for the Commonwealth of Kentucky and the state of Kansas.

Other organizations that might be placed in the same category with universities and research centers are more autonomous research and development laboratories. The Northwest Regional Laboratory, for example, which is a federally funded educational organization, does some contract testing work for states such as Alaska and Utah, in addition to its work under its federal grant. Another example is the American Institutes for Research (AIR), which until recently developed the Medical College Admissions Test (MCAT) under contract for the Association of American Medical Colleges. Yet another example is CASAS, a California foundation, which develops customized tests for adult education programs.[11]

MILITARY TESTING

The U.S. military has played a tremendously influential role in the evolution of the testing industry in the United States in several regards. While we cannot here offer a detailed account of how testing in the U.S. military has evolved over more than eighty years, we summarize that evolution and how it has affected other testing practices in the United States.[12] In the next chapter, we provide a more detailed account of the extent of military testing. For now,

---

[11] The name CASAS was an acronym for California Adult Student Assessment System, organized in 1980 by a consortium of adult education providers and the California State Department of Education, with federal funding, to develop "functional" and adult-oriented tests for students served by adult education programs. Now run under the auspices of an independent nonprofit foundation, CASAS has maintained its name, but the C in the acronym now stands for Comprehensive, since the agency builds tests for adult education programs across the country, rather than just in California.

[12] More detailed accounts of the history of military testing may be found in Sticht (1989); Eitelberg, Laurence, Waters & Perelman (1984); Hale (1982); and Wigdor & Green (1991).

simply to convey the importance of military testing, we note that one military test was reported in 1974 to be administered to "nearly two million applicants [to the military] and high school students, making it the largest volume employment test in the United States" (Eitelberg, Laurence, Waters & Perelman, 1984, p. 19).

Testing in the U.S. military may be divided, very roughly, into four phases: testing during World War I; World War II; post-WWII through the mid-1970s, and post-1976 testing. Just after the United States declared war on Germany on April 6, 1917, a meeting was convened by Robert Yerkes, then president of the American Psychological Association, to discuss how psychologists might contribute to the war effort. Within a month and with the aid of the National Research Council, a tentative plan had been drawn up for psychological examining of recruits. This eventually led to the creation and administration to almost two million men in 1918 and 1919 of the Army Alpha (for literates) and the Army Beta (for illiterates). Since the story of the WWI testing has been told in detail elsewhere (Yerkes, 1921; Camfield, 1969, Gould, 1981; Jonich, 1968; Sokal, 1987),[13] here we focus on the variety of ways in which the WWI testing affected the testing industry and testing practices in the United States. First, the Army testing resulted in an immense amount of popular publicity on testing and how it could be employed in civilian life, both in education and in business and industry (Camfield, 1969; Haney 1984). Second, the Army testing clearly swelled the ranks of people directly involved in psychological testing. At a time when the membership of the APA stood at only 350, more than 500 people were involved in the WWI testing (Camfield, 1969). Third, the Army tests and adaptations of them, as a result of the publicity, provided some of the most profitable products for the nascent commercial testing industry. As late as 1929, over half of the Psychological Corporation's income

---

[13] We note that different accounts of the WWI Alpha and Beta testing do vary on several important points. For example, some accounts indicate that the WWI tests were not actually much used in military assignments and that studies of the test results did not have the effect sometimes attributed to them of spurring passage of the restrictive immigration law of 1924. Nevertheless, Herrnstein seems to us incorrect in stating that "the familiar charge that the [WWI] tests were somehow related to racist and nativist immigration policies . . . is a canard" (Herrnstein, 1990, pp. 125-126). While interpretations of the WWI test results do not appear to have contributed significantly to the passage of the new immigration law, the two were connected in that they clearly were the product of prevailing prejudices about race differences (Gelb, 1986).

was derived from sale of Army Alpha tests (Sokal, 1981). All of this clearly also helped to solidify the place of psychological testing not just as a commercial venture but also as a recognized academic discipline (and of course to boost the careers of several psychologists involved in the Army testing). But finally, the Army test data, and misinterpretations of their meaning by enthusiasts of the new tests, led to considerable controversy over the meaning and value of testing. Most hotly debated was the contention by Yerkes, Terman and others that the WWI tests measured people's innate mental abilities. The most famous exchange of opinion in the controversy over the WWI testing was between Walter Lippmann and Lewis Terman in the pages of the New Republic (the Lipmann-Terman exchange has been reprinted in Block & Dworkin, 1976).

Despite the publicity surrounding the WWI Army testing, the Alpha and Beta tests were dropped by the Army after the armistice, and standardized testing in the U.S. military was not widely resurrected until it seemed that the U.S. would enter the second World War. The War Department was again aided in development of new military tests by the National Research Council and numerous prominent psychologists. The new Army test was the Army General Classification Test (AGCT). The AGCT presented three types of problems: "vocabulary to measure the verbal factor, arithmetic word problems to measure number and reasoning factors, and block counting to measure the space factor" (Dailey, 1953, p. 379). Walter Bingham, the head of the WWII army testing, pointed out perhaps the biggest difference between the army testing in the two wars; unlike the Army Alpha and Beta of the first war, the AGCT made "no pretense of measuring *native* intelligence" (quoted in Hale, 1982, p. 23). The reasons for the change were doubtless several but surely included the controversy over the claims made for the WWI tests, research on mental abilities that had been done during the 1930s (emphasizing multiple abilities rather than one general mental ability; Haney 1984), and the fact that Bingham was far more pragmatically oriented than the status-conscious Yerkes who had headed the Army Alpha and Beta testing in WWI (Mayrhauser, 1987).

The AGCT was standardized in September of 1940 on white male military and Civilian Conservation Corps personnel, with an effort to make the standardization sample representative of the civilian manpower pool — except of course that the sample was restricted to white males. "The 'so-called' rapid learners (those achieving a standard score of 130 or above) were ranked at the top in Army Grade I; the slowest learners (those with a standard score of 69 or below) were placed in Grade V" (Eitelberg, Laurence, Waters & Perelman, 1984,

p. 15). Though as many as ten million recruits were tested with the AGCT, it was used not so much to screen recruits as to assign them to military jobs. During WWII, as in other military conflicts, when demands for manpower were high, test score requirements for military service, and other requirements as well, were adjusted so as to obtain the necessary numbers of people. As after the first World War, civilian versions of the WWII army tests were marketed when the war had ended. The military testing of this era garnered not nearly as much publicity as the WWI testing (Haney, 1984); and unlike the case after WWI, it was continued after the war.

Initially after WWII, the military services developed their own tests to be used in conjunction with the AGCT, but since most covered similar areas — vocabulary, arithmetic and spatial relations — a working group representing the different branches of the services was convened in 1948 to develop a uniform aptitude test. This resulted in creation of the Armed Forces Qualification Test (AFQT) introduced in 1950 in conjunction with the reinstitution of the Selective Service. The new AFQT was modeled after the AGCT and was statistically equated with it. After its introduction, the AFQT was revised in the 1950s and the different branches of the military also used a variety of more specialized tests (see Eitelberg, Laurence, Waters & Perelman, 1984, pp. 17-18, for a summary of this period; also Wigdor & Green, 1991).

In 1974, the U.S. Department of Defense decided once again that all branches should use the same test battery for both screening of enlistees and assigning them to military training and jobs. The battery chosen was the Armed Services Vocational Aptitude Battery (ASVAB), which was already being used by the Air Force and the Marines. A revised version of the ASVAB was introduced in January 1976 for use by all of the armed services.

It may be hard to imagine how a single test battery could be used to assign people to the wide range of jobs encompassed by the four branches of military service, but the ASVAB was designed with ten subtests; thus various subtest scores could be considered separately to assess suitability for different kinds of training and jobs. The ten subtests of the ASVAB are shown in Table 2.3. In addition to its use in military selection and job placement, a separate form of the ASVAB is administered to tenth through twelfth grade high school students as a general vocational aptitude test. In the 1980s, the ASVAB was given annually to roughly 700,000 applicants for military service, as well as over a million high school students (Friedman & Williams, 1982; Office of

Assistant Secretary of Defense, 1987, 1988; Hartigan & Widgor, 1989; Wigdor & Green, 1991).

Table 2.3: Content Areas Tested by the ASVAB

Content Area	Subtest Abbreviation
General Science	GS
Arithmetic Reasoning[*]	AR
Word Knowledge[*]	WK
Paragraph Comprehension[*]	PC
Numerical Operations[*]	NO
Coding Speed	CS
Auto and Shop Information	AS
Mathematics Knowledge	MK
Mechanical Comprehension	MC
Electronics Information	EI

Source: Department of Defense, 1984.

[*] Each of these subtests is used to derive AFQT scores via the formula
$AFQT = AR + WK + PC + 0.5NO$.

The most prominent of the scores derived from ASVAB subtests is the AFQT composite score. As indicated in Table 2.3, this score is simply a composite of four of the ASVAB subtests, dealing with verbal skills (word knowledge, or WK, and paragraph comprehension, or PC) and with math skills (arithmetic reasoning, or AR, and numerical operations, or NO). The AFQT is used by all the services as an indicator of general trainability and thus determines whether an applicant is qualified to enlist or not. Based upon their AFQT scores, applicants are placed into one of the five AFQT categories (previously called mental groups), denoted by Roman numerals I-V (see Table 2.4). Though the exact standards for entrance into different branches of the military have varied over the years, individuals ranking in categories I and II have always been considered above average, those in category III as average and those in categories IV and V as below average (Butler, 1989). The idea of using test score to grade military recruits into "mental categories" dates back to at least WWI, but in 1951 the U.S. Congress enacted into law (10 USC 520) a stipulation that persons scoring in category V on the AFQT (i.e. below the 10th percentile) were restricted from service in any branch of the military (Sticht, 1989, p. 4; see also Wigdor & Green, 1991).

Table 2.4:   AFQT Mental Category Ranges

AFQT Category	Percentile Range	Ability Level
I	93-100	---above average---
II	65-92	---above average---
III	31-64	--- average ---
IV	10-30	---below average---
V	1-9	---below average---

Source: Department of Defense, 1984[14]

As recounted previously, military testing policies and recruitment policies and practices have varied considerably since then, but with the advent of the all-volunteer armed forces following controversy over the Vietnam conflict, there was heightened concern for recruiting high-quality personnel. Thus in the 1970s and 1980s, the U.S. Congress became much more active in prescribing specific AFQT enlistment standards. As Sticht (1989) put it, the Congress "manifested a growing tendency to use mental test scores to micromanage personnel matters in the military services" (p. 4). Basically what the new laws did was to restrict the proportion of recruits in any one year who score in the category IV range to 20%, and to ban military service altogether for non-high school graduates who score below category III, that is, below the 31st percentile, on the AFQT.

These policies turned out to be somewhat ironic because by 1980, it had become apparent that a substantial error had occurred in the norming of the new ASVAB introduced in 1976. When the new form of ASVAB was created, an effort was made to calibrate the AFQT composite scores derived from the new ASVAB to previously used versions, so that there would be a relatively constant meaning in AFQT percentile scores and in the personnel categories defined in terms of those scores. In other words, the calibration was intended to ensure that a 30th percentile score on the 1976 AFQT meant the same thing as a 30th percentile score on versions of the AFQT used in previous years.

This sort of calibration is performed by "equating" two or more versions of the AFQT. There are a number of techniques available for doing this, but the essential idea is quite simple. It is to give both versions of the test

---

[14] Wigdor & Green (1991, p. 47) point out that during a time of scarce military manpower, the 1951 law lowered the minimum AFQT cutoff score from the 13th to the 10th percentile.

to be equated to a representative sample of the population with whom the test is intended to be used in order to determine the equivalence of raw scores on the two tests. For example, if one version is slightly easier, a raw score of 50 questions correct on that version may be equivalent to 48 correct on a more difficult version. Via equating procedures it is possible to adjust derived scores such as percentiles so that they have the same meaning across alternative test versions even if the versions vary somewhat in difficulty.

What happened with the new ASVAB introduced in 1976, however, was that an error occurred in the equating process; that error "inflated the AFQT scores of low-scoring candidates" (Office of the Assistant Secretary of Defense, 1982, p. 6). The scaling error apparently came from at least three sources: 1) one of the equating tests used with Navy and Air Force recruits in the calibration study was scored incorrectly; 2) some Army examinees who did not qualify were incorrectly excluded from the sample used in the calibration study; and 3) some Army recruits were coached in taking one of the equating tests (Ramsberger and Means, 1987, p. 24).

After the problem of the miscalibration — or misnorming, as it is also sometimes called — was discovered, a new accurately calibrated version of the ASVAB was introduced in October 1980. "In addition, the inflated scores for the FY 1976-1980 period were recomputed and the corrected norms were made available" (Office of the Assistant Secretary of Defense, 1982, p. 7).

A number of studies were undertaken to examine how well the hundreds of thousands of recruits who had been mistakenly allowed to enlist — military studies generally referred to them as "potentially ineligibles," or PIs — had actually fared while in military service. Studies looked at how the PIs admitted between 1976 and 1980 compared with control groups of military personnel who had scored higher on the ASVAB on characteristics such as rates of completion of first tour of duty, promotions, eligibility for reenlistment and performance on job proficiency exams. "Overall the PIs performed slightly less well than the controls. Yet the differences were not large and in several cases the PIs performed as well as or even better than the controls" who scored in category III on the ASVAB (Sticht, 1989, p. 61). At a 1987 conference, the Department of Defense's Director of Accession Policy summed up the follow-up studies on the ASVAB misnorming. "Upon looking at their performance," he said in referring to recruits mistakenly allowed to enlist, "we learned that a surprisingly large number of them became successful members of the military. . . . They completed training; their attrition rates weren't unusually high; they were promoted at rates only slightly lower than their higher-scoring peers; and they reenlisted. So the question was not that training grades were somehow flawed but that a quarter of a million people who did not meet the enlistment standards and should not have been able to do the job did in fact do it pretty well" (Sellman, 1987, quoted in Sticht, 1989, p. 62).

It is certainly to the credit of the U.S. military that serious follow-up studies of the ASVAB misnorming were undertaken. But the ASVAB misnorming episode illustrates several important points about the testing industry. The first is that seemingly minor technical issues in the building and norming of tests can have serious implications for large numbers of people. The second is that classifications of people based on test scores are not nearly as accurate indicators of how people will perform in real-life situations as many might imagine. The third is that in the same way that military testing historically has foreshadowed developments in civilian testing, the ASVAB misnorming in the 1976-1980 period foreshadowed a major controversy over the norming of educational tests that was to erupt in the late 1980s. We refer to the Lake Wobegon phenomenon, which we discuss in detail in chapter 7.[15]

OTHER PLAYERS

In addition to for-profit and nonprofit companies, individual researchers who develop and distribute instruments, contract companies, university centers, and the U.S. military, there are a number of other significant players in the testing industry, including:
- Private admissions and licensing boards
- Civil service and other government agencies sponsoring public sector employment testing
- Private companies that do their own employment testing
- Governmental licensing boards, and
- Clinical and counseling testing.

---

[15] There is one other respect in which recent developments in military testing foreshadowed developments in educational testing. In the late 1970s, abuses became apparent in Army recruiting procedures. Because Army recruiters were rewarded in part by how many enlistees they recruited and because enlistment eligibility was tied to AFQT scores, some recruiters "allegedly furnished potential recruits with answers to qualification tests, or coached them while they were taking the tests or doctored the results, all with the intention of enlisting possibly unqualified persons" (Halloran, 1979, p. 37).

Private Admissions and Licensing Boards

Various private organizations either build tests, or contract to have them built, for admission to colleges and graduate training or for certification in a profession. Among the better-known organizations in the admission segment of this category are the College Entrance Examination Board, the Graduate Management Admission Council, the Graduate Records Examination Board, the Association of American Medical Colleges, the Law School Admission Council, and the Law School Admission Services.

A host of organizations use tests to certify candidates applying for admission to various professions. Examples include the National Council of Bar Examiners, the American Institute of Certified Public Accountants, the National Board of Medical Examiners, the American Society of Clinical Pathologists, and the National Council of State Boards of Nursing.

Although we have no precise figures on the number of such agencies, this important non-government gatekeeping component of the testing industry certainly affects large numbers of test takers each year.

Public Sector Employment Testing

Government at the local, state and federal level uses tests extensively for employment and promotion. The federal Civil Service Commission was established in 1883 with the aim of allocating federal jobs to applicants on the basis of "merit" as demonstrated on employment tests, rather than on the basis of political connections. New York and Massachusetts established state civil service exam systems at about the same time, and several more states and several hundred cities followed suit by 1910. Federal civil service testing received a boost from the publicity surrounding the WWI Army testing, but the biggest impetus to state civil service testing came in 1939. In that year the U.S. Congress enacted an amendment to the Social Security Act that required states to maintain merit systems for employees in social security programs. Several federal agencies provided assistance to the states in carrying out civil service testing. "The results of the testing requirement and of federal assistance were striking. By 1949, all but two states had merit systems for public assistance and public health programs" (Hale, 1982, p. 27).

In 1978 the Civil Service Commission had examining jurisdiction over 1.7 million federal workers, and administered 700,000 tests annually (Wigdor & Garner, 1982). At the federal level the Department of State, like the Defense Department, has its own testing programs. Also, the U. S. Employment Service has had a major employment testing program and has assisted states in conducting their own civil service testing programs. State and local governments have a much larger work force than the federal sector. Hence, though more publicity and controversy have centered on federal civil service and military testing, it seems clear that in terms of numbers of employees affected or potentially affected, government employment testing at the state and local levels may have the greater impact. We turn in the next chapter to additional evidence on the nature and volume of public sector employment testing.

Private Sector Employment Testing

In employment settings both public and private, tests are used, often in conjunction with other information, to make personnel predictions or decisions. The 1985 *Standards for Education and Psychological Testing* point out that "competent test use can make significant and demonstrable contributions to productivity and to fair treatment of individuals in employment settings" (p. 59). The *Standards* list the following six kinds of decisions to which tests contribute in those settings:

1. Selecting individuals for an entry level position
2. Making differential job assignments based on test data (classification)
3. Selecting individuals for advanced or specialized positions
4. Promoting individuals within an organization to higher positions (as when test information collected at an assessment center is used to make promotion decisions)
5. Deciding who is eligible for training on the basis of a test of prerequisites
6. Using tests or inventories as diagnostic tools to aid in planning job and career development. (American Educational Research Association, 1985, p.59)

How large is this segment of the testing industry? Friedman and Williams (1982) attempted to gather information on the extent and impact of employment testing in the private sector for the Committee on Ability Testing of the National Research Council of the National Academy of Sciences. They reported:

We know that the use of tests, or systematic use of a variety
of measures of ability or of various processes . . . is scattered
throughout the private sector to help in making decisions on
selection, placement, training, promotion, and retention of
personnel . . . .

There is no way at present, however, to ascertain exactly how
many employment tests are used, in what ways they are used,
how well they are chosen for a given use, or what the overall
effect is. Such information is simply not available, at least
not in any systematic form. (pp. 101-102)

We find that Friedman and Williams' assessment is as true today as it
was a decade ago. However, it seems clear that several dozen companies
specialize in building employment tests for the private sector. The 1988
version of *Personnel Management* published by BNA, in a section headed
Employer Resources, lists 50 companies in the employment testing business,
only ten of which are listed in the 9MMY. However, we are certain that far
more than 50 companies compete in the private employment sector of testing.
For example, when we quickly perused recent copies of the *Training and
Development Journal*, the *Personnel Journal*, the *Personnel Administration
Journal*, and *Training* magazine, we found 11 companies not on the BNA list
advertising tests and testing services. We also talked with the president of one
company that does consulting work in the industrial market (James McSherry of
McSherry Associates). He said that while he could not provide an exact number,
there are far more than 50 companies working in this area.

A 1988 article in *Training* magazine presents a more bullish account of
recent growth in this segment of the testing industry, saying that "all signs
point to a genuine resurgence of employment testing" (Lee, 1988, p. 49). Lee
suggests that employment tests are increasingly being used, not only for initial
hiring decisions, but for a range of other human resource decisions related to
such things as training, promotion and diagnosis of employee weaknesses. He
points to several factors as contributing to the resurgence in employment
testing, including changes in interpretations of the EEOC guidelines and changes
in testing technology. Here is part of Lee's account, in which he quotes an
executive of a company named Personnel Decisions:

It's become a much less costly proposition to develop and validate a test battery that works and is legally defensible. "Ten years ago, if an employer called us and wanted to put together a test battery for salespeople or copywriters or fill-in-the-blank, we told him that it would take $100,000 and six months. Now we're talking about $6,000 and a couple of weeks." And because this test battery will stand up in court, he adds, "even your lawyer can sleep easily." (Lee, 1988, p. 50)

The companies working in the private employee-screening sector publish intelligence tests, clerical aptitude and skills tests, vocational interest tests, manual dexterity tests, personality tests, and training assessment questionnaires. Of the 1,409 tests reviewed in the 9MMY, 45.8% fell in the two categories of Personality and Vocations (Mitchell, 1985). Companies also offer consulting services and customized or packaged pre-employment tests for assessing health substance abuse problems, lifestyle patterns, and reliability or honesty (Bureau of National Affairs, 1988). While we cannot offer a definitive account of each of these niches in the employment testing market, we return in chapter 7 to take a closer look at one of the fastest-growing and most controversial segments of the employment testing industry, namely testing that purports to measure prospective employees' honesty or integrity.

Governmental Licensing Boards

Most states administer tests for licensing or certification for a number of jobs and professions. State boards can develop their own tests, contract for their development, or piggyback on the exams administered by an independent licensing board like the National Council of Bar Examiners. The list of occupations covered by these boards is impressive. For example, Friedman and Williams (1982) report 38 such boards in California and 30 in New York. The jobs covered ranged from dentists to podiatrists, and from automotive repair to cosmetology.

Clinical and Counseling Testing

Clinical testing and tests used in counseling form another significant segment of the testing industry. The *Standards* have separate chapters (7 and 9) devoted to clinical and counseling uses of tests, respectively. In this segment of the market individuals are generally tested one at a time. Clinicians and counselors may test individuals in schools, mental health clinics, hospitals, and prisons, or as part of their private practice. The clinician uses the test results for assessment and decision making about the specific individual. Counselors, on the other hand, facilitate the appropriate and effective use of test results by the test taker (AERA, APA & NCME, 1985).

In the clinical area test results are used to inform a host of important decisions such as "diagnostic classification; presence of neurological impairment; suitability for particular types of treatment; identification of intellectual and personality assets that can be used in rehabilitative, therapeutic or educational planning; eligibility for parole of probation; and evaluation of treatment outcomes" (AERA, APA & NCME, 1985, p.45). Counselors help individuals with questions related to life-span development, "personal and social skills, educational achievement, developed abilities, educational and vocational interests, occupational knowledge and preferences, occupational values, career development, study skills, coping and problem-solving skills, and plans and values for other important roles in adult life, such as relationships with others, work and parenting" (AERA, APA & NCME, 1985, p.55). Advocacy efforts have assured clinical psychologists the right to reimbursement in all major federal insurance plans with the exception of Medicare (Strickland, 1988).

THE FRACTURED MARKET

In this chapter we have sought to provide an overview of the testing industry. Initially, this industry appears to be quite small, with the largest of testing companies having annual revenues only in the hundreds of millions, in contrast with, say, the more general publishing industry where a number of firms have annual revenues in excess of $1 billion (Dun's, 1991). However, as we have shown, the testing industry has dramatic reach, affecting aspects of society ranging from education to employment practices, and from military policies to much of social science research.

Before summarizing the major findings from this chapter, let us take one more broad look at the recent history of the testing marketplace, not in

Table 2.5: Kinds of Tests in Print

Classification	TIP1 Buros, 1961		TIP2 Buros, 1974		TIP3 Mitchell, 1983	
	No.	%	No.	%	No.	%
Achievement Batteries	45	2%	50	2%	74	3%
Business Education	53	2%				
Developmental					87	3%
English	192	9%	131	5%	199	7%
Fine Arts	29	1%	35	1%	33	1%
Foreign Language	92	4%	105	4%	104	4%
Intelligence (& Scholastic Aptitude)	238	11%	274	11%	245	8%
Mathematics	198	9%	168	7%	162	6%
Miscellaneous	233	11%	291	12%	314	11%
Multi-aptitude batteries	20	1%	26	1%	29	1%
Neuropsychological					24	1%
Personality	306	14%	441	18%	576	20%
Reading	159	7%	248	10%	267	9%
Science	106	5%	97	4%	78	3%
Sensory-motor	55	3%	62	3%	51	2%
Social Studies	113	5%	85	3%	81	3%
Speech and Hearing			79	3%	84	3%
Vocations	287	13%	375	15%	487	17%
Totals	2126		2467		2895	

Sources: Buros, 1961, 1974; Mitchell, 1983

Notes: The data for TIP1 and TIP2 are from Buros, 1961 (p. xxix) and those for TIP3 are from Mitchell, 1983 (p. xxvi). However, the classification schemes used in the TIP series have changed somewhat over the years. The classification of "business education" used in TIP1 was dropped in TIP2 and the "speech and hearing" rubric was added. Also the "personality" rubric was listed as "character and personality" in TIP1. Hence for the TIP1 listing we have used the adjusted categorization given in TIP2. In TIP3, the "intelligence" rubric was changed to "intelligence and scholastic ability" and two new rubrics "Developmental" and "Neuropsychological" were added, "principally to reflect changes in the field" (Mitchell, 1983, p. xxvi). Also, while test entries were counted only once in the categorical listings in TIP1 and TIP2, some tests were counted in more than one category in TIP3. While TIP3 contained 2676 separate test entries, the sum of the categorizations for TIP3 shown above is 2895, indcating that as many as 200 tests were double counted. All of these details mean that relatively small changes in the distribution of tests by type (e.g. less than 2%) across the TIP volumes may be artifacts of changes in the categorization schemes employed.

terms of specific test publishers, but in terms of the the kinds of tests published (and in print) during the 1960s, 1970s and 1980s. Table 2.5 shows the numbers and kinds of tests "in print" in 1961, 1974 and 1983 as listed in the *Tests In Print* series of publications. As the notes to this table explain, some caution must be exercised in interpreting these data, because of changes in the test classification schemes used in the *Tests In Print* series. Nevertheless, several broad patterns are apparent. First, and not surprisingly given the increasing social prominence of testing, the total numbers of tests in print increased by about 25%, from 2100 in 1961 to 2700 in 1983 (see note to Table 2.5). But gains in numbers of tests in print were not spread evenly across the rubrics used in the TIP series. The largest gain was apparent in personality tests, which almost doubled in number. Despite such increases in numbers of in-print tests overall and in most categories, interestingly, there were absolute declines in numbers of math and science tests in print between 1961 and 1983. The causes for such changes are likely several. For example, the increase in numbers of personality tests may well reflect increasing application of tests in clinical and counseling psychology. The decreasing numbers of math and science tests, in contrast to the increased numbers of reading tests, may also reflect implicit subject matter priorities in school testing programs (and indicate the influence of federal evaluation requirements connected with Title I programs, which in chapter 5 we show clearly affected the testing marketplace after 1965). But what is absolutely clear is that changes in total numbers and kinds of tests published over the last several decades reflect a wide range of market forces.

Thus our review of the testing industry in this chapter begins to show why we have titled this volume the "fractured marketplace for standardized tests." Different firms are engaged in different segments of the testing marketplace. And even for a single test, different organizations may be responsible for sponsoring, building, administering, scoring and reporting that test. Also, while there have been a significant number of mergers and acquisitions among firms active in the testing marketplace over the last twenty years, it is clear from the new prominence of firms such as Scantron and PRO-ED that the testing industry remains fluid enough to allow the successful entry of new players. And the rapid rise to eminence of firms such as NCS and Scantron shows that computer technology is having an increasing influence on the testing marketplace and that test-related services, such as scoring and reporting of results, are an increasingly important segment of the market, as compared with sales of tests themselves. We discuss some of these themes in more detail in later chapters. But first we turn in chapters 3 and 4 to an examination of both the extent of testing and its direct and indirect costs.

3 THE EXTENT OF THE
MARKETPLACE FOR TESTS

If the nineteenth century in Great Britain was characterized as "the age of examinations," recent decades in the United States might well be called "the age of testing." As Gregory Anrig, president of the Educational Testing Service (ETS), has observed, "There's an old Army saying, 'If it moves, salute it.' Today some reformers seem to be saying, 'If it moves test it.'. . . American schools are going test crazy" (Fiske, 1988, p. 17). It appears that not just schools, but also politicians and policy makers are going test crazy, for 1991 saw numerous proposals for new national tests and testing systems as means of reforming schools and renewing American competitiveness in the international marketplace. In chapters 7 and 8 of this volume we recap and discuss these recent developments, but here in chapter 3, we seek to document the current extent of the market for tests and the way in which it has grown in recent years.

Test use has increased enormously over the last few decades. Like the examinations of the Victorian era, tests in the United States are now used to make a range of important decisions about individuals and institutions. In the field of education, for instance, tests are being used for certification or recertification of teachers, promotion of students from one grade to the next, award of high school diplomas, assignment of students to remedial classes, allocation of funds to schools and school districts, award of merit pay to teachers on the basis of their students' test performance, certification or recertification of schools and districts, and in at least one instance, placement of a school system into "educational receivership." More generally, tests are now widely being touted as instruments of national education reform and renewal. In short, tests are becoming the coin of the educational realm.

Nor is the growing use of standardized testing limited to education. Many states and independent boards build or contract for licensing and certification tests for a wide range of blue-collar and professional occupations, including those of plumber, electrician, police officer, beautician, cosmetologist, nurse, pharmacist, accountant, lawyer, and doctor. In each instance the decisions of a board — based in large measure on a person's test performance — have the force of law. It is illegal for a person who has not been licensed or certified to practice. Moreover, private employers are widely using tests to inform hiring, training, and promotion decisions. These instruments purport to measure traits ranging from literacy to achievement motivation, from numeracy to honesty (the recent upsurge of interest in so-called honesty testing will be discussed later in this volume).

Unlike Victorian examinations, American tests are for the most part developed commercially. However, as in the Victorian era (Bowler, 1983), special preparation and coaching for tests has developed into a highly lucrative commercial enterprise. While standardized commercial testing has been part of the American scene since the 1920s, the last two decades have seen a consistent bull market for testing, with no bear in sight. In order to sketch the dimensions of the testing marketplace, in this chapter we recount a variety of direct and indirect indicators of the extent of the market for tests.

How much testing goes on each year and how has this testing grown? These are important questions but ones that are probably impossible to answer definitively. The reason is that so many different agencies and people administer tests that it is impossible to track all of them down. Hence, the figures presented in this chapter are in many cases merely estimates and sometimes only rough approximations. For such estimations, we explain the exact manner in which we have have derived them and in several instances set bounds on them by calculating low and high estimates.

We begin with the amount and growth of testing in the education sector (for which the data are more plentiful and readily available). After giving estimates of the extent of testing, we present evidence on indirect indicators of the amount of interest in such testing. We then present data on indicators of the extent and growth of testing in the employment sphere for both the public and private sectors. We have no satisfying indicators on the clinical use of tests, so we omit clinical testing from this discussion. The chapter concludes with an overview of the expanding market for testing.

DIRECT INDICATORS OF GROWTH IN EDUCATIONAL
TESTING

Previous estimates have pegged the volume of educational testing per year in the United States at levels ranging between 100 million and 500 million tests (Medina & Neill, 1988; Holmen & Docter, 1972; Houts, 1977; Strenio, 1981; Gay 1989). The 500 million figure comes from Strenio, who reports that in 1930, five million tests were taken per year, in 1960 over 100 million, and in 1981, 400 to 500 million. This last estimate was taken from a 1979 article in *U.S. News & World Report* (cited on p. 297 of Strenio, 1981). No explanations are provided on how these figures are derived.

More recently, Medina and Neill (1988) of the FairTest organization reported that in the 1986-87 school year, 100 million standardized tests were administered. FairTest's figures purport to represent the number of tests given annually, but appear to be based on an uncertain mix of numbers of tests and numbers of students tested. This ambiguity illustrates a definitional problem encountered in estimating the amount of testing. Since many people take more than one standardized test in a given year, we need to distinguish clearly between the *number of tests* administered and the *number of people tested* annually.

However, since much of our source data reports numbers of people tested in specific kinds of testing programs, we need to use some estimate of the number of tests taken by each person in each testing program. For example, if a student sits for a state basic skills test battery that consists of three separate tests assessing reading, math, and listening skills, should the student be counted as taking one test — the battery — or three? Likewise, a student taking the Comprehensive Test of Basic Skills (CTBS) battery may sit for a number of separate tests — e.g. reading, spelling, language, mathematics, reference skills, science, and social studies. Should this count as one or several tests? Since separate scores are typically reported for different portions of a battery — and often may be acted on independently — we decided to consider separately scorable portions of a battery as separate tests.

Also, we should make clear that in estimating the volume of testing in the realm of education, we focus exclusively on the elementary and secondary levels. Though many kinds of standardized tests are used at post-secondary levels, the vast majority of students in the United States are enrolled at the elementary and secondary levels. During the mid- to late 1980s, of over forty million students enrolled in the U.S. schools, only around 12 million were enrolled at the post-secondary level. Also, though testing at the post-secondary level may have increased somewhat in recent years (for example, as a result of the mandate in some states for "rising junior" tests, required of college students in state colleges before they can attain junior standing or major in particular fields), post-secondary testing appears to be much less common than standardized testing at elementary and secondary levels. Thus our estimates cover the bulk of standardized testing in the realm of education.

Finally, we would mention that it would be ideal to focus on one particular year with respect to estimating the extent of testing in the United States. Toward that end we have sought to estimate the extent of testing in 1988. However, since so little data are available on different kinds of testing programs, we actually have had to piece together data from a number of different calendar years. As we explain our methods, we document different data source years. But since available data are drawn from different calendar years, it is probably best to characterize our summary estimates as referring to the volume of annual testing in the mid- to late 1980s rather than in 1988 in particular.

Our overall estimate of the number of standardized tests administered annually in education is an aggregate of the numbers of tests given annually in each of the following types of testing programs:

- State-mandated testing programs
- Traditional school district testing programs
- Tests administered to special populations
- College admission testing programs.

Table 3.1 presents a summary of our estimates for each of these categories, and in the sections below we explain the bases for these estimates. Before turning to this detailed examination, however, it is worth pointing out that overall, we conclude that in the pre-college education sector, between 140 million and 400 million tests are given each year. This estimate represents the equivalent of between three and nine standardized tests administered annually to each of the nation's roughly 44 million students enrolled in public and private elementary and secondary schools.

Table 3.1: Numbers of Tests Given Annually in Late 1980s in Education Sector

STATE MANDATED TESTING PROGRAMS	Low Estimate	High Estimate
Number of students tested	11,000,000	14,300,000
Number of tests per student	3	5
Subtotal	33,000,000	71,500,000
SCHOOL DISTRICT TESTING PROGRAMS		
Estimated enrollment/grade	3,690,579	3,690,579
Adjusted Enrollment @ 80%	2,952,463	2,952,463
No. of grades tested with achievement tests	7	12
Number of achievement tests per student	4	7
Number of achievement tests	82,668,966	248,006,898
Number of grades tested with ability tests	1	4
Number of ability subtests per student	1	2
Number of ability tests	2,952,463	23,619,705
Subtotal	85,621,429	271,626,602
SPECIAL POPULATIONS		
Number of special ed students (aged 3-21)	4,400,000	4,400,000
Adjusted number @ 90%	3,960,000	3,960,000
Number of tests per year	2	5
Number of tests given to special ed students	7,920,000	19,800,000
Number of bilingual students	3,600,000	3,600,000
Number of tests per student	1	3
Number of tests given to bilingual students	3,600,000	10,800,000
Subtotal	11,520,000	30,600,000
COLLEGE ADMISSIONS TESTING		
COLLEGE BOARD		
Scholastic Aptitude Test (2-5 subtests)	3,958,122	9,895,305
Achievement Tests	631,046	631,046
Preliminary SAT (2-3 subtests)	3,276,094	4,914,141
Advanced Placement Tests	369,056	369,056
College-Level Exam'n Program (CLEP)	200,000	200,000
AMERICAN COLLEGE TESTING		
ACT Assessment (4-5 subtests)	4,000,000	5,000,000
Preliminary ACT (4-5 subtests)	600,000	750,000
Subtotal	13,034,318	21,759,548
TOTAL	143,175,747	395,486,150

Sources: see text and appendix 1.

State-Mandated Testing Programs

Under this rubric we include both state-mandated assessment and minimum competency testing (MCT) programs. We arrived at the estimates for state-mandated testing programs using several different sources, but relied primarily on data collected in 1985 for the 1987 Office of Technology Assessment (OTA) report entitled *State Educational Testing Practices* (1987), which gives an overview of all state testing programs. Appendix 1 provides details of how we derived estimates separately for each state, so here we provide only a summary of our methods.

Data on numbers of students tested in state assessment programs were taken directly from the 1987 OTA report. However, the OTA report did not include figures on students tested in state MCT programs; we thus had to piece together data on grade levels tested with estimates of grade level enrollments in each state in order to derive estimates of numbers of students tested in statewide MCT programs. (Because of ambiguities in the OTA data, as explained in the appendix, in some cases we gave high and low estimates.) Next we considered the number of separate tests administered across the states as part of their mandated testing programs. Based on the OTA (1987) report, we used 3 tests per pupil as our lower estimate and 5 as our upper estimate, and multiplied the number of students tested to obtain our overall estimates. As indicated in Table 3.1, these low and high estimates were 33 million and 71 million.

School District Testing Programs

We arrived at our estimates of the numbers of tests administered annually as part of school district testing programs as follows. We started with 1987 public school enrollment data and 1986 private school enrollment data from the 1988 *The Condition of Education* (Stern, 1988). On the basis of these two figures, we estimated that in the late 1980s there were approximately 3.7 million students enrolled per grade in public and private schools (44.3 million over all 12 grades). This compares with a figure of 52 million people aged 0-14 years as counted in the U.S. Census of 1980 (*Information Please Almanac*, 1987, p. 776). This is equivalent to 3,464,000 people per calendar year age under the age of 15 in 1980 — 7% lower than our estimate of 3.7 million per grade level.

After estimating the number of pupils enrolled per grade level in public and private schools, we sought to estimate the number of grades tested in local school district testing programs. Since no systematic national data are available on this point as far as we know, we sought to document the testing practices in a range of school systems, including those of a suburban Massachusetts district, of Topeka, Kansas, and of Boston. On the basis of this information we estimated that a typical school district administers an achievement battery to students in from 7 to 12 grade levels and an ability test in from 1 to 4 grade levels.

To estimate the number of tests students may take in a typical achievement test battery, we examined the catalogs of the three largest publishers of test batteries for the elementary/high school market (referred to by vendors as the Elhi market) to see how many tests make up a typical battery. As a result we used 4 achievement tests per student as a lower bound and 7 as an upper bound estimate. Before producing overall estimates for school district testing programs, we reduced the number of students per grade by 20% to account for several factors. First, it appears that a small number of school systems nationwide may not have such achievement or ability testing programs.[1] Second, some students are excluded from normal achievement testing due, for instance, to their status as special education students or students with limited English language proficiency. The second panel of Table 3.1 presents the results of these assumptions for the estimates of the number of achievement and ability tests taken in school district testing programs per year by students enrolled in public and private schools. As indicated in this table, we thus estimate that from 83 million to 248 million achievement tests have been given annually in recent years. In addition, we assumed that students in such districts took ability tests in from 1 to 4 grades, and that in taking these tests, they took from 1 to 2 separately scorable subtests. This adds three million to 24 million ability tests. Thus, the total number of tests taken per year in the elementary and secondary schools in recent years as part of local school district testing programs is estimated to range from 86 million to 272 million tests.

Before leaving the topic of school district testing programs we should point out that our figures do not reflect the fact that many large districts give

---

[1] In a national probability sample survey of teachers, administrators and testing coordinators, Hall and Kleine (1990) report that 8% of respondents indicated that their schools do not administer norm-referenced achievement tests. Given the way in which the Hall and Kleine survey questions were posed and their data were reported, we cannot be sure what to make of this finding, but it suggests that while over 90% of districts do have norm-referenced testing programs, up to 8% may not.

additional tests over and above the traditional achievement test batteries. For example, in Boston, in addition to the Metropolitan Achievement Tests, the Degrees of Reading Powers Test has been given at certain grades, and tests constructed by the district in reading and math are administered to all students in all grades. Three million students take the Degrees of Reading Power test annually (Stephen Ivens, personal communication, 1988). As another example, in 1985-86 114,000 students in schools across the nation took a test in connection with the National Assessment of Educational Progress (NAEP). Because of the spiral nature of NAEP's sampling of different tests across students, the number of students tested is approximately equivalent to the number of tests administered. However, because these numbers are quite small relative to the standard district testing programs, we have not included special-purpose testing programs in our calculations.

Special Populations

Two special populations of examinees, special education students and bilingual students, are tested extensively. Students in the former group are tested under the provisions of Public Law 94-142. The *Digest of Education Statistics* (Snyder, 1987) reports that 4.4 million students aged 3 to 21 were served in special education programs by the nation's elementary and secondary schools in 1984-85. The number of tests administered to these pupils varies according to the nature of the handicapping condition and also in terms of whether students are undergoing initial diagnosis for placement or are already in a special education program. After consulting with colleagues working in special education, we assumed that between 5 and 10 tests per pupil are used for initial special education classification and 1 to 2 tests are used at least every three years thereafter. The fact of initial heavy testing and then a three-year follow-up complicates estimation of the number of tests administered annually to this population. To arrive at a crude estimate we first deducted 10% of the students classified as special education to eliminate the low-incidence, severely multiply handicapped students who may be little tested with traditional test instruments. This left roughly 4 million students. We then estimated that on average these students took between 2 and 5 tests in any given year, yielding a range of from 8 million to 20 million tests annually.

Another special population of elementary and secondary students are those for whom English is a second language. A 1984 Congressional committee heard that there were 3.6 million such students (Zamora, 1984). If we estimate that each of them takes a minimum of 1 and a maximum of 3 tests per year (the latter is the case in Boston for Spanish speakers), then we have 4 million to 11 million tests administered annually. Altogether then, as shown in Table 3.1, we estimate that between 12 million and 31 million tests are administered annually to special education and bilingual students.

College Admissions Testing

College admissions and related testing is another area considered in our estimates. Before describing how we derived our estimates of the extent of testing in this realm, we should point out that college admissions testing is often not considered as part of the testing of elementary and secondary school students. College admissions tests are not sponsored or generally required by either district or state education agencies, for example. However, there are at least three reasons to view college admissions tests as a significant part of the standardized tests experienced by secondary school students. First, high school students often take such tests in three out of the four high school years (with preliminary tests generally given in sophomore or junior years and the regular tests in junior or senior years). Second, considerable evidence suggests that college admissions tests influence how students study — for example, in taking test preparation courses (a topic to which we return in chapter 7). Third, college admissions tests and results from them have considerable influence on educational policies and programs below the college level. Thus it seems reasonable to consider college admissions testing as an important part of the testing that affects elementary and secondary education.

How much college admissions testing is there? Crouse and Trusheim (1988) estimated that 1.5 million students take the SAT each year and an additional 700,000 take the ACT. To check on the accuracy of these figures we contacted the College Board and ACT directly (Stephen Ivens, personal communication, May 23, 1988; Cinthia Schmeiser, personal communication, May 25, 1988) and were informed that 1,980,000 SATs and 1,000,000 ACTs were given in 1986-87. We thus have relatively firm figures on the number of such college admissions tests given. But there are several ways of counting the number of separately scorable subtests in these testing programs. The SAT has two subtests, the SAT-Verbal and the SAT-Math. Moreover, two subscores are reported for the SAT-Verbal, namely reading and vocabulary. Also, almost all students who take the SAT take the Test of Standard Written English (TSWE). Thus in calculating the number of separately scorable tests involved in SAT testing, we have offered the alternative perspectives of 2 subtests (i.e.. the SAT and TSWE) as a basis for a low estimate and 5 (Math, Verbal Reading, Vocabulary, Verbal Total, and TSWE) as a basis for a high estimate. Similarly, the ACT assessment has four subtests, but since a composite score is also calculated we have used 4 and 5 as bases for high and low estimates. The results, shown in the bottom panel of Table 3.1, indicate that between nearly 4 million and 10 million SAT subtests and 4 million to 5 million ACT subtests are administered annually. Table 3.1 also shows estimates for the numbers of other specialized tests administered in 1986-87 under the auspices of the College Board and the ACT Program. Altogether then we estimate that in 1986-87, 13 million to 22 million college admissions "tests" were administered (with the range in estimates deriving from the number of subtests assumed for each testing program).

In sum then, and as indicated in Table 3.1, we estimate that between 143 million and 395 million tests are administered annually to the nation's population of roughly 44 million elementary and secondary school students, equivalent to between 3 and 9 standardized tests for each student enrolled in elementary and secondary schools.

INDIRECT INDICATORS OF GROWTH IN
EDUCATIONAL TESTING

As far as we have been able to ascertain, no reliable longitudinal data on the number of tests administered exists. We saw that Strenio estimated that between 1930 and 1960 there was an increase of 95 million tests, and between 1960 and 1981 one of 200 million. However, as previously noted, we have little documentation on Strenio's growth estimates. Moreover, as we have seen, our own estimates of the current amount of testing in elementary and secondary schools vary widely, from 143 million to 395 million. Hence, given the paucity of evidence available on the volume of testing over time, we examined four indirect indicators of growth in testing:

1. Recent increases in the numbers of state-mandated testing
   programs
2. Sales figures from test publishers
3. References to testing in the education literature
4. Commentary from analysts of the stock market on testing as a
   growth industry.

STATE-MANDATED PROGRAMS

Figure 3.1 shows a graphical representation of the growth in numbers of state minimum-competency and assessment programs from 1960 through 1985. There was a steady rise in numbers of state-mandated assessment programs, from 1 in 1960 to 32 by 1985. The rise in numbers of minimum competency testing programs at the state level has been even more dramatic. The curve rises sharply from 1 such program in 1972 to 34 by 1985. Naturally, with every state mandate, the number of students tested — and hence the number of tests administered — increased. State testing programs now are the most important market for publishers' group achievement and ability tests (Fremer, 1989).

Sales of Tests

Data on the dollar volume of sales of standardized tests for the elementary/high school market (the Elhi market) is available for the last several decades from *The Bowker Annual of Library and Book Trade Information*. The *Bowker Annual* gets its sales figures from the Association of American Publishers' (AAP) *Industry Statistics Report*. Figure 3.2 shows the reported sales figures for standardized tests for the Elhi market for 1971 through 1990, as reported in the *Bowker Annual* .

Figure 3.2 shows a dramatic growth in test sales, from less than $6 million in 1955 to $128 million in 1990. While this is a substantial growth in test sales even after adjusting for inflation, it should be noted that Elhi test sales of $128 million in 1990, as reported by the AAP, still represents only about 6% of the $15 billion in book publishing sales in the same year.[2]

---

[2] Reported sales for a particular calendar year sometimes vary from one volume of *Bowker* to the next. Since data for the current or most recent year reported in *Bowker* are sometimes identified as preliminary, we have assumed that sales figures for a particular year reported later (which are usually, but not always, higher) usually are correct.

**Figure 3.1: Numbers of States Authorizing Minimum
Competency Testing and Assessment Programs**

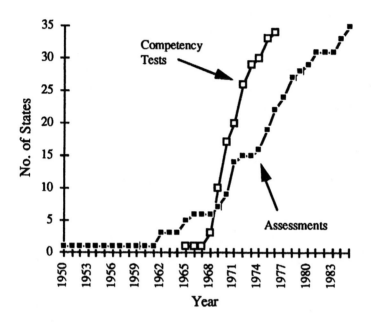

Source: OTA, 1987

Since most publishers treat their sales figures as proprietary, the Elhi
test sales figures cannot be disaggregated by publisher. Further, annual reports
to stockholders by parent companies usually do not break out sales figures for
their testing subsidiaries. Hence, we could find no way of checking the accuracy
of the AAP data reported in *The Bowker Annual*. However, we believe that
these sales figures may be incomplete in several regards.

Figure 3.2: Standardized Test Sales, 1955-1990, in millions of 1988 dollars

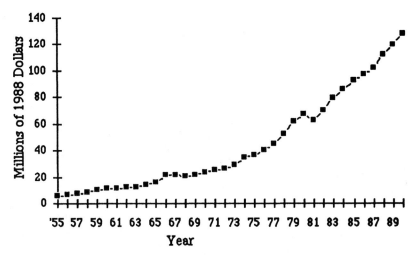

Source: *Bowker Annual of Library and Book Trade Information*, vols. 16-36, 1970-1991.

According to the statistician who compiles the AAP data, statistics on industry sales are based on two sources (personal communication with Robert Winter, May 1991). The first is the census of manufacturers conducted every five years by the U.S. Department of Labor. The second is more detailed data reported by the AAP. Annual data and some subcategory data are based on extrapolations of the 5-year data, informed by actual annual reports of AAP members and others who submit data to the AAP. Thus it appears that annual AAP estimates for particular segments of the publishing industry may be affected by which firms provide annual data to the AAP. For example, the total 1986 figure for sales of standardized tests in the Elhi market for all publishers reported by the AAP was 96.6 million dollars, but the Psychological Corporation (with sales in that year of around $50 million) did not report sales data to the AAP (Fremer, 1989). Since PsychCorp is one of the largest players in the Elhi market, this may have led to an underestimate of sales in that year.

Additionally, the AAP data reported in the *Bowker Annual* do not cover three aspects of the testing that affects elementary and secondary education in the United States. First, they do not encompass some test scoring services (for example the revenues of National Computer Systems, which has a dominant role in the test scoring market). Moreover, they do not include sales figures from companies that are not publishers of tests per se but that build standardized Elhi achievement tests on contract for states and districts (e.g., Advanced Systems in Measurement and Evaluation, Instructional Objectives Exchange, National Evaluation Systems, Scholastic Testing Service). While there is a relatively small number of these companies, they do a significant business — particularly in states with statewide testing programs. Also missing from the AAP estimates are revenues of the American College Testing Program, and the Educational Testing Service, the largest testing company in the United States. While these two firms are not typically viewed as part of the Elhi testing market, their college admissions tests, as we have argued previously, represent an important portion of the testing experienced by elementary and secondary students in the United States.

In sum, the AAP data on elementary and secondary test sales is probably a substantial underestimate of Elhi test sales. They most certainly cover only a portion of the testing industry. Given what the AAP data reveals, and what we know of testing companies not covered in these data, we estimate that in recent years, actual revenues from sales of tests and related testing services may be four to six times higher than those reported in *Bowker* — or on the order of one half to three-quarters of a billion dollars annually.

Revenues of Four Companies

Though comprehensive data on the dollar volume of test sales are not available, we have been able to locate data on revenues of four of the major testing companies over various periods between 1970 and 1991; namely, for Educational Testing Service (ETS) between 1970 and 1991, National Computer Systems (NCS) between 1980 and 1990, American College Testing Program (ACT) between 1972 and 1991 and Scantron between 1980 and 1989 (as previously recounted Scantron became a subsidiary of John Harlan in June 1988). Figure 3.3 shows the revenue trends for these four firms over these periods.

As indicated in Figure 3.3, the total revenues of ETS show a dramatic increase from $35 million in 1970 to $310 million in 1991, representing a compound annual growth rate of about 11%. As mentioned in the last chapter, over the last 20 years, some 85-90% of ETS total revenues have come from testing services it provides to its clients. Though ETS total revenues have risen fairly steadily throughout the last quarter century, increases in the last decade have been sharpest in two of its market segments. Revenues from Graduate and Professional Testing increased from $21 million in 1983 to $45 million in 1990. Over the same period, revenue from teacher and other professional testing tripled from $16 million to $49 million, undoubtedly reflecting the dramatic increase in state legislation mandating teacher certification testing and testing for admission to teacher training. An interesting aspect of the ETS figures is that while ETS is not usually considered a player in Elhi testing, most of its revenues come from college admissions testing of secondary school students. In 1990, the last year for which we have the Elhi sales data from AAP, the ETS revenue from College Board testing alone, $118 million, was nearly as large as the AAP reported for all Elhi test sales ($128 million).

Revenues of NCS have increased even more sharply over the last decade, zooming from $35 million in 1980 to $284 million in 1990 — equivalent to a compound annual increase rate of 23%. While we do not have detailed information on the breakdown of NCS total revenues, it appears that the vast majority of NCS revenues — on the order of 80-90% — come from scanning services, test building and test sales.

ACT has shown more modest revenues over the last 20 years, increasing from $8 million in 1972 to $70 million in 1991. This is equivalent to an annual rate of increase of about 12%, roughly equivalent to ETS's rate of growth in total revenues over roughly the same period. Unlike ETS, ACT actually experienced a period in 1981-82 when total revenues declined. This downturn did not, however, represent a slump in ACT testing business. Rather, it reflected ACT's loss of a major federal contract to process student financial aid forms.

Revenues for Scantron, the fourth company for which data is graphed in Figure 3.3, have been much smaller than those of ETS, NCS and ACT. This is hardly surprising since Scantron was only founded in 1972, whereas the other companies have existed since 1947, 1962 and 1958 respectively. However, between 1980 and 1988 (when it became a subsidiary of John Harlan), Scantron revenues increased from $4 million to $35 million, representing an annual rate of growth of around 30%, considerably exceeding the growth rates of the larger firms.

Though we do not have sufficiently detailed information on sources of revenues for each of these four companies to pinpoint trends very precisely, comparing Figure 3.3 with Figure 3.2 does suggest one generally common trend. For both the four companies for which we have annual revenue data

(ETS, NCS, ACT and Scantron) and for the test publishers reporting to the AAP, the period of the 1980s, after about 1982 or 1983, appears to have been one of unprecedented growth in sales for the testing industry.

Figure 3.3: Revenues of Four Testing Companies

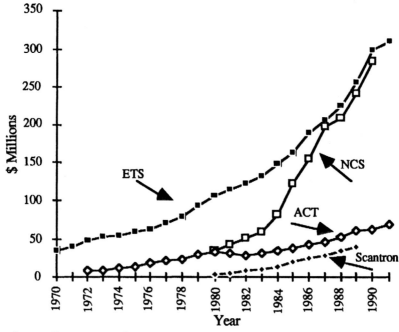

Source: Company annual reports

The Rise in the Price of Test Booklets and Scoring Services

        In order to place test sales data in perspective, we examined the price of the test booklets and the scoring service for the achievement batteries of the three largest publishers in the Elhi market.[3] We did this in order to consider the extent to which reported increases in test sales may be due to increases in

_____

[3] Harcourt Brace, Jovanovich/Psychological Corporation (which publishes the Metropolitan Achievement Test and the Stanford Achievement Test), California Test Bureau/McGraw-Hill (the California Achievement Test and the Comprehensive Test of Basic Skills), and Houghton-Mifflin/Riverside Press (the Iowa Test of Basic Skills and the Stanford-Binet Intelligence Scale).

extent to which reported increases in test sales may be due to increases in volume of testing versus increases in prices of tests and testing services sold. Specifically, we examined costs of test booklets, machine-scorable answer sheets and scoring services as reported in the Mental Measurements Yearbooks or in recent catalogs of the three test publishers. In order to adjust for inflation all costs were converted to constant 1988 dollars (using the yearly CPI as the basis for adjustments). Summary results of these analyses are shown in Figures 3.4 and 3.5 The answer sheet and scoring costs are averages across the three publishers. The booklet cost figures in adjusted dollars are shown in Figure 3.4[4]; the scoring cost figures in constant 1988 dollars, in Figure 3.5.

Figure 3.4: Price per test Booklet in 1988 Dollars

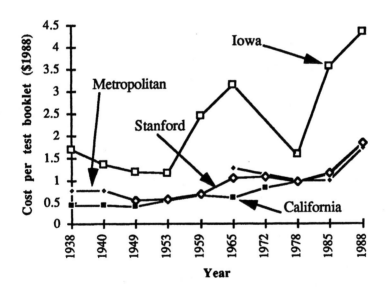

Source: Mental Measurements Yearbooks and catalogs

---

[4] While the Iowa costs appear much larger, the Iowa booklet bundles the test batteries for all the grades. The other two publishers market the booklets separately by grade level.

Figure 3.5: Answer Sheet and Scoring Costs in 1988 Dollars

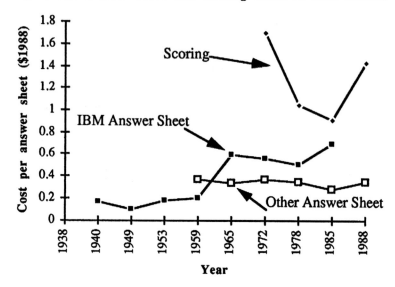

Source: *Mental Measurements Yearbooks* and catalogs

Figure 3.4 shows that the real price of purchasing a test booklet (that is, the constant dollar price) has approximately doubled over the last fifty years. Interestingly, the price of scoring services decreased from 1970 to 1988. These figures compare to a more than four-fold increase in the dollar value of Elhi test sales, as reported by the AAP, from 1971 to 1990. Thus it seems clear that the substantial increase in Elhi test sales over the last twenty years cannot be explained solely by increases in the costs of tests and related services. Instead, the increase is due in large measure to increases in the volume of testing.

The Literature on Educational Testing as an Indicator of Growth

As an indirect way of documenting the increased attention to testing in the educational realm, Haney (1986) charted the number of citations under the rubric "tests and scales" (as indicated by number of column inches) from 1930 through 1985 in the *Education Index*. For comparative purposes, and because curriculum issues should be a central focus of schooling, the numbers of citations under the "curriculum" rubric were also charted. We updated the Haney data through 1987.

Figure 3.6: Education Index Listings Under Testing and Curriculum

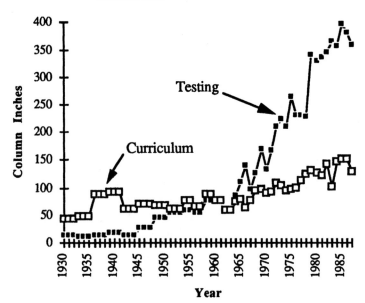

Source: *Education Index*, 1930-1988

As shown in Figure 3.6, the average annual number of column inches devoted to citations concerning curriculum has increased only modestly over the last 57 years — from 50 to 100 inches per year in the 1930s and 1940s to only 100 to 150 in recent years. In contrast, column inches devoted to tests and scales have increased greatly, from only 10 to 30 in the 1930s and 1940s to well over 300 in the 1980s. While these indices are admittedly crude, the data certainly point to the fact that the prominence of testing, as represented in the education literature, has grown dramatically, particularly since the mid-1960s.

When the data shown in Figure 3.6 are considered along with the data on the growth in state testing programs (Figure 3.1) and in testing revenue (Figures 3.2 and 3.3), the conclusion seems inescapable that educational testing has expanded vastly over the last twenty years, in terms of both volume and societal importance.

Corporate and Industry Research Reports

Our search for evidence on trends in testing led us to another indirect indicator of the growth in the testing industry — the evaluations by stock market analysts of companies involved in testing. Independent, publicly held testing companies that offer stock through brokerage houses are analyzed by those houses in *Corporate and Industry Research Reports* (CIRR) (edited by P. Cicchetti). Most of the largest testing companies are not listed on the stock market.[5] Nevertheless, three companies whose primary business is testing — National Computer Systems, Scantron Corporation (SCNN) and London House — have been listed on the stock exchange, and hence have been the subject of analysis by various brokerage houses.

The first two companies, NCS and Scantron, manufacture optical mark reading (OMR) equipment used to score test answer sheets, and market expendable answer sheet forms for machine scoring. NCS also develops tests under contract. Scantron and NCS compete in the Elhi and college market. We discuss London House when we consider the extent of testing in the employment sector. Also, as previously noted, Scantron is no longer an independent corporate entity, but is now a subsidiary of John H. Harlan.

Nevertheless, the following representative descriptions and analyses clearly indicate that stock market analysts are bullish, not only on Scantron and NCS, but also on the testing industry in general (emphasis added):

> *The trend toward objective testing continues to expand and should benefit SCNN* since it is the dominant factor in the lower-volume segment of the educational market. Parenthetically, this market is far from saturated. . . . Given a 15-22% growth potential over the next three years and excellent margins, we consider this stock significantly undervalued. (Sutro & Co. Inc. in Cicchetti, 1988)

> National Computer is the dominant company in the [OMR] market in *a market barely 20% penetrated and growing at 25%*

---

[5] This is because they either are non-profit companies, such as ACT and ETS, or are wholly owned subsidiaries of larger companies, as in the case of Psychological Corporation.

plus per annum. (Drexel Burnham Lambert, Inc., in Cicchetti,
1988)

Greater demands for accountability in education have been a
driving force behind much of the growth in NCS. Mandated
standards are becoming very common, bordering on universal.
. . . There are approximately 45-47 million students in
elementary and secondary schools in some 16,000 districts
containing over 100,000 buildings and about 1.5 million
classrooms. Currently, the installed base of low-end scanners
is only 26,000. (Paine Webber, 1988, in Cicchetti, 1988)

As the leading provider of [OMR] systems, we believe
[NCS's] growth prospects in the educational . . . marketplace
[are] outstanding and will prove rewarding to investors over the
longer term. *External factors have also been important to the
company's growth including a growing concern over the
quality of education in America and the need to make teachers
and administrators more productive within the system . . . .
NCS benefits from the increased use of standardized testing
which has evolved out of a growing national concern over the
quality of our educational system. Over 40 states now use
some form of mandated testing to measure individual
achievement and, more importantly, to identify weakness
within the system itself. OMR technology is well suited to
address this need.* (Blunt Ellis & Lowei, Inc., in Cicchetti,
1988)

The primary interest of stock analysts is in selling stocks.
Nonetheless, their comments on the few companies that represent "pure testing
plays" in the stock market clearly indicate an awareness of the increased demand
for testing in general, and for accountability and mandated statewide testing
programs in particular. Moreover, their estimates of the current annual growth
potential of testing companies (ranging from 15 to 25% per annum) suggest a
recent accelerated growth in testing. For example, the growth in test sales
reported in the *Bowker* volumes, cited earlier, from $25 million in 1971 to $128
million in 1990, could have been achieved by an annual growth rate of only 9%

($25 million growing at 9% per annum compounded over 30 years is $128.5 million). Thus it appears that the testing industry is currently growing faster than it has in the last 30 years.

Standard Industrial Classification Manual

Another indirect indicator of the increasing prominence of standardized testing is provided in the *Standard Industrial Classification Manual* (Executive Office of the President Office of Management and Budget, 1987). The Standard Industrial Classification (SIC) is a set of four-digit codes developed by the U.S. Government and revised in 1987. The SIC

> is the statistical classification standard underlying all establishment-based Federal economic statistics classified by industry. The SIC is used to promote the comparability of establishment data describing various facets of the U.S. economy. The classification covers the entire field of economic activities and defines industries in accordance with the composition and structure of the economy. It is revised periodically to reflect the economy's changing industrial organization. (Executive Office of the President Office of Management and Budget, 1987, p. 2)

The 1987 revision of the SIC system was the first major revision since 1972 and in a sign of the increasing prominence of testing the following new subcategories were added to the classification system:
- Test development and evaluation service, educational or personnel
- Testing services, educational or personnel.

These were included under code 8748 referring to "Business Consulting Services, Not Elsewhere Classified." The 8748 rubric was defined to include a potpourri of other kinds of consulting such as agricultural consulting, radio consultants and traffic consultants.

However, in using various business and industry reference works, we have found that testing companies are rarely classified under the 8748 code. In the InfoTrac General BusinessFile CD-ROM (Information Access, 1990), for example, we found that both ETS and ACT were classified with 8733 as their primary SIC code, referring to "Noncommercial research organizations." In this same reference source, the Psychological Corporation was listed with the primary SIC 2731, referring to "Book Publishing and Printing."[6]

The ways in which companies whose primary business is standardized testing get assigned quite different SIC codes is a notable indication of the fractured nature of the testing industry. Nevertheless, the assignment of the "Test development and evaluation service, educational or personnel" and "Testing services, educational or personnel" subcategories to the 8748 code does provide another indication of the growth of standardized testing as a commercial activity. At the same time, it is revealing that these two new subcategories in the 1987 SIC system fall under the 874 "Management and Public Relations Services" industry group number and not under 873 "Research, Development and Testing Services" industry group number.[7]

THE EXTENT OF STANDARDIZED TESTING IN THE EMPLOYMENT SECTOR

In this section we discuss the extent of testing in government and private industry for employment or licensure. As noted previously, the available indicators in these sectors are not as extensive or detailed as was the case for education. We first examine indicators of the extent of testing in the public sector and then present estimates for the private sector.

Military Testing

Table 3.2 summarizes our estimates of major testing in the military sector. We conclude that at least as of the late 1980s, testing in the military totaled between 20 million and 25 million tests per annum. The most widely used employment test in the country is the Armed Services Vocational Aptitude Battery (ASVAB), which consists of 12 independently scored sub tests as described in the last chapter. In 1979, the ASVAB was administered to approximately 602,000 applicants to military service, as well 965,000 students (Friedman and Williams, 1982), for a total of some 18 million tests.

---

[6] One place where we did find the 8748 code used for a major testing company was *Duns Million Dollar Disc* (Dun's Marketing Services, 1991) in which ETS was listed with both the 8748 and the 8733 codes.

[7] The "Testing Services" referred to under the 873 industry group number pertain to activities of various testing laboratories other than "clinical laboratory testing for the medical profession" (Executive Office of the President Office of Management and Budget, 1987, p. 403).

Table 3.2:   Extent of Testing in Military Public Sector

Test Purpose	1979	1982	1989	Sub-tests	Low Es-timate	High Es-timate
		Numbers Tested			Number of Tests	
Entrance						
ASVAB						
Recruits	601,782		1,000,000	12	7,221,384	12,000,000
Students	965,409		1,000,000	12	11,584,908	12,000,000
CEB		11,000	12,650	7	77,000	88,550
OAR		34,000	39,100	3	102,000	117,300
AFOQT		30,000	34,500	5	150,000	172,500
Subtotal					19,135,292	24,378,350
Promotion	800,000		639,920	1	639,920	800,000
TOTAL					19,775,212	25,178,350

Source: Data on numbers tested from Friedman & Williams (1982) except: 1989
ASVAB estimates, which are from Hartigan, J. & Widgor, A.K. (Eds.) (1989); and
1989 promotion estimates, which are extrapolated from total personnel in military
sector (Bureau of Labor Statistics, June 1989).

In 1989, the ASVAB was administered to approximately 1 million
applicants and a comparable number of high school students (Hartigan, 1989),
for a total of roughly 24 million tests. While the SAT/ACT batteries are often
used for entrance into officer training programs, the various branches of the
service also administer the following tests for the recruitment of officers: Air
Force Officer Qualifying Test (AFOQT/Air Force); Officer Aptitude Rating
(OAR/Navy and Marine Corps); and Cadet Evaluation Battery (CEB/Army). We
estimate that between 397,000 and 456,550 tests are administered annually in
officer selection procedures in the military.

In addition to entrance screening, the military administers tests to
enlisted personnel at almost all pay levels for purposes of promotion. In 1979,
roughly 800,000 enlisted personnel sat for such examinations (Friedman &
Williams, 1982). In 1979, this figure represented 38% of all military personnel.
With no specific comparable data for 1989, we assume that the same percentage
of personnel were tested in 1988 (639,920, or a total 1.7 million). Assuming
further that testing of this nature is job-specific, it may be reasonable to assume
one test per employee, yielding our estimate of between 639,920 and 800,000

tests per year for promotion selection. Thus we estimate that between roughly 20 million and 25 million tests were given annually in the military sector in the late 1980s. However, with decreasing world tensions and cutbacks in the U.S. military in the 1990s, it seems likely that the volume of testing in the military is decreasing at present.

Civil Service

Data on the extent of testing in the civil service at federal, state and local levels are extremely scanty. The civilian workforce is composed of approximately 3 million employees in the federal sector, 4 million in state, and 10 million in local government (*Monthly Labor Review*, June 1989). In the federal sector, approximately 90% of these employees operate under a merit system; 80% are white collar, while 20% are blue collar (Tenopyr, 1981; Friedman & Williams, 1982). At the state and local levels, 50% of all civilian employees are in education (Maslow, 1983).

Federal Sector Until 1979, the U.S. Office of Personnel Management (previously the Civil Service Commission) centrally controlled the testing and evaluation of 1.7 million federal employees. Since 1979, the Office has attempted to decentralize selection and promotion procedures to the individual federal agencies. This has prevented collection of updated and consistent information on the extent of testing within the federal sector.

Table 3.3 presents data on the types and numbers of applications for federal government jobs from 1974 to 1978 for which written tests were required. The numbers of applicants tested (1.6 million) is relatively stable across the five years of the 70s. However, it is likely that the level of federal job testing in the 1970s did not persist into the late 1980s, given the extent of government deregulation under the Reagan administrations, court challenges to job selection procedures, and even some internecine disputes over federal employment testing between different federal agencies. While some of the legislation affecting testing is reviewed in chapter 5 of this volume, it is sufficient to note here that a variety of factors since 1979 make it implausible to assume that the level of federal employment testing in the 1970s persisted into the 1980s. Though we have found no way to estimate the actual volume of federal employment testing in the 1980s, we do have more recent evidence, which we review later in this chapter, on the kinds of testing that seem to be used in government as opposed to other sectors of employment.

Table 3.3: Workload Report for Federal Examinations:
Number of Applications, Selections, and Veterans Selected

Numbers of Applications Requiring Written Tests

Fiscal Year	Steno-Typist	Other Clerical	Summer Employment	Technical Assist(a)	PACE(b)	Air Traffic Controllers	All Six	All Federal Exams
1974	275,201	184,213	60,788	69,630	187,569	23,898	801,299	1,620,798
1975	283,675	173,821	80,053	96,824	219,947	15,794	870,114	1,682,046
1976	260,613	163,248	72,523	56,819	235,333	14,086	802,622	1,676,936
Transition Qtr 76(c)	60,051	43,784	1,563	12,920	23,361	4,933	146,612	348,547
1977	256,789	175,382	65,430	56,236	219,210	18,229	791,276	1,671,119
1978	253,159	176,520	45,111	34,380	166,440	13,055	688,665	1,616,178

Notes:

(a) FY 1976-1978 Technical Assistant data are estimated

(b) Figures for FY 1974 are from the predecessor FSEE

(c) FY 1976 ended 30 June 1976. FY 1977 began 1 October 1976

Source: Data from US Office of Personnel Management; see also Friedman & Williams (1982:126)

State and Local Sector The last known national baseline survey on personnel practices in state and local government was given in 1977 by the U.S. Office of Personnel Management. The survey, *Analysis of Baseline Data Survey on Personnel Practices for States, Counties, Cities* (U.S. Office of Personnel Management, 1979), was sent to 50 states, 2100 cities and 1201 counties, and requested information for the period 1 June 1976 through 30 June 1977. Responses were received from 48 states, 101 cities and 140 county governments. Table 3.4 reports the numbers of applicants tested in 1975 and 1976. If we assume only one test per applicant, these numbers also represent an estimate of the number of tests administered to new applicants in state and local governments in 45 of the 53 states (Washington, D.C., the Pacific Island Trust Territories, and the two personnel systems in Texas were considered as separate states for this survey).

Table 3.4: Number of Persons Tested in State and Local Civilian Public Sector

No. States	Population Range (millions)	1975		1976	
		Low	High	Low	High
10*	0-1	3,415	62,026	3,455	34,860
11	1-3	11,886	56,869	3,000	57,238
12	3-4	22,396	76,400	17,565	77,100
6	5-10	14,308	126,311	21,346	144,195
6	11-20	20,000	128,866	25,000	125,837

*Two respondents within this population range did not provide data.
Source: Office of Personnel Management and Council of State Governments (1979), p. 7.

Other surveys report results as percentages of respondents who prefer certain methods of job selection for entrance and promotion, making any estimate of the current number of tests given extremely tenuous. For example, survey data are available from the 1970s showing state preferences in methods of employee selection procedures by type of occupation. The data indicates that written tests are preferred in selecting applicants for clerical and technical positions, while ratings of training and experience are more common for trades, labor, professional and management applicants.

A more recent survey by the International Personnel Management Association of 519 agency members in 1982, and 389 agency members in 1988, indicated the job testing methods used at all levels of the civilian public sector (local, state and federal), as summarized in Table 3.5. The survey data does not include information on the number of tests developed or administered, or the number of candidates tested. The results in the table are limited to the percent of responding jurisdictions that made any use of each of the testing methods listed. Furthermore, there is no clear explanation for the seemingly anomalous finding that reported use of ratings of training and experience drops markedly, from 82% in 1982 to 38% in 1988.

Table 3.5: International Personnel Management Association Survey Results on Testing Methods

Method	1982	1988
Aptitude Tests	43%	46%
Assessment Centers	NA	33%
Intelligence Tests	16%	21%
In-Basket Tests	24%	28%
Job Knowledge Tests	75%	75%
Performance Tests	69%	52%
Personality Tests	12%	23%
Ratings of Training and Experience	82%	38%
Structured Oral Exams	NA	76%

Source: Personal Communication with Charles F. Sproule, IPMA, May 1989

Licensure

State and federal regulations also require written tests for certification to practice certain professions. Consolidated data on the extent of licensure testing is generally unpublished. While professional licensure has increased since the early 1970s due to greater consumer demand for accountability as well as increased technical development and job specialization, we have found little national data on the extent to which written standardized tests are the instrument of choice in determining professional competency.

However, a 1975 California state report noted that roughly 90% of the licensing boards surveyed (30 boards) used written examinations exclusively

(Friedman, 1982). Data from 1978 indicate that in California there were 110,000 new examinees in that year. In the same year New York state reported 55,473 new examinees, while Florida reported 27,000 (Friedman & Williams, 1982). A 1980 U.S. Government survey estimated that of 800 occupations regulated by licensing procedures, 500 require passing a written test (Greene & Gay, 1980 in Friedman & Williams, 1982).

Job Placement by the U.S. Employment Service (USES)

In addition to testing its own employees and professionals seeking licensure, the federal government assists state employment agencies in the development, validation and administration of guidance and placement tests. The best-known of these is the General Aptitude Test Battery (GATB), which consists of 12 tests and was administered to between 800,000 and 1 million people annually, for a total of 9.6 million to 12 million tests per year, during the late 1980s. In addition to the GATB, USES provides tests in various skill areas, such as typing, dictation, and spelling. However, the current status of USES job placement testing is unclear because of several controversies which broke out over GATB testing polices in the late 1980s. While the following excerpt from the *Federal Register* hardly conveys the passions aroused in debates about validity generalization theory and "race-conscious" adjustment of GATB selection scores (or what critics called race-norming), it does succinctly state the basic facts concerning the case.

In the early 1980s, a new experimental process for using the General Aptitude Test Battery (GATB) was introduced. The process is called Validity Generalization (VG) or VG-GATB (generalizing the validity of the GATB across all jobs in the U.S. economy). Concurrently, to reduce adverse impact that testing has on minority jobseekers in being selected for referral to jobs, a score adjustment procedure was also introduced called within-group conversion.

In 1986, the Department of Justice (DOJ) raised questions about within-group scoring but agreed to withhold legal action pending the outcome of a special review of VG-GATB by the National Research Council of the National Academy of Sciences (NAS). Also, organizations representing groups such as veterans and persons with disabilities have expressed

concerns regarding the use of tests. The NAS study endorsed
the concept of VG and indicated that the GATB compares
"quite well" with other tests.   However, the NAS
recommended that, if the use of VG-GATB would be
continued, it should not be the only referral method used. The
NAS report provided qualified support for the VG-GATB;
however, it provided little basis for resolving the legal
questions raised by DOJ. The NAS report provided useful
operational and technical recommendations in areas such as test
validation methods, additional forms of the GATB,
"coachability" and time limits, test security, and norms. A
number of these areas have implications regarding fairness to
groups such as the less well-educated, older workers, and
persons with disabilities.

Prudence counsels against further use of GATB and similar
tests in screening for referral to employment until an extensive
2-year research project provides assurance that the Department
of Labor has the most scientifically valid and reliable
assessment instrument possible. The GATB may still be used
in vocational counseling where the counselee voluntarily
agrees to such use. (*Federal Register*, 55:142, July 24, 1990,
p. 30126)[8]

Overall Estimate of Public Sector Testing

As this account of the recent bumpy history of the GATB suggests, an
accurate overall estimate of testing in the public sector is impossible. While the
merit system appears to cover the majority of public sector employees (Tenopyr,
1981), data are unavailable on the proportion of merit systems that use
standardized tests. We also do not know the volume of annual testing for
licensure and certification. The most reliable data available had been on the
extent of the use of the GATB, but as explained, after falling into controversy,
the GATB testing program of the Department of Labor was largely suspended in
1990.

---

[8] The NAS report referred to in this passage is Hartigan & Wigdor, 1989.

Thus we conclude that it is extremely difficult if not impossible to estimate the volume of standardized testing in the public employment sector. Knowing the rough composition of the public sector workforce and the general trends apparent in preferences of job selection procedures allow us merely to guess that, excluding licensure and certification testing, the number of people tested for public sector employment in the mid-1980s was probably on the order of 2-4 million people. However, given the recession of the early 1990s, and cutbacks in governmental employment, the extent of public sector employment testing is likely to have substantially diminished since the 1980s.

Extent of Private Sector Employment Testing

Table 3.6 shows a very rough estimate of the numbers of tests administered in the private sector annually in the late 1980s to be between 45 million and 196 million.

Table 3.6: Number of Employment Tests in Private Sector

Industry Sector	% Using Tests[a]	Sector Employment[b]	Low Estimate[c]	High Estimate[d]
Manufacturing	57.7	19,708,000	11,371,516	45,486,064
Public Utilities	77.6	1,016,000	788,416	3,153,664
Hospitals	53.4	3,309,000	1,767,006	7,068,024
Banks	63.5	2,047,000	1,299,845	5,199,380
Insurance	78.2	1,786,000	1,396,652	5,586,608
Other Offices	75.0	11,868,000	8,901,000	35,604,000
Retail Stores	57.5	15,519,000	8,923,425	35,693,700
Trans/Comm	81.7	4,546,000	3,714,082	14,856,328
Other	66.2	17,361,000	11,492,982	45,971,928
Totals	63.5	77,160,000	48,996,600	195,986,400

Notes:
a. Source: Prentice-Hall (1975)
b. Source: 1986 Annual Current Population Survey
c. Low estimate calculated as 1 test per employee per annum
d. High estimate calculated as 4 tests per employee per annum

This estimate is derived from two sources. First is an evaluation of testing procedures in the private sector done in 1975 by Prentice-Hall and the American Society for Personnel Administrators. Responses from 1,339 member companies were analyzed and categorized into the types of businesses listed in Table 3.6. The study reported the percentage of respondents who use standardized tests for selection and promotion, as well as the percentage who do not use written tests at all. To transform these preferences into actual numbers of tests, we acquired data on total annual employment in each of the business types described in the Prentice-Hall survey. These employment data, gleaned from the US Census Bureau's 1986 Current Population Survey, remain fairly stable from year to year and provide a reasonable estimate of the numbers of employees in each of the Prentice-Hall categories.

It may seem somewhat implausible to use 1975 survey data to estimate the volume of employment testing in the late 1980s, but as we will show shortly, the 1975 data are in line with more recent survey results on employment testing and were reported in a manner that allows us to match them with population employment data. Then, in order to derive a very crude estimate of the extent of employment testing, we assumed a range of between 1 and 4 tests per employee per year. This estimate may seem high given that standardized testing is more common for new employees than for employees eligible for retention of promotion, but recall that we consider a separately scorable subtest as a "test." Many employment test batteries actually include six or more separately scorable subtests. Nevertheless, we readily acknowledge that we have no empirical rationale for the range of 1 to 4 tests per employee per year. This crude assumption merely provides some basis for estimating the extent of testing in this sector.

More recent surveys since the 1975 PH/ASPA survey are somewhat contradictory in what they indicate concerning trends in the field of employment testing in the private sector. An excellent review of these surveys through 1982 by Friedman and Williams is contained in Wigdor and Garner (1982).

The state of flux in job selection regulations may have caused changes in testing procedures in industry. This conclusion is suggested, at least, by the results of more recent studies not reviewed in the Wigdor and Garner (1982) volume. The American Management Association found, in a 1985 survey distributed to over 7,000 human resource managers, that most respondents do not test at all, and of those who do, the average annual dollar investment in the total program is only $400 (AMA, 1986). The survey also found that testing is widely used for promotion as well as initial hiring. The same organization, in a 1987 survey of 995 human resource managers, reported somewhat contradictory results. The average investment in testing programs was $23,500 per year, with large companies investing $136,000, mid-size companies $13,900, and small companies $4,500. The 1987 survey also reported that few companies test current employees for promotion, but rather test almost exclusively for job entrance (Greenberg, 1988).

The latest AMA survey, of about 1000 human resource managers, was conducted in 1990 (AMA, 1990). As might be expected, it indicated that generally larger firms (those with sales in excess of $50 million annually) tend to do more testing than smaller firms. Table 3.7 summarizes the results of this survey to show kinds of testing reported by respondents in different business categories. While these results obviously must be viewed with some caution in light of anomalies apparent in previous similar AMA surveys, they suggest several general trends. First, by 1990, across all business categories, testing for drugs appears to have become as common as basic skills or job proficiency testing. Testing for HIV infection, not surprisingly, is most commonly reported by respondents in the health care and medical sector. Four kinds of testing (testing for basic skills proficiency, polygraph testing, psychological or behavior testing and job competency testing) are most commonly reported by those in the "government and military" category. Finally, pencil and paper "honesty" testing is most commonly reported by those in the "wholesale and retail trade" business category. Later, in chapter 6, we return to take a closer look at the emergence of honesty or integrity testing; for now let us simply summarize what we conclude about trends in private sector employment testing.

Standardized testing for employment purposes in the private sector appears to be more common for initial job selection than for job promotion. Also, standardized testing for employment does not seem to be as common in the private sector as in the public sector. Nevertheless, in at least two regards, trends in the private sector appear to be similar to those in the public sector. First, there seems to be greater reliance on multiple assessment techniques for job selection, written testing being part of that process. Second, private sector employment testing, like that in the public sector, clearly has been influenced by challenges to the fairness of employment testing. We comment in more detail on the history of such challenges in the chapter 5. The one realm in which employment testing clearly seems to have increased sharply in recent years is with respect to pencil and paper honesty testing.

Table 3.7: American Management Association 1990 Survey on Workplace Testing

	Whole Sample	Bank'g, Finan., Insur.	Educa-tion	Gov. & Milit.	Health Care & Med.	Manuf. Consum. Goods	Manuf. Indus. Goods	Prof. Ser-vices	Wh'sale & Retail Trade
Number	1021	118	70	73	81	96	230	78	60
Kind of Testing									
Test for Drugs	526	31	11	41	35	77	173	25	28
	52%	26%	16%	56%	43%	80%	75%	32%	47%
Test for HIV Infection	77	2	1	15	34	1	11	3	1
	8%	2%	1%	21%	42%	1%	5%	4%	2%
Test for Basic Skills Proficiency	362	52	22	34	20	36	84	21	25
	35%	44%	31%	47%	25%	38%	37%	27%	42%
Polygraph Testing	38	6	0	15	3	2	0	2	4
	4%	5%	0%	21%	4%	2%	0%	3%	7%
Pencil & Paper Honesty Testing	65	8	2	3	4	8	6	4	18
	6%	7%	3%	4%	5%	8%	3%	5%	30%
Psychological or Behavior Testing	210	32	4	28	5	22	47	13	17
	21%	27%	6%	38%	6%	23%	20%	17%	28%
Job Competency Testing	458	48	41	45	32	49	85	36	21
	45%	41%	59%	62%	40%	51%	37%	46%	35%

Source: American Management Association 1990 Survey on Workplace Testing

Corporate and Industry Research Reports.

Earlier in this chapter we noted that independent, publicly-held testing companies that offer stock through brokerage houses have been analyzed by those houses in *Corporate and Industry Research Reports* (CIRR). One of the three testing companies that have been publicly held and reviewed in CIRR is London House, which designs, develops and markets integrated psychological tests and evaluation systems for businesses. London House also provides its clients with computerized scoring, analysis and interpretation of results. The following description indicates that stock market analysts are also bullish about testing in the business sector (emphases added):

> London House reported an excellent first quarter with revenues advancing 22% — *a reflection of the continued use of testing to make hiring decisions* combined with a more cohesive marketing approach. . . . London House should be able to grow at a 15%-20% annual rate over the next several years. (Blunt Ellis & Loewi, Inc., in Cicchetti, 1988)

Given this evaluation by stock market analysts, it is not surprising that, as noted in chapter 2, London House was acquired by Maxwell and then in 1989 became a part of the Macmillan/McGraw-Hill School Publishing Company.

The Literature on Business Testing As An Indicator of Growth.

Another indirect indicator of the increased attention to testing in the business world is the growth in the number of articles dealing with testing found in the professional literature. Figure 3.7 charts the number of citations, as indicated by number of column inches, under 5 test-related rubrics from 1958 through 1988 in the *Business Periodical Index*. The rubrics were Tests and scales, Ability tests, Employment tests, Intelligence tests, and Personality tests. While growth is not as consistent or dramatic as in the case of the literature covered in the *Education Index* (Figure 3.6), there is an overall upward trend, with an approximate doubling of citations over the 30-year period.

Figure 3.7: Business Periodicals Index Listings Under Testing*

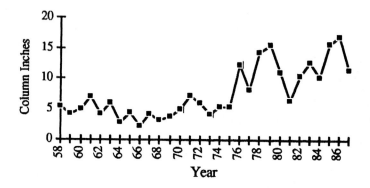

*Citations included under five different rubrics pertaining to testing; see text.
Source: *Business Periodicals Index*, 1958-88

THE EXPANDING MARKETPLACE FOR TESTING

In this chapter we have seen that a wide range of indicators, both direct and indirect, reveal that standardized testing is a large and growing enterprise. As many as 395 million tests are given annually in the education sector. The numbers of states authorizing statewide assessments and minimum competency tests have increased sharply since the 1960s. Though only limited data are available on sales of tests and related services, they clearly indicate that testing is a growth industry. The numbers of references to testing in the education literature indicate a similar upward spiral. Moreover, stock market analysts have been extremely bullish on testing companies that have been publicly traded.

While direct indicators of the extent and growth of testing in the employment sector are elusive, indirect indicators show overall growth in testing over that last thirty years, but apparently with a slowing in the 1970s (resulting from regulation and litigation concerning employment testing), but with some signs of acceleration in the late 1980s.

Why has the market for testing grown so dramatically over the past thirty years? In chapter 5 we consider some of the sources of the demand for tests. Before doing so, however, we stop in chapter 4 to point out that however large the dollar volume of test sales, the broader social investment in the testing enterprise is far more substantial.

4 SOCIAL INVESTMENT IN
EDUCATIONAL TESTING

In this chapter we present ideas on analyzing the costs and benefits of standardized educational testing at the state and local level. The total value of resources devoted to educational testing is much larger than the direct, observable costs of developing, purchasing, and scoring standardized tests. There are significant indirect resource costs that should be included in any attempt to evaluate the social investment in local and state testing programs. In order to make such an analysis fruitful, planners and policy makers need to reorient the way they think about testing in two important ways. First, they should pay closer attention to the fundamental economic concept of marginal value. Second, testing and the time devoted to it should be considered as "inputs" into education, instead of merely as measures of educational "output."

Economists like to compare costs and benefits "at the margin," which simply means comparing the added benefits of doing a little more of something with the added costs of that "marginal" increase in activity. As long as these marginal benefits outweigh the marginal costs, it makes sense to devote more resources to the activity. At the point where the marginal benefits just equal the marginal costs, maximum net benefit has been gleaned from the activity. Any further effort incurs more costs than benefits. This is the fundamental logic of cost-benefit analysis. Much educational testing now seems to be carried out, however, with little regard for this basic economic concept.

Before setting out our discussion on evaluating the social investment in educational testing, we note that there is a fairly long history of evaluations of the benefits of employment testing, dating back at least to the early 1920s when there was a wave of enthusiasm for using the WWI Army tests for purposes of employment selection. Since then some of the key works on evaluating the benefits of selecting employees based on test results have been the Taylor and Russell (1939) tables showing the effectiveness of test use in employment selection under different conditions, Cronbach and Gleser's (1965) *Psychological tests and personnel decisions,* Ghiselli's *The validity of occupational aptitude tests* and the US General Accounting Office's (1979) *Federal employment examinations: Do they achieve equal opportunity and merit principle goals?* Thus, for many decades, it has been widely documented that there are two key circumstances under which employment tests can yield benefits to individual employers. First, the selection procedure, such as an employment test, must be able to predict worker performance (the more predictive validity a test has, the more potentially beneficial it is). Second, the selection ratio, that is the ratio of employee openings relative to the number of applicants, must be less than 1.00. If an employer has ten openings and only ten people apply for those openings, no procedure for selecting among them will yield an advantage.

In the early 1980s the potential benefits of employment testing received renewed and widespread interest, primarily as a result of the work of John Schmidt and Frank Hunter. In the late 1970s, Hunter and Schmidt became known for their work on validity generalization, that is, generalizing validity evidence obtained from general employment aptitude tests used with several specific occupations to a more general class of jobs. Schmidt and Hunter argued that employment tests are more generally valid than had previously been assumed (because, they contended, technical issues relating to sample size, restriction of range and measurement error had not been fully taken into account in previous interpretations of validity evidence from different settings). Extending their work in the early 1980s, Schmidt and Hunter began to make some remarkable claims about the economic returns of employment testing. For example, they argued that using general ability tests to select workers could increase productivity in the U.S. by $90 billion (Hunter and Schmidt, 1982, p. 268).

Though Hunter and Schmidt's work has been widely cited and clearly affected the testing policies of the U.S. Employment Services in the 1980s, subsequent analyses have cast doubt on the claims they have made both for validity generalization and for the economic benefits of employment testing (see for example Hartigan & Wigdor, 1989, and Levin, 1989). We do not recap these various arguments here save to note one of the major points raised by Levin: that a full and reasonable evaluation of employment selection practices ought to look at costs and benefits not just from the perspective of individual employers, but also from the points of view of job applicants and society generally. Such an undertaking is quite difficult, given that the workplace is often the only realm in our society where dollar values are acceptably placed on human qualities. Nevertheless, estimates of gains in productivity for an individual employer cannot be generalized to the society as a whole. Rather than rehashing arguments about the benefits of employment testing, we aim in this chapter simply to take some of the economic concepts raised in evaluations of employment testing and in other realms, and to use them to suggest ways of thinking about evaluating the social investment in educational testing.

As we have documented in chapter 3, the level of standardized testing in elementary and secondary schools has grown enormously over the past three decades. This "if it moves, test it" mentality seems to have evolved in part from the notion that because standardized testing is so inexpensive (often with *direct* outlays of less than $0.80 per student per test hour[1]) and because it holds the promise of providing an "objective" measure of how well schools are performing, it always pays to increase the level of testing, at least it can't hurt. Such reasoning is misleading, however: it ignores the importance of marginal comparisons; it disregards the substantial indirect costs associated with testing; and it makes no attempt to specify the benefits associated with marginal increments in educational testing.

We estimate that the total costs of standardized testing for state and local programs are 4 to 65 times greater than their direct costs (our derivation of this figure is explained later in the chapter). Based upon our estimates of the level of state and local testing, this means state and local governments are investing as much as $20 *billion* annually in their standardized testing programs, usually with little apparent consideration of costs and benefits at the margin. The major part of this chapter analyzes the costs and benefits of the current level of educational testing from the standpoint of marginal value. Such an outlook reveals some interesting results.

A peripheral, but important, point of this chapter views testing as an input into the educational process. As we elaborate in chapter 5, a commonly

---

[1] We detail our estimation procedure below. Please recall that in chapter three we defined a "test" as any separately scorable portion of a test battery. In this chapter we will be discussing costs in the context of testing hours, i.e., the total level of resources devoted to one hour of test administration.

used metaphor for education is that of economic production: the use of resources or "inputs," such as books and other curriculum materials, teacher and student time, and so forth, for the production of an output: student learning. In this metaphor, student learning depends on some factors the schools can control (e.g., curriculum, teacher quality), some factors they cannot(e.g., genetic makeup of the student body, the socioeconomic background of students), and some over which they have only marginal control (e.g, community environment, family environment). In chapter 5, we explain the increasing popularity of this metaphor and the increasing attention to outputs of education, as measured by test results; here we attempt to reverse such thinking so as to consider testing in schools not just as a measurement of outputs but as an input into the schooling process.

Traditionally, the most common indicator of educational output has been standardized test scores. However, this inhibits examination of the relative contribution testing *itself* makes to education as one of many resource-using activities within schools. From this perspective, we need to evaluate our current level of testing "at the margin." And because testing affects educational outcomes, it must be compared to other educational "inputs" in terms of its productivity in improving student learning. It may be more useful to think of standardized testing in this way than as an "objective" (and "inexpensive") measure of how well schools and teachers are doing their job.

COSTS AND BENEFITS: WHAT ARE WE TALKING ABOUT?

Cost-benefit analysis and its variants, such as cost effectiveness and cost utility analysis, have been popular tools of policy analysts at least since the 1960s. As forms of applied welfare economics, these tools were originally used mainly to consider alternative courses of economic investment, but they also have been shown to be useful for evaluating educational and other social programs (Ray, 1984; Levin, 1983).

The idea of these forms of analysis is to compare the costs and benefits of an endeavor. Both costs and benefits are converted to a common metric, usually dollars, so that one can determine the payoff from the endeavor being analyzed. Costs in such an analysis do not refer only to actual monetary exchange or to budgeted amounts. Costs also include the value of all resources invested in an endeavor, be they actual monetary outlays or indirect resource costs. Thus no analytical distinction is made between costs and benefits. The ideal of cost-benefit analysis is to account fully for costs so that they represent the benefits forgone by not investing resources in other ways.

One difficulty with cost analysis is that for many endeavors, such as educational programs, costs typically cannot be determined by actual monetary transactions or budgets because many of the resources used, such as facilities and personnel time, may not be billed directly to, or budgeted for, a particular program. Thus in trying to account fully for all costs of an educational endeavor, that is to fully value benefits forgone by not investing in some other course of action, one must attempt to place values on all these costs.

Perhaps the most difficult part of applying cost-benefit analysis to non-economic endeavors is the problem of how to place a monetary value on benefits, such as increasing students' test scores or their participation in community affairs. Therefore, a variant of cost-benefit analysis called cost effectiveness analysis (CEA) has been more widely viewed as appropriate for educational evaluation. The aim of cost effectiveness analysis is to compare the cost of a program not with dollar benefits, but simply with program effects, measured by whatever unit is appropriate for that activity (Levin, 1983; Catterall, 1990). For instance, the effect of a teacher testing program can be measured by the number of teachers let go because they did not pass the test. In this case, a cost effectiveness analysis would report the cost per teacher laid off as a number to compare with other programs whose aim it was to remove unqualified teachers from the system. With CEA, there is no need to measure the dollar benefits of removing that number of teachers. The outcome has already been defined as desirable; the issue is which of several programs achieves this outcome most efficiently.

Using CEA for testing programs is especially problematic, because CEA implicitly assumes that the outcome is desirable. In the example of teacher tests just cited, where program effectiveness is measured in dollars per teacher laid off, the implicit assumption is that the teachers who pass the test are qualified, and those who fail are not. This is fine if the analyst is willing to make that assumption based on the particular conditions of a certain testing program. However, for our purposes here CEA is insufficient, because it has no power to discern whether a particular program is *worth* its cost, but only whether it achieves its end for less cost than another.[2]

---

[2] The case of attempting to weed out incompetent teachers via so-called teacher competency tests is, in fact, particularly problematic because of both

Given this brief introduction to the ideas of cost-benefit and cost effectiveness analysis, let us now examine the structure of the costs of educational testing and then consider, at least theoretically, the nature of benefits flowing from such investment.

THE COST STRUCTURE OF EDUCATIONAL TESTING

In addition to the obvious direct costs of testing (test purchase and scoring and reporting services), two types of indirect costs are associated with educational testing. Administrative or *transactions* costs are related only indirectly to the achievement of a policy goal but are nonetheless still paid in cash from public or private bourses. The second, and by far larger indirect cost is the opportunity cost of the time that teachers, administrators and students devote to standardized testing in the nation's schools.

The only recent example we have found of a cost analysis of a state-mandated testing program that takes these indirect costs into account was the analysis by Shepard, Kreitzer and Graue (1987) of the Texas Examination of Current Administrators and Teachers (TECAT).[3] In March of 1986, 202,000 Texas teachers and school administrators were given this "basic skills" test to

---

the unclarity of what constitutes teacher competence and the difficulty of establishing any consistent relation between teacher test results and practically any indicator of teacher competence. See Haney, Madaus & Kreitzer (1987) for a discussion.

[3] Fritz Machlup had planned to include a chapter on educational testing in Volume III of his series *Knowledge: Its creation, distribution and economic significance* (see Machlup, 1980, p. 54). Unfortunately, Machlup did not include the chapter in Volume III, and none of the remaining volumes in the planned eight-volume series were completed before his death in 1984. However, part II of Volume III gives an excellent summary of the research on returns to investment in education, both within the economics and education literature.

A computerized search of the ERIC database for 1962-1992 on the terms "COST" and "STANDARIZED TEST*" recovered 114 references, almost none of which provided any actual estimates for testing's dollar cost. Most discussed "costs" in its broader social meaning. One recent article which does give a dollar estimate for the average per pupil annual cost of testing is Bauer (1992). Based on a survey of members of the National Association of Test Directors, Bauer estimates average annual costs of testing per pupil to be $4.79 (the median across the 38 responding districts was $3.73). This estimate was based on reports of direct costs and costs for personnel who administer district testing programs. Thus Bauer's estimate excludes costs of student, teacher and school building administrator time, which, as we will show, clearly constitute the bulk of total costs of testing. See also OTA, (1992, pp. 28-9).

determine whether they were literate enough to keep their jobs. In considering the TECAT, the Texas legislature anticipated costs of $3 million. When the program was implemented, however, the direct cost to the state treasury for test development, administration, scoring, and related Texas Education Agency staff time was $2 million over this estimate; and Shepard et al. concluded that the total tax-supported cost of the TECAT was $35.6 million — or more than ten times the original estimate, and seven times the direct contracted costs for test development and administration. They also estimated that an additional $42 million worth of resources was spent by teachers and administrators privately to pay for TECAT preparation and to score reports.

Shepard et al. divided their cost figures between public (i.e., tax-supported) and private costs. Since our concern here is the total social investment in testing, this distinction is of lesser importance. We organize their data in terms of direct and indirect costs. Table 4.1 shows the distribution of direct and indirect costs, and of indirect transactions costs and indirect time costs. This view of the data shows that the indirect costs of the TECAT were around fifteen times larger than the direct costs of test development and administration. Moreover, the transactions costs alone are comparable to (in fact, slightly larger than) the direct costs of the testing program. What is even more telling, however, is that the value of the time spent by administrators and teachers in TECAT-related activities was thirteen times larger than the direct costs of the test, and comprised almost eighty-five percent of total costs.

The cost analysis of the TECAT is suggestive of the cost structure of standardized testing more generally. However, we could find no similar analysis of a state or local level student testing program. Hence, we undertook to estimate the direct versus indirect costs of such programs. Given the relative importance of the opportunity cost of time that Shepard et al. found with the TECAT, we give special emphasis to this indirect cost in our estimation procedure.

The Value of Time

The major resource that testing consumes beyond its direct costs is time. Estimating the value of time in cost-benefit studies has been somewhat controversial. Different people are likely to assign the same unit of time very different monetary value, and the same person may value different kinds of time (e.g., work, vacation, sleep) differently. In general, however, the appropriate value of time devoted to testing is the value of the next best alternative activity to testing. These alternatives differ between staff and students.

For staff, the most accessible (and probably most useful) measure is their wage rate. While wage rate is often criticized as a poor proxy for the relative value of time spent on non-work-related activities (such as travel or vacation), it is appropriate for valuing time spent on work-related activities. Wage rates are also justified in the sense that they are marginal quantities, at least theoretically. It is well known that the market for teachers and administrators is not freely based on supply and demand, but is subject to intervention by governments and labor unions. That intervention may cause wage rates to diverge from what they would be under a completely free market. However, realizing that teachers and administrators are free, at least in the long run, to leave teaching for other forms of work, it is reasonable, and entirely consistent with previous cost analyses in education, to consider their wage rates as fully representing the costs of their time.[4]

Valuing the time students devote to testing is much more difficult, since there is no explicit market for student time. No one pays students wages for being in school. So we need to come up with a reasonable "shadow" wage that places a value on what an hour of schooling is worth to a student. This may sound like a hopeless endeavor for a several reasons:

- Some people are squeamish about the idea of putting dollar values on education because of its enormous cultural significance in our society; it somehow seems vulgar to attach a dollar figure to the cultural importance of learning.

---

[4] Levin (1983) and others point out that to fully value the time of workers in competitive labor markets, one should use not just the simple wage rate but wages including the value of all fringe benefits.

Table 4.1: The Cost Structure of the Texas Examination of Current Administrators and Teachers (TECAT)

Components of Total Cost		Dollars ($)	% of Total
1.	*Direct Costs*	5,065,000	6.5
	Indirect Costs	72,956,500	93.5
	Transactions costs		
2.	Test Sites	138,500	0.2
3.	Workshop prep	6,000,000	7.7
4.	Workshop sites	100,000	0.1
5.	Private teacher expenses	600,000	0.8
	Subtotal	6,838,500	8.8
	Time costs		
6.	TECAT in-service day	26,260,000	33.7
7.	Teacher study time	38,808,000	49.7
8.	School staff time	1,050,000	1.3
	Subtotal	66,118,000	84.7
Total Costs		$78,021,500	100.0%

Source: Shepard, Kreitzer & Graue (1987)

Notes to line entries:

1. Direct costs of test development, administration and scoring here include the nominal cost of $4.8m plus the $232,000 which the legislature appropriated for Texas Education Agency staff time on the project.

2. Local school districts kept their buildings open to provide test sites for the examination . Shepard et al. estimated these costs to include 1,108 site days at $125/site-day.

3. Shepard et al. estimated that roughly 200,000 or more than 90% of school employees required to take the TECAT participated in test preparation workshops , at an average cost of $30/session /participant.

4. Many school districts provided sites for these preparation workshops (800 site-days at $125/site-day).

5. Some teachers purchased materials for test preparation as well as paying a $15 fee for score reports.

6. Texas schools closed on "TEACAT Monday," the day of the exam. It was considered an in-service day for teachers and thus this cost represents the value of teacher time for that day (202,000 teachers x $130/day).

7. Teachers and administrators each spent an average of 11.55 hours studying for the TEACT. Shepard et al. assign a shadow wage of $16/hour for this time (210,000 x 11.55 hours x $16/hour).

8. Local school district staff spent time in keeping teachers informed about test preparation opportunities, as did the 20 service centers for teacher support. Shepard et al. assumed that a school district with 100 teachers devoted at least 20 hours of administrative time to such activities and estimated the cost at $5/teacher x 210 teachers.

• Students spend their time in school in a variety of activities. They take classes in history, English, math, science, art, music, and gym in addition to talking to their friends, eating lunch and sneaking cigarettes in bathrooms. All of these activities have different values for different students according to their interests and abilities. For any one student, these activities have differing values at various stages in the process of their cognitive and social development. Thus it is questionable to place a single value on an hour of "schooling" across activities or across grade levels.

• Others will argue that our educational system is so inefficient that much of student time is wasted, i.e., not spent on valuable learning. Thus, it is fallacious to argue that testing takes time away from learning. An interesting variant on this point of view sees school as a baby-sitting industry — it is insignificant what students do while they are in school as long as they are out of their parents' hair, so that the parents can do productive work in the society (see Boulding, 1970).

The first criticism is not as fatal as it may at first appear. While education is culturally important, other culturally important activities are given monetary values in our society. An excellent example is "work." There is a strong cultural value attached to having work, yet this does not prevent society from equating particular jobs with particular wage rates. Indeed, the difference between average salaries for people with and without a high school education provides evidence that, as a society, we do not hesitate to place dollar value on the benefit of more rather than less education. According to the U.S. Census Bureau, in 1988 people 25 years old and over with a high school education earned on average $23,046, annually while people without a high school education averaged only $16,508.[5]

---

[5] This income data is from table 29 of the Bureau of the Census, 1990, p. 124-125. We calculated a weighted average of male and female mean earnings in 1989 for people with 4 years high school education and again for those with eight or fewer years. We then adjusted the resulting figures to constant 1988 dollars using the consumer price index.

The second set of criticisms is harder to counter, because they are true. One must be cautious when placing a dollar value on time spent in school, since school encompasses such a wide variety of activities across a broad spectrum of individuals with differing abilities and needs. However, as in all social analyses, some abstraction is necessary to proceed through the muddle of real-world complications. So we apply average values across this broad spectrum. Further, for our mythical youngster sitting atop the peak of the bell curve, an hour of time in high school English class and an hour in math class will be considered equally worthwhile, as will the hours her younger brother spends in each of his second grade classes. While these assumptions are an abstraction from reality, they do not undermine the major point: that student time is worth something and an hour spent taking a test is one less hour students can spend in class learning.

The third argument — that much time is wasted in schools and thus an hour spent under testing is not necessarily a tradeoff with an hour spent learning — is specious. We are not interested in how inefficient schools are, but rather in determining the opportunity cost of an hour of testing. That opportunity cost is the value of the *next best alternative* activity to testing, which is, presumably, learning, regardless of whether such learning is going on or not. Sitting around and wasting time during school has the same opportunity cost as standardized testing does, although it may not have the same benefits.[6] As far as the baby-sitting argument is concerned, we assert that the purpose of schools is to develop talent in young people. To educators such a statement may seem flippant or at least obvious. However, economists have not always been convinced of this point. Only within the past three decades have economists begun to recognize that national expenditure on education is not simply paying the baby-sitter (a "consumption" activity, as economists would say), but is an important *investment* in people. Theodore Schultz was one of the first economists to talk about education as the production of "human capital." In his 1960 presidential address to the American Economics Association, Schultz said:

> Much of what we call consumption constitutes investment in human capital. Direct expenditures on education, health, and internal migration to take advantage of better job opportunities are clear examples. *Earnings forgone by mature students attending school* and by workers acquiring on-the-job training

---

[6] We discuss the benefits of testing below.

are equally clear examples. *Yet nowhere do these enter into
our national accounts.* (Schultz, 1961, p. 1; emphasis added)

As Schultz recognized, one way to measure the value of time spent by
students in school is to estimate the value of earnings forgone by not being in the
workforce (Schultz, 1960, p. 573). There are a number of problems with this
technique. The most obvious is that it only values time for students who are old
enough to work. In this approach, the opportunity cost of time spent in school is
assumed to be zero for elementary school children. This is a serious problem,
given that most educators and psychologists recognize that from the point of
view of human development, early learning is crucial to later success in school.
Intellectual development reaches its peak growth rate during the early childhood
years and thus the early grades— or even the preschool years— are seen as key
in developing intellectual capacity (Bloom, 1964; Hunt, 1961). From this
perspective we should perhaps value time in the early grades more highly than
that in later grades.

In addition, forgone wages do not really measure the opportunity cost
of *learning* in school, but that of merely *being* in school. Moreover, we are
interested not in the value that students *themselves* might place on their time, but
rather in how prospective employers or society more broadly might value that
time. For all of these reasons, any appraisal of the value of student time strictly
in terms of forgone wages is likely to be an underestimate. Given these
limitations, a lower bound for the shadow wage for student time can be
estimated from the median hourly wage rate of 16-19-year-olds. For students in
grades 1-9, this method applies an hourly shadow wage of zero. For students in
grades 10-12, the method values an hour of time at $4.03.[7] To keep things
simple, we compute the weighted average of zero and 4.03 across all twelve
grades, for a result of $1.01. We then apply this estimate to all student time.
This avoids the complexity of making separate estimates for high school and
elementary school students, while preserving our total figures.

In order to calculate an upper bound for the value of student time,
consider the following method. At age 16, a person enters the workforce
without a high school degree. Census Bureau figures give the median income of

---

[7] Table 683 in *Statistical Abstract of the United States*, 1991, p. 418. The
figure is presented in that table for 1989, which we deflate to 1988 dollars
using the consumer price index.

persons ages 15 and over without a high school education as \$7,583 in 1988.[8] For those 25 and over without a high school education, average income in 1988 was \$16,508. We can use these figures to calculate lifetime earnings. Assume that this person works until age 65. With a discount rate of 9%,[9] the present value to the student at age 16 of his expected lifetime stream of income is

$$\frac{7583}{(1+.09)^1} + \frac{7583}{(1+.09)^2} + \cdots + \frac{7583}{(1+.09)^9} + \frac{16508}{(1+.09)^{10}} + \cdots + \frac{16508}{(1+.09)^{49}}$$

or about \$180,729. A second person, also 16 years old, decides to finish high school and not work until age 18. With a high school diploma she can expect to earn about \$14,866 annually until age 25, and after that about \$23,046. But she can't start working until she is 18. At age 16 then, the present value of her expected lifetime earnings is

$$0 + 0 + \frac{14866}{(1+.09)^3} + \cdots + \frac{14866}{(1+.08)^9} + \frac{23046}{(1+.09)^{10}} + \cdots + \frac{23046}{(1+.09)^{49}}$$

or about \$226,164. In a sense, the difference between these two streams of income represents one estimate of the value of time in school to a student. By averaging this difference over the 5,040 extra hours the high school graduate spent in school,[10] one can arrive at an estimate of what an hour of school is worth to a student. The resulting figure is \$9.01.

There are some problems with this figure. First, it is quite sensitive to the discount rate chosen. A discount rate of 1% would raise the figure to \$44.25, while a 14.6% discount rate would lower the estimate to \$4.03, which is the value attached to high school time using our first method. Any present-value calculations are always dependent on the discount rate chosen. However, rates

---

[8] All figures in this section are derived from tables 24 and 29 of the Bureau of the Census, 1990. We calculated weighted averages of salary data presented for males and females in 1989 and deflated these with the consumer price index to 1988 dollars.

[9] This figure is based roughly on recent trends for yields on long-term government bonds, as reported in the *Statistical Abstract of the United States*, 1991. Note that our "discount" rate is not the same as the Federal Reserve's discount rate on short-term adjustment credit, which ran closer to 6.5% in the late 1980s. We use the longer-term yield figure since our aim is to calculate returns over a lifetime.

[10] Seven hours/day times 180 days/year times four years is 5,040 hours.

on long-term government bonds have hovered around 9% over most of the past decade, so we are confident that this estimate is reasonable and stable.

A second problem with this method is that from a strictly economic perspective it overvalues student time because it averages the value of an hour across the four years of high school, and imputes the same value across all eight years before high school. But as we pointed out earlier, from the perspective of human development the lower grades may be more "valuable" than the higher grades. Thus by assigning the same shadow wage to all grades, we seek to capture something of the importance of early childhood cognitive development. We believe that this approach comes closer to measuring the value of *learning* in school and not just *being* in school, for all grade levels.

Any empirical estimates of the value of student time must be based on somewhat heroic assumptions. However, by providing these upper and lower bounds for our student shadow wage, we hope to improve confidence that the true value is contained in the interval.

Transaction Costs

Measurement problems do not end with the value of time. A second theoretical question is, how do we estimate the value of transaction costs? First, we need to establish what transaction costs are involved in educational testing at the state and local level. According to the Shepard study, most of the transaction costs associated with the TECAT were attributable to workshops preparing teachers and administrators to take the examination. The major transaction cost involved in educational testing is the cost of building operation and maintenance during times that are devoted to test-related activities. Since tax dollars are spent on each hour that a school operates, if an hour of school time is spent in taking or preparing for tests, the resources devoted to building operation and maintenance for that hour must accrue as a cost to testing. This point is crucial, because many would argue that building costs are irrelevant if testing occurs during normal school hours since an hour of building operation, whether students are being tested or are square dancing in PE class, is still an hour. From the standpoint of cost-benefit analysis, however, that is incorrect: we are comparing costs and benefits *at the margin* of each activity, and *then* comparing net benefits across activities to see which is more or less productive. The mistake is made in thinking that costs and benefits can be separated: they cannot. Every activity, by definition, has a cost and a benefit inherent to it: the "cost" is what we are missing by putting our energy into this activity instead of another.

That cost changes depending upon which activity we relate it to. So it is necessary to include these opportunity costs as we compare marginal benefits and costs.

It should be noted that not everyone in the school is involved in a test-related activity at the same time. This is problematic, however, only if we consider the school building as the unit of analysis. We resolve this problem by focusing on the per-student per-hour cost of building maintenance. In our estimates, transactions cost is calculated by multiplying the national percentage of total school expenditures devoted to building operation and maintenance by the total expenditure per student per year in public schools.

Valuing In-Class Test Preparation Time

How do we account for the costs of the time students spend *preparing* for tests? This question is an important one in the context of both transaction costs and time costs. There is little doubt that in-school test preparation activities are significant. Several recent surveys show that teachers do spend considerable time directly teaching the test objectives, test taking skills, and even specific test items resembling those on the test (Shepard, 1989; Romberg et al., 1989; Cannell, 1989; Massachusetts Advocacy Center, 1988). The Massachusetts Advocacy Center found that in the Boston public schools, classroom reading instruction has come to imitate reading tests. They found similar results for remediation programs. Romberg et al. surveyed eighth grade math teachers nationally and found that 80% have made instructional changes to accommodate mandated tests. Raivetz (1992, p. 10) reports that in New Jersey, "in urban districts, the test upon which the district is evaluated becomes the district's curriculum." Shepard (1989) found that a wide range of test preparation practices were followed, ranging from simply fostering testwiseness to actually teaching the test. When Shepard asked whether teachers have increased instructional time devoted to teaching the objectives of the test, test directors from the 40 high-stakes states surveyed answered nearly unanimously: *Yes.* A national survey of superintendents, testing specialists, principals and teachers found similar results, with substantial majorities reporting that district curriculums had been changed somewhat or very much to match the content of standardized tests (Hall & Kleine, 1990, p. 7). A more recent national survey of math and science teachers in grades 4 through 12 found that between 12 and 19 percent of respondents reported devoting more than 20 hours of class time per year to preparing students to take the mandated standardized test in their district, and that the majority began test preparation more than a month before the test date (Lomax, 1992, Table 7).

As we will see in the next chapter, the growth in standardized testing in the nation's schools has created a test preparation spinoff industry that is a growing part of the testing marketplace. We will show that there also is great uncertainty over the value, and even the legitimacy, of different kinds of test preparation. For now we merely point to the evidence that schools are spending substantial amounts of time specifically preparing students to take standardized tests, and that, at least according to several accounts, this is a waste of time that might otherwise be used for instruction (Richards, 1989; Haas, Haladyna & Nolen, 1990; Smith 1991). Perhaps the most succinct recent statement of the opportunity costs associated with test preparation is that of Romberg, Zarinnia & Williams (1989, p. iv):

> The tests do have an effect but one more appropriate to the 19th century than pursuit of the NCTM [National Council of Teachers of Mathematics] *Standards*. For any who spend the bulk of their effort pursuing teaching or achievement measured by the yardstick of standardized tests, the opportunity cost is the kind of intellectual engagement recommended by the *Standards* for the development of mathematical power.

Therefore, we believe the evidence is consistent enough to warrant the inclusion of preparation activities in our *upper* cost estimates. As a plausible figure, we assume that for every test battery, teachers and students devote 20 hours of classroom time to test preparation activities.[11] Based on our estimates of the time it takes to give a typical test battery (4 hours, see table 4.3), we estimate that for every hour a student is tested there are 5 hours of concomitant in-class preparation time. We do not include test preparation activities in our

---

[11] See also OTA (1992, pp. 28-9), which found that in one large Northeastern school district teachers reported spending from zero to three weeks preparing students for each test administration. The median figure given here, that is 1.5 weeks, is considerably higher than our assumption of 5 hours of preparation per hour of testing, if we assume 35 hours of instruction per week and four hours of test administration for a typical test battery ((35 hours/week x 1.5 weeks)/4 hours per test administration = 13.125 hours of preparation per hour of testing).

lower-bound cost figures, consistent with our intent to provide a well defined interval between conservative and liberal estimates.

AN ESTIMATED TESTING COST FUNCTION

With this background, we can estimate a cost function for state and local testing that accounts for their direct costs as well as their indirect time and transaction costs. We estimate separate functions for state and local programs since their direct costs differ. As we did in chapter 3, we provide ranges for our estimates. Because of our concern with the value of time, all our estimates are expressed as cost per student per hour tested. This scale also allows us to discuss testing costs and benefits at the margin.

Tables 4.2 and 4.3 provide some of the most recent data we could find on the direct costs of state and local testing programs.[12] Specifically, table 4.2 shows how we took 1984 data on costs of state assessment programs per student tested and adjusted these figures to 1988 dollars using the consumer price index. Table 4.3 summarizes price data on four major achievement test batteries from the mid-1980s, together with data on lengths of these tests in minutes, to show the manner in which we derived estimates of the cost per student per hour of testing time. We did not adjust these test battery costs for the consumer price index because these batteries were still being used in the late 1980s, as far as we can tell, with similar direct costs prevailing. Note, however, that in calculating test costs (including test booklet, answer sheets and scoring) per student per hour, we assumed that booklets are reusable four times. Given this assumption, these data show how relatively inexpensive test booklets themselves are, generally accounting for less than half of the test costs. These data bolster the point made in chapter 2 that for many testing companies scoring is a more important source of revenue than sales of test booklets – especially since every

---

[12] Several features of Table 4.2 are noted, as follows:
  1. Data were not explicitly provided by these states to OTA . We estimated these values using other data the states did provide, as reported in OTA's table IX.
  2. The last column inflates the 1984 values to constant 1988 dollars using the consumer price index.
  3. States not included because they had no assessment program in 1984: Colorado, Iowa, Massachusetts, Montana, Nebraska, Nevada, New Hampshire, New Jersey, N. Dakota, Ohio, Oklahoma, Texas, and Vermont. States not included because OTA did not have any data for them in 1984: Florida, Maryland, New Mexico, New York, Tennessee, Wisconsin, West Virginia.

time a booklet is reused, the test publisher generally sells another answer sheet and scoring service. Note too that in calculating average scoring costs, we obscure the fact that specialized scoring and reporting services can add substantially to the costs of testing. Purchase of specialized services, such as calculation and reporting of results in terms of local norms, or reporting criterion-referenced as well as norm-referenced results, can add substantially to the basic costs of scoring.

In short, tables 4.2 and 4.3 provide raw data on the direct costs of state assessment and local school district testing programs (the latter generally use one of the major batteries for which we have summarized costs, or similar commercial test batteries).

Next we simply employ the data from these tables to derive, as explained in Table 4.4, estimates of the direct costs of state and local testing programs. The low and high estimates of direct costs of state testing programs per student hour tested are based on assuming that one test lasts from 45 minutes (implying 1.33 tests per hour) to one hour (that is, one test per hour). For district testing programs, the low estimate comes from Table 4.3, but the high estimate comes from an independent report of the average cost per student of a testing program in a large urban school district, together with the estimate that this testing program requires three hours of testing.

Table 4.5 shows how we estimate the per hour per student indirect costs of testing. As previously discussed these indirect costs are comprised of transaction costs and costs associated with the time of students, teachers and administrators devoted to testing.

Table 4.2: Cost of State Assessment Programs, 1984

State[3]	Students Tested	Cost/Student ($1984)	Cost/Student[2] ($1988)
Alabama	385,000	2.00	2.28
Alaska	15,000	3.67	4.18
Arizona	461,000	1.73	1.97
Arkansas	100,000	1.90	2.16
California	1,100,000	2.73	3.11
Connecticut[1]	47,500	8.61	9.80
Delaware[1]	67,500	1.91	2.17
Washington DC	84,000	2.00	2.28
Georgia	320,000	1.80	2.05
Hawaii	88,000	2.27	2.58
Idaho	11,971	1.75	1.99
Illinois	7,500	26.67	30.37
Indiana	80,500	3.69	4.20
Kansas	150,000	1.53	1.74
Kentucky	710,000	2.11	2.40
Louisiana	120,000	2.00	2.28
Maine	48,000	10.40	11.84
Michigan	330,000	3.79	4.32
Minnesota	270,000	0.98	1.12
Mississippi	140,000	1.43	1.63
Missouri[1]	17,000	7.29	8.30
N. Carolina[1]	475,000	2.32	2.64
Oregon	25,000	4.00	4.55
Pennsylvania	150,000	3.04	3.46
Rhode Island	1,300	34.62	39.42
S. Carolina	175,000	2.18	2.48
S. Dakota	21,000	3.33	3.79
Utah	7,500	3.08	3.51
Virginia[1]	200,000	8.00	9.11
Washington	110,000	1.36	1.55
Wyoming	8,000	$12.50	14.23
Weighted Cost/Student		**$2.65**	**$3.01**

Source: Office of Technology Assessment, 1987. Adapted from table IX, pp. 77-81.

Notes: see note 12.

Table 4.3: Price Data for Four Major Achievement Test Batteries

Average cost of an answer sheet[1]	$0.35
Average cost of scoring/reporting per student[1]	$1.43

Test	Test Level	$ Price per packet of booklets	Qty	Length of test (min.)	Adjusted $ Cost/ Student/ Hour[2]
California	10	45.50	35	154	0.83
Achieve-	11	45.50	35	175	0.73
ment	12 basic	45.50	35	315	0.41
Test	12 complete	49.70	35	330	0.39
(1986 data)	13 basic	45.50	35	354	0.36
	13 complete	49.70	35	369	0.35
	14-20 basic	44.10	35	408	0.31
	14-20 complete	45.85	35	423	0.30
			Avg:	316	$0.46
Iowa	5	42.00	35	150	0.84
Test of	6	47.10	35	205	0.63
Basic	7 basic	30.00	35	134	0.90
Skills	7 complete	50.52	35	227	0.57
(1986 data)	7 complete +	65.19	35	267	.51
	9-14 basic	3.00	1	135	1.15
	9-14 complete	3.87	1	256	0.66
			Avg:	196	$0.75
Stanford	Primary 1	50.00	35	250	0.52
Achievement	Primary 2	50.00	35	275	0.48
Test	Primary 3	52.00	35	350	0.38
(1984 data)	Intermediate 1	37.00	35	370	0.34
	Intermediate 2	37.00	35	370	0.34
	Advanced	37.00	35	330	0.38
			Avg:	324	$0.41

(continued)

Table 4.3: Price Data for Four Major Test Batteries (cont'd)

Metro-	Preprimer	73.00	35	98	1.41
politan	Primer	73.00	35	134	1.03
Achieve-	Primary 1	73.00	35	215	0.64
ment	Primary 2	77.00	35	225	0.62
Test	Elementary	77.00	35	254	0.55
(1988 data)	Intermediate-basic	57.00	35	244	0.54
Survey	Intermediate-complete	60.00	35	244	0.54
Battery	Advanced 1-basic	37.00	35	229	0.54
	Advanced 1-complete	50.00	35	229	0.56
	Advanced 2-basic	49.00	35	175	0.73
	Advanced 2-complete	50.00	35	175	0.73
Diagnostic Batteries					
Reading	Primer	60.00	35	133	1.00
	Primary 1	66.00	35	52	2.60
	Primary 2	66.00	35	122	1.11
	Elementary	66.00	35	124	1.09
	Intermediate	44.00	35	134	0.94
	Advanced 1	44.00	35	79	1.59
Math	Primary 1	66.00	35	130	1.04
	Primary 2	66.00	35	117	1.15
	Elementary	66.00	35	127	1.06
	Intermediate	45.00	35	175	0.72
	Advanced 1	44.00	35	137	0.92
Language	Primary 1	77.00	35	115	1.22
	Primary 2	77.00	35	130	1.08
	Elementary	77.00	35	150	0.93
	Intermediate	55.00	35	120	1.09
	Advanced	55.00	35	105	1.24
Writing Test					
	Elementary	15.00	35	20	5.66
	Middle/Junior	15.00	35	20	5.66
	High	15.00	35	20	5.66
			Avg:	141	$1.45
		Overall	Avg:	244	$0.77

Source: *Mental Measurements Yearbook*, Volumes IX (Mitchell, 1985) and X (Conoley & Kramer, 1989).

Notes:

1. See figures 3.4 and 3.5 for these values.
2. To obtain the per-booklet cost we divide the test booklet packet cost by the quantity of booklets in each packet. We assume that the booklets are reusable 4 times, so we divide the per-booklet cost by 4. We then add the answer sheet and scoring service costs, divide by length of test and multiply by 60 to get the per hour per student cost. Averages are simple averages.

Table 4.4: How We Estimate the Direct Costs of State and Local Testing Programs Per Student Per Test Hour

State Testing Programs

Low Estimate

	Weighted average cost per student[1]	$3.01
Divided by	Number of tests/student[2]	3
Divided by	Number of tests/hour[2]	1.33
Gives	Direct cost/student/test hour	$0.75

High Estimate

Adjust for	1 test/hour[2]	
Gives	Direct cost/student/test hour	$1.00

District Testing

Low Estimate

	Average cost of one test booklet plus scoring services plus answer sheet per test hour[3]	$0.77

High Estimate

	Average per student cost for a large urban school district[4]	$5.19
Divided by	Number of hours tested[2]	3
Gives	Direct cost/student/test hour	$1.73

Notes:
1. From table 4.2.
2. According to table 4.3, the average time for the four major test batteries is about 4 hours. As we did in chapter 3, we assume 3 to 5 major scorable tests per battery. Thus we use the figures of 45 minutes to 1 hour per test in our low and high estimates.
3. From table 4.3.
4. Office of Technology Assessment, 1992.

Table 4.5: How We Estimate Per Hour Per Student Indirect Costs of Testing[1]

Transaction Cost

Low Estimate		
	Total annual per student expenditure[2]	5091
Adjusted by	10.2% devoted to building operation and maintenance[3]	$519.28
Divided by	Number of hours/school year[4]	1260
Gives	Transaction Cost/test hour/student	$0.41
High Estimate		
Adjust for	5 hours in-class preparation time per hour tested[7]	$2.50

Student Time

Low Estimate[5]		
	Student shadow wage for grades 1-9	$0.00
	Student shadow wage for grades 10-12	$4.03
	Weighted average shadow wage across all grades	$1.01
High Estimate		
	Student shadow wage[6]	$9.01
Adjust for	5 hours in-class prep time per hour tested[7]	
Gives	Student cost/test hour	$54.06

Teacher Time

Low Estimate		
	Average teacher salary[8]	$28,029
Divided by	Number of hours worked	1260
Gives	Teacher hourly wage	$22.25
Divided by	Student/teacher ratio[2]	17.30
Gives	Teacher cost/student/test hour	$1.29
High Estimate		
Adjust for	5 hours in-class prep time per hour tested[7]	
Gives	Teacher cost/student/test hour	$7.74

Table 4.5 Indirect Costs of Testing (continued)

<u>Administrator Time</u>

Low Estimate

	Average administrator salary[9]	$38,480
Divided by	Number of hours worked[4]	1600
Gives	Administrator hourly wage	$24.05
	Number of school building level administrators[2]	126609
Divided by	Number of schools[2]	82081
Gives	Administrators/school	1.54
Adjusted for	50% involved in testing programs[7]	0.77
Divided by	Student/Administrator ratio[2]	317.43
Times	Administrator hours/test hour[7]	0.50
Gives	Administrator hours/student/test hour	0.001
Times	Administrator hourly wage	$24.05
Gives	Administrator cost/student/test hour	$0.03

High Estimate

Adjust for	80% of administrators involved in testing and 1 hour of admin time per test hour[7]	
Gives	Administrator cost/student/test hour	$0.09

1. All data is for 1988 and refers to public schools only.
2. *Digest of Education Statistics*, 1991. These statistics are distributed throughout various tables in the *Digest*.
3. The 10.2% figure is the average percent of total expenditure devoted to building operation and maintenance over the period 1970-1979 nationally in public schools. This is the most recent such data that we could find (*Digest of Education Statistics*, 1991).
4. For teachers and students, 180 days times 7 hours per day is 1260 hours per school year. For administrators, we assume 200 days times 8 hours per day or 1600 working hours per year.
5. Using Schultz's method of valuing student time as forgone wages, for this low estimate we use a zero wage for students in grades 1-9, and the median hourly wage for workers 16-19 years old reported by the Census Bureau for students in grades 10-12 (found in Table 683, *Statistical Abstract of the United States*, 1991; in 1989 this figure was $4.22, which we deflate using the consumer price index to 1988 dollars). So that we do not have to create two separate cost functions for our low estimate, we compute a weighted average of the grades 1-9 and 10-12 and apply this to all students.
6. This estimate is based on the wage differential method described in the text.
7. As described in the text, we estimate 20 hours of classroom time spent by teachers and students in test preparation per major test battery. The average time for battery is 4 hours (see table 4.3). Thus, we estimate that for every test hour, 5 hours of preparation time is spent in class.
8. *Projections of Education Statistics to 2002*, 1991.
9. *Occupational Outlook Handbook*, 1988.

Table 4.6 summarizes our estimates for the direct and indirect costs per student per test hour for state and local testing programs. These estimates indicate that the indirect costs of state testing programs are 3.7 to 65 times larger than their direct costs, while indirect costs of local testing programs are 3.6 to 38 times larger than their direct costs. Further, teacher and student time comprise the largest portion of total costs, ranging from about 66 to 94 percent for both state and local programs.

Table 4.6: Breakdown of Direct and Indirect Marginal Costs for State and Local Testing Programs

| | State Assessment Programs | | | |
| | Low | | High | |
	$	%	$	%
Direct Cost	0.75	21.5	1.00	1.5
Transaction Cost	0.41	11.7	2.50	3.8
Student Time	1.01	28.9	54.06	82.7
Teacher Time	1.29	37.0	7.74	11.8
Administrator Time	0.03	0.9	0.09	0.01
Cost/student/test hour	$3.49	100.0%	$65.39	100.0%
Indirect/Direct ratio	3.7		65.4	

| | District Testing Programs | | | |
| | Low | | High | |
	$	%	$	%
Direct Cost	0.77	21.9	1.73	2.6
Transaction Cost	0.41	11.7	2.50	3.8
Student Time	1.01	28.8	54.06	81.8
Teacher Time	1.29	36.8	7.74	11.7
Administrator Time	0.03	0.9	0.09	0.01
Cost/student/test hour	$3.51	100.0%	$66.12	100.0%
Indirect/Direct ratio	3.6		38.2	

Source: see tables 4.2 through 4.5.

By using the marginal costs from table 4.6 along with our estimates on number of students tested from table 3.1, we can estimate the nation's total resource investment in state and district testing programs in the late 1980s. Table 4.7 presents these calculations.

Table 4.7: Total National Cost Estimates for State and District Testing Programs (millions of 1988 dollars)

		Low	High
State Assessment Programs			
	Number of tests[1]	33.00	71.50
Divided by	Tests/hour[2]	1.33	1.00
Gives	Total test hours	24.75	71.50
Times	Cost/test hour[3]	$3.49	$65.39
Gives	Total Cost of State Testing	$86.38	$4,675.39
District Testing Programs			
	Number of tests[1]	85.62	271.63
Divided by	Tests/hour[2]	1.33	1.00
Gives	Total test hours	64.22	271.63
Times	Cost/test hour[3]	$3.51	$66.12
Gives	Total Cost of District Testing	$225.40	$17,960.18

Notes:
1. See table 3.1. Numbers of tests, total test hours and total cost lines are all given in millions.
2. Based roughly on average length of four major test batteries shown in table 4.3 and our assumption of 3 to 5 major scorable subtests per test battery. The average time per test battery is about 244 minutes, or 4 hours.
3. See table 4.5.

We estimate that the nation devotes between $86 million and $4.7 billion worth of resources annually to state assessment programs, and between $225 million and $18 billion to district testing programs (in constant 1988 dollars). Thus the total investment in state and districts testing is estimated to be between $311 million and $22.7 billion. There is obviously a huge range in these low and high estimates — a 75-fold difference from low to high. We should reiterate that the main cause is the costs of student and teacher time devoted to test preparation that are included in the high estimate. Note, however, that even in our low estimates, which include just testing time and administrative test preparation and value student time very conservatively, the value of student and teacher time still constitute the bulk of the real costs of testing.

How do we judge the significance of these magnitudes? Total national expenditure on elementary and secondary education in 1987-88 was about

$169.7 billion (Snyder, 1991, p. 47). Our testing cost estimates range from 0.18% to 13% of that figure. Thus our high estimate indicates that the equivalent of more than 10% of our national investment in elementary and secondary education is being devoted to the costs of testing. As a comparison, federal government revenues going to elementary and secondary education in 1987-88 were $10.7 billion (Snyder, 1991, p. 47). Thus our high estimate indicates that the cost of testing in elementary and secondary schools — which as we will show in chapter 5 has clearly been spurred by federal education legislation and requirements — is equivalent to more than double the total federal expenditure for elementary and secondary education.

Our low estimate of national cost for testing seems far more modest, "only" $311 million or 0.18% of national investment in elementary and secondary education. By this standard, then, testing costs may seem relatively small. However, this is where the importance of thinking in terms of marginal and not total figures comes in. If we are going to spend even as "little" as $300 million, we certainly hope to get our money's worth. To find out whether we're getting our money's worth with this level of testing requires us to evaluate its costs and benefits at the margin.

COMPARING COSTS AND BENEFITS AT THE MARGIN

Our cost estimation procedure has provided four cost functions, based on our low and high per-student per-hour estimates for state and local testing. In the following discussion we will use the low district-testing estimate as an example of how to compare costs and benefits at the margin. The argument naturally extends to the other three possible cost functions.

Using the district figure, a simple cost function for testing can be written:

$$FC = 3.51h$$

where FC is full cost per year (direct and indirect costs) and h is the number of hours tested per student per year. This function is a simple linear equation, and thus the marginal cost of testing is also its average cost, $3.51.[13] In our discussion, we will call this our "full cost" function, because it includes both direct and indirect costs. Another cost function, which considers only the direct costs of local testing programs, can be defined as

---

[13] See table 4.6 for the derivation of this figure.

$$DC = 0.77h$$

which uses the 0.77 direct cost figure found in table 4.4.

THE BENEFITS OF TESTING

Now that we have testing cost functions, we require a testing benefit function. The fundamental principle of cost-benefit analysis is to choose a level of testing where the marginal benefit is just equal to the marginal cost. The benefits of testing presumably come in two forms: information and motivation. The results of standardized tests provide feedback to students, teachers, administrators and parents regarding student progress and achievement of system-wide curricular goals. Until recently, the most common rationale for testing was to obtain these test results which presumably could be acted on to improve teaching and learning. Lately the importance of the motivational aspects of testing have been increasingly discussed by educational policymakers — that important or high stakes tests may push students to study and teachers to focus their instruction. In chapter 8, we discuss the possible motivational value of high stakes tests; for now in our theoretical discussion of testing's benefits, it is largely a matter of indifference whether those benefits come in the form of information or motivation.

While estimating the indirect costs of testing was elusive, establishing dollar values for these benefits of testing is quite intractable. However, we can draw some interesting if tentative conclusions by hypothesizing what such a benefit function might look like.

We can make three reasonable assumptions about the benefits of testing in a general sense (whether informational or motivational). First, benefits will be zero if no testing is done. Second, no benefits will accrue if students spend all their time in school taking tests. Third, the maximum benefit from testing occurs at some point in between. Figure 4.1 graphs such a hypothetical benefit function. For the purposes of illustration we have made some other technical assumptions concerning the shape of this function.[14] We have chosen a level of

---

[14] The general form for the benefit function shown in figure 4.1 is
$$TB(h) = ah^b - ch,$$
where h is the number of hours tested per student and a, b, and c are parameters that alter the shape of the function. We use a=50, b=0.5 and c = -0.0567 to create the shape shown. Basically, the a parameter shifts the graph up and down; the b parameter alters at what level of h the maximum

benefits commensurate with our direct cost function — that is, the benefits that make current levels of testing appropriate when compared with direct costs. The reader should realize that this level is not based on any evidence. It is not an estimate of what actual benefits are, but simply a hypothetical reference point for the purposes of our discussion. Readers are welcome to experiment with alternative forms and benefit levels. Our main point is not the particular level of benefits, but the relationship between *marginal* benefits and costs.

Figure 4.1: Hypothetical Benefit Function for District Testing

The top panel in figure 4.2 redraws the benefit and cost functions over a range of testing from 0 hours to 5 hours, overlaying the two cost functions: the full cost function (including both direct and indirect costs) and our direct cost function. The lower panel in figure 4.2 charts the marginal benefit and cost curves derived from the total curves in the top panel. According to the fundamental principle of cost-benefit analysis, a school district should choose a level of testing where the marginal cost curve intersects the marginal benefit curve. If school district officials only consider the *direct* costs of testing, this point occurs at h^{dc}, where marginal direct cost is equal to marginal benefit (in our figure, about 3 hours and 12 minutes of testing per student per year). To the

point of the function occurs, and c is chosen to make sure the function equals zero at $h = 1260$, so that our second assumption is valid — that testing all the time leads to no benefits.

right of this point, marginal benefits are lower than marginal costs, indicating that too much testing is being done. To the left of h^{dc}, marginal benefits are greater than marginal costs, indicating that it pays to increase the level of testing until h^{dc} is reached.

However, we have seen that indirect costs are very much larger than direct costs. The marginal full cost function is then a better basis on which to judge an "optimal" level of testing. The appropriate level using the full marginal cost function occurs at h^{fc}, to the left of h^{dc} (or about 41 minutes of testing, as drawn on our graph). *Regardless of the level of benefits, h^{fc} will always be to the left of h^{dc}; using only direct costs to choose a level of testing will always lead to too much testing.*

What is the social cost of this over-investment? In figure 4.2, the welfare loss is indicated by the shaded region above the marginal benefit curve and below the marginal cost curve that includes indirect costs. Given our assumptions about the shape and level of the benefit function, this area is equal to about $5.05 per student per year.[15] If we multiply this per-student loss by the total number of students tested in district testing programs (about 21 million, using our low estimate from table 3.1), we arrive at a net national loss of about $105 million for ignoring the indirect costs of district testing programs. It is important to stress that this loss is *net* of any benefits that derive from such testing — this $105 million is a complete and utter waste of resources.

---

[15]This value is the difference between two areas. The first is the rectangular area in figure 4.2(b) bounded by the horizontal axis on the bottom, the marginal full cost function on the top and h^{fc} and h^{dc} on the left and right. From this subtract the area under the marginal benefit function between h^{fc} and h^{dc}. This calculation requires the use of integral calculus. The formula used to calculate the shaded area is:

$$3.51 (h^{dc} - h^{fc}) - \int_{h^{fc}}^{h^{dc}} (2.5h^{-.95} - 0.0567).$$

Figure 4.2: Relationship between Total and Marginal Functions

(a) Total Benefit, Full Cost, and Direct Cost Curves

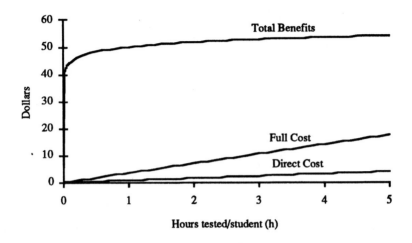

(b) Marginal Benefit, Full Cost, and Direct Cost Curves

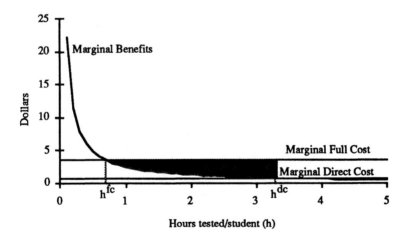

Further, this figure is based on our low cost estimates for district testing programs only. If the same analysis were applied using our upper cost figures and upper estimates for numbers of students tested and further extended to include state as well as local testing, the net national loss for over-investment in these programs would certainly be in the *billions*, not hundreds of millions. However, we caution the reader that our benefit function is *hypothetical* ; these loss estimates should not be considered empirical estimates. Our primary point is that this loss is measured in *missed opportunities* — student and teacher time, primarily, which could be devoted to more productive school activities than testing.

We are in a time when people are deeply concerned with the quality of public schooling in America and with the erosion of our competitiveness in the world economy; enormous federal, state and local budget deficits constrain the allocation of resources for education; more and more standardized testing is being done with no knowledge of its actual benefits; yet the costs of testing, when calculated at all, are severely underestimated because human resource costs are ignored. At such a time, it seems prudent to alter our view of the relationship between testing and education. Testing is not simply a cheap activity for monitoring educational outcomes. Whatever the informational and motivational benefits of testing, testing *changes* the outcomes of education through its use of valuable and scarce resources (student and teacher time).

In chapter 5 we describe some of the broad social forces that have led to our nation's increasing investment in testing. In subsequent chapters we discuss spin off from standardized testing and other developments that raise questions about some of the purported benefits of testing. The main point we wish to emphasize in closing this chapter is that whatever the benefits of testing, be they large, small or non-existent, and whether they come in the form of motivation or information, as long as we fail to take into account the value of student and teacher time invested in testing, we will tend to invest far more than is optimal in the enterprise of educational testing. Comparing costs and benefits at the margin provides some informed basis for choosing a level of testing that makes more effective use of student and teacher time. A second advantage of thinking in these terms is that it requires policymakers and researchers to think more concretely in terms of the actual benefits that justify the substantial indirect costs of testing.

5 FORCES BEHIND THE TESTING MARKETPLACE

According to evidence reviewed so far, it is clear that for close to a half-century, standardized testing in the United States has been increasing at a rapid rate — by over 10% per annum for the last two or three decades. In recent years we may be exceeding even that pace. Why has the testing marketplace grown so steadily?

There is no single answer to the question. But one thing is certain; test vendors alone are not responsible. Instead, a variety of social forces have combined to create the extended bull market for testing — a rate and continuity of growth that has repeatedly attracted the favorable attention of Wall Street, when testing companies have been publicly traded on the stock markets.

In this chapter, we consider broad social forces that have contributed to the bull market for testing under the following four categories:

- recurring public dissatisfaction with the quality of education, and efforts to reform education;
- an array of legislation, at both federal and state levels, promoting or explicitly mandating standardized testing programs;
- a broad shift in attention from a focus on inputs or resources devoted to education toward outputs or results produced by our educational institutions; and
- the increased bureaucratization of schooling and society.

In concluding this chapter, we comment on some of the new forces that seem to be at work in the testing marketplace in the 1990s.

The broad forces discussed in this chapter as driving the testing marketplace are by no means independent. For instance, a specific episode of public dissatisfaction with education often has led to legislation mandating new tests, which in turn focuses the public's attention on school outcomes, or at least on test scores. Similarly, testing legislation often seems to increase the bureaucratization of our educational institutions. Though for ease of discussion we treat then separately, the interdependence of these four broad social forces acting on the testing market should be kept in mind.

DISSATISFACTION AND REFORM

The use of test results to call attention to problems in our schools has a long history. Indeed, the practice precedes the modern era of standardized testing in the United States that began in this century. For example, in the last century pediatrician-turned-education-reformer Joseph Mayer Rice used the results of tests to attack practices of rote instruction in the schools. As a physician in New York, Rice had become interested in the problems of the New York City schools. Following publication of a few articles on education and two years of study of pedagogy in Germany, Rice was commissioned in 1891 by the *Forum* magazine to prepare an appraisal of American public education. In his book *The Transformation of the School: Progressivism in American Education 1876-1957*, Lawrence Cremin (1964), begins with the story of Rice's investigation:

> [Rice] was to place "no reliance whatever" on reports by
> school officials; his goal was to render an objective assessment
> for the public. Rice left on January 7, 1892. His tour took
> him to thirty-six cities and he talked with some 1200 teachers;
> he returned late in June, his notes crammed with statistics,
> illustrations and judgements. (Cremin, 1964, p. 4)

In his articles in the *Forum*, Rice attacked the inefficiency and ineffectiveness of the schools — "the political hacks hiring untrained teachers who blindly led their innocent charges in singsong drill, rote repetition and meaningless verbiage" (Cremin, 1964, p. 5). Rice went on to develop his own tests of spelling — and to administer them to over 30,000 school children. He used the results to attack rote spelling drills and to call for more "progressive education" in which children would be taught in a more meaningful way via a unified curriculum. (For more detail on Rice, see Cremin 1964, Haney, 1984, and the special 1966 issue of the *Journal of Educational Measurement* devoted largely to the work of Rice as a pioneer in American testing.)

The Rice episode was one of the earliest instances in which test results contributed to dissatisfaction over education and to proposals for reform. However, there have been many similar events in this century. In the 1920s, for example, the results from the World War I Army Alpha and Beta intelligence tests were widely used to buttress calls for social and educational reforms. Likewise, during the first third of the century, test results played a prominent role in education as part of a movement which Raymond Callahan (1962) called the "cult of efficiency." Such prominent figures as Edward Lee Thorndike, George Strayer, Elwood Cubberly and Paul Hanus called for the use of standardized tests as a means of making the schools more efficient (Callahan, 1962, Jonich, 1968, Radwin, 1981).

In the first half of the century there were several other instances in which standardized test results were used to support calls for the reform of education. However, because our focus here is on the recent growth in the testing industry, we will skip to the mid-50s and describe briefly the connections between test results, dissatisfaction over education, subsequent reform efforts and their effect on the market for tests.

Since mid-century there have been at least five major cycles of educational reform, all of which have contributed greatly to the growth in testing, namely: (1) the Sputnik episode in the 1950s, (2) the Civil Rights and compensatory education movements in the 1960s, (3) the SAT test score decline in the 1970s, (4) the education reform efforts that emerged in the 1980s, and (5) the national education reform proposals of the early 1990s.

The launching in 1957 of the Soviet satellite Sputnik sparked widespread national concern over our competitiveness with the Soviet Union in the space race and more generally in science and technology. One result of this concern was the passage in 1958 of the National Defense Education Act (NDEA), which, as we will discuss further below, contributed directly to a growth in testing.

In the 1960s, the Civil Rights movement, and efforts to improve education for the disadvantaged (often called compensatory education at the time), also brought increased attention to testing and calls for educational reform. In the next section of this chapter, we trace the relationships between these movements and specific pieces of legislation contributing to the growing testing market. Here we note simply that the Civil Rights and compensatory education movements of the 1960s contributed to increased attention to testing in two quite different ways. On one hand test results of economically disadvantaged students were cited to bolster proposals for protecting the civil rights of minorities and increasing the educational opportunities of disadvantaged children. On the other hand, as civil rights legislation was passed, test results became the touchstone by which many of its mandates (for instance equal opportunity in employment) and the success of compensatory education (such as Head Start, Follow Through and Title I) came to be judged.

In the 1970s, perhaps the most prominent example of the connection between testing and concerns over quality of education was the furor over national declines in SAT scores. From 1963 to 1977, the national average SAT verbal score declined by nearly 50 points, and the math average by about 30 points. This unprecedented decline sparked immense interest and debate over the quality of the education our high school students were receiving. In his preface to the report of a special panel convened to look into the score decline, Sidney Marland, then president of the College Board, wrote: "No topic related to the programs of the College Board has received more public attention in recent years than the unexplained decline in scores earned by students on the Scholastic Aptitude Test" (cited in Wirtz, 1977, p. xii). No one was sure what the decline meant, but whatever the cause, it was widely seen as a serious problem.

The special panel concluded that the decline in average national SAT scores had two causes. First, until about 1970 the fall-off in scores was most likely due mainly to "compositional changes" in the population of students taking the SAT. More students were taking the SAT, and more were of the type that tended to earn lower scores. Second, after 1970 the continuing decline in SAT scores was most likely due to factors unrelated to the demographics of the test-taking population. The panel pointed to indirect evidence implicating six factors as contributing to the score decline during the 1970s (Wirtz, 1977, pp. 46-48):

(1) a significant dispersal of learning activities and emphasis in the schools;

(2) diminished seriousness of purpose and attention to mastery of skills and knowledge . . . in the schools, the home and society generally

(3) more learning taking place via viewing and listening than through "traditional modes" of reading and writing;

(4) changes in the role of the family in the educational process;

(5) disruption of life in the country between 1967 and 1975 by the Vietnam war and other events; and

(6) marked decrease in young people's learning motivation.

Two reports from the Congressional Budget Office (1986, 1987) provide an update on national trends in test scores into the 1980s. However, neither of them garnered nearly as much attention as the Wirtz report.

While six inter-related factors were named as probable contributors in the SAT score decline, the panel seemed to feel that the chief suspects were the deteriorating quality of schools and schooling. The diagnosis — that a variety of ills beset the schools — was common in the 1970s. And among the commonly prescribed remedies was to increase testing. Hence, as we saw in Figure 3.1, the 70s and 80s saw marked increases in state mandated minimum competency and assessment testing programs.

In the early 1980s, low test scores were frequently cited to bolster calls for reform of the nation's schools. And the called-for reforms often included proposals for new testing programs. Our purpose here is not to review recent reform proposals comprehensively, but instead simply to illustrate the recurring cycle of test results being used to bolster reform proposals that include calls for more testing. Therefore, we discuss only two of the more prominent education reform reports of the 1980s, *A Nation at Risk* (National Commission on Excellence in Education, 1983a) and *High School: A report on secondary education in America* (Boyer, 1983). (See Murphy, 1990, for analyses of the broader reform movement of the 1980s, and Stedman & Smith, 1983, for an analysis of early 1980s reform reports.)

A Nation At Risk

Surely the most widely publicized and influential of the education reform reports of the 1980s was *A Nation at Risk*, released in early 1983. The National Commission on Excellence in Education ominously warned, in a much quoted phrase, that "the educational foundations of our society are presently being eroded by a rising tide of mediocrity that threatens our very future as a Nation and a people" (p. 5). The indicators of this "mediocrity" were results from the National Assessment of Educational Progress (NAEP), the SAT score decline, studies of functional literacy, data from the International Assessment of Educational Achievement (IEA) and test scores from the Department of Defense.

Among the recommendations of the Commission was the following:

Standardized tests of achievement (not to be confused with
aptitude tests) should be administered at major transition
points from one level of schooling to another and particularly
from high school to college or work. The purposes of these
tests would be to: (a) certify the student's credentials; (b)
identify the need for remedial intervention; and (c) identify the
opportunity for advanced or accelerated work. The tests should
be administered as part of a nationwide (but not Federal)
system of State and local standardized tests. (p.28)

In the view of the Commission, test results were not only a worthy
source of evidence in diagnosing the ills of the nation's schools, but also part of
the prescription for remedying those ills.

In a follow-up study to *A Nation at Risk*, entitled *Meeting the
Challenge*, the staff of the Commission surveyed the 50 states and the District of
Columbia for their recent efforts to improve education. Though acknowledging
that many reform initiatives were under way prior to the release of *A Nation at
Risk*, the follow-up report recounted that among the reform efforts nationwide,
"action has been taken or proposals made" with regard to "student
evaluation/testing" by 35 states, and with regard to "graduation requirements" by
44 states (p.6). *Meeting the Challenge* also sampled district-level initiatives at
educational reform. Here is a part of what the report recounted as happening in
Dallas, Texas:

Dallas in 1980 announced a plan to end social promotion of
students in grades 1-3 during the 1st year, grades 4-6 in the 2nd
year, and grades 7-12 in 1983. . . . students who enter 9th
grade scoring below the 30th percentile would not be allowed
to take electives, but would be required to double up on
mathematics and reading. Additional teachers have been hired
to carry out the extra duties necessary under this policy. (p.
103)

Though the initiation of these policies in Dallas preceded the 1983
Nation at Risk report, they graphically illustrate how testing became intertwined
with reform efforts in the early 1980s. The Dallas policy, implying that all
students should be above the 30th percentile on a test, foreshadowed a
controversy concerning testing that erupted in the late 1980s. In 1988 another

pediatrician turned educational reformer, John Jacob Cannell, reported on what came to be called the Lake Wobegon phenomenon. Lake Wobegon is the mythical town in Minnesota where all the women are strong, all the men are good-looking and all the children above average. Cannell (1988, 1989) found that all states, and the vast majority of school systems, appear to be scoring above average on nationally normed elementary level achievement tests. (We will discuss the Lake Wobegon phenomenon in more detail in chapter 7.)

The Carnegie/Boyer Report

A second prominent reform report from the early 1980s, *High School: A report on secondary education in America* (Boyer, 1983), was sponsored by the Carnegie Foundation and authored by former U.S. Secretary of Education Ernest Boyer. Focusing on secondary education, the report devoted eight pages to analyses of student test score data in describing the state of secondary education. The study drew on college admissions test data (from the SAT and ACT), results from NAEP, from international comparisons of achievement and from selected achievement batteries, such as the Iowa Test of Educational Development. While using much of the same data as was used in other contemporary reform reports, Boyer presented a more balanced interpretation. He pointed attention not just to the warts and blemishes, but also to the bright spots.

But like most other observers of the education scene in the 1980s, Boyer saw testing as part of the solution to what ails America's educational institutions. Specifically, he recommended a new Student Achievement and Advisement Test (SAAT) reminiscent of the British "O" level tests. The SAAT presumably was to be built and administered by an external agency such as the College Board. The goals of the SAAT would be, first, to evaluate the academic achievement of students on the core curriculum studied, and second, to provide advisement in decisions about work and post-secondary education.

In sum, the Boyer report was another variation on a traditional tune. Test results were used to bolster diagnoses of the ills of American education, and testing programs became part of the prescription for remedying those ills. Both the diagnoses and the prescriptions served to heighten the prominence of standardized testing and expanded the testing marketplace.

National Education Goals and America 2000

In a sort of culmination of diverse proposals for education reform in the 1980s, and after an "education summit" in 1990, U.S. President Bush and the

National Governors Association (NGA) announced six National Education Goals to be achieved by the year 2000:

1. All children will start school ready to learn.
2. The high school graduation rate will increase to at least 90%.
3. American students will leave grades 4, 8, 12 having demonstrated competency in challenging subject matter including English, mathematics, science, history and geography; and every school in America will ensure that all students learn to use their minds well, so that they may be prepared for responsible citizenship, further learning and productive employment in our modern economy.
4. U.S. students will be first in the world in science and mathematics achievement.
5. Every adult American will be literate and will possess the knowledge and skills necessary to compete in a global economy and exercise the rights and responsibilities of citizenship.
6. Every school in America will be free of drugs and violence and will offer a disciplined environment conducive to learning.

(National Education Goals Panel, 1990)

This proposal was followed up in April 1991, with the announcement by President Bush of his "America 2000" strategy for educational reform (Miller, 1991). The proposal called for four tracks of educational reform:

• For today's students: better and more accountable schools
• For tomorrow's students: a new generation of American schools
• For the rest of us (yesterday's students/today's work force): a nation of students
• Communities where learning happens.

Here we do not attempt a review of the details of the America 2000 strategy or of the flurry of activities and commentary that have followed it (for a useful review and pro and con commentary, see the November 1991 issue of *Phi Delta Kappan*.)

Instead we simply note that prominent among the reform proposals of America 2000 (and probably the single aspect of the America 2000 strategy that has aroused the most attention and debate) was a call for new "American Achievement Tests" covering "core subjects" of English, mathematics, science, history, and geography and based on "new world standards." The new nationwide examination system "is intended to foster good teaching and learning as well as to monitor student progress." Also, "Colleges will be urged to use the American Achievement Tests in admissions; [and] employers will be urged to pay attention to them in hiring" (U.S. Department of Education, 1991, p. 11). Additionally the new tests are intended to be used at the national level to help check progress toward the National Educational Goals for the Year 2000.

In sum, the education reform proposals of the early 1990s have continued the tradition of earlier reforms, of viewing testing as a major instrument of educational reform. The America 2000 proposal and many of its offspring differ somewhat from earlier testing proposals in that they call not for traditional norm-referenced multiple-choice tests, but instead for what are now widely called authentic assessments, that is ones that require students to solve a problem or perform a task rather than simply selecting a "correct" answer from a set of given alternative answers. We comment further on this development in chapter 8. But what is clear is that the America 2000 report represents the culmination of a trend apparent in many earlier educational reform proposals, namely the explicit use of tests as instruments of educational reform. Here is how one analyst, in an article on testing and the reform movement in the 1980s summarized the trend:

> Testing has changed dramatically from its former role as an index of educational progress to its current role as an aggressive force in the establishment of educational priorities and practices. . . . informing the public has taken a back set to driving policy and influencing practice. (McClelland, 1988, p. 769-770)

LEGISLATION

Dissatisfaction with the quality of schools, and numerous education reform efforts over many decades, have contributed indirectly to the prominence of standardized tests. A more direct influence has been legislation at both federal and state levels mandating various standardized testing programs. In this section we cannot provide a complete history of all legislation related to testing. Nor can we describe all aspects of the bills we discuss, or their detailed regulations. Instead we simply recap major pieces of federal legislation contributing directly and indirectly to the upsurge in the testing marketplace over the last thirty years.

The National Defense Education Act of 1958

Before World War II the federal government had little direct involvement with education. Immediately after the war, for reasons of national defense, this changed. The first major piece of federal legislation related to elementary and secondary education, the National School Lunch Act, was passed in 1946 to remedy the high rejection rates of draftees during World War II due to nutrition-related deficiencies (Macy & Williams, 1945).[1] The main justification for this legislation was that in the event of another war military manpower needs ought not be adversely affected by poor nutrition.

Ten years later, in response to the Russian launching of Sputnik, Congress passed the *National Defense Education Act of 1958* (NDEA). Section 101 of the NDEA clearly justified the Act in terms of national defense:

> The Congress hereby finds and declares that the security of the nation requires the fullest development of the mental resources and technical skills of its young men and women. [Congress reaffirmed the principle that states and local educational authorities retain control over the primary responsibilities for education but then added that]   the national interest requires that the Federal government give assistance to education for programs which are important to our defense.

The NDEA gave testing its first federal shot in the arm. In a section entitled "Guidance, Counseling and Testing: Identification and Encouragement of Able Students," funds were allocated for local programs (public school and private) for testing students. The NDEA was an important landmark for the testing marketplace in that for the first time the federal treasury became a source of funding for testing at both state and local levels. (Many of the testing provisions in the NDEA were eventually incorporated into the Elementary and Secondary Education Act of 1965, discussed below.) It is surely no coincidence that starting around this time, revenues from test sales began to climb.

Two other factors that contributed significantly to increased national prominence for testing in the 1950s should be mentioned here. The first was the

---

[1] In 1941, the National Nutrition Conference for Defense reported that the first million physical examinations by the Selective Service resulted in 133,000 rejections as unfit for military service from disabilities directly or indirectly connected with nutrition. (Macy, I. G., & Williams, H. H. 1945, *Hidden Hunger*, Lancaster, PA: The Jaques Cattell Press).

founding of the National Merit Scholarship Corporation (NMSC) in 1955. The NMSC used a qualifying test for high school students to identify those "who rank at the upper end of the academic ability scale" (NMSC, 1978).

The second factor was the development of automated optical scanning equipment for scoring multiple-choice tests by E.F. Lindquist and others at the Measurement Research Center (MRC) at the University of Iowa. This paved the way for the fast, efficient and relatively cheap scoring of multiple-choice tests that previously had to be either hand scored by teachers or processed by slower, less accurate mechanical devices. The optical scanning technology helped to expand the testing marketplace by making larger-scale testing programs more feasible and affordable. Moreover, the scoring of test answer sheets became an important source of revenue for companies engaged in testing. As we saw in chapter 2 of this volume, by the 1980s firms such as National Computer Systems (NCS) and Scantron Corporation (SCNN) began to market optical mark reading technology directly to schools so that teachers could score their own answer sheets.

The 1964 Civil Rights Act

The 1964 Civil Rights Act was landmark legislation in many regards, not the least of which was its impact on testing. Title VII mandated nondiscrimination in employment by reason of race, sex or national origin and was widely used to challenge employment testing. The 1972 amendment to the Act extended Title VII's provisions to all public employers as well (see Wigdor, 1982, for a discussion of the impact of the Civil Rights Act on psychological testing and employment discrimination.) The Act also established the Equal Employment Opportunity Commission (EEOC). Starting in 1966, the EEOC issued a series of guidelines on the use of tests in employment selection. Both the 1966 and 1970 EEOC guidelines were based in part on the test standards of the American Psychological Association, the American Educational Association, and the National Council on Measurement in Education (APA, AERA, and NCME). The EEOC guidelines were intended to remedy what was widely seen as abysmally low standards of practice in the field of employment testing in the 1960s and early 1970s. For example Holmen and Docter noted that "spokesmen for test publishers, personnel directors and industrial psychologists agree overwhelmingly that unvalidated tests are commonly used in industry" (1972, p. 146). Under Title VII and the EEOC guidelines, if a plaintiff could show that a test used by an employer has a substantial adverse impact on classes of persons protected under Title VII, then the burden of proof fell on the employer to show that the test is job related and has less discriminatory impact than other available selection procedures. (For a detailed discussion of the evolution of federal guidelines and professional standards, see Novick, 1982.)

The nondiscrimination employment mandate embodied in Title VII and codified in the EEOC guidelines led to a tremendous amount of litigation, much of it concerning employment testing. An employee of the EEOC estimated in the early 1970s that some 15 to 20% of all complaints filed with that agency involved testing, amounting to roughly 1000 cases per year (Holmen and Docter, 1972, p. 146). One review of court decisions on employment testing between 1968 and1977 listed more than 100 federal court decisions, most of them based on Title VII (Psychological Corporation, 1978). (We discuss the important implications for test developers of court decisions reached under Title VII in a subsequent section.) Title VII litigation, along with the development of the EEOC guidelines, led directly to a 1974 revision of the *Joint Standards For Educational Tests and Manuals*. of the American Psychological Association, the American Educational Association, and the National Council on Measurement in Education.

The Civil Rights Act of 1964 also mandated the Equal Educational Opportunity Survey. As will be explained in the next section the report on this survey, which commonly came to be called the Coleman report, helped to move the attention of educational policymakers away from equal educational opportunity defined in terms of school resources toward a focus on educational outcomes as measured by tests.

The National Assessment of Educational Progress (NAEP)

Another milestone in the growth of federal influence on the testing marketplace occurred in 1963. Francis Keppel, then the U.S. Commissioner of Education, approached John Gardner, then president of the Carnegie Corporation, seeking support for a grant to hold conferences to discuss the feasibility of establishing some kind of system to measure the educational level of the U.S. population. This initiative, after many twists and turns, resulted in the National Assessment of Educational Progress (NAEP), which formally began in 1968 (see Greenbaum, Garet & Solomon, 1977, for an account of the early history of NAEP). Though begun with private foundation support, since the late 1960s NAEP has been funded almost entirely by the federal government (Greenbaum, Garet & Solomon, 1977, p. 17).

NAEP has not contributed much to the total volume of tests administered annually in the United States. However, NAEP is an important development in the history of testing in the United States for two reasons. First, although as long ago as 1867 (in the Act establishing the U.S. Department of Education) the federal government was under mandate to collect information about the condition of education in the states and territories, NAEP was the first occasion on which the federal government directly funded, on a continuing basis, the gathering of nationally representative test data. Second, as noted above, NAEP data were used to support calls for educational reform in the 1980s, which in turn usually called for new testing programs. Finally, despite a very limited impact on educational policy-making in its first two decades, it now appears that by allowing state-by-state comparisons of test results, performance on NAEP exercises may focus even more national attention on test scores in the future (Haney & Madaus, 1986). Studies following release of trial state comparisons of 1990 NAEP results in math (called the Trial State Assessment or TSA), released in June 1991, indicated that simple rank-orderings of states based on 1990 results were widely reported in the national press — despite warnings from U.S.Department of Education officials about the meaningfulness of such comparisons (Stancavage, Roeber & Borhnstedt, 1992). One account of press attention given to the release of NAEP TSA results concluded: "Newspaper reports of NAEP TSA reports published the day after . . . press briefings were rife with misinterpretations and erroneous conclusions" (Jaeger, 1992, p. 287). In short it seems likely that current developments in NAEP, and in particular the TSA, are likely to continue to contribute to the prominence of testing in American society.

The Elementary and Secondary Education Act of 1965

If NAEP was a relatively small federal budget item having relatively little impact on educational policy-making in the 1970s and 1980s, the opposite is true of the Elementary and Secondary Education Act of 1965 (ESEA) and its amendments. ESEA represents a watershed in the history of federal government involvement in education. Moreover, federal requirements attached to Title I contributed directly to an expanded national market for tests and related services. We do not attempt to trace the major role of ESEA in the history of federal government involvement in education in the United States (see for example, Bailey and Mosher, 1968, on the early history of ESEA). Instead we focus on the contributions of ESEA to the growth of the testing marketplace.

The main idea behind ESEA was that the United States federal government would provide financial assistance to local educational agencies serving high concentrations of low-income families. During the early 60s, Civil Rights and labor groups lobbying for the passage of ESEA used the fact that children from economically deprived backgrounds were also well below the national average on reading and mathematics tests. For example, Anthony Celebrezze, then Secretary of Health, Education and Welfare, testifying for the passage of ESEA, observed:

> You will find that by the end of the third year [grade] this student [in central Harlem in New York City] is approximately 1.2 grades behind the national average and 1.1 grades behind the New York City average. By the time he gets to the sixth grade, he is 2.1 grades below the national average and two grades below the New York average. And by the time he gets to the eighth grade, he is 2 $1/2$ grades below the New York average. . . .*The student continues to get further and further behind in terms of standardized test norms.* (Celebrezze, 1965, p. 89, Emphasis added).[2]

Disparities in tests scores between economically disadvantaged students and their more affluent peers therefore became an important political lever in the hands of advocates. They used these data to argue that schools and the federal government could and should be concerned with reducing these disparities, the elimination of which would, the argument ran, reduce economic disparities separating the groups.

Since attention had been drawn to achievement disparities in terms of standardized-test performance by advocates of federal funding for schools serving economically disadvantaged children, it is hardly surprising that legislators ended up mandating that efforts to eradicate educational disparities should be evaluated using the same standard (see Kennedy, 1965). Thus, test results became the yardstick used to measure results of ESEA programs and other interventions such as the Head Start Program (Title II of the Economic Opportunity Act of 1964)

---

[2] This conclusion, incidentally, is largely an artifact of the kind of test scale score being discussed, namely, the grade equivalent. The use of percentile rank scale scores generally do not show such an increase in score disparity over grade levels.

and Follow Through (included in a 1967 amendment to Economic Opportunity Act of 1964). This emphasis on test results was clearly reflected in Section 205 (a) (5) of ESEA, which included the provision:

> That effective procedures, including provisions for *appropriate objective measurements of educational achievement*, will be adopted for evaluating at least annually the effectiveness of the programs in meeting the special educational needs of educationally deprived children. (Emphasis added)

By 1975, in response to problems with the variability and the quality of local evaluations of ESEA Title I programs (McLaughlin, 1975), the U.S Department of Education developed six models for districts to use when evaluating their Title I programs (Tallmadge and Wood, 1976). All the models involved the use of either norm- or criterion-referenced test information. To estimate program effectiveness, more than 90% of local Title I evaluations used the norm-referenced Model A. This model required the use of commercially available nationally normed achievement test batteries (Reisner, Alkin, Boruch, Linn & Millman, 1982). Section 222 of the 1978 revision of ESEA required procedures for the evaluation of the effectiveness of local programs. These included a program of periodic testing of basic skills achievement and the publication of test results on basic skills performance by grade level and by school, without identifying the performance of individual children. Since almost every school district in the nation qualified for Title I monies, evaluations of Title I became a major impetus to use nationally-normed achievement tests during the 70s.

Another provision of the 1965 ESEA provided state departments of education with funds for state wide programs designed to measure the educational achievement of pupils. State departments differed in the way they used their ESEA allocations; but many used the new monies for departmental personnel in testing, evaluation or research. It was in the middle 60s that the growth in state assessment programs began, partly reflecting, probably, the impetus provided by ESEA (see Figure 3.1). Amendments to ESEA in 1978, in 1978, included funds to help state and local educational agencies to develop their capacity to conduct programs of testing the basic skills achievement of elementary and secondary school children. This provision seemed to both reflect and reinforce the emphasis at the state level on basic skills testing that began in the early 70s (Ssee Figure 3.1).

Exactly how much the testing industry was affected by Title I is hard to document; however, it is safe to say that the ramifications were considerable. Haney (1984) points to two indicators of the effect of Title I legislation and requirements on the testing industry. First, all major achievement test series revised in the late 70s and early 80s included tables for interpreting results in normal curve equivalents — the metric used to aggregate Title I results across evaluations using the six different evaluation models. Second, local and state officials interviewed about the Title I evaluation system realized that the federal government was promoting the use of norm-referenced tests, even though the officials thought criterion-referenced tests more appropriate (Comptroller General, 1977). In addition, Rudman (1987), the coauthor of the Stanford Achievement Test series, and the Stanford Test of Academic Skills, asserts that in the 70s standardized tests were re-designed to contain a higher density of easier items. The change was made in the interest of test reliability; additional easier items allowed low-achieving students to show more reliably what they knew and could do. This in turn made the tests more useful in the evaluation of programs for the educationally disadvantaged.

Thus it seems clear that though federal legislation promoting standardized testing in education began with the NDEA of 1958, a much more substantial impetus for increased testing was the ESEA legislation and mandates for evaluating programs funded by Title I (which became Chapter 1, under the Education Consolidation and Improvement Act of 1981) in terms of gains on standardized tests. As Clayton (1991, p. 348) noted, "Chapter 1 provisions calling for an evaluation model based on progress on nationally normed tests contributed directly to the growth of the standardized testing industry."

The most recent Congressional reauthorization of Chapter 1 was in 1988, in legislation formally titled the "Augustus F. Hawkins–Robert T. Stafford Elementary and Secondary School Improvement Amendments of 1988," but more widely and briefly called the Hawkins–Stafford Amendments of 1988. This legislation led to a number of important changes in the Chapter 1 system of evaluation and the way in which standardized tests were used in it. One was a change in regulations requiring a shift from fall-to-spring testing (that is testing children in Chapter 1 programs twice in each school year) to annual testing, either fall-to-fall or spring-to-spring. According to one observer, this change alone was expected to halve the "Chapter 1-related testing in most districts" (Stringfield, 1991, p. 325).

At the same time, however, another change in the 1988 Chapter 1 amendments led to increased prominence of test results in Chapter 1 programs. Before 1988, there had been widespread concern that Chapter 1 regulations requiring that funds be targeted on educationally needy children were contributing to fragmented and counterproductive "pull-out" programs in which Chapter 1-eligible children would be pulled out of their regular classrooms to receive small-group instruction from Chapter 1-funded teachers. Because of concern over the value of such practices, the 1988 amendments allowed schools with a large percentage of low-income students (75% or more) to carry out schoolwide Chapter 1-funded projects without the pre-1988 requirement of providing matching funds for non-eligible students (Letendre, 1991). With the increased flexibility of using Chapter 1 funds for schoolwide improvement efforts came the strings that school districts had to review annually the Chapter 1 evaluation results school-by-school and to formulate improvement plans for schools not meeting state-specified standards of progress. Yet the standards of progress specified were defined in terms of NCE gains — thus reinforcing what Clayton (1991) calls the "stranglehold of standardized testing" on Chapter 1. Public identification as being "in need of improvement" was, not surprisingly, seen extremely negatively by school people. Thus, even though the new Chapter 1 evaluation requirements may have lessened the amount of Chapter 1-required testing, they also upped the stakes placed on test results (Davis 1991).

While we cannot here go into a detailed account of the pros and cons of the Chapter 1 evaluation system and its guidelines, several knowledgeable observers have argued that this evaluation system has had educationally undesirable side effects. Here, for example, is how one critic recently summarized his concerns:

> The NCE-gain evaluation model used in Chapter 1
> assessments and for many other evaluations has major pitfalls.
> It can discourage early intervention, increased promotion rates
> and curriculum change. (Slavin 1991, p. 10)

In closing this brief review of Title I (now Chapter 1), we should note that since legislative reauthorization is scheduled for 1993, there is currently much discussion (and several major studies under way) concerning the future of Chapter 1 and the role of testing and assessment in Chapter 1 evaluation.

Indeed, currently a Congressionally-mandated advisory group is considering possible changes to Chapter 1 in light of the prospect for a national testing system (discussed below). But whatever the future of Chapter 1, what is clear in hindsight is that this federal program had a major role, at least through the 1970s and 80s, in promoting the prominence of standardized testing in school systems throughout the country.

The Education for All Handicapped Children Act of 1975 (P.L. 94-142)

Another major piece of federal legislation that contributed substantially to the demand for more testing was The Education for All Handicapped Children Act of 1975 (P.L. 94-142). P.L. 94-142 and its accompanying regulations promoted tests and other evaluation materials to determine individual placement, to assess specific areas of need, and to evaluate the effectiveness of individual educational plans (IEPs) mandated under the law for special needs children. The criteria for determining specific learning disabilities include a severe discrepancy between achievement and intellectual ability in one or more of the following areas: oral expression; listening comprehension; written expression; basic reading skill; reading comprehension; mathematical calculation; mathematical reasoning. Educators turned to standardized tests to measure most of these criteria.

The testing of special needs students in order for local educational agencies to meet the requirements of P.L. 94-142 seems to have provided additional impetus to the market for tests. Between 1978 (the first year in which the law was fully implemented) and 1984, the percentage of students nationally receiving special education under federal law rose from 9 to 11% (Stern 1987). Among the eight categories of handicapping conditions identified under federal law, the largest proportion of special educational students under P.L. 94-142 (more than one third, or more than 4 percent of students nationally in 1978) were identified as learning disabled. This is significant because "learning disability" is almost always identified in terms of students achievement as being significantly below their ability, as measured by standardized tests.

Since 1975 the Education for All Handicapped Children Act has been changed in several major ways. In 1986, amendments extended the right to free and appropriate public education for children with disabilities to include preschoolers aged 3 to 5. In 1990, the Americans with Disabilities Act provided civil rights protections to people with disabilities to cover private-sector employment, public services and accommodations, transportation and telecommunications. Also in 1990, the Education of the Handicapped Act amendments were renamed as the Individuals with Disabilities Education Act (IDEA). Two new categories of disability were added (autism and traumatic brain injury) and various kinds of service coordination were mandated (Hardman, Drew, Egan & Wolf, 1993).

While we have not been able to trace any clear connections between federal special education legislation and test sales, we estimated in chapter 3 that the market for special education testing amounted to between 8 and 20 million tests per year in the late 1980s. Also the prominence of testing and assessment in special education for people with disabilities was indicated indirectly in the IDEA of 1990, which called specifically for nondiscriminatory testing and multidisciplinary assessment (Hardman, Drew, Egan & Wolf, 1993, p. 25). Thus it seems no accident that, as we noted in chapter 2, one of the fastest growing of the mid-sized test publishers in recent years has been PRO-ED, a firm specializing in the special education market.

Other Pieces of Federal Legislation Related To Testing

In addition to these major federal legislative influences on testing in educational institutions in United States, there have been literally dozens of more minor pieces of legislation that have both promoted and, even when not enacted, increased the prominence of testing. Since we cannot trace all such legislation here, in this section we simply outline the extent to which educational testing has been mentioned in proposed federal legislation from the 96th Congress (1979-80) through the 100th Congress (1987-88). The Congressional Research Service of the Library of Congress, at the request of the Honorable Joseph D. Early, aided us in this effort by providing a synopsis of all applicable legislation here. We requested that key words used in the search include such terms as testing, standardized testing, basic skills, assessment, achievement testing, and ability testing.

Both the 96th and 97th Congress saw the introduction of two pieces of legislation responding to a growing demand by consumer advocates for "truth in testing." Both would have required testing companies to provide examinees with performance-related information. Neither was enacted. One of these, H.R. 4949, introduced by Representative Weiss, was modeled after New York's 1979 LaValle Bill (S. 5200). It would have required test agencies to disclose, upon request, the contents of post secondary or professional school admissions tests within 30 days of the release of scores.

Four pieces of legislation containing a testing component were introduced in the 97th Congress; none passed. In addition to the two "truth in testing" bills already mentioned, a bill to amend ESEA (H.R. 252) contained provisions for the establishment of standards of educational proficiency, and directed the Commissioner of Education to make proficiency examinations available to public school students in districts where State proficiency plans were not in effect. This provision of H.R. 252 is the first call — apart from NAEP — for federally sponsored achievement tests. H.R. 252 thus seemed to begin a trend that culminated in a mandate for comprehensive tests of academic excellence in the 1988 revision of ESEA.

The fourth piece of applicable legislation in the 97th Congress, The Productivity and Human Investment Act (H.R. 5461), provided for education for employment for youths not meeting established achievement levels (presumably measured by standardized achievement tests), or those dropping out of school. H.R. 5461 also contained provisions for remedial education to prepare students for a general education development (GED) test.

Ten pieces of legislation concerned with testing were introduced in the 98th Congress; none passed. The direct, indirect references to testing contained in these bills are noteworthy. They indicate, first, a response to growing state and local concerns about educational quality, and second, the growing reliance by legislators on tests as administrative mechanisms in legislation. A brief description of the testing provisions of each bill follows.

- A bill to amend the Defense Production Act of 1950 and labeled the National Defense Education Act of 1983 (H. R. 2483) called for grants to cover the costs of more stringent standards for graduation; certification of teachers in mathematics, science and foreign languages; and competency testing for students in mathematics, science and foreign languages for appropriate placement in undergraduate education programs.
- The Youth Incentive Employment Act (H.R. 5017 and S. 2397) and The Emergency Jobs, Training and Family Assistance Act of 1983 (S. 493) both mention a high school equivalency certificate and incentives for youth with documented educational deficiencies.

- The Professional Development Resources Center Act of 1984
  (H.R. 5586) contained a clause for training teachers to become
  familiar with developments in curriculum, testing and research
  and their applicability to the improvement of teaching skills.
- The Education for Gifted and Talented Children and Youth
  Improvement Act of 1984 (H.R. 5596) called for improving
  methods of identification of such children with particular
  emphasis on minority and handicapped youth who may not be
  so identified through traditional assessment methods.
- The Jobs Corps Amendments of 1983 (S. 2111) is notable in
  three of its provisions. First, it authorized the Secretary of
  Education to develop an intermediate certificate of education
  achievement denoting improvement in the basic skills leading
  to a high school graduation certificate or its equivalent. Second,
  S. 2111 directed the Secretary to establish standards of
  performance for Job Corps centers based in part on numbers
  passing competency tests in mathematics, reading, and
  composition. Third, S. 2111 required each Center to counsel
  and test individual progress in educational and vocational
  programs, and to terminate an enrollee who after six months has
  failed to make satisfactory progress. (S.2397 The Youth
  Incentive Employment Act has a very similar termination
  clause for its intended programs.) S. 2111 is another piece of
  legislation with provisions for a federal level test, this time to
  measure basic skills. It also called for the use of test
  performance in decisions to retain or drop individuals from a
  federally sponsored program, and in continuation or termination
  decisions about the program itself.
- The Secondary School Basic Skills Acts (H.R. 5749 and S. 2422)
  were two slightly different bills that would be introduced again
  in the 99th and 100th Congresses (99th, H.R. 901 and S. 508;
  100th, H.R. 1227 and S. 319) The bills, along with The
  Youth Education and Training for Employment Act (S. 2367),
  were designed to provide LEAs with grants to improve the basic
  skills of economically disadvantaged secondary school students.
  S. 2367 also provided funding to develop testing materials to
  determine the progress of program participants.

Both of the Secondary School Basic Skills Acts used improved performance on a state-approved basic skills test as a criterion for continued funding after the first two years. However, there was a significant change in the language of the House version from the 99th to the 100th Congresses: H. R. 901 and H. R. 1227. Improved performance on a nationally normed basic skills tests was not in the Senate version, which called instead for improvement on a state approved basic skills test. These are the first bills to link continued funding explicitly with improved test performance.

However, the concept of test based funding was not new to Congress. In 1974 in the Amendments to ESEA, Congress directed the National Institute of Education (NIE) to conduct a comprehensive study of changing the allocation of Title I funds from an index of poverty to low pupil achievement as measured by NAEP or by standardized test scores (Harnischfeger and Wiley, 1977). The two approaches differ in that the 70s version allocated funds based on low test performance (what some might view as a negative incentive program), while the 80s version continued funds based on improved test performance.[3]

The 99th Congress saw five bills introduced that had testing provisions, one of which, The Higher Education Amendments of 1985 (P.L. 99-498) was enacted. Of the remaining four bills three were repeats of bills introduced in the previous Congress.[4] The remaining bill, the International Education Reauthorization Act (S. 1926) called for the application of language proficiency tests and standards across all areas of instruction and classroom use.

Nine pieces of legislation that mention testing were introduced in the 100th Congress. Four bills, none of which passed, were repeats. One that did not pass (S. 373), which would have amended ESEA,[5] has provisions worthy of note. First, certain phrases appear throughout that implicitly suggest use of standardized test scores. These include "assessment of educational need," "the aggregate achievement of Chapter 1 children shows inadequate improvement or

---

[3] For a discussion of using test scores as positive and negative incentives in allocating funding for compensatory education see G. F. Madaus, (1979), Testing and Funding: Measurement and Policy Issues (in Schrader, W B., Ed. *Measurement and Educational Policy: New Directions for Testing and Measurement*, Jossey-Bass Inc., 1979 p. 53-62).

[4] The Youth Incentive Employment Act (H. R. 671) and the two versions of the Secondary School Basic Skills Act H.R. 901 & S. 508.

[5] The others were the Youth Incentive Employment Act (. R. 16); and the two versions of the Secondary School Basic Skills Act (H. R. 1227 & S. 319)

decline," "program evaluation," "basic skills improvement," "student achievement," "at-risk students," "increasing the academic achievement levels of all children," "increasing...achievement," "accountability," "improve the achievement of educationally disadvantaged...children," "schools with below average academic performance," and "incentive systems for measurable progress toward specific goals for educational performance improvement." All these imply the use of some type of achievement measure. And commercially available standardized test batteries are the most common measures of such variables.

Second, S. 373 would have authorized the Secretary of Education to approve or develop comprehensive tests of academic excellence to identify outstanding students at the 11th grade. The tests would be given on a voluntary basis, and students who passed would receive a certificate. While this provision died with the bill, a similar breakthrough provision became law in the 100th Congress with the passage of The School Improvement Act of 1987 (P. L. 100-297).

As part of Public Law 100-297. (1988), the *Augustus F. Hawkins-Robert T. Stafford Elementary and Secondary School Improvement Amendments of 1988*, the 100th Congress authorized the Secretary of Education, after consultation with appropriate State and local educational agencies and public and private organizations, to approve "comprehensive tests of academic excellence or to develop such a test where commercially unavailable, to be administered to identify outstanding students who are in the eleventh grade of public and private secondary schools. . . . The tests of academic excellence shall be tests of acquired skills and knowledge appropriate for the completion of a secondary school education." (Public Law 100-297, 1988; p. 102.)

The bill also authorized the Secretary to award students who scored at a sufficiently high level a certificate signed by the Secretary within 60 days of the taking the test. However, while the Congress authorized a national test and a certificate of performance based on the test, it did not provide funds for implementating the program.

P.L. 100-297 was a first of its kind vis-a-vis federal sponsorship testing. After years of strongly resisting a federal level test, the Congress has gone as far as to authorize the Secretary of Education to proceed in this regard. The testing provision is voluntary, and the results are to be used for awarding certificates to students. During the 60s much of the opposition to NAEP centered on the specter of a federal test. This clause in P.L. 100-297 constitutes a milestone in the history of federal legislation. As part of growing acceptance of test results as instruments of educational policy-making, the U.S. Congress has embraced the once alien concept of a federal achievement test. Another bill, the Quality Education Act of 1987 (S. 913), contained a similar national test provision for 12th graders. [6]

P.L. 100-297 also provided for grants to improve educational opportunity, giving priority to projects (1) for students with below academic performance and (2) for incentives whereby continued funding depends upon measurable progress toward specific goals of educational performance improvement.

Of the remaining three bills passed in the 100th Congress, two dealt with NAEP (S. 1700 and 1701). Both provided for state-by-state comparisons of results; on a voluntary basis. This provision reflects a significant change of national political heart regarding education. Until the 100th Congress state-by-state comparisons were considered to be invidious. Before NAEP could be initiated in the late sixties, features were built into NAEP's data collection that made state-by-state comparisons impossible.

The remaining bill enacted in the 100th Congress has the long name, A bill to establish a program of Federal grants to assist local education agencies to establish and provide for a school year of not less than 240 days and to establish Federal grants to recognize achievement in education by local educational agencies (H.R. 3154). This bill directed the Secretary to establish a program of grants to LEAs whose students perform above the national average on national educational competency and achievement exams.

Commentary on Legislation

The foregoing summary of federal legislative initiatives promoting, or indicating increased use of, testing over the five sessions of the U.S. Congress spanning the 1980s presents an incomplete picture of the relationship between legislation and testing in several regards. First, much of the proposed legislation was not actually enacted and therefore, did not have a direct impact on the testing marketplace. Nonetheless, these failed bills are expressions of the increasing prominence of testing as a policy instrument in the minds of policymakers. This trend toward federal legislation sponsoring more testing culminated in 1992 with

---

[6] For a discussion of the implications of such tests see Madaus, 1988.

legislative proposals for an unprecendented new national testing system. This particular development will be discussed in chapter 8.

Second, though we have attempted to provide an overview of recent federal legislation concerning testing, we have not tried to summarize state-level legislation promoting testing. Nevertheless, as indicated in chapter 3, the numbers of state-level testing programs increased sharply after the mid-1960s, and most of the state testing programs were mandated either by state legislation, or by state boards of education under their mandate in state-level legislation.

Moreover, even our discussion of federal legislation mentioning testing probably underestimates the role of federally funded programs in promoting test use. Myriad federal programs mandating research or evaluation concerning children, for example, appear to have the indirect effect of increasing test use. This was documented in a study of the instruments used in federally sponsored research on children (Heyneman and Mintz, 1976). In reviewing over 3500 federal research proposals on children and youth for fiscal year 1975, Heyneman and Mintz identified over 1500 test titles proposed for use in federally funded research projects. Among test titles that could be identified in standard test reference bibliographies, the types of tests most commonly used in federally sponsored research were individual intelligence tests and group administered academic achievement batteries.

We know of no study similar to the Heyneman and Mintz survey in the last ten years. Nevertheless, the fact that standardized tests have been widely used in federally sponsored research on children suggests that the federal influence in promoting test use extends considerably beyond legislation that explicitly or implicitly calls for use of tests. At the same time, the fact that tests are widely used in research and in state-level educational policy suggests that the federal government is by no means the only direct impetus for the increasing prominence of testing.

THE FOCUS ON OUTCOMES OF SCHOOLING

The pattern in recent education reform reports -- using test results to diagnose what is wrong with education and then prescribing more or new kinds of testing as a cure -- and the trend apparent in increasing legislative attention to testing both illustrate a fundamental shift over the last twenty years in how people regard educational quality. The use of test score data by would-be education reformers has a long history, going back at least to the time of Rice. However, for most of this century people have viewed school quality not so much in terms of test scores as in terms of a wide range of facilities, resources, and conditions associated with schools. Thus the perceived quality of a school depended on such matters as how well it was funded, the quality of its physical plant, the characteristics of its teachers and the demographic characteristic of its students.

Observers of the educational scene in America in the 1950s and 1960s — James Bryant Conant (1961) in *Slums and Suburbs*, Francis Keppel (1965) in *The Necessary Revolution in American Education*, for instance — focused attention on issues such as school finance, facilities and the social backgrounds of students attending different schools. In other words, up until the early 1960s, education reformers tended to focus their attention on the inputs of schooling, as opposed to its outcomes.

The release of the *Equality of Education Opportunity* report more commonly known as the Coleman Report after its chief author, helped to prompt a dramatic shift in the way people judged school quality. As mentioned in the last section, the Civil Rights Act of 1964 had mandated a study of the equality of opportunity in the nation's schools. The survey, nationwide in scope, was carried out, results analyzed, and written up in only one year (Coleman et al., 1966).

Though quietly released by the U.S. Office of Education, the findings from the EEO study soon gained notoriety. One of its most startling findings was that school facilities for minority and majority children were not greatly dissimilar. Even more surprisingly, the study found that whatever differences in facilities and school resources existed they had little if any discernible relationship to student achievement. This widely publicized finding was based on the following quotation which is certainly one of the most famous passages in the history of educational research:

> Schools bring little influence to bear on a child's achievement that is independent of his background and general social context; . . .this very lack of an independent effect means that the inequalities imposed on children by their home, neighborhood and peer environment are carried along to become the inequalities with which they confront adult life at the end of school. For equality of educational opportunity must imply a strong effect of schools that is independent of the child's immediate social environment, and that strong

> independent effect is not present in American schools.
> (Coleman, Campbell, Hobson, McPartland, Mood, Weinfield
> and York, 1966, p. 53)

This conclusion — which was popularly and somewhat inaccurately summarized as "schools don't make a difference" — aroused considerable consternation among advocates of education in general and advocates of equal educational opportunity in particular. For some it seemed counter-intuitive. For others it seemed to undercut efforts to equalize school financing. If more school resources are not associated with increased student achievement, many asked, why worry so much about the amount or quality of the resources devoted to schools serving the disadvantaged?

Given such implications, the EEO study received not only remarkable popular attention, but also close scrutiny by the scholarly community. Researchers and educational policy-makers debated, for example, the quality of the analytical methods employed, the nature of the tests used in the study, and the adequacy of information on school resources upon which the study drew. We will not attempt to recount those debates here (see Mosteller & Moynihan, 1972; Jencks et al., 1972; and Madaus, Airasian & Kellaghan, 1980, for a sampling of debates and follow-up studies spawned by the EEO survey and report).

For present purposes however, it is important to note that the EEO clearly contributed to a shift in national attention toward the outcomes of schooling. Frederick Mosteller and Daniel Moynihan, in an introduction to one of many follow-up reports on the EEO described this change as follows:

> . . . before EEOR, "quality of educational opportunity" was
> measured in terms of school inputs, including racial mixture.
> By inputs we mean physical facilities of schools and training
> of teachers; by racial mixture, the Supreme Court's emphasis
> on integration. With the publication of the EEOR it became
> increasingly the practice, even the demand, that equality be
> measured by school outputs; that is to say, by the results of
> tests of academic achievement. (p. 6)

This shift in focus, away from school resources toward school outputs — "measured by tests of academic achievement," as Mosteller and Moynihan put it — clearly contributed to the prominence of standardized tests in the U.S. since the 1960s, and consequently has contributed to the growth in the testing marketplace.

To provide evidence of the extent to which outcomes have become a prominent concern of educational policymakers, we cite three recent examples. First, when U.S. Department of Education officials introduced a fiscal year 1989 budget plan for their department, they proposed making schools and colleges more accountable by linking the level of federal funding to the "attainment of measurable outcomes" (Miller, 2/24/88, p.1). Second, when the Republican Party considered education in its national convention in the summer of 1988, it called for more "practical, down-to-earth reforms that have made a proven difference in actual operation [of schools]." Among the few specific reform proposals spelled out in the Party platform was that of "performance testing, both for students and teachers, [that] measures progress, assures accountability to parents and the public and keeps standards high" ("Excerpts from platform: 'For our children and our future' " *New York Times*, August 17, 1988, p. A20).

The third and even more prominent example of increased attention to outcomes in educational matters is President Bush's America 2000 strategy. In America 2000, the proposal for the new American Achievement Tests is included as part of a "15-point accountability package" through which it is said "parents, schools and communities can all be encouraged to measure results, compare results and insist on change when the results aren't good enough" (p. 11). One prominent advocate of America 2000, Chester Finn, in his book *We Must Take Charge: Schools and Our Future*, argues even more strongly that holding schools accountable for outcomes "is the only kind of accountability worth having in 1991" (Finn, 1991, p. 149).

BUREAUCRATIZATION OF EDUCATION

We have discussed various forces as contributing to the upsurge in standardized testing over the last several decades: dissatisfaction with the quality of education in the nation and calls for reforming schools; legislation calling for more testing for a variety of purposes; and an increased focus on outcomes of as opposed to resources devoted to schools. These help to explain the growing market for testing. Yet each of these influences represents only one perspective on an overarching phenomenon that we believe more broadly explains the recent upsurge in testing. This phenomenon is the growing bureaucratization of American education in this century (see Wise, 1979 and Hall, 1977 for a detailed discussion).

Bureaucracy is a fact of life in large institutions in all industrialized nations. Bureaucracies are present in socialist and capitalist nations, and in government agencies as well as private businesses. Thus we intend in this section neither to attack or to defend the bureaucratic phenomenon. Indeed, literature on the bureaucracy as a social phenomenon is so large that we cannot attempt even an overview of all of it.

Our aim in this section is simply to sketch the outlines of bureaucracy in modern society, to point out some of the ways in which education in the United States has succumbed to the bureaucratic phenomenon, and to describe the ways in which testing seems to have grown as a result of both the successes and the failures of the bureaucratic phenomenon.

The word bureaucracy has come to be something of a pejorative term. Referring to someone as a bureaucrat seems almost akin to deriding the person as pompous, obstructive, and unproductive. Yet the term itself is of remarkably recent vintage. According to the *Oxford English Dictionary*, the introduction of the term bureaucracy into the English lexicon dates back less than 150 years, to Mill's 1848 reference to the "inexpediency of concentrating in a dominant bureaucracy . . . all the power of organized action . . . in the community."

Sociologists and political scientists have been quick to recognize the bureaucratic phenomenon as an essential aspect of modern society. Max Weber, Carl Friedrich, Everett Hughes, Karl Mannheim and others all have helped to define and explain the nature of bureaucracy. Among the essential features of bureaucratic organization are 1) centralization and hierarchical organization of control; 2) functioning of various units within an organization according to generalized, abstract but definite rules that involve the categorizing of problems and people; 3) the definition of procedures in terms that are both formal and impersonal; and 4) selection of personnel on the basis of objective qualifications rather than on the basis of election, family inheritance or social class.

It is easy to see such features in modern schools. In this century the control of schooling has become increasingly centralized; large numbers of local school districts have consolidated to form fewer but larger school systems; state education agencies in most states have increased their influence over local education authorities; and since the 1960s and the passage of ESEA, the federal government has played an increasingly prominent role in education. Another indicator of the growth of the educational bureaucracy is the fact that between 1972 and 1982, the average number of full-time professionals in headquarters of state departments of education increased more than 40% (Campbell, Cunnigham, Nystrand and Usdan, 1985).

Teachers, students and others who inhabit school systems are increasingly organized and classified according to general but abstract rules, such as years of experience in an organization, exams passed, or degrees earned. Formal procedures and abstract regulations now govern many aspects of education — everything from the exact date of birth that makes a child eligible for entry into kindergarten to the number of days a school must be in session in order to meet the requirements of its state education agency.

In most school systems elaborate course requirements, curriculum guides and scope and sequence charts guide what students must study and what teachers must teach. Complex procedures govern the hiring of teachers and other educational personnel; fixed rules have been established for promotion from grade to grade and for high school graduation. Indeed, one of the federal laws mentioned earlier, the Education for All Handicapped Children Act of 1975 (P.L. 94-142), now known as the Individuals with Disabilities Education Act (IDEA), surely represents one of the clearest and most ironic signs of the extent to which bureaucracy has come to characterize education in modern America. For among its other requirements this law sets out elaborate requirements by which school systems are to create *individualized* educational plans for special-needs youngsters. It is a remarkable conflict in perspectives — a federal law setting out standard procedures by which school administrators and teachers must treat children as individuals!

As soon as the features of bureaucracy are noted, it is easy to see the myriad ways in which bureaucracy characterizes modern society in general and modern educational institutions in particular. It also becomes easy to see why standardized testing fits so well with the bureaucratic phenomenon. Externally mandated tests or something like them are an absolute necessity for centrally and hierarchically organized schools.

Standardized tests provide means for categorizing people, educational institutions and problems according to abstract, impersonal and generalizable rules. They expedite formal and impersonal administrative procedures. For instance, if someone certified to administer a recognized intelligence test gives the test to a child using prescribed procedures, the child may be classified on the basis of the resultant score as being of normal intelligence or educably or trainably retarded, and then placed in an "appropriate" instructional group.

Tests surely provide one of the commonest of antidotes to selection of personnel on the basis of political connections, family background or social class. This universalistic feature of tests provides society with a mechanism for the allocation of opportunities on the basis of objective qualifications or "merit." One of the most telling of incidents in this regard is that when a nationwide program was begun in the 1950s to award college scholarships on the basis of scores on standardized tests of verbal and math skills, it was named the National Merit Scholarship program. Scores on standardized tests in modern bureaucratic society represent not just measurements but signs of merit. In education as well as in employment, standardized tests very frequently provide the means by which personnel may be selected not on the basis of patronage, social class, gender or race, but instead on the basis of objective qualifications — or at least on the basis of objective test scores.

NEW FORCES

This chapter has described the four forces that we believe have contributed to the phenomenal recent growth in the testing marketplace: (1) recurring public dissatisfaction with the quality of education in the United States and efforts to reform education; (2) an array of legislation, at both federal and state levels, promoting or explicitly mandating standardized testing programs; (3) a broad shift in attention from a focus on inputs or resources devoted to education toward outputs or results produced by our educational institutions; and (4) the increased bureaucratization of education, schooling, and indeed society more generally.

As we noted in introducing this chapter, these forces often are intertwined in particular historical episodes. For instance, dissatisfaction with political and educational conditions in the United States helped to spur passage of the Civil Rights Act of 1964. This Act also mandated the Equal Educational Opportunity Survey. And the report of findings from this survey helped greatly to focus public attention on the outcomes of schooling, as measured by standardized tests. Moreover many have argued that requirements of the Civil Rights Act and its legislative and regulatory progeny have helped to bureaucratize not just many educational matters, but also matters of employment hiring and promotion, by encouraging that matters of fairness and equity be treated merely in terms of numbers or "quotas."

Without commenting in detail on the merits of such developments, we merely suggest that the four forces identified as contributing to the growth of testing — namely dissatisfaction, legislation, focus on outputs of education and bureaucratization of social institutions — are of sufficient historical influence that they likely will continue into the future. At the same time, it seems clear that these forces are emerging in different ways in the 1990s. Indeed, just as we revise this volume for publication, in the early stages of the 1992 Presidential campaign, it seems apparent that education and testing are receiving unprecedented national attention. As mentioned earlier in this chapter, President Bush unleashed his America 2000 program for educational reform in 1991, with new national tests proposed as one of the major instruments of reform, but now it seems that most of the current crop of Presidential aspirants also are giving ample attention to education and educational reform in their campaigns. In large measure, such concerns seem to stem from widespread dissatisfaction with national economic productivity, but note that current attention to education and to testing coincides completely with forces discussed in this chapter. Continuing dissatisfaction with the quality of schooling in the United States, though often apparently arising out of concerns for matters economic, clearly is contributing to concern for educational outcomes — or to put the matter more like it is usually stated in popular discussions, "what we are getting for our huge national investment in education". Given the continuing political prominence of education, it seems likely that legislative initiatives at both national and state levels will continue to be directed at schools, and already it is clear that some of this legislation will propose use of tests, not just to reform educational institutions but also to guide or control the transition from school to work, at least for young people who do not go on to higher education.

At the same time however, there seem to be two currents in the national discourse concerning education which seem out of synch with the historical forces discussed in this chapter as powering the growth in the testing market over the last several decades. One is that traditional multiple-choice tests are now widely seen as part of the cause of low educational standards. As one recent article reviewing current national educational reform proposals put it, over-reliance on multiple-choice tests in the 1980s "led teachers to emphasize tasks that would reinforce rote learning and sharpen test-taking skills, and discouraged curricula that promote complex thinking and active learning" (Wells, 1991, p. 55). Thus the new national tests called for in the America 2000 project described earlier are not the multiple-choice variety that have dominated the testing marketplace for many decades but instead are to be "authentic" or "instructionally worthy" assessments. What people mean by such terms varies, but the most commonly discussed kinds of alternatives to multiple-choice tests are portfolios of students' work and performance assessments in which people have to perform a task or solve an open-ended problem. We return to the "authentic" assessment movement in chapter 8 to discuss what it may portend for the testing market.

In closing chapter 5, however we should note the other development of recent years which seems somewhat out of synch with past forces behind the testing marketplace. Though variants are called by several names, it is essentially what we see as a movement to deregulate or "de-bureaucratize" schooling in the United States. On one hand, there is at present much interest various programs for organizing education in the United States so that parents and students have more choice in the schools attended (for example via educational voucher and magnet school programs). To some this means breaking the virtual monopoly that public schools have held on the education of American children, so that private schools can compete with public schools, both for students and for public funds supporting education. At the same time, however, many reformers are advocating that even public schools be "restructured," so that educators at the school level have more say in how their schools are run and fewer bureaucratic constraints from local, states and national educational authorities. For instance even the America 2000 report advised that

> The individual school is education's key action-and-accountability unit. The surest way to reform education is to give schools and their leaders the freedom and authority to make important decisions about what happens . . . (U.S. Department of Education, 1991, p. 27).

Such school choice and school restructuring sentiment surely represents something of a change in the prevailing climate of opinion in educational policy-making circles (though, as any student of educational history may testify, there is amply historical precedent for both impulses). But if such rhetoric leads to fundamental changes in the way schools are organized and governed in the United States, it will represent a major change in two of the most clear-cut trends in American education in this century, namely consistent growth in public school enrollments (save for the downturn in enrollments in the 1980s due to demographic changes) and the consolidation of small schools into larger school governance units. Again, however what these movements, toward more school choice and toward "restructured" schools portent for the testing market is a topic we take up in our concluding chapter.

6 SPIN-OFFS FROM THE TESTING INDUSTRY

Like the automotive industry, the testing industry has spawned a number of spin-off companies and endeavors that market products or services related to test preparation, construction, interpretation, administration, and scoring. Some of these endeavors accommodate examinees directly, others target test users in education, business, and clinical and counseling psychology, and still others are directed at people and institutions that are affected by test results. Spin-off products and services from the testing marketplace are highly diverse, ranging from publishers who provide books on how to make, take and interpret tests, to organizations aimed at promoting, and challenging the role of testing in American society. In this chapter, we examine three spin-offs from the testing industry, namely:

- The computer connection;
- Test preparation and coaching; and
- Honesty or integrity testing.

We examine these three spin-offs for two reasons. First, each of these topics has garnered a fair amount of attention in its own right in recent years, and hence is worth examining. But a second and broader reason is that while each is an offshoot of the testing industry, each also suggests something about likely future influences on the role of testing in the United States.

THE COMPUTER CONNECTION

In 1968, Bert Green, Jr., predicted "the inevitable computer conquest of testing" (Green, 1970, p. 194). While computers may not have completely conquered standardized testing, the connections between computer power and testing are strong and growing rapidly. Some of these connections have already been mentioned in chapter 2, where we recounted the the emergence of NCS and Scantron as major players in the testing industry. In this chapter we discuss five practices that serve to link computers and testing, namely:

1 Scoring services;
2 Stand-alone scanners for use at the local level;
3 Computer-Based Test Interpretation;
4 Test Item Pools; and
5 Computerized Adaptive Testing

Scoring services

Since the advent of Lindquist's high-speed optical mark reading (OMR) machine in the 1950s, test scoring has become the largest source of revenue in testing. As we saw in chapter 2, two test scoring companies, NCS and Scantron, are among the seven largest companies in the testing industry. The sales of such scoring services have two components: sales of test answer sheets, and sales of scoring and reporting services. In some cases, such as with most of ETS's tests, answer sheets and scoring are bundled with the costs of the test itself and its administration. However, in other cases, for example with most elementary and secondary standardized testing, purchase of scoring services is separate from the costs of tests themselves. This pattern is seen in *The 1990 Riverside Test Resource Catalog* (Riverside Publishing Company, Chicago. 1990). This Riverside catalog is 156 pages in length, with 70 pages devoted to actual tests and 68 pages to "scoring services." To illustrate the relative importance of the tests themselves versus the scoring services, we note that the catalog gives a price of $68.75 for a package of 35 level-9 test booklets of the complete battery of the *Iowa Tests of Basic Skills*, plus social studies and science, test booklets, or slightly less than $2.00 per test booklet. However, since the test booklets are reusable, say up to three times, the cost per test booklet use may be less than $.50. In contrast, the cost of machine scorable answer sheets for these test booklets is about $.60 per sheet ($21.30 for package of 35), and the costs of scoring services can range from about $1.30 per answer sheet, to more than $4.00 (including basic processing charge and charges for scoring plan selected, norms selected, optional scoring services, and extra copies of any of the various scoring reports offered). In other words, for publishers of reusable test booklets, scoring and reporting services may account for revenues that are two to seven times those from sales of test booklets themselves.

The market for scoring services is not restricted to commercially developed tests. Answer sheets from states' or districts' own tests are frequently scanned under contract with private firms (and sometimes on high-volume scanners owned by state or local education agencies).

Stand-alone scanners

Since a large part of the total costs of testing since the 1950s has been in scoring and reporting, a growing segment of the testing industry since the 1970s is low-volume scanners sold directly to end-users of tests, such as schools or companies. Scantron and Scanning Systems were the first companies to develop desk-top scanners for use at the school and classroom levels to score teacher-made tests. These scanners were designed to "read" test answer sheets and when coupled with a microcomputer and printer, to produce test score reports. In the computer industry such scanners — called OMR, or optical mark recognition, scanners — have been distinguished from optical character recognition, or OCR, scanners and also from bar code readers and graphics scanners. However, since optical scanning technology has been developing rapidly, it is now possible to purchase hardware and software that will allow scanning of marks (such as on test answer sheets), characters, graphics or bar codes on the same machine.

The market for stand-alone scanners, or scanners connected with local personal computers, is based on the idea of simplifying and improving testing by giving schools or employers quick turn-around in the scoring of tests. The machines can also be used for automatic encoding of results from forms pertaining to employee attitudes, attendance records, school grades and any kind of survey. Paine-Webber (Cicchetti, 1987) called the potential of the school market for such stand-alone scanners as "outstanding" and described the market as follows:

> OMR systems offer schools and teachers a very simple, efficient, cost-effective method of improving the testing process. The process is improved because tests can be prepared and graded very quickly and inexpensively; the teacher sometimes has test results in hand quickly enough to correct mistakes before the class is over. There is a national trend toward more testing in schools in an effort to better the [sic] measure of the effectiveness of schools, teachers and the

knowledge and progress of students; this trend should be
beneficial to Scantron. (p. 3)

As indicated previously, the principal source of revenue in the OMR
business in the past has been the sale of the expendable machine-readable answer
sheets. Scantron's policy has been to lend OMR scanners to schools with
enrollments as small as 750 students if they agree to buy a certain quantity of
the company's scannable forms each year (Paine-Webber, in Cicchetti 1987).
The forms are produced at a penny a piece and sold for a nickel or more, "a very
remunerative [margin] on ever-expanding forms sales" (SUTRO & Co., in
Cicchetti, 1988, p. 1).

An ancillary product is the OMR data entry terminal, a device that
transmits information from the scanned forms to a variety of micro-computers
(e.g. IBM PC, Apple), minicomputers, mainframe computers, or data storage
equipment (Paine-Webber, in Cicchetti, 1987). Scanning companies like
Scantron and NCS, as well as smaller independent software firms market
software to schools for computing a host of test statistics such as the mean,
median and standard deviation; performing item analysis; generating frequency
distributions; and producing test reports. As with the stand-alone devices, these
data entry terminals steadily consume paper forms. Further, some data entry
equipment is sold, not "loaned," producing equipment profits (Paine-Webber, in
Cicchetti, 1987).

Apparently the advent of stand-alone scanners has changed the market
for test scoring dramatically in the last decade. A survey in the early 1980s
found that nearly 90% of test scoring for Pennsylvania school districts was done
by commercial vendors (Blurst & Kohr, 1984, p. 6). In contrast, a survey of
large school districts' test scoring practices in 1992 found that 50% of
commercially procured standardized tests (and 96% of locally developed tests)
were machine-scored locally (Bauer, 1992, p. 13).

Another wrinkle in the OMR scanner market for schools is the end-of-
chapter test in textbooks. As a marketing strategy, textbook publishers
sometimes offer end-of-chapter review tests with their books. Scantron and NCS
have developed joint marketing agreements with major textbook publishers to
market forms so that teachers can scan these end-of-chapter tests on OMR
machines (Paine-Webber, in Cicchetti, 1987). These tests are a little noted, but
potentially powerful, spin-off of from the testing industry.

A recent national study of testing practices among grade 4 - 12 teachers found that majorities of teachers at elementary, middle and high school levels used tests supplied with the textbooks used in their classes at least once a month (Lomax, 1992). When asked about the extent to which text-supplied tests influence their own teaching practices, substantial proportions (37-46%) indicated that the text-supplied tests influence the topics they taught, the emphasis given to topics taught and the content and format of teacher-made tests. A companion study of the quality of text-supplied tests (Harmon & Mungal, 1992) indicated, however, that the quality of these tests was very low in that the questions on them tended very largely to focus on low-level factual recall knowledge and only very rarely to more complex aspects of mathematical or scientific reasoning. At the same time, though machine-scoring of tests has become commonplace at the school district level, it appears to be fairly unusual at the classroom level. In the Lomax (1992) survey, only some 8-26% of teachers reported using a scoring machine to score teacher-made or text-supplied tests.   Thus it seems clear that tests that textbook publishers supply to accompany texts they sell are an important and influential aspect of the testing marketplace.

Computer-Based Test Interpretation

A natural extension of OMR scanning, and one of the fastest growing spin-off industries related to testing is that of computer-based test interpretation (CBTI). Attempts to use computers to generate test interpretations date back at least several decades. The Mayo Clinic automated interpretations of the MMPI in the early 1960s. Commercial availability of CBTI began in 1977 with the formation of a company called Psych Systems. Psych Systems was the first to put computer terminals for on-line test administration into the offices of practitioners around the country. Until then practitioners had to send tests away to be scored and interpreted (Moreland, 1987a). Since then, as computer technology has become more sophisticated and available, CBTI has grown enormously.

In particular, the advent of microcomputers in the 1970s led to a proliferation of software of many kinds, including programs for interpreting tests. For instance, listings in *The Educational Software Selector* (TESS) show that the number of software packages listed under the rubric of "test scoring and interpretation" increased by about 50% from 1984 to 1987, (from 15 programs listed in the 1984 edition of TESS to 22 in the 1986-87 edition (EPIE, 1984, 1987).

Despite the proliferation of software, the quality of this new form of test interpretation remains much in doubt. In 1983, for example, the *Wall Street Journal* carried an article entitled "Psychiatrists' Computer Use Stirs Debate" (Hall, 1983). The article recounts how a patient takes a traditional test (e.g. the MMPI) and how proprietary software generates evaluations for psychologists, psychiatrists, personnel officers or special educators. *The Wall Street Journal* characterized the growth of this sector of the testing industry as follows:

> [The] business is growing rapidly. 'God is there a market for it,' says Dr. Joy Stapp, director of the Human Resources Office at the American Psychological Association. She says that nearly all of the organization's 35,000 licensed members perform psychological testing, as do many of the 28,500 members of the American Psychiatric Association. (Hall, 1983, p. 31)

In computer-based test interpretation, a clinician may send a test answer sheet to a company not just for scoring but also for production of an interpretive report. Moreover, in many cases, subjects can take a test while seated at a microcomputer. The microcomputer has software that not only administers and scores the individual's performance, but also produces, either locally or via a phone link to a distant mainframe computer, an interpretive test score report. The latter mode, sometimes described as teleprocessing, is available through companies such as NCS and through the Institute for Personality and Ability Testing (IPAT) (Moreland, 1987). In the teleprocessing of item responses, data are typically transmitted over phone lines via a modem. This can happen in several ways: first by having an individual take a traditional paper and pencil test and then having a clerk keycode responses for transmission; second, by using optical scanning equipment to scan a machine-scorable answer sheet and then transmit results; or third, by having the test administered via computer and having the test-takers' responses transmitted either instantaneously or delayed via batch mode, for processing at a remote site (Moreland, 1987).

The use of the computer to present test questions on-line, process the results, and then generate interpretations of the responses is spreading to a number of applications in psychology and psychiatry, including testing of psychiatric patients; the investigation of particular psychiatric syndromes; psychiatric diagnosis; diagnostic interviewing; career guidance; solving dilemmas in personal decision making; the development of personal construct systems; diagnosis of alcoholism; identification of "Type A" behavior (Jackson, no date). Computer-generated interpretive reports are starting to be used in pre-employment screening of applicants for many jobs involving public trust and safety, such as correctional officials, police officers, nuclear power plant operators, and rail and air crew personnel. In addition, large governmental agencies like the Veterans Administration are beginning to move toward computer-generated interpretive reports.

Computer-generated interpetive reports of test results are also increasingly prominent in education. Many publishers of individually administered tests aimed at the education market now offer software that allows printing out of interpretive reports. In its 1992 catalog, for example, PRO-ED offers a "Software Scoring and Report System" for its *Detroit Tests of Learning Aptitude*, Third Edition. The ad for this system, which runs on several different brands of microcomputers, promises:

> The program converts the student's raw scores into standard
> scores, percentile ranks, and age equivalents and also generates
> composite scores. The program then compares composite
> performance for significant intra-ability differences.
> Comparisons between DTLA-3 performance and achievement
> test performance allow for additional intraindividual
> discrepancy analyses. The program provides a multiple-page
> printout using your 80-column printer, suitable for inclusion
> in the student's record. (*PRO-ED 1992 Catalog, Tests,
> Materials, Books and Journals*, Austin Texas, p. 3)

In 1983, *The Wall Street Journal* named two companies as leading in the market for computer interpreted reports of psychological test results, namely, Psych Systems and Compu-Psych Systems Inc. (since acquired by NCS). However, the same article pointed out that "a new cottage industry in mail-order software is springing up as doctors and researchers rush to market their own tests" (Hall, 1983, p. 31). Also, as noted in chapter 2, one brokerage house identified NCS as the dominant company in the clinical testing market with 30,000 psychologists and psychiatrists as customers.

In addition to the traditional education and employment segments of the testing industry, the general public now constitutes an emerging new market niche for self-administered computer tests and interpretive reports. Psychological instruments designed for administration via personal computer (PC) are now aggressively marketed to the general public. As early as the mid-1980s, it was estimated that one company, Thoughtware, had sales of $8 million in 1984; another, Human Edge, sold an estimated $5 million of its software in 1985 and sales for 1986 were projected at $10 million (Eyde and Kowal, 1985). As PCs in the home become more common, software permitting PC-owners to self-administer various psychological tests will undoubtedly grow.

How large is this spin-off component of the testing industry? As with other components of the testing industry, we have no definitive or comprehensive evidence, but when we turn to indirect indicators, a necessary and much-used recourse in our inquiry into the testing industry, we find strong evidence that the computer connection with testing has increased rapidly in the last decade. Since 1984, for example, Samuel Krug has compiled a reference guide to computer-based products for behavioral assessment in psychology, education, and business called *PSYCHWARE SOURCEBOOK* (1984, 1987, 1989). The purpose of this reference book is "to identify and describe as broad an array of computer-based products available for assessment in psychology, education and business as possible" (Krug, 1989, p. xi). Over the three editions of this *SOURCEBOOK*, the numbers of *PSYCHWARE* products listed have risen from around 200 to 450, an increase of more than 100% in less than a decade.

Several of the classifications Krug uses to describe the "psychware" he lists provide insight into this growing segment of the testing industry. For example, Krug uses the following eight categories to describe products listed:

1. **Career/Vocational.** Describes "products that emphasize career choice or deal with concepts that have special relevance for selection or promotion decisions in the industrial context" (1989, p. xv).

2. **Cognitive/Ability.** Describes "products that feature dimensions of intelligence, abilities, aptitudes or achievement" (p. xv).

3. **Interest/Attitudes.** Describes products that "tend to deal with a broader range of content (e.g. lifestyle concerns, personal belief systems, etc.) than those categorized as Career/Vocational" (p. xv).

4. **Motivation.** Products in this category "emphasize dynamic variables such as Murray's list of manifest needs" (p. xv).

5. **Neuropsychological.** This category "describes products used primarily in the evaluation and localization of organic brain damage or in the remediation of the effects of such damage" (p. xv).

6. **Personality.** Products in this category "emphasize trait or temperament concepts" and "is by far the most frequently selected product category" (p. xv).

7. **Structured Interview.** Products in this category "are often described as intake interviews" (p. xv). They are almost always self-administered and concentrate on background information.

8. **Utility.** "Products in this category are intended to assist in assessment activity, but are not primarily assessment devices" (p. xvi).

For each product listed, Krug indicates in which of these categories it falls, as either a primary or secondary categorization. For the 3rd edition of *PSYCHWARE SOURCEBOOK*, the distribution of products across these categories was as shown in Table 6.1

Table 6.1: Kinds of Psychware Products

Product Category	Percent of products with primary categorization	Percent of products with secondary categorization
1. Career/Vocational	13	5
2. Cognitive/Ability	20	5
3. Interest/Attitudes	3	7
4. Motivation	3	8
5. Neuropsychological	8	10
6. Personality	37	40
7. Structured Interview	9	NL
8. Utility	8	NL

Source: Krug, 1989

Krug also indicates for which of nine kinds of applications each "psychware" product is designed. Easily the most frequently designated application, listed for 35% of the products is "clinical assessment/diagnosis." According to Krug's index of suppliers of "psychware" products, the firms most active in this segment of the testing market (each with ten or more products listed) are:

Consulting Psychologists Press (10 products);
Educational and Industrial Testing Service (10);
Institute for Personality & Ability Testing (17);
Integrated Professional Systems (12);
Life Science Associates (24);
Multi-Health Systems (12);
NCS/Professional Assessment Services (27);
Precision People (16);
PRO-ED (12);
Psychological Assessment Resources (21);
Psychologists Inc. (12);
Sienna Software (10);

Psychological Corporation (14); and

Western Psychological Services (26.

Finally, Krug provides a summary of the types of services offered for each of the products listed: mail-in service via which answer sheets are sent to a remote site for processing; teleprocessing, in which answers are submitted electronically via terminal and/or data transmission equipment; and on-site processing, in which answer sheets are scored locally on the end-user's own equipment. Of these three, types of "psychware" processing services, easily the most commonly offered, for 85% of products listed, is on-site processing, usually via software run on microcomputers.

The sales potential of the computerized "psychware" testing market appears to be enormous and growing, but also raises serious technical and ethical questions, which we will return to in chapter 7.

Test item pools

Another segment of the testing industry with strong connections to the computer revolution is that of marketing test item pools. Item pools, or item banks, are simply large collections of test questions in a given discipline coded by the objective, skill, or content the item is designed to measure and perhaps by other item characteristics, such as grade or age level, for which the item is deemed appropriate. For example, in the 1980s, the Northwest Evaluation Association, a consortium of school districts in Oregon and Washington, developed a bank of more than 16,000 test items keyed to districts' curriculum objectives in reading, language arts, math, and science. This item bank was marketed to other school systems through a firm called Microsystems for Education and Business.

Such item banks are maintained and managed by computer. By having the computer select pre-coded items, a teacher, school system, or state department can build a customized test for specific objectives. By having the computer create tests through random selection, equivalent test forms can be generated for retesting (Jackson,1984). Some of the major test companies are offering to customize tests for clients through the use of their extensive items pools.

While development via test item bank was originally and is still sometimes offered to schools and businesses on a contract basis (that is, a customer provides specifications for the desired test and the vendor builds the test from its proprietary pool of items), computer programs are increasingly being offered to allow schools and businesses to develop and use their own item pools. Assessment Systems Corporation, for example, offers a complete microcomputer-based system for users to develop their own test item pool and build tests from it. A number of firms offer software for virtually every brand of microcomputer that permits users to build their own item pools. Typically, such software gives the user a blank template into which specific test questions can be entered and the correct answers coded; a variety of other codes for each question may also be specified (pertaining, for instance, to the instructional objective, content, and difficulty level of the question). Once a pool of items is built, the user can use the program to generate tests meeting a variety of such specifications.

Such test item banking software programs span a wide range, in terms of both capabilities and cost. At the low end, some programs are available as "shareware," that is, software that may be copied and used gratis, but for which satisfied users are requested to make a donation to the developer. One such "shareware" item bank program for the Macintosh microcomputer, called TestMaker, has been developed by Eric Peters. This program is intended for teachers and allows them to create their own collections of multiple-choice, true/false, fill-in, and essay items.

At the other extreme there are testing software programs costing hundreds or thousands of dollars and allowing the building of tests to be administered not just in traditional paper and pencil format but also via computer. These programs often come with already developed sets of test questions and built-in statistical algorithms to maintain data on how examinees perform on items, and allow creations of tests meeting various statistical specifications. In order to explain such features, we must first, however, examine one of the newest frontiers in standardized testing, namely, what is widely called computerized adaptive testing.

Computerized adaptive testing[1]

Computerized adaptive testing, sometimes called tailored testing, refers to a form of testing in which examinees are not given a predetermined set of test

---

[1] Here we attempt only to provide a brief overview of this form of testing without going into the theoretical unperpinnings of adaptive testing, such as latent trait or item response theory. For fuller treatments of such issues, see Weiss, 1983, or Butcher, 1987.

questions. Instead, depending on their performance on an initial set of test questions, they are given subsequent questions that are either easier or more difficult. In other words, the questions presented in the test are "tailored" or "adapted" so that examinees are presented with questions of appropriate difficulty.

The ideas behind adaptive testing are quite old. Indeed, adaptive testing techniques have long been used in individualized (as opposed to group) testing. Weiss (1983), for example, notes that in the first decade of the 20th century Alfred Binet used adaptive testing techniques. According to his testing protocols, not all examinees were initially presented with identical questions. Instead, the examiner based the questions "on the examinee's ability level as estimated prior to the start of testing" (Weiss, 1983, p. 5). Also, the examiner scored answers as the test proceeded, and the correctness of answers was used to select the questions to be asked next. Finally, Binet's test had a variable stopping rule, so that different subjects tested might be given not just different questions but also different numbers of questions. In the case of the Binet tests, the test was terminated after the examinee had answered a certain number of questions in a row incorrectly.

Thus the essential features of an adaptive test have been experienced by anyone who has ever taken or given a Binet-type intelligence test. Though adaptive testing techniques are still widely employed in individually administered tests, they cannot be used with paper-and-pencil group-administered tests. About the only remnant of such adaptive testing procedures to find its way into group testing practices has been the use of a short "locator" test, after which an individual is given the appropriate level of the full group test.

But since the 1970s, with the increasing availability of computing power, there has been an upsurge of interest in and many new applications of computerized adaptive testing (CAT). As Weiss (1983) put it in the preface to a book on this topic:

> By the mid-1970s, minicomputers (and later microcomputers) made available the power of interactive computing in research laboratories and later in practical testing environments. This development led to implementation of computerized adaptive testing. (p. xiii)

Growing interest in this form of testing was signaled in February 1984 when a new phrase, "adaptive testing," was added to the *Thesaurus of ERIC*

Descriptors. This descriptor was defined as "testing that involves selecting test items according to the examinee's ability as shown by responses to earlier test items" (Houston, 1986, p. 4). Since then, 160 journal articles and research reports have been indexed with this term.[2]

Research on computerized adaptive testing (CAT) and trial CAT programs have emanated mainly from four sorts of institutions: namely; 1) agencies within or directly affiliated with the U.S. Department of Defense; 2) the research oriented major testing companies (i.e. ETS and ACT); 3) a handful of universities with strong research programs in CAT (such as the Universities of Minnesota and Illinois); and 4) a few large corporations with major employment testing programs (such as American Telephone and Telegraph).

The interest of the U.S. Department of Defense in CAT is both theoretical and practical. In the 1970s, the Office of Naval Research, for example, sponsored a series of three conferences on adaptive testing in order to help stimulate research in the field. From a historical perspective, it is hardly surprising that the U.S. military is involved in this new area of testing, since innovations in military testing, dating back to World War I, have been highly influential in both educational and employment testing. But from a practical point of view too, the military has had a keen interest in using adaptive techniques. Adaptive testing is more flexible than traditional group or individually administered testing because recruits can be tested at computers without having to wait for a group to be assembled or a trained test administrator to give the test. Moreover, adaptive testing is less costly, as it reduces testing time, by administering only items of appropriate difficulty, the examinee's ability can be estimated after asking about half the number of items that a conventional test would need (Green, 1984). In 1983, the Defense Department expected to spend $10 million for terminals and $40 million for programs. Despite this cost the DOD expected its testing costs to remain the same because CAT saves heavily on personnel costs (Koenig, 1983).

Given the potential benefits of greater flexibility and efficiency in testing, adaptive testing is also attracting the attention of large corporations. In 1983, Psych Systems Inc. (according to Moreland, 1987, p. 26, "the first commercial enterprise dedicated solely to computerized psychological assessment"), surveyed the testing needs of 4,500 businesses and projected that

---

[2] Specifically a search of ERIC in March 1992 via BRS After Dark, showed 160 ERIC documents indexed with the "adaptive testing" descriptor.

its sales would reach $8 million in that fiscal year (Koenig, 1983). The *Wall Street Journal* described the CAT market as follows:

> Enthusiasts see a market wherever tests are given by paper and pencil. American Telephone & Telegraph Co., for example, gives about 100,000 tests a year. The company already administers tests for keypunch operators and typists by computer and foresees use of adaptive tests by the late 1980s. 'I'm building the staff now,' says AT&T psychologist Mary Tenopyr. (Koenig, 1983, p. 29).

Not surprisingly, other large testing firms are getting involved in adaptive testing. Researchers at ETS, such as Frederick Lord and Howard Wainer, have provided leadership in both the theoretical underpinnings of adaptive testing and in try-outs of its potential in admissions testing. In 1988 ETS and the College Board released new *Computerized Placement Tests,* computer-administered adaptive tests that individualize basic skills examinations in reading comprehension, sentence skills, arithmetic, and elementary algebra for college freshmen. The claim is made that these adaptive tests quickly pinpoint student skill levels using far fewer questions than would be necessary on paper-and-pencil tests. The College Board package also includes Computerized Placement Management Software to use CAT data with placement rules to assign first-year students to particular classes or courses of study. To complete the service, ETS offers a Placement Research Service that will analyze the effectiveness of the placement rules in terms of student grades and modify the rules if necessary (ETS, 1987).

In 1992, ETS announced a "nationwide computerized test network." ETS struck a deal with Sylvan Learning Centers (said to be the largest for-profit educational services company in North America) so that ETS tests can be taken on computers on a walk-in basis at 400 Sylvan sites around the country. The initial ETS test to be offered via this arrangement will be the Graduate Record Examination, scheduled to be offered in Sylvan Centers in the fall of 1992 (Educational Testing Service, 1992).

While the computer has not yet come close to conquering the world of paper-and-pencil standardized testing, the increasing availability of computers in schools and businesses and theoretical developments in adaptive testing point to the increasingly widespread use of computers to deliver adaptive tests.

Conceivably, group-administered paper-and-pencil testing could disappear, to be replaced by "drop-in" assessment centers, at which examinees, via computer, could take any number of admissions or employment tests, any day of the year. While such a prospect is, in our view, fairly remote with respect to schools' standardized achievement testing, the substantial investments of the military and large employers, and major admissions testing programs in computerized adaptive testing, makes this scenario much more likely in these realms of testing.

TEST PREPARATION AND COACHING

Another increasingly prominent spin-off from the testing industry, or more specifically from the increasing social prominence of testing over the last several decades, is test preparation and coaching. Probably the best publicized cases of test "preparation" have been those in which educators blatantly cheated on tests because of pressure on schools to increase students' scores. For example in 1989, the 60 Minutes television program featured a story about an award-winning South Carolina teacher who was fired for preparing students for a standardized test by giving them advance access to the exact questions to appear on the test. Similarly in 1992, an award-winning principal in Lake Forest, Illinois, was fired "after a special hearing officer found that she encouraged faculty members to cheat when administering and scoring standardized achievement tests" (Thomas, 1992, p. 3).

Such cases of outright cheating on standardized tests may be rare, but now clearly commonplace are a variety of efforts to coach or otherwise prepare people to do well on standardized tests. In other words, test preparation and coaching have become a spin-off industry in the testing marketplace. Before describing this industry, it is worth noting that there is ample precedent for it. Whenever testing becomes a major determinant of life chances, an industry grows up to help prepare examinees for high-stakes exams. Test preparation has a long history in the British Isles, for example, dating back to the 19th century when companies called "crammers" abounded. The crammer prepared British and Irish youth for a host of certifying and matriculation exams. Japan has long had its infamous Juku schools to prepare students for important entrance examinations.[3] A gauge of the importance of testing in our society is the

---

[3] For a fascinating review of the examination preparation industry in Japan, see August (1992).

development and growth of a major test preparation industry, targeting examinees, educators, and parents. It is an industry that provides a plethora of products and services running the gamut from direct tutorial help for examinees to "how to" test preparation books; from microcomputer software to mock tests. In order to provide an overview of the test preparation and coaching industry, in this section we describe three types of products and services directed at test preparation, namely:

1. Computer software aimed specifically at raising test scores;
2. Other test preparation materials; and
3. Commercial test coaching programs.

Computer software

In yet another computer connection with testing, a minor industry has developed to produce software for microcomputers to help students prepare for the various standardized tests. Listings in *The Educational Software Selector* (TESS) catalog show that between 1984 and 1986-87 the number of such preparation packages (listed under the "Aptitude Test Preparation" rubric) increased from 27 to 60 (EPIE, 1984, 1987). Actually, however, the number of test preparation programs available for microcomputers was much larger than 60 since many were offered in multiple versions designed for different makes and models of microcomputers. While we have not ourselves seen, much less evaluated, most of these test preparation packages, it appears that many are of questionable quality. Of the 60 listed in the 1986-87 edition of TESS, ten were evaluated using EPIE's systematic evaluation process. Of these ten, eight were rated as "not recommended, but may meet some needs." (EPIE, 1987, pp. 41-47.)

Not surprisingly, test preparation software seems most commonly to be aimed at the largest, best-known tests, such as the Scholastic Aptitude Test or SAT. By the late 1980s, there were at least a dozen software packages available for use on microcomputers to help students raise their SAT scores (Curran, 1988; Kane, 1988; Leonard, 1988). Owen (1985) reviewed three software programs for SAT preparation, and dismissed all of them as largely worthless (the worst, in Owen's view, was one that cost $300; Owen, 1985, p. 119).

Given the apparent market for test preparation software, however worthless, it is not surprising that test sponsors themselves have entered this new market niche. In the fall of 1988, for example, ETS and the College Board introduced interactive software to help students prepare for various admission tests. The College Board claims that its product TESTWISE is "the first SAT test-preparation software offering completely accurate examples of all types of questions on the test" (ETS, 1988, p. 9). ETS has developed similar software for the Graduate Records Examination (GRE) called *Practicing to Take the GRE General Test — Number 4*, and the Graduate Management Admission Test (GMAT). The former is a software version of the popular review book of the same name (ETS, 1988).

Other test preparation material

Like the software industry, book and test publishers have responded to the demand for test preparation material. Every major book store now has a section devoted to test preparation books for a host of admissions, certification, licensing, and job tests. Barrons Educational Series Inc., Cliff Notes, Monarch Press, ARCO, and Barnes and Noble publish test preparation booklets for such tests as the Advance Placement Test, the SAT, the GRE general and area tests, the GMAT, the MCAT, the LSAT, the Miller Analogies Test, the Practical Nurses Licensing Exam, the National Council Licensing Exam for Registered Nurses, the Test of English as a Foreign Language, the Real Estate Licensing Exams, Firefighters Exam, Police Exam, State Trooper Exam, Air Traffic Controllers Exam, Officers Candidate School Exam, the ASVAB, the U.S. Citizenship Test, Correction Officers Exam, and the Securities Exam. One author, Gary Gruber, has 23 different test preparation books credited to him.

As with the test preparation software market, test sponsors themselves have jumped into the test preparation book market. ETS and the College Board, for example, have published actual SAT exams in a series of books called *5 SATs* and *10 SATs*. Though he was highly critical of ETS and the College Board in many other respects in his "debunking" of the SAT in *None of the Above*, Owen (1985) concedes that the ETS/College Board books of actual SAT exams are among the few SAT test preparation books that would "actually help a student prepare for the SAT" (p. 119).

In addition to preparation books for specific tests, a market has also developed for books and materials on general test-taking strategies. These materials are designed to familiarize readers with various item formats, reduce test anxiety, reveal clues to the correct answer, and so on. The prolific Gary Gruber, for example, has authored *Dr. Gary Gruber's Essential Guide for Test Taking for Kids (Grade 3, 4, 5)*. Obviously aimed at test-anxious parent as much as at kids, this single volume is advertised as helping parents to help their children and featuring:

- Development of critical thinking skills to last a lifetime
- Specific preparation for the SAATs, CTBSs, ITBSs, CATs, ERBs, MATs, PSATs, SATs, and Stanford Achievement Tests
- Foolproof methods for zeroing in on correct answers
- The key math rules, concepts and shortcuts children need to know to take any test successfully
- The essential grammar skills and vocabulary lists required for all standardized tests proven reading comprehension techniques
- Easy-to-learn strategies for reducing test-taking strategies in children
- Practical methods for showing children how to realize their true potential at the right age.

As the prominence of standardized testing in education grows, the test preparation market has even expanded to provide teachers and administrators with materials they can use to give students practice for forthcoming tests. Mehrens and Kaminski (1988) identified 12 commercially prepared achievement test preparation programs aimed at teachers and administrators. Major test publishers such as ETS and CTB have produced such materials. ETS, for example, offers two different film strips on test preparation. One is designed to introduce classroom teachers, counselors, and administrators to key concepts of test preparation so they in turn can help students. The second package, aimed at children, features a clown named Buddy who explains in "kids' language" such things as what a standardized test is, how it differs from teacher tests, why children are asked to sit in different seats during the test, and who uses their scores and how. Riverside Publishing Company markets a package of 15 test preparation booklets for student use, covering the following five categories: following test directions, using time wisely, analytical skills in reading, analytical skills in language, analytical skills in math. Similarly, CTB/McGraw-Hill markets CAT Learning Materials, which it describes as follows:

> Use of these materials will improve student learning and help increase levels of achievement . . . Although based on the objectives of the new CAT E&F, they can also be used

successfully with CTB's other widely used tests.
(CTB/McGraw-Hill, 1988 p. 18)

Random House which was taken over by McGraw-Hill, a parent
company of CTB (and which in 1989 became, as noted in chapter 2, a part of the
new Macmillan/McGraw Hill School Publishing Company), markets a series of
practice tests called *Scoring High*. Mehrens and Kaminski (1988) quote from a
letter from an executive of Random House to a school administrator, stating that
the company was proud of the fact that since 1978 over 8,000,000 copies of
Scoring High programs have been used. *Scoring High* consists of mock tests
modeled after such frequently used standardized achievement tests as the
Metropolitan, Stanford, CAT, ITBS, and *Degrees of Reading Power*. It is
designed to let students practice for a forthcoming standardized test of a main line
testing company, by presenting them with a mock test.

Another, largely hidden, dimension of the test preparation market is the
sale of drill and practice ditto masters and workbooks that present students with
multiple-choice questions. Indeed, in some school systems even reading and
math instruction has devolved into test preparation, because instead of having
children read actual books or work to solve real math problems, students practice
test-like reading and math questions. An aspect of this dimension of test
preparation already mentioned is the distribution of end-of-chapter tests that
textbook publishers make to schools adopting their textbook series. As noted
earlier, one brokerage firm views this development as a potentially lucrative
market for OMR companies.

One product that speaks volumes about the recent emphasis on
standardized testing in schools is a package called *Test Buster Pep Rally*,
described as a "unique approach to improving student performance on
achievement tests." The $80 package includes skits, worksheets, practice tests,
cheers, songs, games, jokes and "other unique test preparation activities for use
with grades 1-6," all centered around a motivational half-hour assembly program
called "test buster pep rally." In partial answer to the question, "Why
implement a program that prepares students for taking achievement tests?", Test
Buster author Robert Brown points to the increased emphasis on test scores and
accountability and the use of scores for decisions that have far-reaching effects on
students. An ad for the package points out that *Test Buster Pep Rally* "makes a
nice compliment [sic] to 'practice test' programs." In other words we now have
a market for complements to practice test programs -- spin-offs of spin-offs!

We know little about sales of such materials, or about how their use affects teaching and learning. Nevertheless, some research to which we will return in chapter 7, and considerable opinion, holds that overemphasis on test preparation in schools has a negative impact on teaching and learning. But whatever the impact of these materials, there is little question that test preparation products represent an important and lucrative spin-off of the testing industry.

Test coaching

An even more visible form of test preparation is the modern American equivalent of the 19th century British crammers, namely test coaching companies. We have already mentioned computer programs and printed materials designed to help people prepare to take standardized tests, but a third kind of test preparation is offered through a host of commercial test coaching "schools." The most extensive investigation into coaching for standardized admissions tests in the United States was that undertaken by the Federal Trade Commission (FTC) in the late 1970s. The FTC inquiry, which was prompted by potentially false advertising claims, found that "commercial coaching schools exist . . . in every state and in virtually every major city and college campus throughout the country for all standardized admission examinations" (FTC, 1978, p. 35).

The FTC analysts observed:

> Although the coaching school industry may not be large in terms of annual sales by some standards, the industry structure already exists which enables it to reach any of the approximately 2,500,000 individuals who annually will be taking a standardized admission examination. It has the potential to grow quite rapidly and to exceed annual sales of one-half billion dollars. Furthermore there are almost no entry barriers to this industry. (FTC, 1978, pp. 35-36)

The FTC inquiry found the test coaching industry so extensive that it concentrated its investigation on coaching for just two examinations (the SAT and the LSAT) in four major cities over a two-year span (1976-1978). Despite this limited focus, the investigation documented the existence of 21 commercial entities. Courses lasted between 6 and 40 hours, for which students were charged fees ranging between $40 and $250.

In addition to such commercial test coaching, the FTC study documented the existence of substantial non-profit test coaching activities: "There are a large number of undergraduate colleges and universities that offer preparation for admission tests to graduate schools" (FTC, 1978, p. 41). After noting the irony and potential hypocrisy of undergraduate institutions offering coaching for graduate admissions tests, the FTC study pointed out that most test preparation courses offered by colleges and universities cost substantially less than those of commercial test coaching schools. But the FTC inquiry uncovered the fact that one university offered a test preparation course for a fee comparable to that charged by for-profit entities for an examination (the SAT) that the same institution "uses in determining, at least in part, who will gain admission" (FTC, 1978, p. 44). Regardless of the efficacy of that university's test prep course, such a practice clearly raises ethical and conflict-of-interest questions, as the FTC inquiry noted.

Considerable controversy surrounded the FTC inquiry, primarily because of the statistical methods employed in the initial FTC study to estimate the effects of coaching. In chapter 7 we return to discuss the controversy over the effects of test coaching and present our own view of the the efficacy of coaching. Here we simply recap some of what we have learned about the nature of this test coaching spin-off from the testing industry.

According to both the FTC (1978) inquiry and Crouse and Trusheim (1988), the largest test coaching company nationwide, with over half the market, is the Stanley H. Kaplan Educational Centers LTD. Kaplan founded his test-coaching business in Brooklyn in 1938. According to a 1984 account:

> Last year Stanley H. Kaplan Educational Centers grossed $35 million in sales by offering instruction on a variety of topics to 88,000 students at its 124 permanent centers and 250 temporary ones, according to Mr. Kaplan. The firm, he said expects enrollment to reach 97,000 this year.
>
> The Kaplan company is best known for its preparation courses for college, graduate-school and professional-school admissions tests including the S.A.T., the Graduate Record Examination sand the Law School Admission Test.
>
> But it also has a growing roster of preparation courses for licensing examinations in such fields as accounting, nursing,

dentistry and medicine. In the last few years, it has also developed "self-improvement" programs such as speed reading and instruction in English as a second language.

Kaplan fees range from $50 to $1,800 for yearlong courses that ready students for professional licensing tests. The average fee is $350 for courses that prepare students for college and graduate school admissions tests, the firm's most popular courses, Mr. Kaplan said. (Toch, 1984, P. 15)

According to a 1988 account, Kaplan's firm was then grossing about $60 million per year and its student clientele was growing at 15 percent per year (Jakubovics, 1988). Ads for Kaplan's services at its centers across the country have long run in Sunday newspapers and in college publications across the country. A typical ad in the *New York Times* (June 6, 1988) proclaims in bold letters "I want for your kids what I wanted for my kids — 250 more points on the SAT." In 1984, the Kaplan firm was reportedly purchased by the Washington Post Company, for an undisclosed amount (Toch, 1984). Thus it is not surprising that in 1992, full-page ads for Kaplan began appearing in *Newsweek* magazine, also a Washington Post Company subsidiary.

In an attempt to learn more about the test coaching or tutorial segment of the testing industry, we contacted Stanley Kaplan by phone in 1989. He indicated that he has been in business since 1938, and until 1970 his only center was in Brooklyn. Students came to Brooklyn from all over the East Coast for his service. In 1970 he began to expand, opening a second center in Philadelphia. From 1970 through 1975, 50 additional centers were established; from 1975 to 1980 the number of centers doubled to 100. As of 1989 he reported 130 permanent and 400 temporary centers from coast to coast. Mr. Kaplan stated that throughout the 50 years he has been in business, revenue has never gone down.

Mr. Kaplan indicated that the demand for his services directly reflects social and economic conditions. He offered the following example: enrollment in preparation courses for the LSAT rose 40% in 1988 and was rising even faster in 1989; enrollments in GRE courses are also on the rise. Students see jobs in law or realize that jobs in high technology require Master's or doctoral degrees. Enrollment in the MCAT and GMAT courses has declined. Mr. Kaplan feels that the decline in MCAT enrollments reflects the high cost of medical education and the lower rewards brought about by the rise of health maintenance organizations (HMOs). He concluded that students who previously would have been pre-med students now "would rather sue than be sued." He attributed GMAT enrollment declines to the market crash and ensuing layoffs by financial and stock companies, which make management degrees less attractive. Similarly, an expanding market is preparation for Nursing Boards by foreign students who wish to come to America because of the nursing shortage. A final indicator of the success of Kaplan's services is an ad in the July 31, 1988, *New York Times* for a national director of instructor development whose job would be "to create and implement teacher training and evaluation programs for instructors preparing young adult and adult students to take standardized tests."

As indicated previously, the Kaplan chain is not the only company in the test coaching business. The FTC study found that after Kaplan, the next largest coaching firms were John Sexton, Amity and Evergreen. Since the FTC inquiry, another test coaching chain, Princeton Review, has sprung up in New York, which by the mid 1980s had established branches in the greater New York area, Los Angeles, Chicago and Boston (Owen, 1985, p. 138). By 1992, Princeton Review has grown to have 60 offices nationwide operating programs in 400 locations, and is reported to gross around $30 million per year (Katzman, personal communication, July 12, 1992). One notable difference between this new player in the test coaching business and its predecessors is that Princeton Review makes little pretense about being an educational organization. Its avowed aim is more to teach students how to beat the SAT and the other tests for which it preps students — and of course to make a tidy profit in doing so. Here is how a 1989 article on Princeton Review (entitled "Cranscam") described Katzman's approach:

> Katzman says he based "more than 50 percent" of his teaching
> on having students "get inside the heads of the test-makers"
> and figure out the right answers, or at least improve their odds
> without actually learning much of substance. (Hammer, 1989,
> p. 16)

Not surprisingly both Kaplan and Princeton Review have been exploiting the computer connection with testing. As early as 1984 Kaplan said that his firm was looking for software that would employ a problem solving approach to test preparation (Toch, 1984). Princeton Review not only maintains computerized databases on its student clients, but also undertakes detailed independent analyses of the tests it coaches students for, and has plans in the works to develop its own computerized adaptive tests (Katzman, personal communication, July 12, 1992).

Nationally organized test coaching companies are not the only players in this market niche. The Yellow Pages of major cities list a range of test preparation services (most frequently under the "Tutoring" rubric). For example, nine companies that specifically offer test preparation courses appear in the Boston yellow pages. Some of the companies are well established with a number of centers in the metropolitan Boston area; most, however, are local enterprises. Coaching for tests like the SAT and ACT has become so popular that many public schools, responding to parental demand, are now offering this service to their college-bound students.

As with other segments of the testing industry, systematic evidence on the size of the test coaching industry is hard to come by. The most systematic inquiry into the commercial test coaching business was the 1978 inquiry previously mentioned. However the test coaching business has changed markedly since then. According to the 1978 FTC study, for example, the Kaplan chain had total annual sales of nearly $8 million in 1975-76 (p. 37), but more recent published accounts put Kaplan revenues at $60 million in 1988. Scanty though the evidence may be, in Figure 6.1, we show a graph of apparent growth in revenues for Kaplan and Princeton Review This data suggests that the commercial test coaching business may be one of the fastest growing spin-off segments of the test marketplace over the last decade or two. In less than 20 years Stanley Kaplan Educational Centers grew from a single center in Brooklyn to a nationwide chain with total revenues surpassing those of all but a handful of testing companies. And Princeton Review has grown from an idea of a couple college graduates in less than a decade to surpass the revenues of all but the largest test producers.

Figure 6.1: Revenue Growth for Stanley H. Kaplan Educational Centers and Princeton Review

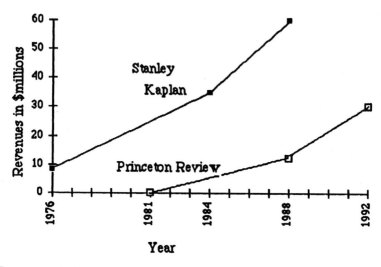

Sources: see text

HONESTY TESTING

Another newcomer in the testing market has been the so-called "honesty" or "integrity" test. An ad that appeared in the April 1988 issue of *Personnel Administration* aptly illustrates the emergence of this new market niche. Above a banner headline stating: "The honest [sic] truth about Polygraph testing," the ad highlighted the fact that the U.S. Congress had put an end to polygraph screening. The ad asserts that Congress' action proclaimed "the beginning of a new era in employee screening and testing methods."

To appreciate the full import of this 1988 advertisement, some background information is needed. In March of 1988, a U.S Senate bill barred the use of polygraph tests to screen job applicants for most jobs. The House had passed a similar bill in November. The American Psychological Association (APA) supported the bill.[4] It was passed in part because of expert testimony that polygraph screening is not valid, and that because of the low base

---

[4] The Senate version exempted security guards and nuclear power plant employees. At the time of the Monitor report the two bills were in joint committee to iron out differences. The APA opposed exempting any industry from the bill's provisions.

rate of dishonesty among potential employees, the number of false positives — honest applicants labeled dishonest by the polygraph — is unacceptably high. In other words the polygraph is biased against honest applicants. An article appearing in the April, 1988, issue of the APA *Monitor* described the problem this way:

> Although the real rate is probably much lower, assume that the polygraph screening identifies 90 percent of the dishonest applicants and 80 percent of the honest applicants, and that 20 percent of applicants have in fact withheld something in their past that would disqualify them, for a base rate of 20 percent.

> If 1,000 people are tested, 800 are honest and 200 dishonest. Assuming the test is 90 percent accurate in detecting dishonesty, 180 of the 200 dishonest people will be detected. But 20 percent of the honest people, or 160, will be inaccurately branded dishonest. So while 340 people were said to be dishonest, only 180, or 53 percent, actually were. (Bales, 1988a, p. 10)

The thrust of the ad discussed above is that the product promoted, the *Wilkerson Pre-Employment Audit* (WPA), a "paper-and-pencil psychological indicator," can be used in lieu of the polygraph. The ad is remarkable for a number of reasons. First, its timing with respect to Congressional action is noteworthy. Given that the ad appeared in April, the company must have anticipated the bill's passage. Second, the implication is clear that while the polygraph will certainly be challenged, the paper and pencil *Audit* will not. Third, the justification for purchasing the WPA product — because it accurately predicts the results of a polygraph 97% of the time — is extraordinary. The unwary consumer is not informed that one of the prime bases for the banning of polygraphs was the high rate of misclassification of employees. Yet the alleged 97% correspondence between results of the *Wilkerson Pre-Employment Audit* and polygraph results suggests that the *Audit* would have a misclassification rate nearly as high as or possibly higher than that of the outlawed criterion measure the *Audit* compares itself with.

In 1988 in the *APA Monitor*, Bales quoted the APA's Director for Science Alan Kraut and reported that the APA's Committee on Psychological Tests and Assessments remains

> "seriously concerned" about the widespread use of integrity tests for pre-employment screening, because "there is simply not enough known" about the tests. In spite of the research done to date, the committee concluded, "no adequate data-base now exists to support the use of honesty tests"(1988b, p. 1).

Because of such concerns, two independent studies of honesty or integrity testing have recently been undertaken. The first completed was titled *The Use of Integrity Tests for Pre-employment Screening* and released by the Office of Technology Assessment of the U.S. Congress in September 1990. In addition to the 1988 Congressional ban on polygraph testing, the OTA identified three broader factors contributing to the growth of such testing. First is the belief of some test publishers and employers that use of such tests can reduce employee theft and counterproductive behavior. (One estimate in 1989 had pegged the annual loss to U.S. businesses from nonviolent crimes, including theft, vandalism, and bribery, at $40 billion; the estimate appeared in a book published by one of the major producers of integrity tests.) Second, the OTA study suggested that there was increased concern among employers about "negligent-hiring lawsuits," in which companies are sued for hiring dangerous or incompetent employees. Third is the argument that if paper-and-pencil integrity tests are "accurate and reliable, they can be cost-effective tools for employee screening" (OTA, 1990, p. 3).

The OTA noted that there is some ambiguity as to exactly which instruments ought to be classified as honesty or integrity tests. Some "overt honesty tests" ask applicants directly about past acts of theft or dishonesty, but other more general personality tests sometimes used in "integrity screening" ask much less obviously relevant questions, regarding for example whether the applicant likes to take chances. Despite such ambiguities the OTA study estimated that some 5000 to 6000 business establishments "use honesty tests in the process of screening and selecting job applicants for employment" (p. 1). As noted in chapter 3, the 1990 AMA survey on workplace testing indicated that paper-and-pencil honesty testing is apparently most common in the wholesale and retail trade business category (reported by 30% of respondents) than in any other business sector (none of which showed more than 8% of respondents reporting such testing).

After reviewing published research on the validity of integrity testing (and some unpublished research that was not reported because it was deemed proprietary by the test publishers), the OTA reached the following conclusion:

> Given the paucity of independent research results, problems
> identified in published reviews and in the OTA's review of a
> sample of validity studies, and unresolved problems related to
> the definition and measurement of underlying psychological
> constructs, OTA finds that the existing research is insufficient
> as a basis for asserting that these tests can reliably predict
> dishonest behavior in the workplace. (OTA, 1990, p. 10)

Just six months later, however, the American Psychological Association's Task Force on the Prediction of Dishonesty and Theft in Employment Settings reached a somewhat different verdict on this sort of testing (Task Force, 1991; Robb, 1991). The Task Force identified 45 companies selling integrity tests, and, like the OTA report, estimated that some 5000 companies were using them to test five million people per year. The vast majority of the companies identified by the Task Force appear to be extremely small operations, not previously mentioned in standard reference works on testing such as the *Mental Measurements Yearbook* series. The only three large or medium-sized test publishers identified in the report as selling integrity tests are:

> National Computer Systems (Hogan Personnel Selection Series and
>   Employee Reliability Index);
> Consulting Psychologists Press (Personnel Reaction Bank); and
> London House (Employee Attitude Inventory and Personal Outlook
>   Inventory).

The APA Task Force report observed that promotional claims for honesty tests, as perhaps for all other procedures used for preemployment screening, vary from the circumspect to the fraudulent.

> We have seen a number of promotional brochures that are so
> clearly overblown as to make a test expert cringe in

embarrassment. In the most flagrantly hucksterish of these, all problems associated with test use remain unmentioned, and the purported reduction in actual theft that can be achieved is wildly exaggerated. (Task Force, 1991, pp. 20-1).

Despite these findings, the APA Task Force report substantially softened its conclusions, as compared with that of the OTA: for it observed that while the evidence on the validity and fairness of integrity tests is weak or nonexistent, such tests are probably more valid and efficient, and less harmful, than alternatives that employers might otherwise use — such as interviews or surveillance.

So apparently, despite extensive investigations into this new niche in the testing marketplace by both the OTA and the special APA Task Force, and despite their similar findings that little if any evidence exists to support claims made for such tests, neither agency took or recommended any concrete action to intervene in the market for these tests.

In our concluding chapter 8, we will discuss a variety of options that exist for dealing with imperfections in this and other realms of the testing marketplace; but first in chapter 7 we will examine the implications of the fractured testing marketplace for test quality and use.

7 TEST QUALITY AND THE FRACTURED MARKETPLACE FOR TESTING

In previous chapters, we have seen that the marketplace for testing has been expanding rapidly over the last several decades. From a business point of view, standardized testing appears to be more successful than ever, with more tests sold for more different purposes than ever before. Moreover, as we have recounted, a variety of spin-off industries (e.g. computer products and services, books and commercial test coaching courses) have grown up around the burgeoning testing market. Despite their commercial success, the quality of many tests and test-related services appears to be increasingly questionable. The testing marketplace is so large and diverse that it is impossible assess the quality of all tests and related services; in this section, we simply attempt to describe what we see as five problem areas in the testing marketplace: the Lake Wobegon phenomenon, the marketing of tests, the purchase of tests by government agencies via the RFP process, computer-based test interpretations, and test preparation and coaching. In the concluding part of this section we try to assess the significance of these problems in the testing marketplace. Before setting out on this itinerary, however, we first delineate what we mean by quality in testing.

QUALITY IN TESTING

The quality of a test may be judged from many different points of view, such as ease administration, cost and commercial success. The perspective of prime concern to us, however, is that of test validity and its implications for use of tests as instruments of educational and other social policies. As the 1985 *Standards for Educational and Psychological Testing* of the American Educational Research Association (AERA), the American Psychological Association (APA), and the National Council for Measurement in Education (NCME) emphasizes, "Validity is the most important consideration in test evaluation" (AERA, APA and NCME, 1985, p. 9).

Test validity refers to the quality of inferences made from test results. Though many people, including ourselves, sometimes speak in shorthand of the validity or quality of a test, what is really at issue is not just a test itself, but rather the quality or accuracy of inferences drawn from the results of the test. Thus, from a scientific point of view, a test as a measurement device or inferential aid must be judged not in isolation but in terms of how it is used. As the 1985 *Standards* indicates, validity refers "to the appropriateness, meaningfulness, and usefulness of the specific inferences made from test scores" (AERA, APA and NCME, 1985, p.9).

There is far more that could be said about the issue of test validity, different kinds of validity evidence, and standards of validity evidence.[1] We return to some of these issues later in this section. For now, prior to discussing problem areas in the testing marketplace, we simply want to state our concern about tests and related services that allow, or even encourage, false and misleading inferences from test results. Tests, as inanimate instruments, are not in and of themselves good or bad, valid or invalid. It is the manner in which tests are used, and the way in which inferences are drawn from and decisions based on results, that determine the worth of inferences drawn from the test.

As we will see, five particular problem areas in the testing marketplace appear to be undermining the quality of inferences drawn from tests.

THE LAKE WOBEGON PHENOMENON

Lake Wobegon is the mythical town in Minnesota popularized by Garrison Keillor in his National Public Radio program "A Prairie Home Companion." It is the town where "all the women are strong, all the men are good-looking, and all the children are above average." Though Keillor's "Prairie

---

[1] It should be noted, however, that the key reference on the topic of test validity since the 1985 *Standards* is Messick's (1989) chapter on the topic. Messick's main contribution to the theory of test validity is to note that a thorough consideration of test validity must include not only the inferences implicit in test use, but also the consequences of test use.

Home Companion" ceased production after a 13-year run, it appears that Lake Wobegon in a sense has gone national. For according to a 1987 report by John Cannell, the vast majority of school districts and all states are scoring above average on nationally normed standardized tests (Cannell, 1987). Since it is logically impossible for all of any population to be above average on a single measure, it seems clear that something is amiss, that something about nationally normed standardized tests or their use has been leading to false inferences about the status of learning in the nation's schools.

Cannell is a physician by training and not a specialist in education or educational measurement. His original (1987) report was published by "Friends for Education," the foundation he established to promote accountability in education. A revised version of Cannell's report was published in the summer 1988 issue of *Educational Measurement: Issues and Practice* (Cannell 1988), together with responses and commentary from representatives of major test publishers and officials of the U.S Department of Education (Phillips and Finn, 1988; Drahozal and Frisbie, 1988; Lenke and Keene, 1988; Williams, 1988; Qualls-Payne, 1988; Stonehill, 1988). Cannell's charges regarding misleading test results were hotly debated in this and in other forums. Some people doubted whether the Lake Wobegon phenomenon was real (that is, whether large majorities of states, schools and districts were in fact scoring above the national norms on the tests),while most observers accepted the reality of the phenomenon but disputed what caused it. Among the causes suggested and debated were problems in the original norming of the tests, outdated norms, lack of test security, manipulation of populations of students tested, artificial statistical manipulation of test results, and teachers and schools teaching to the tests, either purposely or inadvertently. The publicity surrounding the Lake Wobegon phenomenon was sufficiently widespread that the U.S. Department of Education funded researchers at the Center for Research on Evaluation, Standards and Student Testing (CRESST) to investigate. On the basis of a survey of state directors of testing, Shepard (1989) concluded that the conditions for inflated test results — such as high stakes being pinned on test results, efforts to align curriculums to the tests, and direct teaching to the tests — existed in virtually all of the states. And on the basis of an analysis of up to three years of test results from 35 states from which they were available, Linn, Graue and Sanders (1989) essentially confirmed Cannell's basic finding that test results across the nation are implausibly inflated — Lake Wobegon has gone national. For instance, they found that "for grades 1 thru 6, the percentage of students scoring above the national median in mathematics ranges from a low of 58% in grade 4 for the 1985 school year to a high of 71% in grade 2 for the 1987-88 school year. . . " (p. 8). Linn, Graue and Sanders concluded that the use of old norms is one of the factors that contribute to the abundance of "above average scores" (p. 23), but also pointed out that in situations in which the same form of a test is used year after year, "increased familiarity with a particular form of a test" (p.24) likely contributes to inflated scores.

> The practice of using a single form of a test year after year poses a logical threat to making inferences about the larger domain of achievement. Scores may be raised by focusing narrowly on the test objectives without improving achievement across the broader domain that the test objectives are intended to represent. Worse still, practice on nearly identical or even the actual items that appear on a test may be given. But as Dyer aptly noted some years ago, "if you use the test exercises as an instrument of teaching you destroy the usefulness of the test as an instrument for measuring the effects of teaching (Dyer, 1973, p. 89; Linn, Graue and Sanders, 1989, p. 25).

The problem was illustrated even more clearly in a subsequent study reported by Koretz, Linn, Dunbar & Shepard (1991), which compared test results on one "high-stakes" test, used for several years in a large urban school district, with those on a comparable test that had not been used in that district for several years. They found that performance on the regularly used high-stakes test did not generalize to other tests for which students had not been specifically prepared, and again commented that "students in this district are prepared for high-stakes testing in ways that boost scores . . . substantially more than actual achievement in domains that the tests are intended to measure" (Koretz, Linn, Dunbar & Shepard, 1991, p. 2). To put the matter bluntly, teaching to a particular test invalidates the test results as indicators of more general learning.

While educational researchers were essentially confirming Cannell's initial charges, the intrepid physician was continuing his own investigations. In late summer 1989, Cannell released a new report, entitled *The "Lake Wobegon" Report: How Public Educators Cheat on Standardized Achievement Tests.* This time Cannell presented more recent instances of the Lake Wobegon phenomenon and a variety of evidence on outright fraud in school testing programs, including a sampling of testimony from teachers concerned about cheating on tests. After presenting results of his own survey of test security in the 50 states (concluding that security is generally so lax as to invite cheating), Cannell outlined methods to help people detect whether cheating is going on in their school districts, and "inexpensive steps" to help prevent it.   Without debating Cannell's prescriptions, we note his conclusion. How, he asks, can legislators and school boards across the nation be expected to undertake needed reforms in the nation's schools, when the principal yardsticks on which they rely are providing them with a falsely rosy picture of the condition of the schools? It is a question that clearly points out the intersection between test quality and matters of public policy. When conditions of the testing marketplace undermine the validity of inferences drawn from tests, they also may seriously undermine the educational and employment policies of the nation.

THE MARKETING OF TESTS AND RELATED SERVICES

In his 1989 report on the Lake Wobegon phenomenon, Cannell recounts an incident that helped spark his concern about standardized testing. As a physician treating adolescent patients with serious self-esteem problems, Dr. Cannell noted discrepancies between results of testing by clinical psychologists to whom he had referred patients, and test results for those patients reported by the schools they attended. How, he wondered, "could so many children test below average on independent testing, but do well on their official school achievement test?" (Cannell, 1989, p. 2). After finding that education officials could offer little explanation for anomalously high student and district test results, Cannell, pretending to be a school superintendent from a small southern district who was interested in improving its test scores, telephoned a large commercial test publisher:

> Within a few minutes, a saleswoman implied that our district's scores would be "above average" if we bought one of the "older" tests! She further intimated that our scores would go up every year, as long as we "didn't change tests." Something was very wrong. What was an "older test?" How could she know that our district would be above the national average? The district whose name I used is a poor rural southern Virginia district.   How could she guarantee yearly

improvements 'as long as we didn't change tests?' She couldn't know if this district's schools were improving or not. (Cannell, 1989, p. 3)

Cannell's experience illustrates a second problem area in the testing marketplace, namely the manner in which tests are sold and bought. In this section we discuss the traditional means by which tests and related services are marketed, via salespeople and promotional materials. In the next section we discuss a newer means by which tests are bought and sold, via the Request for Proposals or RFP process.

Direct Sales

Though two of the major test publishers (ETS and ACT) do not have a sales staff, the other major test publishers and companies like NCS and Scantron have a sales force that markets their tests and/or services directly to potential buyers such as school districts. For example, The Psychological Corporation (1988) divides the country into sales regions, which are in turn split among six to ten sales persons; CTB/McGraw-Hill (1988) has four sales regions with between 8 and 10 representatives in each. Riverside Press (1988) and SRA (1988) list consultants for their products in five geographical regions. These salespeople are important marketing agents. For example, Paine Webber, commenting on Scantron's investment potential, pointed to the increased productivity of its sales organization and the company's belief that sales per salesperson could double over the next several years. Not surprisingly, perusal of publishers' catalogs reveals that many of the salespersons for educational tests are former teachers who are knowledgeable about schools and teacher needs; but what is far less prominent in the advertisements is whether such salespeople are trained in educational measurement. For example, in its 1992 catalog, *Resources for Measuring Educational Performance*, the Psychological Corporation describes each of the 40 members of its national sales staff. Though almost all are said to have some kind of teaching or educational administration experience, not a single one is listed as having a doctorate in educational measurement or testing (though six out of 40 are listed as having a PhD or EdD).

Whatever their backgrounds, the prime object of such salespeople's work is the selling of tests to potential buyers at the school district or state level. Typically, decisions to purchase a test series are not made by any one person in a school system or state. Rather they tend to be made by committees composed of members ranging from classroom teachers to school administrators and one or two testing or evaluation specialists (Cowden, 1981; Shepard 1989). While such specialists often are charged with attending to technical evaluation of candidate tests' technical qualities, including validity and reliability evidence, it is clear that validity evidence rarely appears to be the key factor in determining whether or not a test series is purchased. Instead, how well a test appears to match the local curriculum, ease of administration, the availability of certain reporting scales (such as grade-equivalents or normal curve equivalents), the size of the discount offered, the promise of free workshops devoted to test interpretation, or extra copies of test results are factors that may tip the scale toward a particular publisher's test.

The most recent study we know of on how schools select tests is Shepard's survey. She concluded that "without question, published norm-referenced tests are selected to achieve the best match possible between the test content and the state's curriculum" (p. 9). As one state test director commented, "if the test is not aligned with our curriculum, it just gets discarded immediately" (p. 9). This sort of strategy in school districts' efforts to find their way among test series marketed to them at first would hardly seem ill-founded. It is natural for a school system to prefer a test that matches its curriculum. But from the point of view of validity of norm-referenced inferences, such a practice contributes to biases. The reason for this is simply that when national test series are normed, publishers seek to obtain norming data on a nationally representative sampling of all school districts, not just school districts whose curriculum is aligned with the test that is being normed.

Shepard's report of the survey of state test directors provides little indication that Cannell's experience — of test salespeople explicitly marketing a test on the grounds that it will make a school system look good — is commonplace. Cowden's study concerning district level test purchasing decisions did, however, reveal that "on some occasions, a new test may be selected because it is reputed to be easier and promises to make a school district look better in the eyes of the community" (Cowden 1981, p. 8).

Whatever the frequency of these two strategies in the selling and buying of tests — that an easier or nonsecure test can make a school system look better, or that a test's content matches a school system's curriculum — the key point is that either practice tends to undermine the validity of inferences made from test results with regard to schools' and school systems' standing on national norms.

Advertising

A second obvious means of communication in the selling and buying of tests is advertisements and other promotional materials aimed at potential buyers of tests. In 1984, the APA convened a meeting of 23 test publishers to discuss the current status of psychological and educational testing, explore mutual concerns and examine the status of testing from the professional and policy rather than technical points of view (APA, 1984). One of the concerns of the meeting was the advertising of tests. The group was asked to address the following questions:

- What are the reasonable bounds on advertising of tests?
- What are the obligations of publishers to acknowledge limitations of tests?
- What are some of the abuses that can occur in advertising?
- What might be done to review the situation in test advertising?

The reason for such questions is that advertising is a major marketing mechanism for testing and spin-off companies, both large and small, to sell their products. Most companies have catalogs that, in addition to product descriptions and promotion, contain ordering information and forms. Advertisements for tests appear in the professional publications aimed at those who buy or use tests. Even the mom-and-pop operations can afford ads in pertinent professional journals. To our knowledge, however, despite the fact that some ads for tests have been found to be clearly fraudulent (as with some ads for honesty tests discussed in the previous chapter), little independent critical scrutiny is directed at advertising for tests and related services.

The APA reportedly uses its *Casebook on Ethical Standards of Psychologists* as the basis for screening ads in the APA's two dozen publications. The ethical code specifies that in advertising, individual psychologists (a) may not list APA membership as a credential; (b) may not partially disclose or misrepresent themselves or their product; (c) may not say something that creates false expectations; (d) may not present individuals, services, or products in their ads as being better than others; and (e) may not use a computer-generated test interpretation as a hard diagnosis or a substitute for a professional relationship (APA, 1984). In addition, the *Standards for Educational and Psychological Testing* (AERA, APA and NCME, 1985) contains one standard dealing with test advertising:

Promotional material for a test should be accurate. Publishers should avoid using advertising techniques that suggest that a test can accomplish more than is supported by its research base.

At least theoretically, therefore, test advertisements appearing in APA, AERA and NCME publications might be challenged under the ethical principles and/or the test standard listed above. However, these organizations appear to have little role in monitoring the accuracy of ads for tests and related services. In 1988, for example, of some 1500 telephone and letter inquiries to the testing office of the APA, only six dealt with "complaints about testing ads or products" (Committee, 1990). Of the three organizations sponsoring the *Standards*, only the APA has guidelines for accepting ads. Ads must be in good taste, must conform to pertinent standards from the *Ethical Standards of Psychologists* (APA, 1974), and must not claim that the product does something for which it was not developed. However, though some ads are rejected as inappropriate for a particular APA publication, and others are occasionally sent to legal counsel for an opinion (APA, 1984), the content of ads in APA publications is not verified. Other than the 1988 statistic cited above, we have no figures on the number of ads for tests challenged by readers or by other companies, or on the number of test ads rejected by APA publications. But it seems clear that the APA is unlikely to take a more active role in monitoring accuracy of ads for tests. For example, though the APA Task Force on honesty testing described in the last chapter found that some ads for such tests were "fraudulent" and "flagrantly hucksterish," the group's recommendation was simply that "test publishers adopt and enforce standards ensuring that the promotional claims made . . . rest on a firm empirical foundation" (Task Force, 1991, p. 21).

We do not know how many professional organizations other than APA have a formal policy on accepting ads for their publications. Nor do we know of a comparable system within other professional organizations that permits an ethical challenge to a test ad appearing in an organization's publication; but perusal of ads for tests and related services appearing in a variety of publications suggests to us that standards of truth in advertising related to testing are virtually non-existent.

Most advertising-related regulations in the United States emerge from the Federal Trade Commission, and test advertising falls under these strictures (Rothschild, 1987). Until 1983 the FTC merely looked at ads and made a judgment about whether they were deceptive or unfair. In 1983 three major changes were made in the way the FTC evaluates deception and unfairness. First, it now must prove that an ad actually deceives. Second, a "reasonable consumer must be deceived." Finally, it is not enough merely to deceive; the deception must lead to material injury; that is, it must influence consumer decisions (Rothschild, 1987).

If a competitor or consumer group wanted to challenge a particular testing ad it presumably could do so through the FTC. Alternatively, it could ask that the ad be reviewed by the National Advertising Division (NAD) of the Better Business Bureau. If NAD does not resolve the issue, the National Advertising Review Board, a self-regulating agency of the advertising industry, becomes a court of appeals (Rothschild, 1987). Test advertising has been the subject of very little FTC or NAD scrutiny (we are aware of only two FTC inquiries concerning testing). We know of no equivalent in testing to the publicized challenges to ads for products like deodorants, soft drinks, mouthwashes, and fiber cereals. Certainly, however, from a public policy point of view, test advertising merits the same scrutiny as do ads for Ban roll-on deodorant, Pepsi or Listerine. The stakes associated with many tests are substantially higher than those associated with which cola tastes better, whether one's deodorant is really dry, or whether gargling with a mouthwash cuts down on colds.

According to FTC standards, ads can be challenged not only for sins of commission, but also for those of omission. An ad can fail to give all the relevant information, and if this happens the FTC can require a company to add certain information. This practice, called affirmative disclosure, is illustrated by the following case:

> The FTC proposed a rule that antacid ads should contain warnings of contraindications. There was no implication that there had been a deception but, rather, that it was difficult for consumers to learn about possible side effects of product usage. For example, Alka-Seltzer contains large amounts of sodium and is therefore dangerous for people on sodium-restricted diets. Older people are most likely to be on such a diet and are most likely to use the product; the FTC staff felt that there was a high level of inadvertent misuse and therefore pressed for hearings on the issue. (Rothschild, 1987 p. 201)

We found one study that dealt with ads for psychological testing software (Eyde and Kowal, 1985). The study focused on promotional material for software marketed to the general public. The three programs reviewed in this study allowed a personal computer user to self-administer several psychological tests. Eyde and Kowal cite the following promotional claim for one of the products, *Sales Edge* by Human Edge Software:

> We've tested our Strategy Reports against the expert analysis
> of hundreds of real-world situations and, in any given
> situation, our 'hit rate' (incidence of accuracy) betters the
> thermometer in your medicine cabinet and the odometer in
> your car. (p. 326)

Eyde and Kowal concluded, however, that despite this claim there was little evidence for the reliability and validity of *Sales Edge*.

A second product reviewed by Eyde and Kowal, also marketed by Human Edge Software, is *Mind Prober*,™ which is "shrewdly marketed psychological software for the masses (Caruso, 1984, September 24), which Johnson [the author] wanted Toys-R-Us to distribute" (Eyde and Kowal, 1985, p. 323). Ironically enough, however, the following ad for *Mind Prober* appeared in the September 1984 edition of *Psychology Today* (at that time an APA publication):

> Read any good minds lately? With *Mind Prober*™ you can. In
> just minutes you can have a scientifically accurate personality
> profile of anyone. This new expert systems software lets you
> discover the things most people are afraid to tell you. Their
> strengths, weaknesses, sexual interests and more.

This ad apparently survived the APA ad screening process, despite the fact that lay consumers without expertise in psychology to evaluate the promotional claim are promised a scientifically accurate personality profile of anyone in minutes. Eyde and Kowal quote from another ad for *Mind Prober* that appeared in the November 19, 1984, issue of *InfoWorld*, a newsweekly for microcomputer users:

> We'll Get You Inside Her Head, the Rest is Up to You. It's a
> situation every guy has faced. There she is. The perfect

woman. Or close enough. The problem: How to insert
yourself into her psyche . . . that's a tremendous advantage in
figuring out how to get what you want from someone.
Anyone. In a business situation. Or a personal situation.
Mind Prober. It delivers the goods. What you do with them
is up to you. (p. 323)

Eyde and Kowal conclude that the claims for *Mind Prober* are
questionable.

A sequel to Mind Prober was brought to market by a company called
Neuralytic Systems. It is called *Dr. Shrink*,™ and could be purchased in the late
1980s for $49.95. Its promotional material, mailed to a "few select computer
owners" and offering an introductory discount price of $36.95, is revealing, to
say the least. First, from it we learn that *Mind Prober* sold nearly a quarter of a
million copies and was named "Best Selling New Educational Software of 1985"
(Neuralytic Systems, 1988). Second, *Dr. Shrink* promises that "you can learn
more about a person in 10 minutes than many people will find out in a lifetime.
It's almost like looking into an X-ray of someone's personality." (It must have
momentarily slipped *Dr Shrink*'s "mind" that X-rays are interpreted by
radiologists, not the patient.) Third, the promotional material claims that *Dr.
Shrink* will reveal ANY (emphasis in original) person's "Deepest, innermost
secrets. Hidden loves and hates. Private sexual fantasies." Fourth, it promises
that after you try *Dr. Shrink* "you will know why this software is used by trial
lawyers, clinical psychologists, college professors, top salespeople, famous
writers, psychiatrists in private practice, professional negotiators and business
consultants," and that "it is no surprise that this program has even touched
nerves inside the FBI and the CIA!" Fifth, the promotional material does carry
the following affirmative disclosure: "WARNING!!! This program provides
explicit information about people's forbidden sexual fantasies. It should not be
used by young people under the age of 18." Finally, the promotional material
points out that status of the authors, Drs. Jim and Kathy Johnson, "leaders in
the development of personality software is recognized by the press: *TIME*,
Newsweek, *FORTUNE*, *The Wall Street Journal*, *The New York Times*,
SUCCESS, *InfoWorld*, *Personal Computing*, NBC's Today Show — The list
goes on and on."

As we saw in the last chapter, self-administering testing software for
the general public is an expanding and potentially lucrative market. In some

ways such software is the equivalent of over-the-counter medicines, except that the medicinal products are reviewed for efficacy and safety by the Food and Drug Administration. Further, promotional materials for such medicines are widely subjected to challenge and to affirmative disclosure.

We have discussed examples of a number of testing ads to give readers an appreciation for the types of promotional material for tests and test-related products that is now in circulation. While a detailed analysis of test advertising is beyond the scope of this book, a few comments are in order. First, very few of the ads we have seen address what we feel should be the central issue in test purchase, the validity evidence that supports a particular use or claim. Very few ads make direct claims about a test's validity or accuracy, though many imply it. The ads promise many things: ease of administration, fully integrated reports in as little as six minutes, distinguished authorship, improved quality of information, measurement of this trait or that type of person, results returned in 10 days (or minutes), improved student self-esteem, guidance of children to a brighter tomorrow, computer-generated interpretations, improved instruction, decreased gap between measurement and achievement, step-by-step procedures for in-depth counseling, and up-to-date national norms. This list too goes on and on. All of the ads claim directly or indirectly that the product marketed measures some trait or construct, but we found only few that referred to the existence of validity evidence. And when validity evidence is mentioned, the wary test consumer would have to go to considerable lengths to actually locate and then evaluate it.

Second, the issues of validity evidence and affirmative disclosure regarding potential test misuse in ads for tests and ancillary products clearly warrant far more serious and critical scrutiny. One of the questions raised at the APA/Publishers meeting in the early 1980s concerned affirmative disclosure. The group asked, "What obligations do publishers have to acknowledge limitations of tests?" Unfortunately no answer was forthcoming. One of the problems with affirmative disclosure is getting agreement on what constitutes misuse, and, on the flip side of the coin, what constitutes sufficient evidence of validity to warrant use or support a promotional claim. At the APA/Publishers meeting it was pointed out that "tests do differentiate among and can hurt people." We have to ask who is looking out for the interests of the consumer relative to promotional material for tests and related products and software. While the Eyde and Kowal (1985) review calls attention to problems of validity and reliability of certain instruments, it appears in *Computers in Human*

Behavior, a journal not nearly as readily available to the general public as is *Psychology Today* or *InfoWorld* where the products are promoted. Of course not all tests are marketed to the general public, but even many professional users are at a disadvantage in finding and evaluating evidence for the validity of many common uses of tests. For some of the more recently developed "honesty" or "integrity" tests, validity studies are not widely available because the companies view them as proprietary. Indeed, despite their somewhat differing conclusions about validity of tests, both the OTA and the APA Task Force noted their inability to obtain research evidence on the validity of some such tests. If neither an agency of the U.S. Congress nor a task force of a prestigious professional association could get access to such information, it is extremely unlikely that a prospective purchaser of a test would fare better. Further, if a product like *MindProber* can be advertised in an APA publication, then professional self-regulation of promotional materials in APA surely needs to be tightened considerably.[2]

It is interesting to note that the publishers at the 1984 APA meeting reached consensus "that test advertising was not an area of great concern and that it did not need future action" (p.10). This is a remarkable conclusion after the meeting raised a range of serious issues about advertising. To us it seems that there is a clear need for action in the regulation of test advertising. We concur with the conclusion of an earlier APA committee set up to look at ethical practices in industrial psychology, which said:

> There are too many questionable practices in the advertising
> and promotion of tests. We feel, however, that the Code itself
> is explicit enough, and that the problem here is one of
> compliance and enforcement rather than of revision of the
> Code. (APA, 1967, p. 71)

It appears that Wayne Holtzman's observation of 30 years ago remains true in the 1990s. Writing in 1960 on why the APA principle on test publication and advertisement "is violated more flagrantly than any other in our code of ethics," Holtzman observed, "the enthusiastic author and obliging

---

[2] In 1988, the APA severed its connection with *Psychology Today*. (See "Sale won't put PT and field asunder," and "PT's sale closes era of effort, controversy," APA Monitor, July, 1988.)

publisher cannot resist the temptation to sell the test as the latest word, the answer to eager personnel executives' problems" (Holtzman, 1960, p. 249).

Commercial advertising of tests thus continues to be a major influence serving to undermine the validity of tests. While it could be argued that the lack of attention to validity questions in test ads does not affect validity of test use for good or ill, but merely ignores the matter, this seems to us an unlikely proposition. Advertising clearly affects consumers' behavior in myriad ways beyond just the products they buy. A long history of research shows that advertising and mass media affect not just discrete decisions but attitudes and cognitive structures as well (Schramm and Roberts, 1974; Greenfield, 1984). An ad promising a test to measure something that a purchaser wants to measure thus may well have as much influence on how the typical test user interprets test results as any cautionary scientific report warning of incomplete validity evidence. But science does make for good salesmanship. As one advertising executive put it, "No one yet has succeeded in making an advertisement by setting in type a research report" (Fox, 1985, p. 182, quoting Walter Weir).

That advertising regarding testing is fairly immune to the scientific strictures regarding validity evidence is, however, not terribly surprising. As we reported in chapter 2, though figures on test sales industry-wide are hard to come by, total revenues from test publishing and test-related services in recent years appear to be on the order of a half-billion dollars annually. Though this is a significant sum, it is worth noting in contrast that in 1980, ten individual ad agencies each had domestic billings in excess of a half-billion dollars (Fox, 1985). And when it comes to the potential for professional standards to influence practice, it is notable that while the profession of psychologists promulgated its first set of ethical standards in 1953, the advertising profession, under pressure from a nascent consumer movement and facing the prospect of unwanted governmental regulation, created its own set of ethical standards in the 1930s (Fox, 1985, pp. 89-90, 125-126). And as a further caution on the likelihood of academic research to resist the influence of advertising, it is worth noting that two of the nation's best-known social scientists of this century — J.B. Watson and George Gallup — abandoned promising academic careers to go to work for advertising firms. (Watson went to work for J. W. Thompson in the 1920s, and Gallup joined Young & Rubicam in the 1930s; Fox, 1985.)

THE RFP PROCESS

Whatever the limitations of traditional means of buying and selling tests — via ads and salespeople marketing their wares to schools and businesses — within the last three decades a major new avenue of commerce has developed in the testing marketplace. It is the Request for Proposals, or RFP, process by which government agencies typically purchase products and services. The requesting agency issues a notice of a RFP via some publication (notices for federal government RFP's are listed in the *Commerce Business Daily*) or issues a RFP directly to vendors possibly interested in providing the needed goods or services. Interested vendors then submit proposals. The winning proposal is typically selected after review for features such as technical merit, cost-effectiveness and quality of proposed personnel.

The exact process varies from agency to agency, but the RFP process as a procurement mechanism seems to have evolved generally out of efforts to make the business of government more efficient and less subject to cronyism. The RFP process, however, when used by governments to obtain tests, poses threats to the valid use of tests. These threats are quite different from those associated with traditional channels of commerce in the testing marketplace, but in several ways may be more dangerous.

As noted in chapter 3, state testing programs constitute a large new niche in the testing marketplace. Once an educational testing program is mandated by a state legislature or state board of education, the state department of education is typically charged with implementation. Most state departments do not have the capability to develop, administer, and score state level Elhi tests, teacher certification tests or other large-scale tests. Therefore, they issue a Request For Proposal to potential vendors, soliciting competitive bids for test development, administration, scoring, and reporting. The RFP spells out the scope of work, time line, and budget guidelines.

The RFP process has altered the face of educational testing. Competition among publishers for school district adoption of their Elhi tests was (and still is) intense. Before the advent of state testing legislation, the districts were free to purchase or reject the test of any vendor, usually one of the large test publishers described in chapter 2. The RFP process has greatly enlarged the role of a new set of vendors in the testing marketplace, many of whom do not have off-the-shelf products to sell. Instead, these vendors bid to build a "customized" state test from scratch. Traditional test publishers may try to compete for state testing contracts by offering an off-the-shelf test with discounts to the state off the catalog price, and often offer to extend the discount to any local district that adopts the same test for its testing program. Extending the discount is a marketing device to entice districts to use the state-adopted test in grades not covered by the state testing program. Such marketing strategies seem, however, to have been relatively unsuccessful in promoting off-the-shelf tests for statewide contracts. The reason is that vendors offering custom-built tests can hold out the promise of building a instrument that precisely meets the state's curriculum or content specifications. Given the apparent success of new test-building companies (such as National Evaluation Systems and IOX, discussed in chapter 2), it is not surprising that some of the traditional test publishers, such as CTB-McGraw-Hill, have gone into the business of modifying their national tests to meet state specifications.

Whether the test is off-the-shelf or customized, however, once the state contract is awarded, local districts can no longer choose not to use the state test: the successful bidder has a guaranteed monopoly. Such a situation is not necessarily bad. Having one statewide testing program instead of a multitude of local ones has several potential benefits. Economies of scale, for example, offer the prospect of building or buying a better test. And the availability of comparable test results throughout a state seems universally attractive to state-level policy-makers. Nevertheless, statewide educational testing carried out via the RFP process carries with it several weaknesses that tend to outweigh the potential benefits. In the paragraphs below we discuss these weaknesses: inhibition of the validation process, cost- and corner-cutting, diffusion of responsibilities, and promotion of legal defensibility.

Inhibition of the Validation Process

The RFP process tends to canonize the status quo in testing and inhibit serious test validation research. To meet the demands of state programs for mass testing and fast feedback of test results, vendors, at least until very recently, have tended to base their instruments on the optical mark reading technology, which in turn requires that the selection format be used for test questions: rather than supplying an answer, students select one and fill in a box on an answer sheet. The only widespread exception to this pattern have been RFPs for constructing and scoring writing samples.

Quite apart from the form of testing that is developed via the RFP process, the key problem is that the process almost inevitably tends to treat validation as a one-time technical matter. Via a single RFP, a contractor may be asked to develop a new test, try out and revise it, validate it, and devise and set up test administration procedures. Contracted validation efforts, as we explain below, often are reduced to formula investigation efforts, with the results — a "valid" test — very largely preordained.

The problem is that validation simply cannot be done via a one-shot contracted research effort. Serious validation research ought to be an ongoing, additive process of accumulating evidence to support — or refute — particular kinds of inferences or decisions. It simply cannot be done via a single study following a recipe. Validation includes the whole test development process but extends beyond it. An inference made from a test is not simply true or false but must be seen as claiming only greater or lesser degrees of probability, and as always open to revision. Validation calls for multiple lines of evidence using multiple methodologies. Validation is hermeneutic, a search for the meaning behind a test score. It calls for iconoclastic speculation, suspicion, doubt, autonomous judgment, deliberate hard-mindedness, open-ended intensive enquiry, discernment, and a willingness to follow the evidence wherever it may lead. Validation is ultimately a scientific enterprise (Madaus, 1990). All of this poses a real conflict for contractors who are basically technicians, not scientists. Contractors called on to validate their own tests cannot afford to have the detachment of a skeptical inquirer, or to admit to the limits of their presuppositions and methods. They are forced to have can-do mentalities, which focus more on delivering a product that can, as we explain below, stand up in court than on searching for meaning behind a test score.

Cost- and Corner-Cutting

The RFP process also encourages the use of a test not necessarily for its quality or actual function, but for minimal development cost. Often, because of budget restrictions, states allocate highly limited funds to mandated testing programs. To give some idea of the difference in magnitude of resources that may be devoted to independent versus contracted test development, we note the following contrast. In Congressional hearings in 1979, the Educational Testing Service presented testimony indicating that development of a new form of an existing test (i.e., for which content and statistical specifications were already in-hand) cost between $50,000 and $100,000 ($50,000 was the figure given for a new form of a Graduate Record Examination Advanced Test, and $92,000 for a new form of the Graduate Management Aptitude Test; U.S. Congress, 1979, p. 108). In contrast, when Alabama mandated development of new tests to certify prospective teachers, a budget of less than $1 million was allocated to develop from scratch and validate 26 different tests for different certification areas (Madaus, 1990).

Small budgets mean that what can be done in the test validation process is limited, and test-building contractors design their programs accordingly. If vendors are to meet their contractual obligations and make a profit, there isn't time or money to design and implement an integrated, multifaceted, ongoing validation strategy. Contractors are also acutely aware that pursuing certain lines of evidence is a risky business, given the possibility of legal challenge (Yalow, Collins, and Popham, 1986). Finally, investigating disconfirming hypotheses about their products poses a real conflict of interest for contractors. What if the facts did disconfirm: how could they tell the state?

The lure of RFP money is a temptation for vendors to ignore awkward questions about the worthiness, relevance, or equity of the testing program. Potential vendors who question the value of the enterprise will lose the business to someone else. For example, ETS refused to bid on the lucrative Texas and Arkansas recertification testing program for in-service teachers. Gregory Anrig (1987), the president of ETS, announced publicly that the NTE could not be used for decisions regarding retention or termination of in-service teachers. He questioned, and we feel rightly, the wisdom of using a paper and pencil test for that purpose. This instance of withholding services, represents, according to Anrig, the first time any test producer in the United States took such action. Nevertheless, other contractors bid on both the Texas and Arkansas projects; the tests were built and administered, and used to make high-stakes career decisions about tens of thousands of experienced teachers.

Cost-cutting brought about by low bidding and limited funds, coupled with the entrepreneurial bottom-line mentality of a commercial enterprise, can result in the test being viewed as just another product that must be mass produced as cheaply as possible under tight timeliness. Rudman (1987) offers one indication of this phenomenon (not due merely to the RFP process). He points to the fact that test authorship by recognized measurement and curriculum specialists is being phased out in at least two publishing houses. These publishers are converting their writing and development of standardized achievement tests to in-house production by full-time staff. He suggests that this move parallels what happened in the development of textbooks, where the books are written by teams of editors whose names rarely, if ever, appear on the covers of the books. Rudman points out that judgment of appropriate content for textbooks is diminished in the face of political considerations, the pressure to ease vocabulary loads, and other business related-compromises. He worries that "organizations whose economic interests lie outside of psychological and educational measurement can have the same effect on tests that they have had on textbooks" (p. 10). As test companies are swallowed up by large publishing houses and become just another subsidiary, the economic interests of the parent company can cloud psychometric and measurement issues.

Contracted test building often seems to imply that to meet contract obligations and still make money, vendors must cut corners and produce tests that are just good enough for the state agency's purpose. This leads to the paradox that "just good enough for the purpose" can result in the building of "imperfect" products — products that are no better than they need to be (Boorstin, 1973). The problem with this is that what is good enough for the purpose may be determined as much by the fact of state sponsorship as by validity evidence. Mandate by state law or regulation (most of the new state tests developed over the last two decades have been mandated by state legislatures, state boards of education or other regulatory commissions) lends a legitimacy to a test that would be missing if the same test had been privately sponsored. If the state says a test is to be used for a particular purpose, buys one, and uses it to make high-stake decisions, then in the eyes of many, the test must do what it purports to do. Policymakers, members of the media, the general public, test users and even test vendors treat the test as if what it measures is transparent. They uncritically accept the test as authoritative. But, the meaning behind a test score and its suitability for high-stakes inferences or decisions is opaque until revealed through validation.

Diffusion of Responsibilities

A third implication of government-sponsored test building via RFP is diffusion of responsibility for test development and use. A test may be mandated by a legislature or executive, planned by an executive branch agency such as a state department of education, constructed by an independent contractor (usually advised by some sort of advisory group), administered and scored by other agencies and used by still others (such as accreditation agencies and the press) who know little about other phases of the test planning and development process. This sort of fracturing of responsibilities for testing and test use means that few people, if anyone at all, may have detailed knowledge about the entire process. Given the fractionation of responsibilities, it now seems virtually impossible to adhere to the "essential" principle set out in the 1974 *Standards for Educational and Psychological Tests* (reiterated word for word in the 1986 APA *Guidelines for Computer-Based Tests and Interpretation*):

> A test user should consider the total context of testing in interpreting an obtained score before making any decisions (including the decision to accept the score). (APA, AERA and NCME, 1974, Standard J1.1)

The diffusion of responsibilities for the testing process often becomes apparent when litigation arises over a particular testing program and that program is subjected to close scrutiny.   In one court case in which one of the authors was involved, for instance, it became apparent only after the case went to trial that state officials had not known precisely what a contracted firm had been doing in developing and scoring a test for their state. In another case, concerning the Illinois Insurance Agent License Exam, the Golden Rule Insurance Company charged the State of Illinois and the Educational Testing Service with racial discrimination and violations of various provisions of the Constitution. ETS sought to be excluded from the lawsuit on the grounds that it was merely a contractor doing the state's bidding. Initially a lower court ruled that ETS had acted as a private contractor and hence was not subject to Constitutional due process and equal protection limitations. But on appeal, the appellate court found that "ETS, by virtue of becoming an integral part of the state-licensing function, was subject to the constitutional limitations of the Equal Protection and Due Process clauses" (Rooney, 1987, p. 10). The Golden Rule case was settled out of court shortly after the appellate court ruling. For details of the Golden Rule settlement, or the controversies and disputes that followed in its wake, the interested reader is referred to the summer 1987 edition of *Educational Measurement: Issues and Practice*, and to follow-up exchanges in that journal between Patrick Rooney, Chief Executive Officer of Golden Rule, and Gregory Anrig, President of ETS. Here, it is worth noting how the case highlighted the blurring of roles and responsibilities that can arise from contracted test development. Though ETS saw itself merely as building a licensing test on contract for a state agency, the plaintiff in the case, and ultimately the appellate court, ruled that via its test building, the test builder had become a part of the state licensing function.

Promotion of Legal Defensibility

A fourth way in which government testing via the RFP process has undermined valid testing is through promotion of the criterion of "legal defensibility" in test development. With increasing numbers of lawsuits concerning both educational and employment tests, it is not surprising that state agencies contracting for test building have sought to include safeguards to protect themselves against litigation. Thus delivery of a "legally defensible" test is frequently a requirement in RFPs calling for test development. Moreover, some contractors advertise their services as providing not only technical expertise, but also "legally defensible programs" (see for example the ad on page 2 of the summer 1987 issue of *Educational Measurement: Issues and Practice*).

The focus on legal defensibility as a criterion for test development tends, however, to circumscribe the validation process. Legal precedent on what constitutes a legally defensible test directs inquiry away from the essential question that should undergird all test validation — how correct are the inferences made from peoples scores? — toward the quite different question of how evidence can be gathered that will stand up in court. The problem with this diversion of attention is that a test can be legally defensible but not valid (Madaus, 1990).

The concept of a legally defensible test has emerged from a quasi-legal, quasi-scientific approach of the courts to employment and educational testing litigation. To explain that evolution, a digression is necessary here.

Title VII of the Civil Rights Act of 1964 required nondiscrimination in employment with respect to race, color, religion, and national origin. The act also established the Equal Employment Opportunity Commission (EEOC). In 1966 and 1970, and again in 1978, the EEOC issued guidelines on the use of tests in employment decisionmaking. (See Novick, 1982, and Wigdor, 1982, for fuller discussions of the evolution of the federal employment testing guidelines). The 1966 and 1970 EEOC guidelines were based in part on the testing standards created by the American Psychological Association, American Educational Research Association, and the National Council on Measurement in Education. Nevertheless, the 1970 EEOC guidelines set fairly stiff criteria for establishing the legality of employment testing procedures. They specified that the use of any test that adversely affects the hiring, promotion or other employment opportunities of classes protected under Title VII constituted employment discrimination unless:

1. The test had been validated to show its relevance for specific jobs through predictive validity studies; and

2. It had been demonstrated that alternative employment selection
procedures having less discriminatory impact were unavailable
for use.

The nondiscriminatory employment mandate embodied in Title VII of
the Civil Rights Act of 1964, and its implementation via EEOC Guidelines, led
to a tremendous amount of litigation, much of it concerning employment
testing. *Summaries of Court Decisions on Employment Testing 1968 - 1977*
(Psychological Corporation, 1978) listed more than 100 court decisions, most
based, at least in part, on Title VII.

The first half of the 1970s was the period of greatest deference by the
federal courts to the EEOC Guidelines' interpretation of Title VII
nondiscrimination in employment mandate. In the 1971 *Griggs v. Duke Power*
case, the U.S. Supreme Court ruled against the use of tests that had the effect of
discriminating against Title VII protected classes since the tests had not been
shown to be "demonstrably a reasonable measure of job performance" (Wigdor,
1982, p. 39). And, in what has been identified as the high point in the Supreme
Court's bowing to the EEOC Guidelines, in the 1975 *Albemarle Paper
Company v. Moody* case the court ruled against the use of employment tests
that had discriminatory impact, and had not been shown to have a reasonable
relationship to important job skills.

In 1976, however, in what is widely cited as a turnabout decision, the
Supreme Court in the case of *Washington v. Davis* gave its imprimatur to a
much more flexible interpretation of job relatedness. This case concerned a
Constitutional challenge to an entry-level police exam in Washington D.C. (The
Civil Rights Act was not extended to cover public employees until shortly after
the case was filed.) Results on the police exam had been shown to exclude more
blacks than whites and had not been shown to be related to police officers'
success on the job. Nevertheless, in affirming a lower court ruling, the U.S.
Supreme Court endorsed the interpretation that the job-relatedness requirement
could be satisfied by showing the relationship between the test and the training
for the job, without showing a relationship between test performance and actual
on-the-job success. In other words, what the court recognized in the Washington
v. Davis case was a sort of training-related validity.

This line of reasoning was extended to the testing of teachers in the case
of *United States v. South Carolina*. The decision was ultimately affirmed by the
U.S. Supreme Court in 1978. In question was South Carolina's use of cut-
scores on the NTE to determine certification and classification of teachers. The

state raised the cut-scores on the NTE several times, resulting in increasingly disproportionate disqualification of candidates from historically black colleges:

> During the 1967-68 academic year approximately 3% of the candidates from predominantly black colleges were disqualified for failure to meet the minimum NTE score while less than 1% of the candidates from predominantly white colleges were disqualified.   When South Carolina raised certification requirements in 1969-70, approximately 41% of the candidates from predominantly black colleges were disqualified while the disqualification of candidates from predominantly white colleges remained less than 1%. (Strassle, 1985, p. 495)

The state of South Carolina had commissioned the Educational Testing Service to conduct a validation study of the NTE for use in teacher certification. The study, which documented a relationship between the content of the NTE and the content of state teacher training programs, was accepted by the federal district court as demonstrating the job-relatedness of the NTE for use in initial teacher certification.   ETS summed up the South Carolina validation study and the court's interpretation of it as follows:

> The study involved 356 faculty members from 21 colleges and universities in South Carolina who, convening as members of panels, looked at the tests under controlled conditions and made judgments about the relationship between the tests and the curricula of teacher-training institutions in the state. According to the federal district court, the study's findings indicated that the tests are "a fair measure of the knowledge which teacher education programs in the state seek to impart." It found that there is ample evidence in the record of the content validity of the NTE . . . . The NTE has been demonstrated to provide a useful measure of the extent to which prospective teachers have mastered the content of their teacher-training programs. (ETS, 1984, pp. 147-48)

In January 1978, the U.S. Supreme Court affirmed, without comment, the lower court's decision in the South Carolina case. In effect, *United States v. South Carolina* established curricular validity of teacher tests as the prime basis for determining their legal permissibility, even if they have disparate impact on blacks and other classes protected under Title VII of the Civil Rights Act. As this case law has evolved it has become clear that a contractor wishing to build a legally defensible teacher certification test simply has to show that the test content corresponds to skills and knowledge in the state's teacher training curricula, as rated by people involved in teacher training.

Given the rapid proliferation of litigation in federal courts concerning employment discrimination in the 1970s, several federal agencies cooperated to produce the 1978 *Uniform Guidelines on Employee Selection* (43 F.R., No. 166, 38290-38296). One portion of these guidelines, known as the "four-fifths rule" or the "80 percent rule," had widespread influence on employment discrimination litigation in general, and employment testing lawsuits in particular. What this rule did was to set out a clear criterion for judging the prima facie evidence of adverse impact:

> A selection rate for any race, sex or ethnic group which is less
> than four-fifths (or eighty percent) of the rate for the highest
> group will generally be regarded by Federal enforcement
> agencies as evidence of adverse impact, while a greater than
> four-fifths rate will generally not be regarded . . . as evidence
> of adverse impact. (Sec. 6D)

This rule implies that if, say, on a job promotion test whites pass at a rate of 80%, but only 50% of blacks pass, the difference constitutes adverse impact, since 50/80 = 62.5%, which is less than 80%. In actual application, of course, the use of the four-fifths rule is more complex (see Feinberg, 1989, for an excellent discussion of the use of statistical evidence by the courts not just in employment discrimination lawsuits, but also in other areas of the law). But the rule was one of the most widely cited sections of the 1978 *Uniform Guidelines:* a seemingly straightforward criterion of adverse impact; and because under civil rights law and federal guidelines, the prima facie showing of adverse impact shifts the burden of proof from plaintiffs to defendants. The rule thus has had a dramatic impact on litigation over employment testing.

As a result of these developments and two 1981 cases, *Contreras v. City of Los Angeles* and *Guardians Association of the New York City Police Department v. Civil Service Commission,* the key question determining legal defensibility of employment tests has become, "What constitutes passable evidence in the eyes of the court that the test is legal?" In effect, by the early 1980s the following steps had emerged as a strategy to ensure a legally defensible employment test:

1. Perform an analysis to determine skills required on the job or, if in training, required for the job.
2. Write or select test items to match those skills;
3. Select a cut-off score on the test made up of such items to determine employment (or promotion) eligibility.

Note that because of the four-fifths rule, the first two steps in this formula become critical from the perspective of equal employment opportunity only if the cut-off score selected yields differential pass rates that fail to meet the rule. If they do, then the burden of proof falls on the employer to show that the content of the test reflects job requirements. But even if test content cannot be shown to match skills required on the job, a fallback defense for employment tests, accepted in the *Washington v. Davis* case by the Supreme Court, has been to show that test content reflects content of training already required for the job.

Another wrinkle on building a legally defensible test, especially one used by states to control graduation or promotion of students, is showing that the test has instructional validity — a kind of extension of the "training-related validity" recognized in *Washington v. Davis* and the "curriculum validity" legitimized in the South Carolina case. The concept of instructional validity, which had not explicitly been recognized in previous versions of the APA, AERA and NCME test *Standards*, emerged from a decision in the Florida minimum competency testing case, *Debra P. v. Turlington* (1979). In *Debra P.* the judge ruled that the test could be used for decisions about awarding high school diplomas only if it could be shown that students had an opportunity to learn the skills covered in the test. In other words, the judge held that for the high school graduation test, it was not enough to show that the material or skills tested were found in the curricular materials. He also demanded evidence that the content and skills were actually taught in the schools.

What seems to us to have happened is that, as the concept of a legally defensible test has become more refined in reaction to federal guidelines and court decisions, with different kinds of content validity evidence (job-related, training, curricular and instructional) being recognized, we have lost sight of the essential validity question — whether the inferences, decisions, and descriptions made on the basis of test results are adequately supported by a range of evidence. Instead, concern for legal defensibility has focused attention on alternative kinds of content validity evidence just as specialists in educational measurement such as Messick and Cronbach, and the test *Standards* (AERA, APA and NCME, 1985) have increasingly emphasized the pre-eminence of construct validity in any thorough test validation effort. Though it is clearly recognized that content evidence can contribute to construct investigations, an exclusive focus on content evidence carries two major problems.

First, reliance on content validity evidence ignores the fact that as the 1985 *Standards* (AERA, APA and NCME, 1985) point out:

> A variety of inferences may be made from scores produced by a
> given test, and there are many ways of accumulating evidence
> to support any particular inference. Validity, however, is a
> unitary concept. (p. 9)

Hence, the focus on only one type of evidence, prompted by the legal defensibility strategy, tends to short-circuit the test validation inquiry by avoiding looking for alternative kinds of validity evidence.

Second, when someone enters into an inquiry aimed at <u>confirming</u> a test's validity, even the limited content-related inquiries that are undertaken can be manipulated, either purposely or inadvertently, to obtain the results desired. As standards of evidence recognized by the courts for establishing job-relatedness have focused on a well-recognized set of content-related evidence, inquiries aimed at producing legally defensible tests have come to follow a standardized methodology that is biased in favor of positive, rather than disconfirming, answers about test validity (Madaus and Pullin, 1987). Very often evidence as to job-relatedness is based on teachers' or supervisors' judgments about the degree of match between test content and the job (or the curriculum, training, or instructional practice). Such judgmental ratings can be significantly altered by features of the rating process such as (1) the particular wording of the rating scale used, (2) the statistical procedures used to combine ratings, or (3) the selection criteria for panelists (Madaus and Pullin, 1987; Poggio, Glasnapp, Miller, Tollefson and Burry, 1986).

Indeed, it is highly ironic that content validity studies have come to depend so heavily on judgmental ratings, because in another arena of testing research, analogous judgmental ratings have been severely criticized. After one of the most thorough reviews available of judgmental versus empirical methods of detecting test item bias, Arthur Jensen reached the following conclusion:

Many items judged by test critics to be "culturally unfair" for some particular group actually show the group to be less disadvantaged on those items than on other items that were not judged to be so culture bound. It is easy to demonstrate with evidence that culture bias in test items cannot be judged in terms of an item's content or face validity. Thus claims of test bias cannot be supported by subjective judgements regarding item content . . . . The determination of bias must be based on objective psychometric and statistical criteria. (Jensen, 1980, p. 371)

Similarly, despite the emphasis on judgmental content validity (whether item content is compared with training, curriculums, or instructional practices) flowing from growing concerns about legal defensibility of employment and education tests, we argue that adequate validity evidence cannot be gathered solely via judgmental content validity studies.

COMPUTER-BASED TEST INTERPRETATION

A fourth problem area in testing is computer-based test interpretation (CBTI), which, as noted in chapter 6, constitutes a major and growing dimension of the testing industry. A variety of important validity and consumer-protection questions surround CBTI as this technology becomes increasingly more common in education, clinical diagnosis, pre-employment screening and the retail computer software market. Here we undertake only a brief description of questions relating to the validity of and proprietary rights claimed for CBTI. (For a more in-depth treatment of these important issues see Butcher, 1987; Matarazzo, 1983; Moreland, 1985a & b, 1987a & b; Eyde and Kowal, 1985, 1987; Edye, Moreland, Robertson, Primoff, and Most, 1988; Jackson, nd; Eyde, Kowal and Fishburne, 1984, 1987).

Proprietary Questions

The computer-based interpretation of a person's test performance depends on the decision rules incorporated in the software. To protect vendors' proprietary interests against piracy, the algorithms for interpretive decision rules are typically locked in the black box of the software, and are not readily available for review. In contrast, however, Standard 5.11 of the 1985 *Standards for Educational and Psychological Testing* (AERA, APA, and NCME 1985) states:

Organizations offering automated test interpretation should make available information on the rationale of the test and a summary of the evidence supporting the interpretations given. This information should include the validity of the cut scores or configural rules used and a description of the samples from which they were derived.

Comment:

The release of cut scores or configural rules is a very desirable practice. When proprietary interests result in the witholding of such algorithms, arrangements might be made for an external review of these algorithms under professional auspices, which ensures adequate protection of any proprietary material. (p. 37)

Despite the serious uses for which many CBTIs are intended, few if any of the CBTI programs now on the market meet this standard. Instead of adhering to the scientific standard of making interpretative algorithms available for peer review, CBTI software vendors far more commonly appear to hold to the view that such algorithms, encoded in computer programs as part of a larger software package, should be withheld on proprietary grounds. And despite the comment cited above, as far as we know no alternative arrangements have been established by any professional organization for allowing professional peer review of such algorithms while protecting proprietary interests.

Similar questions about the tensions between proprietary claims of test publishers and independent scrutiny of validity evidence have been raised with regard to honesty tests discussed in chapter 6. Though the two independent reviews of honesty testing reached somewhat different conclusions about the validity and utility of honesty tests (as recounted in chapter 6, the review by the Office of Technology Assessment, 1990, was somewhat more critical of honesty tests than that of the APA Task Force, 1991), both reviews noted the problem that proprietary claims of honesty test publishers greatly limited the independent scrutiny of validity evidence for such tests. Some publishers of honesty tests refuse to disclose to reviewers not just test validation studies but even the scoring keys used to evaluate answers to questions on these tests. As the APA Task Force noted:

It is . . . important that all relevant information be made available to test reviewers, including normative data and information about test-construction procedures. We strongly recommend that honesty-test publishers do all in their power to ensure that their tests receive adequate reviews. Any resistance to appropriate peer review of tests is a professional dereliction, and one of considerable consequence. If test publishers wish to retain their identity with the field of psychological measurement, they must be professionally responsible and accountable, whatever their proprietary interests. (Task Forces, 1991, p. 22)

Validity Questions

Standard 5.11 implicitly acknowledges the essential question underlying the use of CBTI, the validity of the interpretations offered users. If the CBTIs are used to make differential classifications of people, then the validity of those differential classifications ought to be established. However, Moreland (1987) points out that despite the many CBTI systems marketed for personality inventories, "viewed in proportion to their availability, far fewer validity studies have been completed on those systems" (p. 388).

In light of very meager direct validity evidence on CBTI systems, Eyde, Kowal, and Fishburne (1987) offer an indirect method for examining their validity. They simply compared the accuracy, relevancy, and usefulness of the output of seven MMPI CBTI systems for patients in a military hospital. Basically, they looked at how clinical psychologists rated the accuracy of the narrative statements or sentences produced by the seven CBTI systems to whom they sent patient test scores. The psychologists used case histories of the patients as the criterion in making their ratings. The summary of their findings is illuminating:

The study showed that the output of CBTI systems for the MMPI was found to vary in relevancy, accuracy, and usefulness using file drawer histories or self-report data for subclinical normal, neurotic, characterological, and psychotic profile types. The output of CBTI systems was found to differ in the accuracy of both clinical and subclinical normal code types. Raters showed considerable agreement in their global and sentence-by-sentence ratings of accuracy and relevancy.

> For the most highly rated CBTI systems, moderate validity
> levels were found for the narrative output. (p.44)

The conclusions of Edye et al. point to the importance of being able to inspect the heart of CBTI software, that is, the decision algorithms that are used to turn patterns of test scores into interpretations. The decision algorithms contained in the seven different systems they studied produced different interpretations for the same test data. Thus, the critical interpretation on which an MMPI user might act is, unfortunately, dependent to a large degree on the choice of vendor of software for interpreting MMPI results.

In a review of *Medicine & Culture: Varieties of Treatment in the United States, England, West Germany, and France* by Lynn Payer (Henry Holt & Company, 1988), Leonard Sagan (1988) makes the following point:

> To be scientific, medicine should have at least two
> characteristics: The efficacy of medical practices and procedures
> should have demonstrated validity and there should be little
> difference in them from one community to another. Just as
> physicists measuring the speed of light come to the same
> conclusion in France, Brazil or China, patients with similar
> symptoms would receive at least approximately the same
> examination, diagnosis and treatment everywhere. (p. 11)

If we view MMPI scores as "symptoms" of people who take this test, Payer's advice suggests that if they are reliable, given the same MMPI scores, CBTI systems for the MMPI ought to result in highly similar interpretations. The evidence presented by Edye et al. indicates that this standard of reliability is not very well met by the seven CBTI systems they compared. Moreover, even if the systems met this standard of reliability, validity is by no means guaranteed, for a test interpretation may be reliable, but not valid. But reliability is a sine qua non for validity.

While it is true that test interpretation, like medical diagnosis, is partly artistry on the practitioner's part, CBTI must be firmly rooted in science if it is to be valid. If interpretations or recommendations for classification or treatment based on identical test performance differ notably from one vendor's software to another, then we must question the scientific basis of CBTI. At the very least, we need to ask whether such differences are primarily due to the attempt to codify the artful diagnostic rules of different authors, which are grounded in their different experiences with different populations (age, gender, race, SES, condition, etc.) in different settings (hospitals, schools, private practice, etc.).

The problem for some CBTI systems may be deeper than their encoding of interpretations of different practitioners. For example, Moreland (1985b) makes this sobering observation:

> The advent of the microcomputer has changed things greatly from the time when tens of thousands of dollars worth of equipment and considerable programming expertise were needed to get into the CBTI business . . . . Gone are the days when the tremendous investment necessary to develop and market CBTIs virtually guaranteed that they had been developed by experts whose interpretations stayed as close as possible to the empirical data available for thoroughly investigated instruments. Many CBTI systems are now authored by individuals who have no special qualifications. They have never published a scholarly paper on either the test or the CBTI in question. Nor do they have any credentials that indicate any special expertise as practitioners. The CBTIs by such authors often stray far from available empirical data, with some employing completely idiosyncratic scoring procedures or interpretive algorithms. Perhaps even worse, highly detailed, well written, empirical-sounding CBTIs are now available for tests for which validity data are practically nonexistent. Indeed, some of these poorly validated tests cannot be purchased apart from their CBTIs. (p. 226)

Krug provides a somewhat tongue-in-cheek but also sobering account of why unreliable CBTI systems, yielding test interpretations that are of highly doubtful validity, may readily reach the testing marketplace:

> The basic problem is that many expert systems [for CBTI] are not really very expert. Although a number of these products have been carefully designed and developed, a frightening number have been developed along the lines of what might be termed the "creationist" perspective. That is, on Monday, the system developer (SD) begins the process by selecting and ordering a new microcomputer system. On Tuesday the

system is installed and made operational. On Wednesday the SD learns to program in BASIC. On Thursday, the SD develops an interpretation program for the MMPI or some other well-known instrument. On Friday, the SD places an ad for the new system in the APA *Monitor*. On Saturday, the SD fills the first order and begins to develop the documentation for the system. But then on the seventh day the SD rests (and the documentation is never quite completed). (Krug, 1987b, p. 21-22)

Moreland (1985b) offers three suggestions to help protect potential CBTI consumers from such products. First, find out about the author's qualifications and record of scholarship with the instrument in question. Second, examine published documentation for the interpretive system. Yet Moreland also admits that "documentation providing decision rules for interpretive statements is almost unheard of because most CBTI developers are concerned lest their work be pirated" (p. 229). However, he advises that at least the general interpretive approach behind CBTI be documented. Finally, the consumer should find out whether there are scholarly reviews of the system and check the reviewers' credentials. As reasonable as these suggestions are for some users, they seem to us unlikely to be practical for many others who lack resources and access to the necessary information. This raises the question of what else might be done to protect consumers from shoddily developed (though usually slickly packaged) CBTI systems, which promote misinterpretation of test results. This is a question to which we return in chapter 8 where we discuss what might be done to help mend the fractured marketplace for testing.

TEST PREPARATION AND COACHING

Coaching for tests has a long history. In his book on *China's Examination Hell*, Miyazaki (1976) recounts the extent to which special preparation for Chinese civil service examinations had become institutionalized in the Ming and Ch'ing eras, when the Chinese examination system had reached its most complex form:

Because not very many places in the classics were suitable as subjects for examination questions, similar passages and problems were often repeated. Aware of this, publishers compiled collections of examination answers, and a candidate

who, relying on these compilations, guessed successfully
during his own examination could obtain a very good rating
without having to work very hard . . . . Reports from
perturbed officials caused the government to issue frequent
prohibitions of the publication of such collections of model
answers, but since it was a profitable business with a steady
demand, ways of issuing them surreptitiously were arranged
and time and time again, the prohibitions became mere empty
formalities. (Miyazaki, 1976, p. 17)

Without attempting to recount a history of special preparation and
coaching for tests, we point out here simply that, as noted in chapter 6, test
preparation and coaching in the United States in the last thirty years or so seem
to represent a "profitable business with a steady demand," and as such, a fast-
growing spin-off segment of the testing market. Test preparation and coaching
take many forms, including orientation materials that test publishers themselves
distribute, study guides for particular tests, software programs to help people
practice for particular tests, and commercial courses aimed at preparing students
to take particular exams. What we wish to address here, however, are the
implications of test preparation and coaching for the valid use of tests.

Some kinds of test preparation and coaching can wholly undermine test
validity. The most obvious is usually called cheating, as when test-takers get
advance access to test questions and are able simply to memorize answers
without knowing the broader skills or content that test performance is intended
to represent. This is the kind of "preparation" that, Cannell argues, lies behind
the Lake Wobegon phenomenon, and thus he has subtitled his latest report,
discussed in chapter 6, *How Public Educators Cheat on Standardized
Achievement Tests*.

At the other extreme, some kind of test preparation can actually enhance
test validity. Perhaps the clearest example of this is with young children for
whom the marking of machine-scorable answer sheets may be more difficult than
the problems or content that the tests are intended to measure. If practice in
using machine-scorable answer sheets is not provided, test results may reflect
children's clerical skills more than their word knowledge or letter recognition
skills.

Between these extreme implications of coaching for test validity, there
is much ambiguity. In part, this stems from the fact that in recent controversies

over test coaching and preparation (DerSimmonian and Laird, 1983; FTC, 1978, 1979; Kulik, Kulik and Bangert, 1984; Messick, 1980, 1981; Messick and Jungeblut, 1981; Owen 1985; Slack and Porter, 1980; Becker, 1990; Cole, 1982; Bond, 1989), numerous issues have become intertwined. As Messick (1981) observed:

> The controversy over whether or not coaching works for tests of scholastic aptitude such as the College Board SAT is in actuality a multitude of controversies — over the meaning of scholastic aptitude, the meaning of coaching, the nature of the fundamental research questions, the adequacy of empirical evidence for coaching effectiveness, the possible implications of effective coaching for student performance and test validity, and the consequent ethical imperatives for educational and testing practice. (p. 21)

We cannot here review all the issues that have become intertwined in debates about coaching for tests. Though it often is difficult to disentangle such issues, we attempt here to focus on just two aspects of the test preparation and coaching controversy that have direct implications for test validity: (1) coaching's effectiveness, and (2) efforts to distinguish legitimate from illegitimate forms of coaching. In the final section of this chapter, we return to discuss coaching in light of some of the other problem areas in testing discussed previously.

The Effects of Coaching

Test coaching clearly has contributed, as we saw in chapter 6, to generating a sizable spin-off industry with the marketing of hundreds of books, software programs, and commercial test preparation courses. It is difficult to talk about the "effects" of such a range of products and services, but from the point of view of test validity, a key issue is whether any such coaching has significant effects on individuals' test scores. If not, coaching's effects on the goodness of inferences made from scores would presumably be minimal (though in some cases the mere existence of test coaching, or knowledge that individuals partook of it, might affect inferences). In other words, if preparation and coaching do not significantly change people's test scores, implications for test validity would be less than if they do.

The literature on the effects of test preparation and coaching will not be reviewed thoroughly here. However, it seems clear that — though a number of studies have found no statistically significant effect of special preparation and coaching on test scores (e.g. Dear, 1958; Frankel, 1960; Alderman and Powers, 1979) — other studies going back more than half a century have found that special preparation can significantly improve scores. Gilmore (1927), for example, investigated "how much a student's score in [Otis group] intelligence tests might be increased as a result of coaching" and concluded that "students can be coached to the point of increasing their standing and score in intelligence tests even in case of the material used in coaching being only similar and not identical with that of the basic test" (p. 119, 121). Vernon (1954), summarizing results on the effects of practice and coaching on intelligence test results, concluded that practice on parallel test forms resulted in gains of 5 to 10 IQ points (with diminishing return to exposure to multiple forms).

More recently, research has shown that instruction in taking machine-scorable tests affects test results more for younger children than older ones (Gaffney and Maguire, 1971). But even for older students (all presumably with substantial experience with machine-scored tests), a variety of research studies and syntheses of research — including Roberts and Oppenheim (1966), FTC (1979), Slack and Porter (1980), Messick and Jungeblut (1980), Messick (1981), Dersimonian and Laird (1983), Kulik, Kulik and Bangert (1984), Zuman (1987), Curran (1988) and Becker (1990) — have shown significant effects of coaching on test scores. It has been demonstrated that the largest effects of coaching have been found in studies that are, from an experimental design point of view, relatively less well-controlled (Messick,1981; Dersimonian and Laird,1983); but even when taking the vagaries of experimental design into account, the bulk of evidence clearly indicates that some kinds of coaching and special preparation can be effective in raising test scores. However, even the same kind of coaching appears to be differentially effective for different kinds of students and different kinds of tests.

What remains unclear from this literature, however, is the importance of gains engendered by test coaching, and whether they are likely to threaten the validity of inferences made from scores. These are issues to which we return in a moment, but first we recount a debate that has emerged, largely since Cannell's 1987 report, about the ethics and legitimacy of different kinds of test preparation and coaching.

Test Preparation and Coaching: Legitimate or Illegitimate?

The rise in test preparation and coaching activity, coupled with increasing evidence that coaching can be effective in raising scores and with widespread publicity about the Lake Wobegon phenomenon, have aroused interest in the question of what constitutes legitimate as opposed to illegitimate test preparation and coaching.

One of the first to set out a delineation of kinds of coaching was Pike (1978), who distinguished ten "components" via which instruction (intermediate-term or short-term) might affect test performance and argued that "drill on sample test questions [is] academically unsound" (p. 73). More recently Shepard and Kreitzer (1987), after reviewing test preparation practices for the Texas Examination of Current Administrators and Teachers (TECAT), classified such activities into three categories, the first two considered legitimate, the last not: (1) content teaching which includes overviews of test content, substantive presentation of rules of grammar, principles of good writing, and detailed explanations or examples; (2) teaching to the test that includes familiarization with test format, scoring rules, advice about guessing strategies, and anxiety reduction techniques; and (3) practices that include advice on how to hide one's ignorance or pretend to know, and exploitation of the test specifications to eliminate wrong answer alternatives without knowing the material.

Mehrens and Kaminski (1988) argued that the line between legitimate and illegitimate test preparation is not so clear. To help illuminate the distinction, they set out a continuum of seven types of test preparation:

1. General instruction on objectives not determined by looking at the objectives measured on standardized tests;
2. Teaching test-taking skills;
3. Instruction on objectives generated by a commercial organization where the objectives may have been determined by looking at objectives measured by a variety of standardized tests, (the objectives taught may or may not [involve] test-taking skills);
4. Instruction based on objectives (skills, subskills) that specifically match those on the standardized test;
5. Instruction on specifically matched objectives (skills, subskills) where the practice (instruction) follows the same format as the test questions;
6. Practice (instruction) on a published parallel form of the same test; and

7. Practice (instruction) on the same test. (pp. 10-11)

Mehrens and Kaminski argue that practices (6) and (7) are never legitimate, but that the ill-defined line between legitimate and illegitimate test preparation is somewhere between practices (3) and (5). In contrast to this judgment, they note that in one survey a majority of teachers rated the use of an old version of a test to practice for a current version as "not at all a form of cheating" (Gonzalez, 1985, cited in Mehrens and Kaminski, 1988, p. 41).

After describing their types of test preparation, Mehrens and Kaminski (1988) analyzed four sets of commercially published test preparation materials: Riverside Press's *Improving Test-taking Skills*, Random House's *Scoring High in Math and Reading* and *Scoring-High CAT*, and CTB/McGraw-Hill's *CAT Learning Materials*. They found that both the *CAT Learning Materials* and *Scoring High on the CAT* matched the *California Achievement Test* (CAT) so closely that use prior to testing would jeopardize inferences "from the test scores to a broader domain that the test samples" (p.31). In other words, these authors' conclusion is that use of some widely available test preparation materials has the effect of undermining the validity of inferences that may be drawn from a test.

Another writer to comment recently on illegitimate test preparation is Cannell (1989), whose concerns over the Lake Wobegon phenomenon in elementary school achievement testing were discussed above. Cannell's advice on prevention of cheating on standardized tests includes a warning against using a given version of a test for more than one year, and preventing teachers from seeing advance copies of tests. Thus it is clear that Dr. Cannell sees dangers of "cheating" where others, such as Mehrens and Mehrens and Kaminski, see only preparation activities that limit the range of inferences to be made from test scores.

Even more recently, Smith (1991) shed additional light on the "meanings of test preparation" as a result of an intensive 15-month study in two elementary schools in Arizona. From observing and talking with elementary school educators, and reviewing literature of test preparation practices, Smith derived a typology of eight kinds of meanings of test preparation "in action." These were:

1. No special preparation
2. Teaching test-taking skills
3. Exhortation
4. Teaching the content known to be covered by the test
5. Teaching the test

6 Stress inoculation

7. Practicing on items on the test or parallel forms

8. Cheating

Smith pointed out that the sorts of test preparation engaged in by teachers may change over time as a result of pressure to raise scores. With sufficient pressure, teachers will engage in test preparation activities that they would prefer not to spend instructional time on. Many such activities are ones that Cannell and Mehrens and Kaminski clearly would condemn as cheating or illegitimate. But Smith argues that teachers' reality, shaped largely by direct experience within the classroom, is very different from that of educational reformers such as Cannell or testing experts such as Mehrens.

> To chastise teachers for unethical behavior or for "polluting" the inference from the achievement test to the underlying construct of achievement is to miss a critical point: The teachers already view the indicator as polluted. Our extensive contact with teachers in this study, close analysis of their beliefs about testing, and a theoretical sampling of other sources of data and alternative sites led us to conclude that teachers see fundamental discrepancies between true educational attainment and information conveyed by test scores. (p. 538)

As Smith puts this point more pithily, at the end of her article: "You can't cheat a cheater, which from the teacher's point of view is the standardized test itself and those who use its results fallaciously or for inappropriate purposes." (pp. 541-2)

The increasing commentary and debate about the meaning, effects and legitimacy of various kinds of test preparation and coaching are surely signs of trouble in the testing marketplace. But it is clear that different parties involved in standardized testing hold markedly different views as to what is appropriate and legitimate when it comes to test preparation. Smith pointed this out with respect to how the differing concerns of teachers and testing experts shape attitudes towards preparing elementary school children for achievement tests. These competing realities clearly also apply in preparation practices for other kinds of tests. Note, for example, that Mehrens and Kaminski flatly denounce "practice (instruction) on a published parallel form of the same test" as "never legitimate." Meanwhile, the College Board has been marketing books of old

Scholastic Aptitude Tests — and apparently with some commercial success as the books, titled *Five SATs* and *Ten SATs*, have both gone through several editions (e.g. College Board Staff, 1988). If Mehrens and Kaminski are correct — that practice on a published parallel test form is "never legitimate" — it would appear that the College Board's publishing venture is promoting illegitimate test preparation.

The apparent disagreement over the appropriateness of giving students practice on test items parallel to those on tests they have to take is particularly ironic in light of findings that this practice is effective. As a result of their meta-analysis of some 40 coaching studies, Kulik, Kulik and Bangert (1984) argued that "practice on parallel forms of a test" is one of the most effective forms of coaching (p. 444). Similarly, when Zuman asked students enrolled in a commercial test preparation program to rate various ways in which they had been helped, on average they rated "Gave me practice on problems similar to real SAT" far more highly (a mean of 4.1 on a scale in which 4 = "quite a lot") than substantive learning: teaching of logical reasoning, vocabulary, geometry, algebra, and arithmetic were all rated 3.0 or below (where 3 = "somewhat,") (Zuman, 1987, p. 106). Additionally, in her meta-analysis of nearly two dozen previous studies of the effectiveness of coaching for the SAT, Becker (1990) found that "practice and instruction on answering particular item types" showed significant advantage over other types of coaching such as practice in taking complete tests of instruction in general test-taking skills (Becker, 1990, p. 395).

Whatever the frequency, effectiveness, or legitimacy of different kinds of test preparation, it seems clear that because of the growing emphasis placed on standardized tests, questionable test preparation is increasingly being offered not just by commercial entities but also by public schools. Consider, for example the recent testimony of Albert Shanker, President of the American Federation of Teachers (AFT). In his weekly *Where We Stand* column in an article entitled *Exams Fail the Test* (NY Times, April, 24, 1988), he confessed, "I never thought that I'd ever be writing a column warning about standardized tests, but I am." Much of the cause for recanting his previous endorsements of standardized tests was Shanker's concern over the ill effects of test preparation in the schools.

> Since the reputation of a school, its principal, its teachers and
> the school board and superintendent depends largely on these
> tests scores, schools are devoting less time to reading books,
> writing essays and discussing current events and more and

> more time to teaching kids strategies for filling in blanks and choosing the answers to multiple-choice questions. This destroys much of the value of these tests, which only tell you something if they are an independent measure of what students know. . . .
>
> School districts are now engaged in a process called "curriculum alignment." This means that course content, textbooks, lesson plans, etc. are all being geared to items that will be on the test . . . . Coaching and testing time has increased so much that it is significantly taking away blocks of time from teaching and learning. (Shanker 1988, p. 7)

One recent news account quoted Jay Comras, who developed test preparation materials for the National Association of Secondary School Principals as saying that 84-85% of schools currently offer test preparation instruction (Marklein, 1992). And a variety of research in the past few years has shown that test preparation is coming to inhabit not just specialized test preparation courses, but also instruction in general in both elementary and secondary schools. Some of this literature has been previously mentioned in chapters 4 and 6 (e.g. Shepard, 1989; Romberg, Zarinnia & Williams, 1989; Smith 1991; Haas, Haladyna & Nolen 1990; Hall & Kleine, 1990, 1992; Lomax, 1992; and Raivetz, 1992), so here let us mention merely some of the findings from several additional studies not previously mentioned. In a statewide survey of testing practices in North Carolina, Gay (1990) found that 20-25% of teachers in grades 3, 6, 8 and 10 reported that their colleagues were not just preparing students to take tests but were actually "teaching the test," for example by copying standardized test materials and using them to teach their classes. Similarly in another statewide survey, Monsaas (1992) found that among grade 1-7 teachers in Georgia, 94% reported that they frequently or sometimes would engage in "teaching general test-taking skills that will help on all standardized tests"; and 64% reported using commercially available test preparation materials. While results from such surveys vary in terms of how questions are posed (e.g. whether teachers are asked about test preparation activities they themselves or their colleagues engage in) and what populations of teachers are surveyed (e.g. teachers in states with high-stakes testing programs or teachers of economically disadvantaged students who are subject to Chapter 1 evaluations), the general trend of findings from such studies seem clear. It is that the majority of teachers and schools in the United States are now engaging in some form of specific test preparation as a normal part of instruction, and some of the "preparation" is, to be charitable, of dubious educational value.

MINOR MOLD OR MAJOR BLIGHT?

From a market perspective, as we saw in chapters 3 and 6 of this volume, standardized testing seems to be a thriving enterprise, with many more new tests, spin-off industries, and new companies entering the testing market over the last few decades. However, in this chapter we have pointed out that in terms of the validity of inferences drawn from tests, all is not well in the burgeoning market. Specifically, we reviewed five problem areas in the testing market:

- The Lake Wobegon phenomenon
- The marketing of tests and related services via salespeople and promotional materials
- The RFP process via which government agencies purchase tests and testing services;
- Computer-based test interpretation; and
- Test preparation and coaching.

In each area we pointed to what we view as serious problems tending to undermine the validity of inferences drawn from test results. Still, it could be argued that the problems are fairly small in comparison to the size of the testing marketplace, and that the enterprise is basically healthy. Indeed, given the widespread concern about the health of the nation's schools and the productivity of the nation's workforce, it might appear that the imperfections of standardized tests are fairly insignificant since tests represent one of the few policy instruments available for assessing and effecting change and improvement in the schools and in the workplace. Hence, in this concluding section of chapter 7 we step back to assess whether the problems to which we have directed attention are simply minor mold or a major blight on the testing marketplace.

We address this question by examining to what degree these problems distort our view of schools and students. Regarding the coaching issue, we have pointed out that some kinds of coaching may actually increase test validity; and it is still is true, as Messick (1981) observed, that so far no studies of preparation and coaching have systematically evaluated the implications of effective coaching for test validity.

Nor is there much clear evidence on the potential distortions introduced by the Lake Wobegon phenomenon. We thus attempt to assess the magnitude of these distortions by comparing them to other documented changes in test performance. One useful metric is the standardizedized growth expectation (SGE) implicit in many nationally normed standardized tests. The SGE has been defined by Stenner et al. (1978) to mean the amount of growth (expressed in standard deviation units) that an average student must demonstrate over the course of one year in order to maintain an average or 50th percentile ranking. This can easily be calculated by examining norms for any test form for which multiple grade norms are available. For example, if a raw score of 25 is equivalent to the 50th percentile in spring grade 4 norms, one need only look in spring grade 5 norms to find the next grade level's percentile equivalent for that raw score. Suppose this was the 33rd percentile. If a student received exactly the same raw score in grade 5 as in grade 4, his or her percentile ranking would have dropped 17 percentile points (from 50 in grade 4 to 33 in grade 5). Conversely, in order to maintain his or her relative standing in the norms tables from one year to the next, the student would have to gain the equivalent of 17 percentile points. Using tables for normal distributions, it is easy to see that this student would have to gain 0.44 standard deviation units in order to maintain his or her 50th percentile standing on this test (because 17% of the area under a normal curve lies between $z=0$ and $z=-0.44$).

Since the idea of a standardized growth expectation (SGE) introduced by Stenner et al. (1978) has not received widespread attention, we hasten to point out that it is directly analogous to the idea of effect size, which has come to be widely recognized in educational research because of the increasing prominence of meta-analysis. Meta-analysis refers to the statistical analysis of the summary findings of many empirical studies. With the proliferation of research studies on particular issues, statistical analysis and summary of patterns across many studies on the same issue has proven to be a useful tool in understanding patterns of findings on the same research issue (Glass, 1977; Glass, McGaw & Smith, 1981; and Hunter & Schmidt 1990 are three of the basic reference works on meta-analysis). In meta-analysis, effect size is defined as the difference between two groups' mean scores expressed in standard score form, or — since the technique is generally applied to experimental or quasi-experimental studies — the difference between the mean of the treatment group and the mean of the control group, divided by the standard deviation of the control group (Glass, McGaw & Smith, 1981, p. 29). Mathematically this is generally expressed as:

$$\text{Effect size } \Delta \;=\; \frac{\bar{x}_t - \bar{x}_c}{\sigma_c}$$

where:

$\bar{x}_t$ = mean of the treatment group;

$\bar{x}_c$ = mean of the control group; and

σ_c = standard deviation of the control group

The SGE is thus directly analogous to the idea of effect from the meta-analysis literature in that it represents the difference in mean performance of two groups expressed in standard scores. The only difference is that while the effect size in meta-analysis is used to compare the means of "treatment" and "control" groups, we are using the SGE to compare the performance of groups of students to derive national norms for standardized tests at the various grade levels.

We have calculated such SGEs implicit in norms for six nationally normed test series published during the 1980s, namely the MAT, the CAT, the SAT, the ITBS, the CTBS and the SRA. The specific edition forms and documents for these major test series from which we drew our data are listed below.

MAT6: Metropolitan Achievement Tests, Survey Battery, Multilevel National Norms Booklet (1986) The Psychological Corporation/ Harcourt Brace Jovanovich.

CAT: California Achievement Tests, Forms E and F, Norms Book, December through February (1986); Norms Book, March through June (1986). CTB/McGraw-Hill.

SAT: Stanford Achievement Test Series, Multilevel National Norms Booklet (1989). The Psychological Corporation/ Harcourt Brace Jovanovich

ITBS: Iowa Test of Basic Skills, Forms G/H. Teacher's Guide Levels 5 and 6; Teacher's Guide Levels 7 and 8; Teacher's Guide Levels 9-14 (1986) Riverside.

CTBS: Comprehensive Tests of Basic Skills Forms U and V.
Norms Book Grades K-3; Norms Book Grades 4-6 (1982-1983)
CTB/McGraw-Hill.

SRA: SRA Achievement Series. Answer Keys, Norms and
Conversion Tables. (1985, 1979,1978) . Science Research
Associates.

Detailed data concerning SGEs calculated for each of these major test series, and a discussion of practical issues in calculation of SGEs from published sources, may be found in the appendix. Here we present only tabular and graphical summaries to show how SGEs for Total Reading and Total Math scores change over the grade levels. Table 7.1 show the SGEs for the six test series mentioned above, together with the minimum, maximum and mean SGEs for each grade, calculated across these test batteries. Figure 7.1 shows the mean SGEs for these six test series across grades 1-12 for Total Reading and Total Math scores.

As shown in the table and figure, student "growth" as reflected in SGEs declines steadily from grade 2 through grade 12 on both Total Reading and Total Math scores, from around 1.3-1.4 standard deviation units in grade 2, to approximately a half standard deviation unit in the upper elementary grades, and to 0.25 to 0.10 of a standard deviation during the high school years. Note that though there is some variation in the SGEs implicit in the norms for these six major test series, this general pattern of decelerating SGEs shows up in all test series and is apparent regardless of whether we consider the minimum, maximum, or means of SGEs across the test series (as indicated in Table 7.1). Note, too, that though the general deceleration in SGEs is apparent in both Total Reading and Total Math scores across the grade levels generally, for grade 1 the reading SGEs are greater tham those for math, then there is a tendency for math scores to show higher SGEs in grades 2- 8, but then in grades 11-12 the reading SGE tend slightly to exceed the math.

Table 7.1: Standardized Growth Expectations for Six Achievement Test Series (for Total Reading and Total Math scores by grade level)

		Grade level											
		1	2	3	4	5	6	7	8	9	10	11	12
Total Reading													
MAT6 (1986)		2.05	1.18	0.85	0.31	0.39	0.28	0.33	0.26	0.10	0.08	0.23	0.15
CAT (1986)	Winter (Dec.-Feb.)		1.75	0.92	0.33	0.56	0.47	0.36	0.47	0.39	0.20	0.23	0.13
	Spring (Mar.-June)	2.33	1.28	0.65	0.26								
SAT (1989)			1.40	0.65	0.39	0.53	0.20	0.33	0.28	0.20	0.10	0.15	0.10
ITBS (1986)			1.08	0.85		0.61	0.61	0.47	0.41	0.28			
CTBS (1983)			1.28	0.65	0.56	0.47	0.33						
SRA (1985)		1.28	1.04	0.53	0.50	0.41	0.39	0.26	0.23	0.28	0.23	0.23	0.10
	Minimum	1.28	1.04	0.53	0.26	0.39	0.20	0.26	0.23	0.10	0.08	0.15	0.10
	Maximum	2.33	1.75	0.92	0.56	0.61	0.61	0.47	0.47	0.39	0.23	0.23	0.15
	Mean	1.89	1.29	0.73	0.39	0.50	0.38	0.35	0.33	0.25	0.15	0.21	0.12
Total Math													
MAT6 (1986)		1.56	1.35	1.13	0.56	0.68	0.39	0.31	0.39	0.08	0.23	0.20	0.13
CAT (1986)	Winter (Dec.-Feb.)		1.88	1.18	0.74	0.71	0.44	0.50	0.47	0.39	0.18	0.10	0.05
	Spring (Mar.-June)		1.56	1.00	0.56								
SAT (1989)			1.23	0.77	0.68	0.56	0.41	0.31	0.41	0.13	0.15	0.08	0.05
ITBS (1986)			1.23	0.92	0.96	0.81	0.81	0.61	0.50	0.36			
CTBS (1983)			1.75	1.28	0.85	0.65	0.56						
SRA (1985)		1.08	1.04	1.08	0.71	0.58	0.53	0.33	0.36	0.23	0.31	0.10	0.10
	Minimum	1.08	1.04	0.77	0.56	0.56	0.39	0.31	0.36	0.08	0.15	0.08	0.05
	Maximum	1.56	1.88	1.28	0.96	0.81	0.81	0.61	0.50	0.39	0.31	0.20	0.13
	Mean	1.32	1.43	1.05	0.72	0.67	0.52	0.41	0.43	0.24	0.22	0.12	0.08

**Figure 7.1: Average Standardized Growth Expectations, Total
Reading and Total Math**

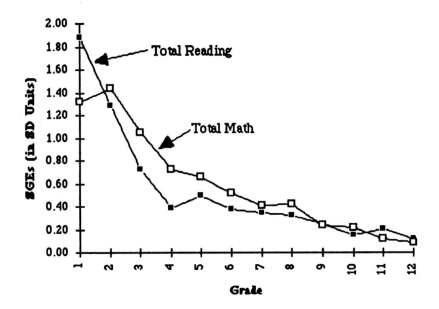

The causes of the general pattern of decelerating rate of growth are probably several, including normal de-acceleration in human (and other animal) growth with age, and the fact that, while in the early grades much of schooling is focused on reading and math instruction, through the grade levels there is a broadening of instruction, so that by the high school years, relatively little of the typical school year is focused directly on the sort of reading and math skills covered on such nationally normed tests. Our purpose here, however, is not to try to explain the pattern of results shown in Table 7.1 and in Figure 7.1. We simply want to use the results shown there as a useful backdrop against which to weigh possible distortions in test results caused by some of the problems discussed earlier.

Let us first revisit the Lake Wobegon phenomenon, described earlier in this chapter. Recall that Linn, Graue and Sanders (1989) reported on their attempt to investigate the phenomenon in test results. They analyzed data from

35 states from which statewide nationally normed test results were available. Though data on all grade levels were not available from each state, these investigators did analyze results by grade level for both Total Reading and Math scores (weighting by numbers of students for whom results were reported in each state). The number of states for which usable results were available ranged from a high of 22 for grade 8 to a low of 5 for grade 12. Though the authors did not present detailed numerical results by grade level, we have shown in Table 7.2 the grade level results Linn, Graue and Sanders (1989) did report.

Table 7.2: Percentages of Students Scoring Above National Median for Selected Grade Levels

	Grade level	School year	Percentage of students scoring above national median	Normal curve deviate from 50th% (in SD units)
Reading	2	87-88	71	0.55
	4	85-86	58	0.20
	8	85-86	55	0.13
	9	86-87	48	-0.05
Math	3	87-88	60	0.25
	5	85-86	52	0.05
	11	86-87	60	0.25
	12	85-86	49	-0.03

Source: Linn, Graue and Sanders, 1989.

The first four columns of this table come directly from Linn, Graue and Sanders (1989, pp. 8-9). To their data, we have added normal deviates (in standard deviation units) from the median, in order to allow comparison with previously presented data on SGEs. Two aspects of Table 7.2 are noteworthy in comparison with the SGE data. First, the Linn, Graue and Sanders (1989) results of possible Lake Wobegon effects show a similar de-acceleration across grade levels from a high of 0.55 standard deviation units in grade 2 reading to a low of -.03 units for grade 12 math (though as Linn, Graue and Sanders, 1989, p. 7, note, the grade 12 average was based on reports from only 5 states).

Second, and more importantly, note the substantial magnitude of possible Lake Wobegon effects shown in this table in comparison to the standardized growth expectations shown in Table 7.1.   Across the grade levels (except for grade 12 reading and math and grade 5 math), they are of magnitude comparable to the standard growth expectations. In the extreme, the Linn, Graue and Sanders (1989) data show a possible Lake Wobegon effect of 0.25 for grade 11 math, roughly double the average grade 11 math SGE of 0.12.

It should be reiterated that the results of Linn, Graue and Sanders (1989) may not be exclusively attributable to the Lake Wobegon phenomenon. Their data came from only 35 of the 50 states and is not claimed to be a nationally representative sample. Nevertheless, to the extent that their results do represent Lake Wobegon "effects" (whether they are due to use of old test norms, curriculum alignment, teaching to the tests or outright cheating), these results indicate that the Lake Wobegon phenomenon may substantially distort in our view of schools' performance — a distortion roughly equivalent to the amount that students' scores, on average, might change in one-quarter to one-half of a full year.

The SGE perspective also sheds light on the effects of coaching discussed earlier. Recall that we mentioned the Kulik, Kulik and Bangert (1984) meta-analysis of well-controlled studies of the effects on achievement and aptitude test scores of students taking practice forms of tests. They found that the effects of practice were substantial, ranging up to 1.0 standard deviation or more in size. From their meta-analysis they concluded:

> The size[s] of gains . . . were larger when identical forms of a test were used for practice and criterion measurement and were smaller when parallel forms were used. Second, the size of the effect increased with the number of practice tests given. And finally, . . . gains were larger for subjects of high ability than they were for subjects of low ability. (Kulik, Kulik and Bangert, 1984, p. 435)

The average effect sizes found were 0.42 standard deviation units in 19 studies in which subjects had one practice trial on a test identical to the criterion test, and 0.23 in 21 studies in which subjects had one practice trial on a test parallel to the criterion measure. Grouping results in terms of whether subjects were K-8 or 7-12 grade level, Kulik, Kulik and Bangert did not find significant differences by grade level. Whether practice was for elementary or secondary students, effects averaged 0.20-0.22 standard deviations in size. From some perspectives, effects of these magnitudes would not appear to be terribly substantial. For example, in some major educational program evaluations in the 1970s (e.g. see Haney, 1977, regarding the national Follow Through Planned Variation experiment), one-quarter of a standard deviation was the effect size that was used as a rough measure of educational as opposed to statistical significance. However, if we compare effect sizes of 0.20 with the data depicted in Figures 7.1 and 7.2, we see that an effect size of 0.20 from one practice trial on a parallel test form is equivalent to about one-half of a full year's reading SGE for grades 4-6, and at the high school level an effect size of 0.20 is equivalent to one full SGE or more.

These results suggest two things. First, the Kulik, Kulik and Bangert (1984) findings clearly show that whatever the other possible causes of the Lake Wobegon phenomenon, practice on parallel tests could easily have caused the possible Lake Wobegon effects reported by Linn, Graue and Sanders (1989). Second, if simply giving students practice on parallel forms of of a test can change their scores by the equivalent of one-third to more than one-half of how much they might normally change in a full year, at least as represented on SGEs reflected in test norms, then surely coaching can cause major distortions in what such test scores tell us about student learning.

Finally, the SGE perspective may be used to illuminate the literature on coaching for the SAT referred to earlier. Among studies mentioned were Messick and Jungeblut's (1980, 1981) and Becker's (1990) reanalyses of previous SAT coaching studies. The main finding of the Messick and Jungeblut reanalysis was a significant relationship between amount of time spent in coaching for the SAT and size of effects estimates. Generally what they found was that "arithmetically increasing amounts of score effect were associated with geometrically increasing amounts of student contact time" (Messick, 1981, p. 38). Thus it was suggested that 10 hours of SAT verbal coaching was associated with an effect of 8 or 9 points, 20 hours with 13 points, 30 hours with 16 points, and 50 hours with 19 points (the corresponding estimates for SAT math coaching and scores were 10 hours, 12-13 points; 20 hours, 21 points, 30 hours, 25 points; and 50 hours, 31 points). Another way of interpreting the pattern found by Messick and Jungeblut is to say that increasing amounts of coaching time are associated with de-accelerating score gains. Note that this is analogous to the pattern shown in Figures 7.1 and 7.2 for reading and math test SGEs across the grade levels. And indeed, this is the sort of pattern that led Messick to observe that "this developmental pattern of gradual and diminishing increases in response to coaching and instructional experiences is just about what one might expect with measures of stable though developing abilities" (Messick, 1981, p. 40). Messick pointed out that given the distribution of SAT scores, normally with a standard deviation in the neighborhood of 100, a coaching effect of 20 points is equivalent to around a fifth of a standard deviation (p. 46), and even to suggest that "the functional characteristics of any SAT coaching programs that prove to be effective would have direct implications for instructional practice" (p. 50).

Becker's (1990) analysis of previous studies of the effectiveness of coaching for the SAT was both more detailed and wider-ranging than that of Messick and other previous analysts. Though she used a metric for comparing study outcomes, which is somewhat unusual in the meta-analysis literature — namely the standardized mean-change measure — this measure is computed in standard deviation units, just like the effect size and the SGE. Becker analyzed study outcomes in terms of some 20 study characteristics having to do with both study design and content of coaching studied. She found, like Messick and others, that coaching effects were larger for the SAT-M than for the SAT-V. However, unlike Messick, she did not find that duration of coaching was a strong predictor of the effects of coaching. Instead, she found that of all the coaching content variables she investigated, "item practice," that is coaching in which participants were given practice on sample test items, was the strongest determinate of coaching outcomes. Overall, she concluded that among 21 published comparison studies, the effects of coaching were 0.09 standard deviations of the SAT-V and 0.16 on SAT-M. Here is how Becker herself summarized this finding:

> When all published results from comparison studies were analyzed, findings were consistent with a very simple model of coaching effects. Advantages for the coached groups of 9 SAT-V points and 16 SAT-M points (on the population score scale) were predicted. If we consider these studies to provide the most rigorous evaluation of coaching's potential, we must expect only modest gains from *any* coaching intervention. This is the clearest finding of the synthesis. (p. 405, italics in original)

Gains of this magnitude may indeed be modest from the perspective of individual college aspirants who seek to better their chances for admission to prestigious colleges by taking coaching courses.   But from the broader perspective of educational policy, the SGE data cited previously cast these findings in a very different light. In grades 10, 11, and 12, a full year of change is associated with SGEs of 0.15, 0.21, and 0.12 for Total Reading scores and 0.22, 0.12, and 0.08 for Total Math scores. Thus according to Messick and Jungeblut's results, SAT coaching of only some 20 to 50 hours seems to produce effects equivalent to a whole year of learning for high school students (including perhaps 1000 or more hours of schooling during the school year), at least as the effects of schooling are reflected on Total Math and Total Reading test scores.[3] Thus, despite Messick's suggestion that effective coaching may be simply good instruction effectively developing students' verbal and math abilities, it is entirely clear that something very different is happening in typical high school instruction than in coaching; for the latter can be 20 times as

---

[3] It may at first seem inappropriate to use SGEs for reading and math achievement tests to estimate the amount of growth that high school students typically show on the Scholastic Aptitude Test. However, data on SAT score changes for students who took the SAT in both junior and senior years of high school from 1977 through 1982 (Donlon, 1984, pp. 63-64) indicate that average SAT score gains are fairly consistent with SGEs calculated from achievement test norms. For instance, when SAT verbal score gains from junior to senior year are linearly extrapolated to estimate a 12-month gain, the resulting estimate is a 20-30 point increase. The extrapolation is necessary since SAT repeaters typically take the SAT in spring (March, April, May or June) of junior year and fall (November or December) of senior year. At the same time, it should be noted that calculating SGEs from data on the population of juniors and seniors taking the SAT in any particular year yields somewhat smaller SGEs for junior to senior year SAT changes. This is almost surely due to the fact that students who take the SAT in their junior year in high school are somewhat more able than those who take it in their senior year. Data for national "norming" of the SAT in 1960 and in 1966, indicate SGEs (or effect sizes) from junior to senior year of around 0.30 for the SAT-Verbal and 0.22 for the SAT-Math (calculated from data reported in Donlon 1984, p. 172). Thus the SGEs calculated from the national norms data for the SAT (in 1960 and 1966) are fairly consistent with the SAT score changes for students who took the SAT in both junior and senior years of high school from 1977 through 1982.
    It is of course somewhat surprising that the growth on the Scholastic Aptitude Test from junior to senior year appears to be larger than growth on reading and math achievement tests from junior to senior year, but we put aside discussion of this finding to another time and place.

effective in increasing SAT scores — that is, can produce in less than 50 hours gains equivalent to increases generally shown over a full calendar year including some 1000 hours of high school instruction.

Indeed, from this perspective, even if we accept Becker's slightly lower estimates, effects of coaching that rival in magnitude the amount of gain evident normally over a full year of maturation and school instruction can hardly be viewed as modest. Whatever the validity of coached scores for individual students — a matter to which we return below — it is clear that test coaching and preparation can substantially distort judgment of school quality in terms of SAT scores. Though the practice of using SAT scores as gauges of school quality may be regarded as erroneous by some observers, including ourselves, SAT scores are widely viewed and used as indices of the quality of the nation's schools by people ranging from the U.S. Secretary of Education to local real estate brokers (Stickney, 1986). Given this practice, it is clear that score changes that may be produced by coaching and preparation are sufficiently large to produce substantial distortions in the views of schools afforded by SAT scores.

Apart from the way SAT scores may be used — or misused — as indices of school quality, what of the likely implications of coaching and preparation for the validity of SAT scores as measures of students' "developed abilities" (Donlon, 1984, p. 37), since that after all is what developers of the SAT claim for it? Despite much previous speculation and controversy over the implications of coaching for the validity of SAT scores (e.g. Slack and Porter, 1980; Messick and Jungeblut, 1981; DerSimonian and Laird, 1983), as we observed earlier, no previous studies of coaching for the SAT have systematically examined implications of coaching for the validity of SAT scores in predicting college performance. Hence we have little direct evidence on the implications of SAT coaching for the validity of SAT scores as measures of students' developed verbal and math abilities. Nevertheless, several kinds of indirect evidence indicate that scores elevated by coaching for a specific test such as the SAT may undermine valid inferences from individuals' scores.

First, we note the implications of the foregoing discussion of the relative magnitudes of time and gains associated with SAT coaching versus time and gains associated with high school instruction. The fact that score gains per hour of instruction time can be 10-20 times greater for short-term coaching than for high school learning casts considerable doubt on the claims that the SAT measures "general intellective skills [that] develop gradually over a number of years as a result of everyday experience as well as formal education [and] may be relatively difficult to enhance markedly in late adolescence through brief courses of intervention'"(Messick, 1981, p. 24). Though the capability of coaching to affect SAT scores by 10-30 points may seem small relative to the measurement error that might typically be plus or minus 30 to 60 points, it seems very large in comparison to the sort of gains students typically show as a result of high school instruction and maturation.

The apparent susceptibility of SAT scores to change as a result of short-term coaching in contrast to longer-term high school instruction certainly raises doubts about the validity of the SAT as measuring general skills that develop only gradually. Nevertheless, the fact that some students (in all coaching studies, experimental subjects are to some extent self-selected) can show substantial increases (relative to typical change over a year of high school) does not necessarily indicate that the improved scores are less highly predictive of success in college, as Messick (1981) has pointed out. Unfortunately, few coaching studies have looked directly at the question of the predictive validity of coaching studies.[4] There are, however, other instances in which educational programs have been aimed at increasing students' scores on particular standardized tests, which suggest that scores elevated by "targeted" instruction do not have the same predictive value as test scores that have not been so elevated.

One prominent example of this phenomenon comes from the national evaluation of the Follow Through (FT) program. In this evaluation, the effects of different models of early elementary education were compared in terms of how they affected student performance on the Metropolitan Achievement Test (MAT). Though the full story of the FT evaluation, which lasted more than ten years and cost over $50 million (Haney, 1977), cannot be recounted here, what is worth noting is that after the evaluation came to be focused closely on MAT as the prime outcome measure, the main substantive conclusion of the evaluation was that over the K-3 grade levels, "models that emphasize basic skills succeeded better than other models in helping children gain these skills" as measured on the MAT (Stebbins, et al., 1977, volume IVA, pp. 135-155).

---

[4] Mallone (1965) did look at this issue and found that while coached students seemed to do less well at service academies than test scores would have predicted, at other institutions of higher education, college standings did not seem lower than the test scores would have predicted. See also Messick (1981), who points out the difficulty of conducting follow-up predictive validity studies on coached students who may scatter to attend many different institutions of higher education.

In particular, the Direct Instruction model of the University of Oregon appeared to be the most successful of the 20 FT models in boosting children's MAT scores. Though effect sizes varied across different sites and different MAT subtests, the largest effects estimates for the Direct Instruction "treatment," derived from multiple regression analyses controlling for a range of background factors, were that this model accounted for around 10% of the variance in children's end-of-third-grade MAT language and math computations subscores (Haney, 1977, p. 313-314). These were equivalent to effect sizes of approximately one-third of a standard deviation. However, after children left the Direct Instruction program, the gains rapidly faded. As Becker and Engelmann (1976) noted in follow-up studies, "there were sizeable losses against national norms from the third to fifth or third to sixth grades." Becker and Engelmann concluded, "there is a clear implication that compensatory programs cannot be expected to maintain gains after the programs are stopped" (Becker and Engelmann, 1976, pp. 12-13). Another way of interpreting this situation is to say that scores increased as the result of an intervention targeted directly at improving performance on a particular test cannot be expected to have the same predictive validity as scores for students whose initial performance was not enhanced by an intervention targeted specifically at those test scores.

The extent of the problem of invalidation of test results when instruction focuses specifically on boosting scores on a particular test was shown with data from the study reported by Koretz, Linn, Dunbar & Shepard (1991), described earlier. As recounted earlier in this chapter, these investigators compared test results on one "high stakes" test used for several years in a large urban school district, with results on comparable tests which had not been used in that district for several years. Specifically, they tested separate samples of third grade students on both an alternate form of the districts high-stakes test and on a different achievement test covering the same content. Table 7.2 shows a summary of their results for two comparisons. In the first, these investigators compared students results on the district's high stakes test, with the student scores on an alternate form of the same test. In the second, and with a separate sample of third graders, they compared scores on the district high-stakes test with students scores on a different achievement test covering the same material, but which had not been regularly used in the district for several years. As these data indicate the students' scores were higher on the high-stakes test regularly used in the district than on either the alternate form or alternate test. Koretz, Linn, Dunbar & Shepard (1991) showed differences in student performance in these two comparisons only in terms of mean (or median) student percentile scores (and also grade equivalent scores). What we have done in Table 7.2 is to convert the the percentile differences to z-score or standard deviation differences so that we can compares them with the SGE data described earlier. Thus, as indicated in Table 7.2, the results of Koretz, Linn, Dunbar & Shepard (1991) indicate that third grade test results on this district's high-stakes test were inflated, on average, by about 0.10 to 0.18 standard deviation units for reading scores and 0.31 to 0.41 for math. By comparing these data to the SGE's shown in Table 7.1 (across six major test series, the average SGE was 0.73 for Total reading and 1.05 for Total Math), it is possible to estimate that the degree of distortion apparent on this district's test results was, for reading and math respectively 15 to 25% and 30 to 39% of the amount that students could be expected to increase in scores over the course of a full year.

Table 7.3: Magnitude of Distortion in High-stakes Test Results

	Average %ile scores and differences	
Comparison 1	(n=620)	(n=707)
High stakes district test	42	61
Alternate form	35	46
Difference (in %ile points)	7	15
Difference (in z-scores)	0.18	0.31
Comparison 2	(n=749)	(n=721)
High-stakes test	42	67
Alternate test	38	51
Difference (in %ile points)	4	16
Difference (in z-scores)	0.10	0.41

Source: Koretz, Linn, Dunbar and Shepard, 1991, Tables 3 and 4.

Though the relevance of these findings from one elementary education intervention program and another high stakes school district testing program to coaching for college admissions testing may be limited, the phenomenon they illustrate is more common — namely that the effects of an intervention or educational program aimed at raising scores on a particular test in the short run, likely will not persist over the long haul and may not be apparent in the short run even on other similar tests.

In sum, though there is little direct evidence on the validity of test scores resulting from special preparation and coaching, we have reviewed three kinds of indirect evidence indicating that test scores boosted through targeted instruction and coaching do indeed have diminished validity. The rates of gain associated with at least some SAT coaching programs in comparison with the gains associated with schooling and maturation more generally, the phenomenon of test scores gains associated with test-targeted educational interventions fading out after the intervention ceases, and the failure of results on school district high-stakes tests to generalize to other tests, all suggest that the validity of "coached" scores is not the same — either as indicators of individual student learning or as indices of quality of educational programs — as for scores that have not been enhanced by intervention targeted specially at raising those scores.

More generally, though we have found no way to gauge the extent of distortions that may be introduced into the testing marketplace by problems of various test marketing schemes, the RFP procurement process, or computer-based test interpretations, the evidence reviewed concerning the potential magnitude of distortions introduced by the Lake Wobegon phenomenon and by targeted test preparation and coaching are potentially quite severe. The distortions are of sufficient magnitude to undermine substantially inferences that may be drawn from test scores both about the quality of schools and other educational programs and about the learning of individual students. Thus, though the problems we have identified in the testing marketplace may not represent a major blight on the entire enterprise of testing, neither do they represent merely minor mold that can be safely ignored. Hence in the next, and concluding, chapter of this volume, we turn to consider alternative strategies for mending the fractured marketplace for testing.

8 MENDING THE FRACTURED MARKETPLACE

As previous chapters have recounted, the market for tests has not only been expanding rapidly in recent decades, but also has been changing sharply in structure — into an increasingly fractured marketplace. In this concluding chapter, we describe the various ways in which the testing marketplace is fractured via a summary of the major points raised in previous chapters. Then we outline recent proposals for developing new national testing systems; for even as we have been writing this volume, unprecedented plans have been announced, and legislation proposed, to develop a national examination system employing "new" assessment methods. Finally, in the last portion of this concluding chapter we discuss various strategies for mending the fractured marketplace for tests and explain why proposals for a new national system of achievement tests, at least as embodied in current proposals, seem to us quite unlikely to produce results that are either highly valid from a measurement point of view or promising from the standpoint of improving teaching and learning.

FRACTURES IN THE TESTING MARKETPLACE

We began this volume by showing that the commercial side of standardized testing in the United States has received remarkably little serious scrutiny. Though tests are increasingly prominent in the social life of the United States, very little attention has been given to the markets by which tests get produced, sold and used. This blind spot in the national discourse about testing is particularly odd, since market forces are so widely seen as having a major influence on many facets of our life — not just on economic conditions but also on aspects of social welfare ranging from health care to recreation.

Thus we continued in chapter 2 to show that the testing industry is composed of not just a half-dozen of the better-known test publishers, but also around three dozen medium-size and hundreds of smaller test publishers (though some of these are actually large firms publishing only a few tests). In addition to such "publishers", the marketplace for tests involves a variety of other organizations and agents, including sponsors, developers, groups that score tests and produce interpretative reports, and a wide range of "users" of test results. For a particular testing program, the parties involved and the relations among them often are far more complex than the relatively simple relations between buyers and sellers in other markets.

To illustrate this point, let us describe some of the range of organizations and individuals involved in the Scholastic Aptitude Testing (SAT) program. The SAT has long been sponsored by the College Board, an organization of institutions of higher and secondary education. Thus the SAT is also widely known as the "College Boards." But the organization that develops and administers the SAT, as recounted in chapter 2, is the Educational Testing Service. The bodies that create the market for the SAT are institutions of higher education, which require applicants to submit SAT scores in order to be considered for admission. These institutions often seem to have felt that this requirement added to their prestige, since the SAT and the College Board itself grew out of a group of elite institutions. Moreover, "there was little bother and no cost to colleges in requiring applicants to take the tests" (Valentine, 1987, pp. 70-71).

The people who pay for the SAT — and provide the main source of income for both the College Board and ETS — are students who seek admission to institutions of higher education. And the "users" of SAT test results are many. The traditional and most obvious users of SAT results are college admissions officers, but since scores began being released to SAT takers themselves in the 1950s, students too are in an important sense users of SAT results. Moreover, given the popular awareness of the SAT, a wide range of others have become users, including real estate agents, educational policy-makers (who often use SAT averages as gauges of educational quality), and the considerable test preparation industry described in chapters 6 and 7. Two of the more surprising users of SAT results not previously mentioned have been the U.S. Secretary of Education and the National Collegiate Athletic Association (NCAA).

The Wall Chart

If the SAT score decline helped to popularize use of admissions test scores as indicators of educational quality, as described in chapter 5, the U.S. Secretary of Education's introduction in 1984 of a "wall chart" of rankings of the states in terms of educational quality effectively institutionalized their use as indicators of the educational quality of the states. As one article on the "Lessons from the Wall Chart" put it, the U.S. Department of Education's publication of the large wall chart "signaled a revolution of sorts in the reporting of facts and trends in American education" (Ginsburg, Noell & Plisko, 1988, p. 1).

For more than a century the U. S. Office of Education (and its successor, the U.S. Department of Education) had published statistics on the condition of education in the nation, including many kinds of data for each of the states. However, the wall chart was the first time that the Department of Education published state-by-state comparisons of not just educational resources or processes but "outcomes" as measured by college admissions test scores.[1]

Though Department of Education officials had planned a small, carefully controlled press conference for release of the 1984 wall chart (in part for fear of embarrassing low-ranking states), the release of the new document quickly turned into a national media event, widely covered by print, radio and television journalists. As Department of Education officials later wrote, no one in the Department "involved in the project was prepared for the degree of interest generated" (Ginsburg, Noell & Plisko, 1988, p. 4). Serious questions were raised about the meaningfulness of state comparisons of college admissions test scores, because the prime factor explaining states' SAT averages seemed to be the percentages of high school graduates in the states taking the SAT; yet state rankings on SAT and ACT scores quickly became hot topics of political debate in a number of states around the country.[2] The wall chart, and the publicity surrounding it, also led to adoption of a plan by chief state school officers for developing a sounder and more systematic basis for state comparisons of student learning.

---

[1] Ginsburg, Noell & Plisko (1988) comment that release of the wall chart had the "effect of completing the shift started by the Coleman report to assess education primarily in terms of outcomes rather than inputs" (p. 6).

[2] Ginsburg, Noell & Plisko (1988) discuss five major complaints raised about the wall chart data and five "positive" impacts that they saw the wall chart as having on educational policy-making in the U.S.

Whatever the complaints about and consequences of the wall chart, this episode clearly indicated that the highest education official in the nation, the U.S. Secretary of Education, was willing to use college admissions test scores for a purpose for which they had never been intended and for which they had not been validated. Indeed, independent research on the wall chart data quickly showed that the states with the highest college admissions test scores tend to be those in which smaller proportions of students take the tests. Nearly three-quarters of the variation in 1982 state average SAT scores was shown to be accounted for by the percentage of eligible high school seniors in the states taking the SAT (Powell & Steelman, 1984).[3] Not surprisingly, sponsors and developers of college admissions tests objected to the Department of Education use of state averages to rank the states. Here is how ETS President Gregory Anrig summarized his "serious reservations" about using SAT scores to make state comparisons, in a letter to Secretary of Education Lauro Cavazos:

> The SAT is not designed to reflect the outcome of instruction in high school and therefore is not sensitive to a great many changes in the high school curriculum or to changes in subject matter. . . . Annual SAT scores are based on a self-selected sample of test takers and are not likely to reflect the results obtained if given to a representative sample of students. Large differences in scores over the years have to a large degree been the result of changes in the make-up of the student population taking the test and not changes in scholastic ability of high school seniors. . . . Given the tenuous relationship of SAT scores to changes in high school instruction and the lack of representativeness of the scores, the state rankings are likely to be in serious error and small changes from year to year meaningless. (Gregory Anrig, letter to Lauro Cavazos, April 12, 1990)

Despite such cautions, Cavazos went ahead with release of the wall chart rankings based on SAT and ACT scores in 1990, as Secretaries of

---

[3] Similar studies have shown the pitfalls in trying to use school average SAT scores as indices of school quality (Fetler, 1991), even though the practice is widespread.

Education had done every year since 1984. As Department officials had explained, they were well aware of many problems in state rankings on SAT and ACT scores; but when they wanted to compare student performance in the 50 states, they found that these scores "proved the best available alternative" (Ginsburg, Noell & Plisko, 1988, p. 3).[4]

Given this inappropriate use of college admissions test scores by the highest federal education official in the nation, despite the opposition of test sponsors, it was not surprising that others also used admissions test scores to pursue their own agendas, even though the SAT and ACT admissions tests had never been validated for the uses to which they were put.

Proposition 48

Another major example of the use of college admissions test scores for purposes for which they were not intended is embodied in what has widely come to be called Proposition 48, passed by the convention of the National Collegiate Athletic Association (NCAA) in January of 1983. Proposition 48 (which became effective in 1986) changed the rules governing the eligibility of students to compete in Division 1 intercollegiate athletics. The new rules allowed freshmen to participate in intercollegiate sports only if they had attained at least a 2.00 high school grade point average in a core curriculum of 11 academic subjects and a 700 combined verbal and math score on the SAT or a 15 composite ACT score (Greene, 1984, p. 110).

Like the wall chart, Proposition 48 generated a storm of controversy and numerous criticisms (Humphries, 1983; Farrell, 1986). It should have been obvious to the college presidents who proposed the new NCAA eligibility rules that ACT and SAT scores were never intended — or validated — by the test developers as yardsticks to determine athletic eligibility. Indeed, via both press releases and direct communications to NCAA officials, ETS and ACT expressed disapproval of this use of their college admissions tests.[5] To explain how this

---

[4] It should be noted that with availability of sounder comparative achievement test data on states in 1991 (via the Trial State Assessment of the National Assessment of Educational Progress), U.S. Secretary of Education Lamar Alexander discontinued the wall chart series.

[5] In a press release and a letter to the NCAA Executive Director, both dated January 19, 1983, ETS President Gregory Anrig warned that using a fixed cutoff score on college admissions tests would have effects that "may not have been fully realized." And in a press release in 1990, Anrig said "Since the introduction of Rule 48 seven years ago, I have repeatedly stated my

new use of test scores came about despite the disapproval of test sponsors, some background needs to be provided.

Intercollegiate athletics, at least at the level of Division 1 NCAA schools, has become increasingly competitive over the last several decades. Colleges compete fiercely to recruit blue-chip high school athletes, sometimes bending their own college admissions rules in the process (and NCAA recruiting guidelines as well). Also, by the early 1980s it had become clear that some college sports programs exploited student athletes, by giving them the opportunity to play intercollegiate sports but providing them with little education.

Before adoption of Prop 48, NCAA rules had decreed that to be eligible for varsity athletics, incoming freshmen needed to have attained a high school grade point average of 2.00 — irrespective of what courses had been taken. But the proposers of Prop 48 (and the 1983 NCAA convention itself) clearly felt that tightening up academic requirements simply in terms of grades and courses would not be a sufficient remedy for the ills of big-time college athletics. This view was doubtless bolstered by the fact that these ills included documented instances of the doctoring of student transcripts. So in addition to stiffening the high school grade requirement (by requiring a 2.00 average in academic subjects), Proposition 48 also required minimum SAT or ACT scores.

Just as in the case of the wall chart, it appears that this new use of college admissions test scores was mandated for a very practical reason. The NCAA wanted to address the problem of academic integrity in intercollegiate sports, and it decided to use colleges admissions tests simply because these were the only instruments available. These two examples of the use of SAT and ACT scores for functions for which the tests were never intended nicely illustrate the complexity of the testing marketplace, and the difficulties in reforming it. An instrument may be very carefully developed, and the research supporting its use for its intended purposes may be very elegant; indeed the SAT and ACT admissions tests are clearly among the most carefully developed and thoroughly researched of tests. But once such an instrument is used — particularly if it

opposition to its use of a fixed cutoff score on nationally standardized admissions tests as a determining criterion for athletic eligibility, especially when other equally valuable information, such as high school grades, is available." (ETS, Statement of ETS President Gregory R. Anrig on NCAA Legislation, January 3, 1990).

gains a degree of legitimacy in popular opinion — it may well be applied, arguably as one of few available tools, as a lever for changing social policy. This may be done not out of ignorance — in the examples of the wall chart and Proposition 48, clearly the U.S Secretary of Education and the college presidents involved in the NCAA decision knew that college admissions tests had not been validated for the purposes to which they put them — but rather out of concern for a greater good. In the case of the wall chart, it was to spur public attention to the need for educational reform and improvement. In the case of Prop 48, it was the need to reform intercollegiate athletics. And in both cases, college admissions test scores were seized upon simply because they were viewed as one of the few instruments available for pursuing the reform agendas at hand.

This general sentiment, that standardized tests can be useful instruments of education reform and indeed educational policymaking more generally, is one of the key forces behind the growth in standardized testing over the last several decades. As recounted in chapter 3, testing in the United States has been increasing sharply. Though it is impossible to document that growth precisely, a number of indicators suggest that the volume of testing in the education sector has increased steadily over the last several decades (particularly since around 1960) and that the number of tests administered annually may be rising by 10-20% annually. Evidence on the extent of testing in the employment sector is still more elusive than that on education. It appears that after some diminution in volume of employment testing in the 1970s and early 1980s (as a result of litigation and uncertainty over the requirement for job-relatedness under the EEOC guidelines), it is now increasing substantially (see, for example, Lee, 1988, "Testing makes a comeback.")

In chapter 4, via examples pertaining to state and local school district testing programs, we showed that though the direct costs of testing are substantial, the indirect social investment in testing is much larger still. We estimated that the total social costs of state testing programs are at least six to ten times greater than the direct or obvious costs. Moreover, estimates indicate that the implicit costs of student time devoted to testing and test preparation amount to a substantial portion of the nation's investment in education. In light of these costs, we argue that people need to consider not just the full resource costs of testing but also the marginal value of testing as compared with alternatives to which these resources might be put.

In chapter 5, we sought to describe some of the social forces behind the upsurge in testing in recent decades. In the realm of education, one of the clearest influences has been recurring public dissatisfaction with the quality of schooling and consequent reform efforts that frequently have become embodied in state and federal legislation mandating more or new testing. More broadly, since the 1950s there seems to have been a widespread shift in the manner by which policymakers judge the quality of schools. Instead of using resources or inputs as criteria, many now tend to focus on the outcomes of schooling. Since standardized test results are the most obvious indicators of educational outcomes, this shift has focused additional attention on test results. Finally, standardized objective testing was shown to fit well with the rise of bureaucracy. Standardized tests provide means for selecting and categorizing people in organizations according to formal and impersonal rules, and so provide the basis for treating people, both in schools and in the workplace, according to "objective" qualifications rather than on the basis of election or family or social class.

In chapter 6, we described several spin-off segments of the testing marketplace. The increasing influence of computer technology on testing was noted as affecting not just test development and scoring, but increasingly also test administration and even test interpretation. In a related development, there has been a tremendous growth in the test preparation and coaching industry. This segment of the testing industry now includes dozens of computer programs aimed at helping users prepare for standardized tests, hundreds of books and manuals (many published by test publishers themselves) with the same aim, and numerous companies selling test preparation services. Finally, we noted that since the 1988 Congressional ban on polygraph testing, there has been a rapid growth in the marketing of so-called honesty or integrity tests — another clear example of entrepreneurial test-makers responding to a market opportunity.

Some standardized testing still follows the model that has existed at least since World War II, in which a commercial publisher — perhaps aided by some subject-matter experts serving as test authors — builds a test (achievement, aptitude, personality) and seeks to market it to schools, counselors, psychologists or employers. Yet as our analysis has shown, with the volume of testing increasing rapidly over the last twenty years, the nature of the testing market has changed. Specific tests are now often mandated by legislative bodies and executive agencies of government. Courts often are involved in adjudicating disputes over both employment and educational testing. Government agencies at both federal and state levels are variously developers, sponsors, users, and regulators of tests. The federal government, for example, publishes the *General Aptitude Battery* (GATB) and the ASVAB, but also regulates employment testing via the *Uniform Guidelines*. In many instances, the spin-off market for tests may involve agencies, independent of either the test maker or the test buyer, in scoring and interpreting test results or preparing people who are to take the tests.

As we have argued in chapter 7, this increasing fracturing of the testing marketplace poses new threats to the reasonable and valid use of test results. Tests mandated by state agencies, for example, often seem to gain credibility, even absent reasonable validity evidence, simply because they are mandated by a state agency. Similarly, even when a good test has been developed, and supported by adequate validity evidence and is responsibly administered and scored, reasonable and valid use of its results may nevertheless be severely undermined by inappropriate test preparation, by misleading or inaccurate algorithms for interpreting the results, or by application of results in ways never intended. Though evidence on the extent to which these factors may distort test results is scanty, we showed in chapter 7 that factors such as the Lake Wobegon phenomenon and targeted test preparation and coaching may change test results by the same magnitude as could be expected from a full year of schooling or more. Thus, we have argued that such influences represent not just minor mold on an otherwise healthy enterprise, but sources of major distortions, as seen for example in efforts to use test results to judge the quality of schools and educational programs, and in the use of tests to judge the qualifications of individuals "objectively".

RECENT PROPOSALS FOR NEW NATIONAL TESTS

In chapter 5 we described several prominent proposals for reforming education the United States, including:

- *A Nation at Risk*, released in early 1983;
- *High School: A Report on Secondary Education in America*
    (Boyer, 1983);
- the "National Education Goals," announced in 1990, by President
    Bush and the National Governors Association (NGA);
- the *America 2000* plan for educational reform, announced by
    President Bush in April 1991.

As noted in chapter 5, one of the key proposals in *America 2000* was for new "American Achievement Tests" covering "core subjects" of English, mathematics, science, history, and geography and based on "new world standards." These new tests were to be used to foster good teaching and learning; to monitor student progress; for college admissions, and for making hiring decisions. Since we have set out our criticisms of the *America 2000* proposals for new American Achievement Tests elsewhere (Haney, 1991), we simply summarize our concerns here. The proposal that one test or even one set of tests can be used for such a wide range of purposes is ill-conceived and evidences considerable ignorance of the evolution of testing. Moreover, it violates professional and legal standards of educational and employment testing and defies even simple logic, for tests aimed at improving teaching need totally different characteristics from those intended to inform hiring decisions. In short, trying to use one test for the range of purposes set out in *America 2000* is like trying to use one tool — say a screwdriver or a hammer — for jobs ranging from brain surgery to pile driving. It is of course physically possible to attempt it, but even a cursory glance tells us that the effort will not be successful.

Nevertheless, the basic idea of a new national testing system set out in America 2000 was furthered by the release on January 24, 1992, of a report by the Congressionally mandated National Council on Education Standards and Testing (NCEST), entitled *Raising Standards for American Education.* The NCEST concluded that "national [education] standards and a system of assessments are desirable and feasible mechanisms for raising expectations, revitalizing instruction, and rejuvenating educational reform efforts for all American schools and students" (p. 8). This conclusion was reached in the following passage from *Raising Standards for American Education* (which we quote at some length, so as to set out the Council's rationale fully):

> ... the Council concluded that high national standards tied to assessments are desirable. In the absence of well-defined and demanding standards, education in the United States has gravitated toward de facto national minimum expectations. Except for students who are planning to attend selective four-year colleges, current education standards focus on low-level reading and arithmetic skills and on small amounts of factual material in other content areas. Consumers of education in

this country have settled for far less than they should for far less than do their counterparts in other developed nations.

High national standards tied to assessments can create high expectations for all students and help to better target resources. They are critical to the Nation in three primary ways: to promote educational equity, to preserve democracy and enhance the civic culture, and to improve economic competitiveness. Further, national education standards would help to provide an increasingly diverse and mobile population with shared values and knowledge.

The Council recommends standards for students and standards for schools and schools systems. *Student standards* include specification of the content - what students should know and be able to do - and the level of performance that students are expected to attain - how good is good enough. The Council envisions that the *national standards* will include substantive content together with complex problem-solving and higher order thinking skills.

To ensure that students do not bear the sole burden of attaining the standards and to encourage assurances that the tools for success will be available at all schools, the Council also recommends that *states establish school delivery standards.* System performance standards should also be established. School delivery and system performance standards would attest to the provision of opportunities to learn and of appropriate instructional conditions to enable all children to reach high standards.

In endorsing the concept of national standards for all students, the Council stipulates several characteristics these standards should have:

• Standards must reflect high expectations, not expectations of minimal competency.

- Standards must provide focus and direction, not become a national curriculum.

- Standards must be national, not federal.

- Standards must be voluntary, not mandated by the federal government.

- Standards must be dynamic, not static.

The Council's intent in recommending the establishment of national standards is to raise the ceiling for students who are currently above average and to lift the floor for those who now experience the least success in school, including those with special needs. States should work toward reducing gaps in students' opportunities to learn and in their performance, such as those now associated with race, income, gender, and geographical location.

Having reached consensus that standards are desirable, the Council then determined that it is not sufficient just to set standards. Since tests tend to influence what is taught, assessments should be developed that employ the new high standards. The considerable resources and effort the Nation expends on the current patchwork of tests should be redirected toward the development of a new system of assessments. Assessments should be state-of-the-art, building on the best tests available and incorporating new methods. In order to measure individual student progress and to monitor achievement in attaining the National Education Goals, the new system of assessments should have two components -

• individual student assessments, and

• large-scale sample assessments, such as the National Assessment of Educational Progress.

The key features of both components would be alignment with high national standards and the capacity to produce useful, comparable results. In addition, the system of assessments should have a number of other features.

- The system of assessments must consist of multiple methods of measuring progress, not a single test.

- The system of assessments must be voluntary, not mandatory.

- The system of assessments must be developmental, not static.

As these features are put in place, technical and equity issues need to be resolved, and the overriding importance of ensuring fairness for all children needs to be addressed. Resolving issues of validity, reliability, and fairness is critical to the success of the new system.

The Council concludes that the United States, with appropriate safeguards, should initiate the development of a voluntary system of assessments linked to high national standards. These assessments should be created as expeditiously as possible by a wide array of developers and be made available for adoption by states and localities. The Council finds that the assessments eventually could be used for such high-stakes purposes for students as high school graduation, college admission, continuing education, and certification for employment. Assessments could also be used by states and localities as the basis for system accountability.

In the Council's view, it is desirable that national content and performance standards and assessments of the standards be established. Doing so will constitute an essential next step to help the country achieve the National Education Goals. Moreover, developing standards and assessments at the national level can contribute to educational renewal in several ways. This effort has the potential to raise learning expectations at all levels of education, better target human and fiscal resources for educational improvement, and help meet the needs of an increasingly mobile population. Finally,

standards and assessments linked to the standards can become
the cornerstone of the fundamental, systemic reform necessary
to improve schools. (National Council on Education Standards
and Testing, 1992, pp. 2-5, italics added)

Before commenting on the NCEST report recommendations and
recapping what has happened since it was issued, we should note that the
Council's recommendations in part reflect a broader movement in American
education away from traditional multiple-choice standardized tests towards what
are variously called "authentic" or performance assessments. As we have shown
in previous chapters, the influence of standardized multiple-choice tests has
grown enormously over the last several decades. In the last year or two, it has
been widely argued that multiple-choice tests have tended to emphasize
memorization and "lower-order" thinking skills. Increased pressure on students,
teachers and schools to raise test scores during the 1980s has driven "teachers to
emphasize tasks that would reinforce rote learning and sharpen test-taking skills,
and discouraged curricula that promote complex thinking and active learning"
(Wells, 1991, p. 55). Indeed, in 1984 one testing specialist argued that the
influence of multiple-choice testing on teaching and learning was the "real"
source of bias in tests (Frederiksen, 1984).

As a result of increasing recognition of this phenomenon, proponents
of new national tests now generally are calling for new forms of assessment,
which they call "authentic" or "instructionally worthy." What different people
mean by this term varies, but the most commonly discussed alternatives to
multiple-choice tests are portfolios of student work and performance assessments
in which students have to perform a task or solve an open-ended problem (see,
for example, Wolf, LeMahieu & Eresh, 1992). The kind of performance
assessment most commonly employed at present is the essay test, and there is
some evidence that teachers do find essay tests more instructionally useful than
multiple-choice tests of writing skills (Suhor, 1985). A report by the Office of
Technology Assessment (1992) provides a useful summary of recent activities in
the states regarding performance assessment. Not surprisingly, the most
common form of statewide assessment, other than multiple-choice testing, is
essay testing. States appear to be moving only very gingerly into using other
kinds of performance testing.

This is not the place to go into detail on the pros and cons of different kinds of assessment and their feasibility and validity for different purposes. However, several general points are worth noting.

Alternative Assessments Not Novel. First, many of the assessments that are being touted as new alternatives to multiple-choice tests are not at all new (Haney & Madaus, 1989).[6] Testing via essay and oral examinations, for example, has a much longer history than multiple-choice testing, which was a creation of the 20th century (Madaus & Kellaghan, 1992). Indeed, multiple-choice testing widely replaced such alternative forms of assessment in the late 19th and early 20th century because of the expense of using, and the difficulties in standardizing, these kinds of assessments when used with large numbers of people.

This does not mean that we ought not pursue inquiry into alternative forms of educational assessment. As the National Commission on Testing and Public Policy (NCTPP, 1990) noted, "Testing programs should be redirected from over-reliance on multiple-choice tests toward alternative forms of assessment" (p. 26). As the NCTPP recommended:

> A major cause for the distortion of test results and the ill effects of testing over the last several decades has been that the same test, or kind of test, has been asked to serve many important but different functions. Therefore, we recommend that testing for different purposes be differentiated and disentangled. Specifically, we urge that assessment of the effectiveness of social institutions — such as schools and training programs — be differentiated from assessment of individuals in order to help them. (p. 30)

---

6 The main problems with such performance testing, as noted for example by Chester Finn, are that "other kinds of tests and evaluations one would like to see given are more cumbersome, time-consuming, costly, and at least as vulnerable to manipulation. They are subject to uneven standards among those conducting and evaluating them — people rather than machines — and to the extent that they are not administered in a controlled setting, may invite more cheating" (Finn, 1991, p. 168). Later we comment more on the "corruptibility" of performance assessments. Also, see Madaus & Kellaghan (1991) for a discussion of the problems encountered in England and Wales when performance assessments were employed on a large scale in 1991.

Alternative Assessments Will Involve the Same Crowd. Second, even if the movement away from multiple-choice testing towards "performance" testing does continue, it surely will not put traditional test-makers out of business, for large producers of multiple-choice tests have perceived the opportunity for selling performance tests and have moved quickly to create products for this potential market. As a December 1991 article in *Business Week* put it, however, traditional test publishers think the performance testing movement may be just the latest educational fad.

> The big test publishers are hedging their bets. CTB MacMillan/McGraw-Hill, Houghton Mifflin's Riverside Publishing and Harcourt Brace Jovanovich have launched their own versions of performance-assessment exams within the last 18 months. . . . The publishers won't discuss sales of their new products, but Maryland is trying out a McGraw-Hill test this year. (DelValle, 1991, p. 110)

The big test publishers are, of course, embracing performance assessment not as a replacement for their traditional multiple-choice test wares, but as tools that can be used in addition to traditional tests. The 1992 catalog of HBJ's Psychological Corporation, *Resources for Measuring Educational Performance*, for example, listed "performance assessment" prominently on its cover, but inside advised:

> The Psychological Corporation has devised systems that integrate the results of multiple-choice, open-ended, and performance components in meaningful ways, allowing the user to analyze measured achievement, compare performance across formats and groups and combine results where desired. (Psychological Corporation, 1992, p. 11)

Three further points about the nascent movement away from multiple-choice tests towards performance tests — regarding the need to validate them for particular purposes, their motivational power, and susceptibility to corruption — are relevant to the national assessment system proposed in the NCEST report. So before setting out these points, let us briefly recap what has happened since release of the NCEST report in January 1992.

Update on National Education Standards and Assessments. The U.S. Senate passed legislation (S. 2) on January 28, 1992, just four days after release of the NCEST report, essentially endorsing the report's recommendations for creation of national education standards and assessments . However, the U.S, House of Representatives has not been so quick. In early 1992, the House Subcommittee on Elementary, Secondary and Vocational Education held hearings that included critical commentary and questions about the desirability and feasibility of the NCEST proposals.[7] On May 20, the House Committee on Education and Labor reported to the full House its Neighborhood Schools Improvement Act (H.R. 4323), described as "the Education and Labor Committee's response to America 2000."

As of this writing (July, 1992) the Education and Labor Committee's proposed bill has not been acted on by the full House of Representatives. And given that the United States is in the midst of a Presidential election, it is hard to predict what will happen with such politically prominent legislation. Worth noting, nevertheless, are important substantive differences between the House bill pending and the NCEST report proposal (essentially adopted in the Senate bill) that have important implications for any new national testing system.

The NCEST panel had recommended *national* student performance standards and assessments, but only *state-level* school delivery standards. This difference seems somewhat illogical on its surface. In light of widespread inequities in school finance and staffing, requiring all students nationwide to meet the same performance standards while allowing states to set their own school delivery standards seems a sure recipe for unfairness to students in ill-financed and ill-staffed schools. What the Congressional hearings made clear was that there was no reasoned basis for this recommendation of the NCEST panel. Rather, the reason was purely political; state governor members of the Council had objected to national school delivery standards as an infringement on states' responsibilities for education (and also as a possible threat to state budgets). So what the pending House bill does is to call for development of voluntary national school delivery standards.

---

[7] Two of the authors of this volume (Haney and Madaus) testified before the House Subcommittee on Elementary, Secondary and Vocational Education, essentially criticizing the NCEST report (Haney, 1992; Koretz, Madaus, Haertel & Beaton , 1992). Because the Subcommittee hearings on the NCEST report have not been published as of this writing, we cannot give a citation for the printed record of those hearings.

In addition, while the NCEST report and the Senate legislation had endorsed expeditious creation of new assessments, the House bill calls for development of voluntary national content standards prior to assessments; independent evaluation, through the National Academy of Sciences, of school delivery standards; of whether model assessments meet recognized technical standards for validity, reliability and fairness, and of alignment of assessments with content standards. From a measurement point of view, clarifying what is to be assessed and evaluating the technical quality of assessments before developing a large-scale program makes eminent sense.

Thus the House position seems much more reasonable in both regards than that of the NCEST report. Whatever will happen with this legislation will be known by the time this book is published; meanwhile, let us return to our general points about testing and assessment in general.

Validation for Purpose

Returning now to more general comments, pertinent to both multiple-choice tests and alternatives to mutiple choice tests, the NCEST proposals and many recent suggestions to use performance assessment as key instruments for educational reform call for using the same tests or assessments for several different purposes. The NCEST report, for example, recommended five different purposes to be served by the new system of assessments; but the five, if examined closely, actually encompass more than a dozen quite different purposes (p. 27). This problem is exactly the same, in our view, as that with the multiple aims proposed in America 2000 — though the NCEST group did at least add the disclaimer that "it is unlikely that all of these purposes can be accomplished with the same test or assessment instrument" (p. 27).

From a measurement point of view, the fundamental problem with proposals for using one or even several tests or assessments for purposes ranging from improving teaching and learning to informing college admissions and employment hiring decisions and even spurring national educational reform is that such tests require, as we have argued earlier, fundamentally different characteristics. Proposals such as the NCEST report ignore the fundamental notion of test validation — that tests and assessments must be validated not in the abstract but for particular functions, with regard to both how the results are used and the consequences of such use.

But what is reasonably clear in the recent spate of attention to new national tests as levers for educational reform is that many would-be educational reformers see a different role for tests and assessments than that which has generally been envisioned. In the past, tests have widely been viewed as sources of information. Test results have been seen as providing information that can be used by a variety of parties — students, parent, teachers, educational administrators and policymakers — to help inform their thinking and make decisions.

Now, however, tests and assessments have come to be widely viewed not simply as sources of useful information, but as instruments of reform in and of themselves. As one recent commentator put it, "No longer are tests geared primarily to probing and ultimately correcting the weaknesses of students; now they are mutating into policy weapons for spurring a dubious brand of change in local school districts" (Kaplan, 1992, p. 2). There is of course a fairly long history of using tests as instruments of reform (note for example the introduction of the original college boards in 1900 as a means to reform the process of admissions in to elite colleges, as briefly recounted in chapter 2). But now business leaders, governors and even the President of the United States have latched on to new national tests as key instruments to spur education reform. While there are significant variations in current proposals for new national tests, the common rationale behind numerous proposals was aptly summed up in a recent review on "the scramble for a national test":

> Advocates of national testing agree that the stakes in the current system of assessment are not high enough. They believe that the only way to motivate students and schools to improve is to provide them with feedback about where they rank according to objective, national standards. Underlying the rhetoric is a kick-in-the-pants approach. (Wells, 1991, p. 54)

The idea of jolting the educational system of the United States into major reforms by holding it accountable via high-stakes tests does seem to be increasingly popular. While we have described various problems with high-stakes testing elsewhere (Madaus, 1989), here we simply summarize two major points relating to 1) the idea that high-stakes tests motivate students; and 2) historical evidence on the corruption of test results when numerous high stakes are attached to results.

The Motivation Argument

If there is a theory implicit in both the *America 2000* and the NCEST *Raising Standards* reports as to how new national tests will help students learn, it is that if we kick students in the pants hard enough with tough national tests, they will be motivated to learn more. This "theory" is elaborated by others, such as Chester Finn, who devotes one section of his recent book on educational reform to a discussion of the merits of internal versus external incentives for improving student learning. Asking, among other things, whether we can really ever expect to make algebra more seductive than television or chemistry more beguiling than rock music, he implicitly answers his own questions when he states that "When it comes to academic learning, I believe that external consequences are the main determinant of how hard we work" (Finn, 1991, p. 125).

The problem with this theory as a strategy for school reform is that, though there is some evidence that tests and examinations do help motivate some students to study (or at least to prep for tests), there is little evidence that lack of motivation to do well in school is a key problem in students' learning. One major study of motivation and student effort in a large urban school district, for example, concluded:

> Students in our studies reported that evaluations of their performance in school were central to their life interests. . . . Evaluations of performance were seen as affecting important material sanctions in the future, in the form of jobs and careers, as well as important social sanctions in the present in the form of the opinions of parents, counselors, and friends. Moreover these sanctions were considered as very important by most students. . . .
>
> Low-achieving students, as well as minority group students, were just as likely as high-achieving students and Anglo students to report that evaluations received in school were influential. Since most students in our studies perceived evaluations of their school performance as being influential, low student effort and low achievement in school cannot be attributed to lack of influential evaluations. (Natriello & Dornbush, 1984, pp. 137-8)

Thus it appears that the theory that new national tests will increase student learning via higher stakes attached to test results is based on a faulty premise. If low student achievement in school cannot be attributed to lack of influential evaluations currently, it is hard to envision how more influential evaluations via national tests and external sanctions could possibly improve matters.

The other problem with the "kick-em-the-pants with tough tests" theory of motivation is that students are likely to be motivated by high-stakes tests only if they think that have a reasonable chance of succeeding on them. If they do not, testing may instead contribute to disillusionment, decreased motivation and even dropping out of school. In a survey of students in grades 2 through 11 in four large states, for instance, Paris, Lawton, Turner & Roth (1991) found a "negative impact [of testing] on students that can be summarized in three general trends: growing disillusionment about tests, decreasing motivation to give genuine effort [on tests], and increasing use of inappropriate strategies" (p. 14). Moreover, in a second survey in another state, the same investigators found that:

> the results of standardized tests become increasingly less valid
> for low achievers, exactly the group who are most at risk for
> educational problems and who most need diagnostic testing.
> Their scores may be contaminated by inappropriate motivation
> and learning strategies that further debilitate their performance
> and affirm a self-fulfilling prophecy of low scores. Apparently
> in their efforts to decrease personal anxiety and increase the
> protection of their own self-esteem, they relinquish effort and
> appropriate strategies on standardized achievement tests. (p.
> 16)[8]

More generally, the motivation argument ignores available evidence on how sanctions attached to high school graduation have worked in recent decades. High school graduation already has attached to it many seemingly strong incentives. With minor exceptions, people have long had to possess a high school diploma in order to go on to college, to gain other than fairly menial employment or even to join the armed forces of the United States (young people can enter the military without a regular high school diploma, but for those who

---

[8] On the connection between high stakes testing and high school dropouts see also Catterall (1989) and Kreitzer, Madaus & Haney (1989).

do not, entrance requirements are much stiffer). How well has this range of incentives served to motivate students to complete high school? Not terribly well, obviously, since 25% or so of students nationally continue to drop out of school prior to high school graduation. If incentives currently attached to the high school diploma do not serve to motivate these students' physical presence in schools (and after all, seat-time is all that is required in some schools to win a diploma), then it is extremely unlikely that hastily developed new tests of doubtful validity, and with smaller incentives attached, will motivate them either to stay in school or to work hard while there.

Corruption of High-Stakes Test Results

Another major problem in the proposed use of new national tests for functions ranging from making decisions about individual students to holding schools accountable is that high-stakes test results tend to become corrupted over time. In a broad sense, what seems to have happened in recent national discourse about testing and assessment is that, as many observers have become aware of the distortion of test results via the Lake Wobegon phenomenon (recounted in chapter 7), the consensus seems to be that the answer to this problem is to develop new kinds of national tests.

This seems to us an unfortunate and short-sighted reading of recent educational history in the United States. Beginning around the mid-1960s, the stakes attached to results of traditional standardized achievement tests have increased steadily (for example via developments discussed earlier in this volume, such as Title I evaluation requirements, the minimum competency testing movement and the shift to hold schools accountable in terms of outcomes, as measured by test results). With this increasing emphasis on test results, schools and teachers (particularly those serving large proportions of traditionally low-achieving students) increasingly focused instruction on the tests, sometimes using highly questionable techniques. But as we have shown in chapter 7, instruction targeted specifically at test results changes the meaning of those results.

Some proponents of new national tests, recognizing that this has happened, are now calling for alternative "instructionally" worthy kinds of assessments, such as performance tests. But it seems to us that this is the wrong inference to make from recent experience. As Finn (1991, p. 168) notes, alternative kinds of assessments are "at least as vulnerable to manipulation" as multiple-choice tests. Madaus (1988), for instance, explains how the validity of Primary Leaving Certificate essay examinations in Ireland in the 1940s was vitiated via students' memorizing stock responses that could be adapted to almost any essay question.

An even older example of corruption of performance tests comes from the fate of the "payment-by-results" scheme used in England in the last century. In May of 1862, the British Parliament passed the Revised Code under which schools would be paid not just on the basis of student attendance, but also on the basis of "results of the examination of individual children" by school inspectors (Connell, 1950, p. 205). The main sentiments behind the payment by results plan, such as calls for more efficiency in funding education and better educational accountability, appear to have been remarkably similar to those now motivating the current scramble in the United States for new national tests (Rapple, 1991). One backer of the Revised Code told his colleagues in Parliament that it would allow the public "to know exactly what consideration they get for their money." He continued:

> I cannot promise the House that this system [payment by
> results] will be an economical one, and I cannot promise that
> that it will be an efficient one, but I can promise that it will
> be one or the other. If it is not cheap, it shall be efficient; if it
> is not efficient it shall be cheap (quoted in Connell, 1950, p.
> 207)

The examinations to determine school payments were entirely "performance-based" — actual reading from a school book, newspaper or modern narrative, writing from dictation, and solving of open-ended arithmetic problems. The examinations were to stress the abilities of pupils to exercise such skills "in such a manner as will really enable them to employ those attainments in the practical business of life" (p. 210).

The payment by results scheme was much debated and was revised in the 1870s and 1880s (in part to provide additional payments for students passing examinations in specialized subjects such as history and geography, or what now

would likely be called higher order skills and knowledge). Finally in 1890 the
payment by results plan was abandoned altogether in England.[9]

The full story of this scheme in England cannot be told here;[10] suffice
it to say that the main reasons for its demise appear to have been the
administrative burden it imposed, the success over time of efforts to cram
students for the exams (and the concomitant increases in government
expenditures), the plan's effects in stifling teaching and "overpressuring" of
students, and ultimately the corruption of examination results. One critic
likened the scheme to "the payment of gardeners for planting in or out of season,
a shrubbery of evergreens for show on a special occasion, no matter of its dying
off immediately after" (quoted in Sutherland, 1973, p. 251).

It is worth recounting briefly the comments of one of the more eloquent
of opponents of the payment by results scheme in England, Matthew Arnold.
Though at the time Arnold was a School Inspector in the Education Department,
he spoke out repeatedly about the ill effects of the scheme on pupils, on teachers
and on teacher training:

> In a country where everyone is prone to rely too much on
> mechanical processes, and too little on intelligence, [the
> Revised Code] inevitably gives a mechanical turn to the school
> teaching. . . It attempts to lay down to the very letter, the
> requirements which shall be satisfied in order to earn grants.
> The teacher in consequence is led to think, not about teaching
> his subject, but about managing to hit those requirements.
> (quoted in Connell, 1950, p 225)

Arnold viewed schools as centers of culture and believed that their
general role in civilizing pupils was far more vital than the mere teaching of
skills and knowledge. Thus he argued that the government should support a
school "not as a mere machine for teaching reading writing and arithmetic, but as

---

[9] Payment by results started later and lasted longer in Ireland than in England,
but appears to have had many of the same effects on schools (Madaus,
Ryan, Kellaghan, & Airasian, 1987).

[10] For useful recent accounts of payment by results in England, see Rapple
(1990; 1991). Sutherland (1973) provides a broader account, which shows
the complexity of political considerations surrounding payment by results;
and for more on Arnold, see Connell (1950).

a living whole with complex functions, religious, moral and intellectual" (quoted in Connell, 1950, pp 213-14).

As far as we know, not even the most extreme proponents of educational voucher systems are advocating anything akin to the English payment by results scheme. But recent experience with accountability testing in the United States clearly shows that the stakes attached to test results do not have to be nearly as tangible as financial rewards to lead to corruption of results. For example, Corbett & Wilson (1991) recount how a statewide testing program in Pennsylvania began with low stakes attached, but after comparative school results were published in the newspapers, the implicit stakes rose swiftly as public perceptions of school quality came to be based on test results. As Corbett and Wilson (1991) point out, the stakes attached to a testing program are not something inherent in a formal program, but rather reside in people's perceptions. When Pennsylvania educators regarded the statewide test results as important, they began to target instruction to raising scores, via methods that not only raise doubts about the validity of results, but also, according to Corbett and Wilson, impeded serious educational reform.

Thus, whatever the exact form of assessment, be it multiple-choice testing or some manner of alternative assessment, and whatever the ostensible consequences attached to assessment results, one of lessons from early English experience with test-based school accountability still pertains. As one early student of English educational history warned more than 80 years ago:

> Whenever the outward standard of reality (examination results) has established itself at the expense of the inward, the ease with which worth (or what passes for such) can be measured is ever tending to become in and of itself the chief, if not sole, measure of worth. And in proportion as we tend to value the results of education for their measurableness, so we tend to undervalue and at last to ignore those results which are too intrinsically valuable to be measured. (Holmes, 1911, p. 128)

STRATEGIES FOR MENDING THE FRACTURED MARKETPLACE

What then can be done, in light of the fractured marketplace for testing, to improve the valid use of tests and to prevent their misuse? Though there are a variety of technical developments and research endeavors that we believe to be

relevant to this question, in this volume we focus mainly on broad policy
alternatives that might be pursued or have already been proposed or actually tried.
Specifically we discuss the following possibilities:

- Greater reliance on the marketplace
- Professional standards and peer review
- Litigation
- Education of test users
- Government regulation
- An independent auditing agency
- Development of new kinds of tests and assessment strategies.

After considering these strategies for improving the marketplace for
testing, we offer in conclusion some general suggestions for the ends we think
need to be sought in improving testing regardless of which strategies may be
employed.

Greater Reliance on the Marketplace

One of the more popular remedies for social and economic ills, at least
since the inauguration of the Reagan administration in 1980, has been to rely on
free market forces and competition to increase efficiency in production and
distribution of goods and services. But this strategy for reforming the testing
marketplace seems to us to have little promise of success.

Standardized testing and assessment already represent a fairly open
marketplace, with relatively few regulatory constraints. In some new segments
of the market, such as honesty testing, small companies have clearly been able
to respond to market opportunities and quickly bring new tests and services to
market. Even some of the large test publishers have been shown to be fairly
nimble in quickly responding to new opportunities (such as Psychological
Corporation in bringing out new performance assessments).

Moreover, the very fracturing of the market leads us to think that
deregulation in the interest of freeing the invisible hand of market forces holds
little potential for improving testing. For the ideal of a free market is that there
are large numbers of independent consumers who may chose among competing
products. Yet this ideal is very far removed from actual practice in the realm of
testing. Tests, for example, are very rarely bought, taken and used by any one
group of consumers. The tests may be mandated by one agency (e.g. a college
or employment agency), paid for and taken by others (e.g. high school students

seeking college admission, or prospective employees) and used by still others (admissions officials or employment counselors). In addition to this diversity of roles at the consuming end of testing, there appears to us to be increasing fracturing on the production end also. Different agencies may sponsor, develop, administer, score and interpret a single test.

Thus it seems to us that the relatively direct transactions between buyer and seller, between producer and consumer, posited in the ideal of a free market make greater reliance on market forces a strategy of doubtful utility for improving testing.

Professional Standards and Peer Review

Perhaps the oldest existing mechanisms seeking to promote standards and quality in the testing marketplace are professional standards concerning testing, and professional peer review of tests and related materials. Efforts by psychologists to develop professional standards for tests and test use have a long history, dating back to 1895. Though individual psychologists suggested standards for tests several times early in this century, the first official promulgation of standards for tests did not come until the 1950s. The first formal code of ethics for psychologists, which touched on testing in several places, was adopted by the American Psychological Association (APA) in 1952. And after an initial version prepared by the APA was revised, in 1954 the APA, the American Educational Research Association (AERA), and the National Council on Measurements Used in Education (the forerunner of the National Council on Measurement in Education or NCME) produced the *Technical Recommendations for Psychological Tests and Diagnostic Techniques*. The next year the AERA and NCME collaborated to produce the 1955 *Technical Recommendations for Achievement Tests*.

These codes of professional standards have gone through several revisions in the last 40 years, with different editions of the APA's ethical standards or principles being issued in 1963, 1967, 1977, and 1981, and different versions of the APA, AERA and NCME standards for tests and testing being issued in 1966, 1974 and 1985. We have traced the evolution of these standards elsewhere (Haney & Madaus, 1990) and will not recap their history here, save to note several limitations in their application. Additionally, since 1985, the Joint Committee on Testing Practices of the American Psychological Association, the American Educational Association, and the National Council on Measurement in Education has set up two working groups concerning test standards. One has prepared a *Code of Fair Testing* that details the responsibilities of test publishers, test users and test takers. The second is the Test User Qualification Working Group (TUQWoG), which is considering whether some mechanism might be developed to allow access to test materials to qualified users.[11].

The other long-standing effort to bring the power of professional self-governance to bear on the testing marketplace has been the *Mental Measurements Yearbooks*, which not only have served as the pre-eminent bibliographic sourcebooks on testing, but also contain reviews of test and test manuals by people active in the world of testing.[12] This series was begun by Oscar Buros, with publication of the *Nineteen Thirty-eight Mental Measurements Yearbook* (Buros, 1938) which later became know as the first Mental Measurements Yearbook. Altogether, over the next 40 years, Buros edited eight *Mental Measurements Yearbooks* or MMYs (Buros, 1940, 1949, 1953, 1959, 1965, 1972, 1978), *Tests in Print* (1961, 1974) and several other volumes of specialized test bibliography.

After Buros' death, the MMY project was transferred to the University of Nebraska where James V. Mitchell edited *Tests in Print III* and the *Ninth Mental Measurements Yearbook* or 9MMY (Mitchell, 1985). Subsequent editions of *Tests in Print* and *Mental Measurements Yearbook* continue to be produced by the University of Nebraska Press under several different editors. Thus, would-be purchasers of tests have long had easy access to bibliographies of information on tests and to independent critical reviews of tests that they might consider purchasing. Nevertheless, the professional standards, ethical codes and test reviews appear to have had only limited impact on the testing marketplace. Larger test publishers and test contractors unquestionably pay attention to the *Standards* (Holmen and Doctor, 1972; Buros, 1974). Perhaps the clearest example of how seriously the major publishers regard the Standards is the *ETS Standards for Quality and Fairness*. These internal Standards adopted by the ETS Trustee's "reflect and adopt the Standards for Educational and Psychological Testing" (p. vii). "Adherence to the Standards is regularly

---

[11] As of 1992, there is a movement under way by the three professional organization that have sponsored the test standards to revise the 1985 *Standards*.

[12] In the mid-1980s a second series of publications reviewing tests was begun by the Test Corporation of America, a subsidiary of Westport Publishers. See for example Keyser & Sweetland (1987).

assessed through a carefully structured audit process and subsequent management review" (p. iii). This compliance is monitored by a "Visiting Committee of persons outside ETS that is comprised of distinguished educational leaders, experts in testing and representatives of organizations that have been critical of ETS in the past" (p. iii).[13]

Nevertheless, the overall impact of these professional standards and peer review mechanisms appear to have been small, particularly among small publishers and users of tests. Shortly before his death Oscar Buros commented:

> The nonobservance of the APA-AERA-NCME and MMY Standards by test authors, publishers, and users is shocking. When will test users make it unprofitable for publishers to market tests without reporting even the barest essentials of the data which were considered minimal forty-nine years ago? (Buros, 1974, p. 757)

An APA survey reported by Singleton (n.d.) found that the 1974 *Standards* had a weak impact on the manuals of major test publishers. A study on test distribution practices revealed that test publishers generally seem to violate the *Standards* (Oles and Davis 1977). Holmen and Docter (1972) found that test publishers have criticized the *Standards* as "somewhat unrealistic, overly demanding, and impossible to meet without unwarranted investment" (p.49).

Our own review of the testing marketplace has revealed that there remain numerous instances in which the test *Standards* seem to have been totally ignored. With regard to the wall chart episode recounted earlier, for example, consider just two of the prescriptions from the 1985 *Standards* . In a section on "professional standards for test use", Standard 6.3 prescribes that

---

[13] Even though we credit ETS for its effort to develop internal standards of quality control consistent with the test *Standards* and with some degree of external oversight, we should point out that a recent court case has raised questions about the extent to which ETS follows its stated policies. In a case in which ETS had failed to release a student's SAT scores because of suspected cheating, a New York court ruled that "by failing to make even rudimentary efforts to evaluate or investigate information furnished by Brian [the student suspected of cheating], information that was clearly relevant to a rational decision-making process, ETS reduced its contractual undertaking to an exercise in form over substance." (Peter Dalton v. ETS, 1992, p. 17)

When a test is to be used for a purpose for which it has not
been previously validated, or for which there is no supported
claim for validity, the user is responsible for providing
evidence of validity. (p.42)

In the same section, Standard 6.8 maintains:

When test results are released to the news media, those
responsible for releasing results should provide information to
help minimize the possibility of the misinterpretation of test
results. (p. 42)

When U.S. Secretaries of Education released wall charts from 1984
through 1990 ranking the states by average college admission test scores, they
were, it seems eminently clear to us, violating both of these standards. They
were using test scores for purposes for which college admissions tests had not
been validated, and indeed had been told explicitly by test sponsors that states'
averages on such tests were not valid for the purpose of comparing educational
outcomes of the states. Yet the U.S. Department of Education made no
professional effort to present evidence on the validity of college admissions tests
for comparing educational quality in the states, beyond the argument published
in 1988, four years after initiation of the wall chart series, that statewide average
college admissions test scores "proved the best available alternative" for doing
what they wanted to do (Ginsburg, Noell & Plisko, 1988, p. 3). Moreover, in
releasing the wall charts at press conferences year after year for nearly a decade,
the U.S. Department of Education clearly violated Standard 6.8; not even the
simplest of precautions, like reporting confidence intervals around rankings, were
employed to help prevent misinterpretation of small and meaningless differences
in state averages.

The latest version of the *Mental Measurements Yearbook* (the 11th)
provides another example of a clear violation of professional standards
concerning testing. The 1985 *Standards* made several references to computerized
tests and test interpretations, but because computer applications regarding testing
were increasing rapidly in the 1980s, two of the standing committees of the
APA decided to develop a special set of guidelines regarding computer
applications as they related to testing. This resulted in the 1986 APA

Guidelines for Computer-based Tests and Interpretations (which are reprinted in Butcher, 1987).

The *Guidelines* were intended to provide an interpretation of the 1985 *Standards* as they relate to computer-based testing and interpretation, and to indicate the nature and extent of professional responsibilities in this field. While we do not try to summarize the *Guidelines* here we note that they clearly specified that computer-based testing ought to be subject to the same sort of scholarly peer review as paper-and-pencil tests:

> Adequate information about the [computer] system and reasonable access to the system for evaluating responses should be provided to qualified professionals engaged in a scholarly review of the interpretive service. When it is deemed necessary to provide trade secrets, a written agreement of nondisclosure should be made. (Guideline 31, from Butcher, 1987, p. 430)

This guideline appears, however, to have had little effect on the field of computerized testing, as noted in the introduction to the most recent MMY:

> There has been a dramatic increase in the number and type of computer-based-test-interpretative systems (CBTI). We had considered publishing a separate volume to track the quality of such systems. Our hopes to do so were frustrated, however, by the difficulty we encountered in accessing from the publishers the test programs and more importantly the algorithms in use by the computer-based systems. (Kramer & Conoley, 1992, p. xi)

If even the Buros Institute, which is surely the pre-eminent agency for scholarly review of tests and test-related materials, cannot get access to computerized testing systems for review purposes, it is clear that the *Guidelines* are simply not being followed by producers of such systems.

If the test standards and peer review processes have had limited impact on the testing marketplace in general and specifically at the highest levels of government, the main reasons are: 1) problems of nonadherence and lack of enforcement; 2) problems of interpretation and reliance on professional judgement; 3) politicization of education in general and testing in particular.

Problems of nonadherence and lack of enforcement. One reason why existing professional ethical codes and test standards have had little impact on the testing marketplace is that such professional strictures can easily be ignored and are not accompanied by any systematic enforcement mechanism. The APA has developed a mechanism to consider complaints concerning possible violations of the APA ethical code by its members. And on occasion, APA members have been expelled from the organization for violations of ethical standards concerning testing (APA, 1967; for discussion see Haney & Madaus, 1990). However, while an individual violating the standards may be banished from the APA, the APA has no way of assuring that the offending test or related service is removed from the market. Moreover, though the AERA and the NCME have participated in developing the various standards for tests and testing for almost 40 years, neither of them, as far as we have been able to determine, has ever applied any sanction, even among their membership, to enforce the standards and in fact neither has developed mechanisms to do so.

Occasionally there have been calls for more stringent enforcement of testing standards. In 1950, an APA committee on test standards was charged with studying "the feasibility of and methods of implementing a Bureau of Test Standards and a Seal of Approval to apply and enforce test standards, but took no action because of the complexity of the issue" (Singleton, n.d.). In 1975, a federally sponsored project on the Classification of Exceptional Children made a proposal along similar lines:

> Because psychological tests of many kinds saturate our society and because their use can result in the irreversible deprivation of opportunity to many children, especially those already burdened by poverty and prejudice, we recommend that there be established a National Bureau of Standards for Psychological Tests and Testing [responsible to the Secretary of Health, Education, and Welfare]. (Hobbs, 1975, p.237)

Proposals like the 1975 call for federal intervention to curtail "poor tests and testing [which] may be injurious to opportunity as impure food or drugs are injurious to health" (Hobbs, 1975, p.238) met with little response. Despite the apparent gap between standards and practice, there seems to be no professional enthusiasm for concrete proposals to enforce standards on educational and psychological testing.

This is in part because the notions of self-governance and professional judgment on the part of individual professionals are part of their self-image. As Arlene Kaplan Daniels has observed, professional "codes do not simply fulfill the function suggested by the professional ideology. Rather, they are part of the ideology, designed for public relations and justification for the status and prestige which professions assume vis-a-vis more lowly occupations" (Daniels, 1973, p. 49). This ideological, as opposed to functional, role of professional standards is of course not unique to professions associated with testing. In medicine, law and religion, as well as in other professional arenas, professional associations are often extremely slow to discipline members who violate professional norms, not just because individual self-governance is part of the credo of professionalism, but also because publicized disciplining of too many members of one professional group is often seen as casting a bad light on all its members.

Problems of interpretation and reliance on judgement. A further set of problems with the various editions of the APA-AERA-NCME test *Standards* (and the more recent *Code of Fair Testing*) is that they are so general in nature that they are open to various interpretations, depending on the judgement of the person doing the interpreting. For example, the 1985 *Standards* do not clearly spell out the documentation or evidence required to support claims that a test meets a particular standard.

In an analysis of the 1985 *Standards* , Della-Piana (1985) shows how developers can interpret the standards to avoid providing evidence for key inferences about people or institutions made on the basis of their products. He shows how a contradiction between the key validity standards let developers argue that they do not have to provide evidence to support certain inferences. Della-Piana points out that Standard 1.1 reads as follows:

> Evidence of validity should be presented for the major types of
> inferences for which the use of a test is recommended. A
> rationale should be provided to support the particular mix of
> evidence presented for the intended uses. (Primary)

Given its *primary* categorization, Standard 1.1 should, as the *Standards* state, "be met by all tests before their operational use and in all test uses, *unless a sound professional reason is available to show why it is not necessary or technically feasible to do so in a particular case* (p. 2; italics added). The italicized clause in the description of what is meant by a *primary* standard might by itself let a test developer off the *primary* hook. However, when considered with *secondary* Standards 1.9 & 1.23 — (desirable but beyond reasonable expectation) — Della-Piana argues that the developer is given a large loophole for not providing validity evidence for specific inferences intended to be made from test performance. For example, Standard 1.9 prescribes that:

> When a test is proposed as a measure of a construct, evidence should be presented to show that the score is more closely related to that construct when it is measured by different methods than it is to substantially different constructs. *Secondary* (p. 15)

Likewise, Standard 1.23 prescribes that:

> When a test is designed or used to classify people into specified alternative treatment groups (such as. . . educational programs). . . evidence of the test's differential prediction for this purpose should be provided. *Secondary* (p. 18)

Thus two important types of inferences, one dealing with construct validity and the other with placement in treatment groups, fall under the *secondary* categorization. According to Della-Piana this contradiction between a *primary* and a *secondary* standard give a test developer wide latitude to argue that certain inferences made from their instruments need not be backed up by validity evidence. Whether one agrees with Della-Piana's analysis or not, the important point is that the 1985 *Standards* will be interpreted and used by developers and users in ways that are most advantageous to their particular position.

Messick (1989) in his chapter on validity in the revised version of *Educational Measurement* (Linn, 1989) makes a similar point about the unclarity of the 1985 *Standards*:

> The comments accompanying the validity standard leave the door open for an interpretation that there exist circumstances under which only one kind of validity evidence — be it content-related, for instance, or criterion-related — may not only be feasible but also adequate for a particular applied purpose. This selective reliance on one kind of validity

evidence, when it occurs, is tantamount to reliance on one kind of validity as the whole of validity, regardless of how discredited such overgeneralization may have become and of how much acceptance is voiced of validity as a unitary concept. (p. 166)

The flip side of the *Standards* ' vagueness is the emphasis they place on the role of professional judgment in interpreting the individual standards. The 1985 Standards state that the document "is intended to offer guidance for such judgments."(p. 2.) It goes on to state that the purpose of publishing the *Standards* was to:

> Provide criteria for the evaluation of tests, testing practices, and the effects of test use. Although the evaluation of the appropriateness of a test or application should depend heavily on professional judgment, the *Standards* can provide a frame of reference to assure that relevant issues are addressed. The *Standards* does not attempt to assign precise responsibility for the satisfaction of individual standards. To do so would be difficult, especially since much more work in testing is done by contractual arrangement. However, all professional test developers, sponsors, publishers, and users should make reasonable efforts to observe the *Standards* and to encourage others to do so. (p.2)

Further, the *Standards* state that "evaluating acceptability involves the following: professional judgment that is based on a knowledge of behavioral science, psychometrics, and the professional field to which the tests apply. . . (p.2). Finally, the 1985 *Standards* recognize that "in legal proceedings and elsewhere, professional judgment based on the accepted corpus of knowledge always plays an essential role in determining the relevance of particular standards in particular situations"(p.2).

This emphasis on "professional judgement" fits well with the ideology of professionalism. It reinforces the perception that the various test standards and ethical and fairness codes sponsored by the APA, the AERA and the NCME have served not so much to alter actual practices of testing and test use as to bolster the image of these groups as professional organizations. However, as Messick (1988, p. 165) aptly points out, "In the absence of enforcement mechanisms, where is the protection against unsound professional judgment? And how could one tell the difference, if not on the basis of the validity principles and testing standards themselves?"

Politicization of Testing. A third and more general reason for the lack of impact of the test *Standards* on the testing marketplace is simply the increasing political prominence of both education and educational testing. As we showed in chapter 3, the prominence of testing in the educational field nationally has been increasing steadily over the last three decades or so; and as we showed in chapter 5, this growth is clearly associated with growing national concern for education, as evidenced in legislation at both federal and state levels. As the political prominence of education has risen (with most U.S. Presidents and presidential aspirants ever since Lyndon Johnson aspiring to be "education" presidents), it is not surprising that the politics seems increasingly embroiled in matters of testing, both educational and employment. Thus it is worth pointing out that the main justification set out by defenders of the U.S. Department of Education's wall chart series (and its use of college admission test scores has been in essence a political justification.

> We believe that the publication of the wall chart, with its acknowledged flaws, has helped validate state-by-state comparisons as a means of holding state and local school systems accountable for education. In fact of all the lessons learned from the wall chart, the most important has been establishing this validity. (Ginsburg, Noell & Plisko, 1988, p. 1)

Though these authors, all from the U.S. Department of Education, use the word validity in defending the wall chart's utility, they are using it in a *very* different sense than we do in discussing the measurement validity of tests and assessments. In essence, it seems to us, what they are really claiming is that the wall chart episode helped to establish the political viability of state comparisons of test data. Doubtless, the wall chart comparisons of state average college admission test scores did help to pave the way for acceptance of such comparisons via the Trial State Assessment of the National Assessment of Educational Progress; but our point here is simply that the obvious violation of the test *Standards* by the U.S. Department of Education has been rationalized not on the basis of measurement validity but primarily on the basis of political "validity."

Litigation

The main mechanism via which the test *Standards* have been applied to particular uses of tests has been litigation. Indeed, the test *Standards* have regularly been cited in both due process and equal protection court cases for more than two decades. However, there are reasons, in our view, why that litigation is not likely to be a reasonable strategy for mending the fractured marketplace for testing.

First, as discussed in chapter 7 above, given the manner in which federal court cases concerning testing have evolved in the recent past and the way in which test contractors have responded, surely it will become increasingly difficult for plaintiffs to succeed in challenging testing practices. As we have recounted, there is more and more precedent for the courts to accept various content validity studies to establish both the job-relatedness of employment tests and the instructional and curriculum validity of educational tests. Aware of this evolution in judicial reasoning, test contractors now promise legally defensible tests, but may do so, as we have argued, by focusing on content-related validity studies, without ever examining directly what should be the key validity issue, namely the goodness of decisions, inferences or classifications drawn from test scores (Madaus, 1990; Haney, Madaus & Kreitzer, 1987).

A second reason for skepticism about testing litigation as a viable policy instrument is that litigation is time-consuming and expensive. Court cases concerning both employment and educational testing have been known to drag on for years and to cost hundreds of thousands of dollars. One such federal court case, in which one of us has been directly involved (and which will be discussed further below), was initiated in 1979, and as of 1992 is *still* pending trial.

The third reason for rejecting litigation as an attractive policy alternative for improving testing is that litigation and resulting court decisions usually seem to represent extremely blunt policy instruments. The main vehicle via which both educational and employment cases have reached the federal courts is claims of discrimination against classes protected under Title VII, as recounted in chapter 7. But if a test were to be totally lacking in validity and reliability, and to represent merely the random assignment of numbers to individuals, there could be no claims of discrimination under Title VII because there would never be any statistically significant disparate impact on identifiable classes of individuals.

Moreover, when testing practices are subjected to judicial scrutiny and court opinion is rendered, one party wins and the other loses, and court opinions often have had the effect of either approving or disapproving a range of uses of testing without differentiating the reasonable from the unreasonable uses. In the *Larry P.* IQ testing case in California, for example, when the court outlawed the used of standardized intelligence tests for placement of minority students in classes for the "educably mentally retarded," it quite effectively banned the use of such tests by school psychologists who might have used the results reasonably and responsibly (Haney, 1985).   Similarly, the wave of employment testing discrimination cases in the 1970s had, in the view of many observers, a chilling effect on all employment testing practices, good and bad alike (see for example Wigdor's 1982 account).

In sum, litigation arguably has been one of the few avenues available in the past by which advocates have been able to limit the use of educational and employment tests in curtailing educational and employment opportunities of classes protected under Title VII. But the courts have clearly been reluctant to intervene in testing cases when testing practices were interpreted to be matters of professional practice. Moreover, if test validity is viewed ultimately as a matter of scientific inference, the courts surely represent a poor forum for deciding matters of science. But whatever the pros and cons of court decisions on testing in the past, recent Supreme Court decisions regarding heightened standards for proving illegal discrimination clearly suggest that litigation will have less influence on testing practice in the future than it has in the last several decades.

Education of Test Users

A fourth possible strategy for improving testing practice is better education of test users concerning the nature and limitations of testing.   This strategy would inform would-be users of results as to the nature and limitations of standardized test results. Studies have shown that some likely users, such as teachers, are not very knowledgeable about some of the technology of testing, with misinterpretations of grade-equivalent scores and even percentile scores quite common. This has led to suggestions that users of test results ought to be better educated about testing, and a variety of organizations, ranging from NCME and the NEA to the National Parent Teacher Association and various government agencies, have published numerous guides to testing for teachers, parents and the public (see for example, Haney, 1979, for a review of some two dozen such guides).

While we are not opposed to educating users on the topic of testing, this policy alternative seems of limited potential for several reasons. First, so many different people, in many different occupational roles, are users of test results that it is hard to conceive how such a goal might be pursued in practice. Second, freedom-of-information laws are making virtually all citizens actual or potential users of test results. When a high school student takes a college admission test, for instance, he or she receives notification of his or her score and uses that knowledge, perhaps to make a decision about where to apply for college. Similarly, a citizen who reads of his or her school system's average on a statewide test may in a real sense be a user of test results. Also, an employer who requires prospective employees to take an employment screening test is surely a user of the results.

In short, it seems to us that testing has become so pervasive that virtually all members of society are actual or potential test users in the sense that they are provided with data on test results and make inferences from those data. Thus while better education of people on the nature, value and limits of standardized tests would surely be useful, the number and range of test users in modern America is so great that this strategy does not have a very sharply focused target or great policy leverage. If there is a specific group upon which the education strategy might most advantageously be focused, it would seem to be policy-makers in both the education and employment sectors, who often influence testing practices and policies. This is an issue to which we return below.

A third reason for reservations about educating users about testing is that though this seems an attractive goal in the abstract, what is unclear is exactly *how* potential users ought to be educated. For example, a review of a variety of general educational materials on testing by one of the authors some years ago concluded:

> Several stripes of observers are concerned with getting more information on testing into the hands of parents and the public. Their motivations for doing so, however, are markedly different. The do-it-yourself test authors would put the tools of "scientific" psychology into the public's hands — though

according to prevailing standards of psychology their works seem more like astrology or scientism than real science. The mini-textbook authors would make the public into mini-experts on educational testing, apparently in the belief that since testing is an important and valuable activity, people should know more about it. The consumer advocates, on the other hand, believe that parents and the public should know more about standardized testing not simply for the sake of their own enlightenment, but so that they can judge for themselves the quality of standardized testing programs, and maybe even take action to reduce wasteful testing in the schools. (Haney, 1979, p. 22)

Finally, one clear limitation of this strategy for improving test use is that some of the most prominent misuses of test results in the recent past surely have not come about because of lack of knowledge. The wall chart and Prop 48 incidents, for example, did not happen simply because the U.S. Secretary of Education and college presidents (who promulgated Prop 48 through the NCAA) did not know better. They knew that the college admission test results they were using were not intended or validated for the functions to which they were put. As we have argued, they seem to have done what they did simply out of a sense of a greater good, and a feeling that college admissions test scores were the only powerful levers available for promoting that good. Thus it seems clear that informing them more fully on the limits and validation of test results would not have prevented their actions.

Government Regulation

When markets go awry, whether they deal in stocks and bonds or in corn and barley, a common recourse is to seek some kind of government intervention or direct regulation. Thus we now have a range of federal and state regulatory agencies overseeing commerce ranging from foods and drugs (the Food and Drug Administration) to interstate transport (the Interstate Commerce Commission). Indeed, in chapter 7 we have noted the apparent anomaly that while our society requires product warning labels on things so relatively unimportant as personal deodorants and food coloring, no warning labels are federally required on test instruments that may determine whether someone gains employment or is classified as mentally retarded.

Thus it is not surprising that government regulation of testing has been called for in the past, perhaps most notably by the federal Project on the Classification of Exceptional Children mentioned earlier (Hobbs, 1975). Though the National Test Bureau proposed by this Project was never created, government mandates have impinged on testing in a variety of ways. As we have previously shown, federal regulations ranging from requirements for education of special populations to evaluations of federally funded programs have had a clear impact on the nature and extent of testing in the United States over the last two decades. Also, as we have shown, testing in the U.S. military has had a long and pervasive influence on civilian testing in both the employment and education sectors. But perhaps the clearest examples of direct government regulation of testing have been the EEOC's Equal Employment Opportunity Guidelines and New York State's Standardized Testing Law of 1979. Since we have previously described the EEOC's Guidelines (now the *Uniform Guidelines*) and the evolution of resulting court cases concerning employment testing, here we will simply recap some of the basic facts concerning the New York law and apparent implications of this instance of government regulation of tests.

During the 1970s a variety of so-called "truth-in-testing" legislative proposals were filed in several states and in the U.S. Congress. Though specific proposals varied, all were backed by advocates of testing reform and generally proposed that 1) individuals taking various admissions examinations have access, not just to the resulting test scores, but also to corrected test questions; 2) test sponsors file information on test development, validity and cost with specified government agencies; and 3) test publishers give individual test takers information on the nature and intended uses of test results prior to testing and guarantee right of privacy concerning individuals' results.[14]

Legislative proposals along these lines were vigorously opposed by test publishers and professional organizations such as NCME, and in most cases were not enacted. The only state to pass a "truth-in-testing" law was New York in 1979. Test publishers' reactions to the New York law varied markedly. Most complied with its provisions, but one withdrew some of its tests from the market in New York, and one (the Association of American Medical Colleges or AAMC, sponsor of the Medical College Admissions Test) immediately sued the

---

[14] This account of "truth-in-testing" proposals and debates about them is necessarily very brief. For more detail see Brown & McClung, 1980, Strenio, 1980, New York State, 1980, U.S. Congress, 1980a &1980b, and Haney 1984, 1990, 1992.

state, charging that the disclosure provision of the law constituted an illegal expropriation of copyrighted material and that disclosure of test items would prevent their re-use.[15] A federal court in New York quickly gave the AAMC a waiver from the requirements of the law, pending outcome of the lawsuit. The ETS and College Board initially not only complied with the New York law, but also began voluntary disclosure nationwide of the corrected test questions for some administrations of some of their tests (such as the PSAT and the SAT). After the law's passage, ETS, the College Board and other publishers also entered into discussions with New York legislators, which led to amendments to the New York law. These had the effect, among other things, of making compliance easier for low-volume testing programs. The AAMC lawsuit was initially decided in favor of the AAMC in 1990, but that summary judgement was overturned on appeal in 1991. Meanwhile, ETS, the College Board, the Graduate Management Admissions Council (GMAC) and the Graduate Records Examination Board had filed a lawsuit in 1989 similar to the AAMC suit (charging that the New York law violated federal copyright law and that disclosure of test items prevented re-use). In early 1992 the GMAC filed an addendum requesting summary judgement exemption in order to offer more administrations of the GMAT in New York. But after an analysis of previously disclosed items from the SAT, the GRE and the GMAT showed that test developers were already doing what they had said could not be done — that is, re-using previously disclosed items — the court declined to give the GMAC the same waiver that it had granted to the AAMC eleven years earlier.

Since the New York testing law represents a specific example of legislative attempts to regulate the testing industry, several things are worth noting about it. First of all, the case clearly suggests that legislation to regulate testing can lead to very, very lengthy litigation -- the AAMC case is now more than 10 years old and remains unsettled. Second, the New York law applied only to admissions tests and passed primarily because of the lobbying efforts of well-organized student advocacy groups. It did not apply to other sorts of tests, which

---

[15] The lawsuit brought by the Association of American Medical Colleges against the state of New York in 1979 remains as of the summer of 1992 unsettled. Since we are discussing a form of disclosure here we would be remiss if we failed to note that one of the authors (Haney) has been retained by the State of New York as an expert witness in both the AAMC and ETS-College Board-GRE Board-GMAC cases.

on rational and public policy grounds it might well have, but instead focused on tests of particular interest to politically active students. Third, some of the provisions of the law did not appear to work out in practice as some its advocates had predicted. For example, some of the backers of the law had argued that the disclosure provisions would make access to test preparation materials more equitable, rather than limiting access to students who could afford expensive test preparation and coaching courses. Nevertheless, follow-up studies with regard to at least one test showed that the students who did avail themselves of the disclosure provisions of the law tended to be the more affluent and well-to-do. Fourth, the New York law and similar legislative proposals in the 1970s clearly did prompt some test publishers to adopt some provisions of the New York law (such as disclosure of test questions after administration, for at least some test administrations). Fifth, though publishers initially presented a highly unified front in opposing the New York law, once it was enacted they reacted in markedly different ways: with compliance in some cases, with lawsuits against the state in other instances, and with withdrawal of their tests from New York in another. Indeed, the varied reactions of publishers to the New York law might themselves be viewed as a sign of the fractured nature of the testing marketplace.

A final important lesson from the New York case is that some of the indirect outcomes of government regulation of testing may be of wider consequence than the direct outcomes. For example, though the ETS and the College Board still have a lawsuit pending against New York with regard to the "truth-in-testing" law, some of the requirements of the law have led to nationwide disclosure of some test forms and to revisions in the way the SAT is scaled.

The New York law, the history of the EEOC guidelines and experience with government regulation of other business activities thus suggest considerable caution about the regulatory strategy for mending the fractured testing marketplace. As a practical matter, government regulation of testing strikes us as somewhat unlikely, given that prevailing political opinion over the last decade, at least in Washington, has been to reduce rather than to enlarge the sphere of government regulation of business activities. Finally, turning to government regulation to mend the testing marketplace would be a somewhat perverse development since, at least in our view, some of the most obvious abuse of testing over the last several decades (e.g. in the wall chart episode and in the use of isolated test results to determine whether students receive their high school diplomas) has been brought about by government officials and policies.

An Independent Auditing Agency

Given the problems apparent with policy alternatives previously discussed, we are intrigued with the idea of an independent auditing agency for testing (Madaus, 1985). A variety of possible models are available for such an independent auditing or oversight agency, for example:

- Consumers Union
- Underwriters Laboratories
- Public advocacy agencies, such as the Center for Auto Safety or the Center for Science and the Public Interest.

Indeed, we are sufficiently interested in these possibilities that, as part of a project separate from the preparation of this volume, we are examining the feasibility of such agencies. We have not completed this examination as of this writing and so cannot comment here on its results. But we can already describe what we envision as some of the main limitations of this approach and note some potential applications of the idea.

Any independent auditing agency regarding testing would surely find it almost impossible to address the full range of problems in the testing marketplace identified in this volume. For example, such an agency could hardly exert much influence on many of the small-scale publishers who market low-volume tests for limited markets. Also, it seems extremely unlikely that such an agency could deal with some of the unintended uses of test results (such as realtors' use of local schools' SAT score averages as indices of school quality; though a prestigious independent agency might have some power to curb prominent misuses of tests such as the U.S. Department of Education's wall charts).

Second, it is unclear what the audience might be for such an agency. Agencies such as the Consumers Union, the Center for Auto Safety and even the Underwriters Laboratories (UL) have fairly well-defined audiences. In the case of Consumers Union it is members who subscribe to the *Consumer Reports* and who may purchase the products reviewed. "Consumers" of tests are not nearly so well-defined; (colleges, for example, may be the actors who require college admission tests and presumably use their results, but applicants are the ones who actually pay the fees for the tests). Thus, the Consumers Union model appears to be of limited relevance for many kinds of testing.

The activities of the Center for Auto Safety and the Center for Science and the Public Interest are directed at quite different audiences: legislators and governmental regulatory agencies such as the FDA and the Department of Transportation, for instance with regard to the setting of government standards for food additives or auto emission standards. Since we have substantial reservations about government regulation of testing, these agencies have little possible relevance for a possible auditing or advocacy agency regarding testing.

Nevertheless, it seems that independent auditing or review of testing programs and test use have considerable potential. Here we can cite two examples. The first concerns a controversy over the GATB recounted in chapter 3. After a dispute arose between the U.S. Departments of Labor and Justice over the GATB testing program, a special review of the issues in dispute was undertaken by the National Research Council of the National Academy of Sciences (which resulted in the 1989 Hartigan & Wigdor report). This review produced "useful operational and technical recommendations" that led to major changes in the GATB testing program — and probably prevented what could have developed into a messy and surely embarrassing legal dispute between two departments of the executive branch of the federal government.

The second example concerns the new national system of tests and assessments proposed in the NCEST report. This document proposed that the new tests be reviewed, for example, for "technical merit (validity, reliability, fairness)" by a reconfigured National Education Goals Panel and a new body called the National Education Standards and Assessments Council, or NESAC. While the NCEST report suggests that "the Goals Panel and NESAC would be allowed substantial latitude in their operation and would be as independent of the U.S. Congress, the U.S. Department of Education and other federal agencies as permissible by law" (NCEST, 1992, p. 36), the members of the Goals Panel would almost all be politicians (including eight Governors and four members of Congress), and the Goals Panel itself would appoint members of NESAC. In our view this is hardly the sort of truly independent monitoring body that could seriously evaluate of the validity, reliability and fairness of national tests. Much more akin to what we have in mind is what is proposed in the pending House bill described earlier, namely independent evaluation of new assessments in terms of clearly identified standards regarding validity and reliability (and alignment of assessments with content standards) through the auspices of the National Academy of Sciences.

In sum, we are intrigued with the possibility of some kind of independent auditing agency with regard to testing, and are studying it further. We are aware of several major limitations of this approach to mending the fractured marketplace for testing; but already we have seen instances (such as with regard to the GATB) and proposals (such as those of the House Education and Labor Committee) that suggest to us the promise of serious, independent scrutiny of socially important testing programs.

Development of New Kinds of Tests and Assessment Strategies

One of the most venerable strategies for solving problems associated with current standardized tests current tests is to develop new or better kinds of tests or assessment strategies. As we have argued elsewhere (Haney & Madaus, 1989), the build-a-better mousetrap mentality appears to be alive and well in testing. Numerous individuals and agencies over the last several decades have sought to promote new and better tests or alternatives to tests. In the 1970s, criterion-referenced tests were widely touted as useful alternatives to norm-referenced tests (see "The criterion referenced testing cause" in Haney, 1984, pp. 621-622). The relatively new field of cognitive sciences and the rapidly developing field of computer technology have also been widely cited as likely sources for the development of new and better tests (Tyler & White, 1979; Wigdor & Garner, 1982, McBride, 1985; Madaus 1986). However, as we saw in chapter 7, whatever the potential of computer technology for improving testing, it has also promoted some highly questionable developments (for example, in the form of CBTI).

Now it appears that performance assessment is widely viewed as a remedy to past ills of standardized tests. Yet it is clear to us that some of the approaches to assessment being touted recently are not altogether new (Haney & Madaus, 1989). More generally, we are skeptical that new technologies of testing and assessment will solve the educational and employment problems associated with standardized testing. For it must be remembered that such problems are not always products of the testing technology itself, but often of the educational and broader social context in which this technology is used. Thus with regard to both current standardized tests and possible new or alternative assessment techniques, *what forms* of assessment are used usually makes far less difference than *how* they are used.

CONCLUSION

No one of the policy alternatives just discussed seems to us to provide easy solutions to the problems posed by the increasingly fractured testing marketplace. Professional standards and peer review of test materials have clearly had limited impact on test use and practice in the past. Legislation and litigation, for all their problems, have been useful both in preventing some abuses of testing and in promoting testing as an alternative to less reasonable forms of policy-making, such as nepotism.

Unfortunately, litigation is extremely costly and slow, and — given the recent evolution in court decisions — seems less likely to be successful in the future. Greater education of would-be users of tests surely would be helpful, but there are now so many users of test results, for so many different purposes, that it is uncertain how this option would best be pursued. Government regulation of some forms of testing doubtless has been helpful in preventing the use of testing to undermine the rights of some classes of citizens. But given apparent problems and unanticipated consequences associated with past governmental attempts to regulate testing, and the current dearth of political enthusiasm for government regulation of any kind, this does not seem a promising policy option.

Greater reliance on market forces seems a strategy unlikely to help mend the fractured marketplace, if for no other reason than because the market for tests *is* so fractured. There are very few instances in which testing practices represent a simple exchange between buyer and seller or producer and consumer. Some kind of independent auditing agency may be attractive, but would be unlikely to solve the range of problems now apparent in the testing marketplace. Though many people are working to develop new or alternative kinds of assessment for use in both the education and employment sectors, strictly technological solutions seem to us unlikely to solve the problems of the testing marketplace.

In sum, our review of various policy options that might be applied to help mend the fractured marketplace for testing suggests that none of these strategies is likely to have a major impact on the full range of the testing market. Given our review of the social forces behind the testing marketplace, this conclusion should not be surprising, for some of these forces represent broad historical currents rather than short-term or explicit policies.

Standardized multiple-choice tests surely represent one of the most notable accomplishments of applied psychology in the 20th century. If numerous social problems are now associated with this technology, this is due not so much to the technology as to the social reality that more weight is now being placed on this technology than any human contrivance can bear. Thus it seem to us that if there is a general strategy useful in helping to solve the problems of the fractured marketplace for testing, it is to reduce the weight placed on this technology. In the employment sector, for example, it seems clear that in occupational selection and referral, reliance should be placed not just on employment tests, but on alternative paths toward employment. To reduce the over-weighting of employment tests we thus need to rely not just on alternative modes of assessment, but also on a balancing of competing social aims (National Commission on Testing and Public Policy, 1990; Hartigan & Wigdor, 1989).

Similarly, in the realm of education, the general strategy that seems to us most promising is to disentangle the myriad functions (e.g. student evaluation, instructional guidance, and school and teacher evaluation) that the same standardized testing program is often expected to perform. Instead we need to use different mixes of assessment strategies and technologies as appropriate to different functions. For instance, our assessments of individual student learning will likely be more valid and useful if we avoid using the results of the same assessments as indices of school or teacher quality.

In short, in the market for testing, the medium of standardized multiple-choice tests has too often become the message because different media have not also been employed. To the extent that we regain more balanced approaches to assessment, reflecting a wider range of the modes by which we ought to judge student learning, employee competence, and educational quality, to that extent will the distortions now associated with standardized tests be reduced. Or, to put our general conclusion more succinctly, the more we can de-emphasize the particular medium of standardized testing, the more we will be able to perceive the valid messages that this medium can convey to us.

REFERENCES

Alderman, D. L., & Powers, D. E. (1979). *The effects of special preparation on SAT-Verbal scores* (ETS Research Report RR-79-1). Princeton, NJ: Educational Testing Service.

American Educational Research Association, American Psychological Association, & National Council on Measurement in Education. (1985). *Standards for educational and psychological testing.* Washington, DC: American Psychological Association.

American Management Association. (1986). *Hiring costs and strategies: The AMA report.* New York: Author.

American Management Association. (1990). *The AMA 1990 survey on workplace testing.* New York: Author.

American Psychological Association. (1953). *Ethical standards of psychologists.* Washington, DC: Author.

American Psychological Association. (1959). Ethical standards of psychologists. *American Psychologist, 14,* 279-282.

American Psychological Association. (1967). *Casebook on ethical standards of psychologists.* Washington, DC: Author.

American Psychological Association. (1977). *Ethical standards of psychologists.* Washington, DC: Author.

American Psychological Association, American Educational Research Association, & National Council on Measurement in Education. (1966). *Standards for educational and psychological tests.* Washington, DC: American Psychological Association.

American Psychological Association Committee on Professional Standards Committee on Psychological Tests and Assessment. (1986). *Guidelines for computer-based tests and interpretations.* Washington, DC: American Psychological Association.

American Psychological Association. (1981). Ethical principles of psychologists. *American Psychologist, 36,* 633-638.

American Psychological Association. (1984). Minutes of an Annual Test Publishers' Meeting of the American Psychological Association. *Annual Meeting of the APA*. Washington, DC: Author.

Anastasi, A. (1988). *Psychological testing*. (6th ed.). New York: MacMillan.

Angoff, W. H. (1971). *The College Board admissions testing program: A technical report on research and development activities relating to the Scholastic Aptitude Test and Achievement Tests*. New York: College Entrance Examination Board.

Anonymous (1984, Spring). NCS acquired unit of Westinghouse. *Mergers and Acquisitions*, p. R53.

Anrig, G. R., Daly, N. F., Futrell, M. H., Robinson, S. P., Rubin, L. J., & Weiss, J. G. (1987). *What is the appropriate role of testing in the teaching profession?* Washington, DC: National Education Association.

August, R. L. (1992). Yobiko: Prep schools for college entrance in Japan. In R. Leestma, & H. J. Walberg (Eds.), *Japanese educational productivity*. Ann Arbor: Center for Japanese Studies, University of Michigan.

Bailey, S. K., & Mosher, E. (1968). *ESEA: The office of education administers a law*. Syracuse, New York: Syracuse University Press.

Baker, F. (1971). Automation of test scoring, reporting and analysis. In R. Thorndike (Ed.), *Educational measurement*. (2nd ed.) (pp. 202-234). Washington, DC: American Council on Education.

Baker, F. (1989). Computer technology in test construction and processing. In R. Linn (Ed.), *Educational measurement*. (3rd ed.) (pp. 409-428). New York: Macmillan.

Bales, J. (1988a, August). Polygraph Screening Banned in Senate Bill. *APA Monitor*, p. 10.

Bales, J. (1988b, August). Integrity Tests: Honest Results? *APA Monitor*, pp. 1,4.

Bangert-Drowns, R. L., Kulik, C. C., Kulik, J. A., & Morgan, M. (1991). The instructional effect of feedback in test-like events. *Review of Educational Research, 61*(2), 213-238.

Bauer, E. A. (1992). NATD survey of testing practices and issues. *Educational Measurement: Issues and Practice, 11*(1), 10-14.

Becker, B. J. (1990). Coaching for the Scholastic Aptitude Test: Further synthesis and appraisal. *Review of Educational Research, 60*(3), 373-417.

Block, N., & Dworkin, G. (Eds.). (1976). *The IQ controversy*. New York: Pantheon.

Bloom, B. S. (1964). *Stability and change in human characteristics*. New York: Wiley.

Blurst, R. S., & Kohr, R. L. (1984). *Pennsylvania school district testing programs.* Harrisburg, PA: Pennsylvania State Department of Education. (ERIC No. ED 269 409)

Bond, L. (1989). The effects of special preparation on measures of scholastic ability. In R. Linn (Ed.), *Educational measurement, 3rd Ed.* (pp. 429-444). New York: MacMillan.

Boorstin, D. J. (1973). *The Americans: The democratic experience.* New York: Random House.

Boulding, K. E. (1970). *Beyond economics: Essays on society, religion, and ethics.* Ann Arbor, MI: The University of Michigan Press.

Bowker Annual. See R. R. Bowker Co.

Bowler, R., F. (1983). Payment by results: A study in achievement and accountability. *Dissertation Abstracts International, 44.* (University Microfilms No. 83-14852)

Boyer, E. (1983). *High school: A report on secondary education in America.* New York: Harper & Row.

Bureau of Labor Statistics (1989). Statistical tables. *Monthly Labor Review, June.*

Bureau of National Affairs. (1988). *Preemployment testing in personnel management.* Washington, DC: Author.

Buros, O. K. (Ed.). (1938). *The nineteen thirty eight mental measurements yearbook.* Highland Park, NJ: Gryphon Press.

Buros, O. K. (Ed.). (1940). *The nineteen forty mental measurements yearbook.* Highland Park, NJ: Gryphon Press.

Buros, O. K. (Ed.). (1949). *The third mental measurements yearbook.* Highland Park, NJ: Gryphon Press.

Buros, O. K. (Ed.). (1953). *The fourth mental measurements yearbook.* Highland Park, NJ: Gryphon Press.

Buros, O. K. (Ed.). (1959). *The fifth mental measurements yearbook.* Highland Park, NJ: Gryphon Press.

Buros, O. K. (Ed.). (1961). *Tests in print: A comprehensive bibliography of tests for use in education, psychology, and industry.* Highland Park, NJ: Gryphon Press.

Buros, O. K. (Ed.). (1965). *The sixth mental measurements yearbook.* Highland Park, NJ: Gryphon Press.

Buros, O. K. (1974). *Tests in print II.* Highland Park, NJ: Gryphon Press.

Buros, O. K. (Ed.). (1974). *The seventh mental measurements yearbook.* Highland Park, NJ: Gryphon Press.

Buros, O. K. (Ed.). (1978). *The eighth mental measurements yearbook.* Highland Park, NJ: Gryphon Press.

Business Periodical Index. See H. W. Wilson.

Butcher, J. N. (Ed.). (1987). *Computerized psychological assessment: a practitioner's guide.* New York: Basic Books.

Callahan, R. E. (1962). *Education and the cult of efficiency.* Chicago: Chicago University Press.

Camfield, T. M. (1969). Psychologists at war: The history of American psychology and the first world war. *Dissertation Abstracts International, 30.* (University Microfilms No. 70-10766)

Campbell, R. F., Cunningham, L. L., Nystrand, R. O., & Usdan, M. D. (1985). *The organization and control of American schools.* (5th ed.). Columbus, OH: Merrill.

Cannell, J. J. (1987). *Nationally normed elementary achievement testing in America's public schools: How all 50 states are above the national average.* Daniels, WV: Friends for Education.

Cannell, J. J. (1988). Nationally normed elementary achievement testing in America's public schools: How all 50 states are above the national average. *Educational Measurement: Issues and Practice, 7*(2), 5-9.

Cannell, J. J. (1989). *The 'Lake Wobegon' report: How public educators cheat on standardized achievement tests.* Albuquerque, NM: Friends for Education.

Catterall, J. S. (1989). Standards and school dropouts: A national study of tests required for graduation. *American Journal of Education, 98*(1), 1-34.

Celebreeze, A. (1965). *Education Act of 1965: Hearings before the Committee of Education and Labor.* Washington, DC: U.S. Congress House of Representatives.

Chapman, P. D. (1980). Schools as sorters: Lewis M. Terman and the intelligence testing movement, 1890-1930. *Dissertation Abstracts International, 40.* (University Microfilms No. 80-11615)

Cicchetti, P. (1987). *Corporate and industry research reports.* Eastchester, NY: JA Micropublishing, Inc.

Cicchetti, P. (1988). *Corporate and industry research reports.* Eastchester, NY: JA Micropublishing, Inc.

Cicchetti, P. (1989). *Corporate and industry research reports.* Eastchester, NY: JA Micropublishing, Inc.

Clifford, G. J. (1968). *Edward Lee Thorndike: The sane positivist.* Middletown, CT: Wesleyan University Press.

Cole, N. (1982). The implications of coaching for ability testing. In A. K. Wigdor & W. R. Garner (Eds.), *Ability Testing: Uses, consequences and controversies.* Washington, DC: National Academy Press.

Coleman, J. S., Campbell, E. Q., Hobson, C. J., McPartland, J., Mood, A. M., Weinfield, F. D., et al. (1966). *Equality of educational opportunity.* Washington, DC: U.S. Government Printing Office.

College Board Staff. (1988). *Ten SATs*. (3rd ed.). New York: College Board.

Committee on Psychological Tests and Assessment. (1990). *Testing inquiries received by the APA in 1988*. (Unpublished report). Washington, DC: American Psychological Association.

Comptroller General. (1977). *Problems and needed improvements in evaluating Office of Education programs*. Washington, DC: U.S. Government Printing Office.

Conant, J. B. (1961). *Slums and suburbs: A commentary on schools in metropolitan areas*. New York: McGraw-Hill.

Congressional Budget Office. (1986). *Trends in educational achievement*. Washington, DC: Government Printing Office.

Congressional Budget Office. (1987). *Educational achievement: Explanations and implications of recent trends*. Washington, DC: Government Printing Office.

Connell, W. F. (1950). *The educational thought and influence of Mathew Arnold*. London: Rutledge and Kegan Paul.

Conoley, J. C., & Kramer, J. J. (Eds.) (1989). *The tenth mental measurements yearbook*. Lincoln, NE: The Buros Institute of Mental Measurements, University of Nebraska-Lincoln.

Corbett, H. D., & Wilson, B. L. (1991). *Testing, reform and rebellion*. Norwood, NJ: Ablex.

Cooley, W. W., & Bernauer, J. A. (1991). School comparisons in statewide testing programs. In R. E. Stake (Ed.), *Advances in program evaluation*. (pp. 159-170). Greenwich, CN: JAI Press.

Cowden, P. (1981). *Private influences in the public governance of education: The case of private testing firms in American schools*. Cambridge, MA: Huron Institute.

Cremin, L. (1964). *The transformation of the school*. New York: Vintage.

Cronbach, L. J. (1975). Five decades of public controversy over mental testing. *American Psychologist, 30*, 1-14.

Cronbach, L. J. (1984). *Essentials of psychological testing*. (4th ed.). New York: Harper & Row.

Cronbach, L. J., & Gleser, G. C. (1965). *Psychological tests and personnel decisions*. Urbana, IL: University of Illinois Press.

Crouse, J., & Trusheim, D. (1988). *The case against the SAT*. Chicago: University of Chicago Press.

CTB/McGraw Hill. (1988). *The testing company and more*. Monterey, CA: Author.

Curran, R. G. (1988). The effectiveness of computerized coaching for the PSAT and the SAT. *Dissertation Abstracts International, 49*. (University Microfilms No. 88-11615)

Dailey, J. T. (1953). Review of the Army general classification test, first civilian edition. In O. K. Buros (Ed.), *The fourth mental measurements yearbook*. Highland Park, NJ: Gryphon Press.

Daniels, A. K. (1973). How free should professionals be? In E. Freidson (Ed.), *The professions and their prospects*. (pp. 39-57). Beverly Hills, CA: Sage.

Davis, A. (1991). Upping the stakes: Using gain scores to judge local program effectiveness in Chapter 1. *Educational Evaluation and Policy Analysis, 13*(4), 380-388.

Dear, R. E. (1958). *The effect of a program of intensive coaching on SAT scores*. Princeton, NJ: Educational Testing Service.

DelValle, C. (1991, December 16). Are multiple-choice tests about to flunk out? *Business Week*, p. 110.

DerSimonian, R., & Laird, N. M. (1983). Evaluating the effect of coaching on SAT scores: A meta-analysis. *Harvard Educational Review, 53*(No.1), 1-15.

Donlon, T. (Ed.). (1984). *The College Board technical handbook for the Scholastic Aptitude Test and Achievement Tests*. New York: College Entrance Examination Board.

Drahozal, E. C., & Frisbie, D. A. (1988). Riverside comments on the Friends for Education report. *Educational Measurement: Issues and Practice, 7*, 12-16.

Dun's Marketing Services Inc. (1989). *Duns million dollar directory*. Parsippany, NJ: Author.

Dun's Marketing Services Inc. (1991). *Duns million dollar disc*. Parsippany, NJ: Author.

Dyer, H. S. (1953). Does Coaching Help? *College Board Review, 19*, 331-335.

Eckstein, M. A., & Noah, H. J. (1989). Forms and functions of secondary-school leaving examinations. *Comparative Education Review, 33*(3), 295-316.

Education Index. See H. W. Wilson.

Educational Testing Service. (1987). *Educational Testing Service annual report*. Princeton, NJ: Author.

Educational Testing Service. (1987). *ETS standards for quality and fairness*. Princeton, NJ: Author.

Educational Testing Service. (1992, March 20). *ETS announces nationwide computerized test network (press release)*. (Available from Educational Testing Service Information Services).

Eitelberg, M. J., Laurence, J. H., Waters, B. K., & Perelman, L. S. (1984). *Screening for service: Aptitude and education criteria for military entry*. Office of Manpower, Installations and Logistics of the US Department of Defense.

EPIE Institute. (1984). *TESS the educational software selector.* (1984 ed.). New York: Teachers College Press.

EPIE Institute. (1987). *TESS the educational software selector.* (1986-87 ed.). New York: Teachers College Press.

Executive Office of the President, Office of Management and Budget. (1987). *Standard industrial classification manual.* Springfield, VA: National Technical Information Services.

Eyde, L. D., & Kowal, D. M. (1985). Psychological decision support software for the public: Pros, cons, and guidelines. *Computers in Human Behavior, 1,* 321-336.

Eyde, L. D., & Kowal, D. M. (1987). Computerised test information services: Ethical and professional concerns regarding U.S. producers and users. *Applied Psychology: An International Review, 36*(3-4), 401-417.

Eyde, L. D., Kowal, D. M., & Fishburne, F. J. (1987). Clinical implications of validity research on computer-based test interpretations of the MMPI. In A. D. Mangelsdorff (Ed.), *Practical Test User Problems Facing Psychologists in Private Practice* New York: American Psychological Association.

Farrell, C. S. (1986, January 22). NCAA votes to bar varsity competition by freshmen with low test scores. *Chronicle of Higher Education, 31*(19), 1,30.

Federal Trade Commission-Boston Regional Office. (1978a). *The effects of coaching on standardized admission examinations.* Boston: Author.

Federal Trade Commission-Boston Regional Office. (1978b). *Staff memorandum of the Boston Regional Office of the FTC: The effects of coaching on standardized admission examinations.* Boston: Author.

Federal Trade Commission-Bureau of Consumer Protection. (1979). *The effects of coaching on standardized admission examinations. Revised statistical analyses of data gathered by the Boston Regional Office of the FTC.* Federal Trade Commission.

Feinberg, S. E. (Ed.). (1989). *The evolving role of statistical assessments as evidence in the courts.* New York: Springer-Verlag.

Fetler, M. E. (1991). Pitfalls of using SAT results to compare schools. *American Educational Research Journal, 28*(2), 481-491.

Finn, C. E. J. (1991). *We must take charge: Our schools and our future.* New York: Free Press.

Fiske, E. (1988, April 10). America's Test Mania. *New York Times,* pp. 16,20.

Fox, S. (1985). *The mirror makers: A history of American advertising and its creators.* New York: Vintage.

Frankel, E. (1960). Effects of growth, practice, and coaching on Scholastic Aptitude Test scores. *Personnel and Guidance Journal, 33,* 713-719.

Fremer, J. (1989). Testing companies, trends, and policy issues: A current view from the testing industry. In B. Gifford (Ed.), *Testing and the allocation of opportunity: Vol. I.* (pp. 61-80). Boston: Kluwer.

Friedman, T., & Williams, E. B. (1982). Current uses of tests for employment. In A. K. Wigdor, & W. R. Garner (Eds.), *Ability testing: Uses, consequences, and controversies: Part II. Documentation section.* Washington, DC: National Academy Press.

Gaffney, R., & Maguire, T. (1971). Use of optically scored answer sheets with young children. *Journal of Educational Measurement, 8*(2), 103-106.

Gale Research. (1989a). *Ward's business directory of U.S. private and public companies. Vol. 1, Over $11.5 million in sales.* Detroit, MI: Author.

Gale Research. (1989b). *Ward's business directory of U.S. private and public companies. Vol. 2, From $.5 to $11.5 million in sales.* Detroit, MI: Author.

Gamel, N. N., Tallmadge, G. K., Wood, C. T., & Brinkley, J. L. (1975). *State ESEA Title I Reports: Review and analysis of past reports and development of a model reporting system and format.* (RMC Report No. UR 194). Mountain View, CA: RMC Research Corporation.

Gay, G. H. (1989). Standardized tests: Irregularities in the administering of tests affect test results. *Dissertation Abstracts International, 51.* (University Microfilms No. 90-20156)

Gay, G. H. (1990). Standardized tests: Irregularities in administering of tests affect test results. *Journal of Instructional Psychology, 17*(2), 93-103.

Gelb, S. A. (1986). Henry H. Goddard and the immigrants, 1910-1917: The studies and their social context. *Journal of the History of the Behavioral Sciences, 22*(1), 324-332.

Gifford, B., & Wing, L. C. (Eds.). (1992). *Test policy in defense: Lessons from the military for education, training and employment.* Boston: Kluwer Academic Publishers.

Gilmore, M. E. (1927). Coaching for intelligence tests. *Journal of Educational and Psychological Measurement, 19,* 319-330.

Ginsburg, A. L., Noell, J., & Plisko, V. W. (1988). Lessons from the wall chart. *Educational Evaluation and Policy Analysis, 10*(1), 1-12.

Glass, G. V. (1978). Standards and criteria. *Journal of Educational Measurement, 15,* 237-261.

Gonzalez, M. (1985). Cheating on standardized tests: What is it? In P. Wolmut, & G. Iverson (Eds.), *National Association of Test Directors 1985 Symposia* (pp. 4-16). Portland, OR: Multnomah ESD.

Gould, S. J. (1981). *The mismeasure of man.* New York: W. W. Norton & Company.

Green, B. F., Jr. (1970). Comments on tailored testing. In W. H. Holtzman (Ed.), *Computer-assisted instruction, testing and guidance.* New York: Harper and Row.

Green, B. F., Jr. (1984). *Computer-based ability testing.* Washington, DC: APA Scientific Affairs Office.

Greenbaum, W., Garet, M. S., & Solomon, E. R. (1977). *Measuring educational progress: A study of the national assessment.* New York: McGraw Hill.

Greene, L. S. (1984). The new NCAA rules of the game: Academic integrity or racism? *Saint Louis Law Journal, 28*(1), 101-151.

Greenfield, P. M. (1984). *Mind and media: The effects of television, video games and computers.* Cambridge, MA: Harvard University Press.

Haas, N. S., Haladyna, T. M., & Nolen, S. B. (1990, April). *Standardized achievement testing: War stories from the trenches.* Paper presented at the Annual Meeting of the National Council on Measurement in Education, Boston, MA.

Haladyna, T. M., Nolen, S. B., & Haas, N. S. (1991). Raising standardized test scores and the origins of test score pollution. *Educational Researcher, 20*(5), 2-7.

Hale, M. (1982). History of employment testing. In A. Wigdor, & W. Garner (Eds.), *Ability testing: Uses, consequences and controversies* (pp. 3-38). Washington, DC: National Academy Press.

Hall, C. (1983, December 6). Psychologist's Computer Use Stirs Debate. *Wall Street Journal,* p. 31.

Hall, E. T. (1977). *Beyond culture.* Garden City: Anchor Books.

Hall, J. L., & Kleine, P. F. (1990, April). *Educator perceptions of achievement test use and abuse: A national survey.* Paper presented at the Annual Meeting of the National Council on Measurement in Education, Boston, MA.

Hall, J. L., & Kleine, P. F. (1992). Educators' perceptions of NRT misuse. *Educational Measurement: Issues and Practice, 11*(2), 18-22.

Halloran, R. (1979, October 14). Recruiting inquiry by army nears end. *New York Times,* p. 37.

Hammer, J. (1989, April 14). Cramscam. *New Republic,* pp. 15-18.

Haney, W. (1977). *The follow through planned variation experiment, Volume 5: The follow through evaluation; A technical history.* U.S. Department of Health Education and Welfare, U.S. Office of Education.

Haney, W. (1979). *A Review of publications on testing for parents and the public.* (National Consortium on Testing Staff Circular No. 5). Cambridge, MA: The Huron Institute.

Haney, W. (1981). Validity, vaudville and values: A short history of social concerns over standardized testing. *American Psychologist, 36*(10), 1021-1034.

Haney, W. (1985). Making testing more educational. *Educational Leadership, 43*(2), 4-13.

Haney, W. (1991). We must take care: Fitting assessments to functions. In V. Perrone (Ed.) *Expanding student assessment.* (pp. 142-163). Alexandria, VA: Association for Supervision and Curriculum Development.

Haney, W., & Madaus, G. (1986). *Effects of standardized testing and the future of the National Assessment of Educational Progress.* Chestnut Hill, MA: Boston College Center for the Study of Testing, Evaluation and Educational Policy.

Haney, W., Madaus, G., & Kreitzer, A. (1987). Charms talismanic: Testing teachers for the improvement of American education. *Review of Research in Education, 14*, 169-238.

Haney, W., & Madaus, G. F.(1990). Evolution of Ethical and Technical standards. In R. K. Hambleton, & J. N. Zaal (Eds.), *Advances in educational and psychological testing* (pp. 395-425). Boston: Kluwer.

Haney, W., & Madaus, G. F. (1992). Cautions on the future of NAEP: Arguments against using NAEP tests and data reporting below the state level. In *Assessing student achievement in the states: Background papers* (pp. 363-408). Stanford, CA: National Academy of Education.

Haney, W. M. (1984). Testing reasoning and reasoning about testing. *Review of Educational Research, 54*(4), 597-654.

Haney, W. M. (1992). *Testimony of Dr. Walter M. Haney before the Subcommittee on Elementary, Secondary and Vocational Education, February 4, 1992.* Boston College Center for the Study of Testing, Evaluation and Educational Policy.

Haney, W. M., & Madaus, G. F. (1989). Searching for alternatives to standardized tests: The whats, whys and whithers. *Phi Delta Kappan, 70*(9), 683-687.

Hardman, M. L., Drew, C. J., Egan, M. W., & Wolf, B. (1993). *Human exceptionality: Society, school and family.* (4th ed.). Boston: Allyn and Bacon.

Harmon, M. E. (1992). *Study of textbook supplied tests.* Chestnut Hill, MA: Center for the Study of Testing, Evaluation and Educational Policy.

Harnischefeger, A., & Wiley, D. E. (1975). *Achievement test score decline: Do we need to worry?* Chicago: CEMREL, Inc.

Hartigan, J., & Widgor, A. K. (Eds.). (1989). *Fairness in employment testing: Validity generalization, minority issues and the general aptitude test battery.* Washington, DC: National Academy Press.

Hastings, J., Runkel, P., Damrin, D., Kane, R., & Larsen, G. (1960). *The use of test results.* Urbana, IL: Bureau of Educational Research, University of Illinois.

Hazlett, J. A. (1974). A history of the National Assessment of Educational Progress, 1963-1973; A look at some conflicting ideas and issues in contemporary American education. *Dissertation Abstracts International, 35.* (University Microfilms No. 75-06135)

Hernstein, R. J. (1990). On responsible scholarship: A rejoinder. *Public Interest, Spring 1990*(99), 120-127.

Heyneman, S. P., & Mintz, P. (1976). *The frequency and quality of measures utilized in federally-sponsored research on children.* Washington, DC: Social Research Group, George Washington University.

Hobbs, N. (Ed.). (1975). *The futures of children: Report of the project on the classification of children.* San Francisco: Jossey-Bass.

Hoffmann, B. (1962). *The tyranny of testing.* New York: Crowell-Collier.

Holmen, M. G., & Docter, R. (1972). *Educational and psychological testing: A study of the industry and its practices.* New York: Russell Sage Foundation.

Holmes, E. G. (1911). *What is and what might be: A study of education in general and elementary in particular.* London: Constable.

Holtzman, W. (1960). Some problems of defining ethical behavior. *American Psychologist, 15*(3), 247-250.

Hopkins, K. D., George, C. A., & Williams, D. (1985). The concurrent validity of standardized achievement tests by content area using teachers' ratings as criteria. *Journal of Educational Measurement, 22*(3), 177-82.

Houston, J. E. (Ed.). (1986). *Thesaurus of ERIC descriptors 11th Edn.* Phoenix, AZ: Oryx Press.

Houston, J. E. (Ed.). (1990). *Thesaurus of ERIC descriptors 12th Edn.* Phoenix, AZ: Oryx Press.

Houts, P. L. (1977). *The myth of measurability.* New York: Hart Publishing Company.

Humphries, F. S. (1983). *Academic standards and the student athlete.* Paper presented at the Annual Forum of the College Board, Dallas, TX. (ERIC No. ED 247 854)

Hunt, J. M. (1961). *Intelligence and human experience.* New York: Ronald Press.

Hunter, J. E., & Schmidt, F. L. (1982). Fitting people to jobs: Implications of personnel selection for national productivity. In E. A. Fleishman, & M. D. Dunnette (Eds.), *Human performance and productivity: Vol. 1 Human capability assessment* (pp. 233-284). Hillsdale, NJ: Lawrence Erlbaum.

H.W. Wilson. (1958-1988). *Business Periodical Index.* New York: Author.

H.W. Wilson. (1932-1987). *Education Index.* New York: Author.

Information Access Co. (1990). *Infotrac General Business File Disc.* Foster City, CA: Author.

Information Access Co. (1990). *InfoTrac National Newspaper Index.* Foster City, CA: Author.

Jackson, D. N. (no date). *Computer-based personality testing.* Washington, DC: APA Scientific Affairs Office.

Jaeger, R. (1992). General issues in the reporting of NAEP Trial State Assessment results. In *Assessing student achievement in the states: Background papers* (pp. 285-344). Stanford, CA: National Academy of Education.

Jakubovics, J. (1988, December). Stanley Kaplan: Master Tutor, Entrepreneur. *Management Review,* pp. 16-17.

Jencks, C., Smith, M., Acland, H., Bane, M. J., Cohen, D.,& Gintis, H. (1972). *Inequality: A reassessment of the effect of family and schooling in America.* New York: Basic Books.

Jensen, A. R. (1980). *Bias in mental testing.* New York: Free Press.

John H. Harland Company. (1989). *Annual report.* Atlanta, GA: Author.

Johnson, O. G., & Bommarito, J. W. (1971). *Tests and measurements in child development.* San Francisco: Jossey Bass.

Jonich, G. (1968). *The same positivist: A biography of Edward L. Thorndike.* Middletown, CT: Wesleyan University Press.

Kane, K. (1988). Software to raise SAT scores. *Family and Home Office Computer,* pp.

Kaplan, G. (1992). Testing: Gambling with reform? *R&D Preview,* 7(1), 2-3.

Kelleghan, T., Madaus, G. F., & Airasian, P. W. (1982). *The effects of standardized testing.* Boston: Kluwer-Nijhoff Publishing.

Kennedy, R. (1965, January 26). *Congressional Record,* p. 513.

Keppel, F. (1966). *The necessary revolution in American education.* New York: Harper & Row.

Keyser, D. J., & Sweetland, R. C. (Eds.). (1987). *Test critiques compendium*. Kansas City, MO: Test Corporation of America.

Koenig, R. (1983, April 18). Interest rises in testing by computer. *Wall Street Journal*, p. 29.

Kohn, S. (1977). The numbers game: How the testing industry operates. In P. L. Houts (Ed.), *The myth of measurability* (pp. 158-182). New York: Hart Publishing Company.

Koretz, D. M., Linn, R. L., Dunbar, S. B., & Shepard, L. A. (1991, April). *The effects of high stakes testing on achievement: Preliminary findings about generalization across tests*. Paper presented at the Annual Meeting of the American Educational Research Association, Chicago, IL:

Koretz, D. M., Madaus, G. F., Haertel, E., & Beaton, A. E. (1992). *Statement before the Subcommittee on Elementary, Secondary and Vocational Education, February 19, 1992*. RAND, Boston College and Stanford University.

Kramer, J. J., & Conoley, J. C. (Ed.). (1992). *The eleventh mental measurements yearbook*. Lincoln, Nebraska: University of Nebraska Press.

Kreitzer, A., Madaus, G., & Haney, W. (1989). Competency testing and dropouts. In L. Weis, E. Farrar, & H. Petrie (Ed.), *Dropouts from school: Issues, dilemma and solutions* (pp. 129-152). Albany, NY: State University of New York Press.

Krug, S. E. (1984). *PSYCHWARE: A reference guide to computer-based products for behavioral assessment in psychology, education, and business*. Kansas City, KS: Gale Research Company.

Krug, S. E. (Ed.). (1987). *Psychware sourcebook*. Kansas City, MO: Test Corporation of America.

Krug, S. E. (Ed.). (1989). *Psychware sourcebook*. Kansas City, MO: Test Corporation of America.

Kulik, J. A., Bangert-Drowns, R. L., & Kulik, C. C. (1984). Effectiveness of coaching for aptitude tests. *Psychological Bulletin*, 95(2), 179-188.

Kulik, J. A., Kulik, C. C., & Bangert-Drowns, R. L. (1984). Effects of practice on aptitude and achievement test scores. *American Educational Research Journal*, 21(No. 2), 435-447.

Kulm, G. (Ed.). (1990). *Assessing Higher Order Thinking Skills in Mathematics*. Washington DC: American Association for the Advancement of Science.

Kulm, G., & Malcom, S. M. (Eds.). (1991). *Science Assessment in the Service of Reform*. Washington DC: American Association for the Advancement of Science.

Lee, C. (1988, December). Testing makes a comeback. *Training*, pp. 49-59.

Leiter, J., & Brown, J. S. (1985). Determinants of elementary school grading. *Sociology of Education, 58*, 166-80.

Lenke, J. M., & Keene, J. M. (1988). A response to John J. Cannell. *Educational Measurement: Issues and Practice, 7*, 16-18.

Leonard, J. (1988). Software to help students preparing for taking the SAT. *Electronic Learning, 7*(4).

LeTendre, M. J. (1991). The continuing evolution of a federal role in compensatory education. *Educational Evaluation and Policy Analysis, 13*(4), 335-338.

Levin, H. M. (1983). *Cost-effectiveness: a primer.* Beverly Hills, CA: Sage.

Levin, H. M. (1989). Ability testing for job selection: Are the economic claims justified? In B. R. Gifford (Ed.), *Test policy and the politics of opportunity allocation: The workplace and the law* (pp. 211-232). Boston: Kluwer Academic Publishers.

Linn, R. L., Graue, M. E., and Sanders, N. M. (1989, March). *Comparing state and district test results to national norms: Interpretations of scoring 'above the national average'.* Paper presented at the Annual Meeting of the American Educational Research Association, San Francisco, CA.

Linn, R. L., Graue, M. E., and Sanders, N. M. (1990). Comparing state and district test results to national norms: The validity of claims that "everyone is above average". *Educational Measurement: Issues and Practice, 9*(3), 5-14.

Lomax, R. G. (1992). *The influence of testing on teaching math and science in grades 4-12: Appendix A: Report of a national teacher survey.* Chestnut Hill, MA: Boston College Center for the Study of Testing Evaluation and Educational Policy.

Lublin, J. S. (1989, May 18). McGraw-Hill sets venture with Maxwell, wins promise he won't make hostile bid. *The Wall Street Journal,* p. B7.

Lyman, R. (1989). Give 'em the razor, sell 'em the blades. *Graphic Arts Monthly,* (January), 74-76.

Madaus, G. F. (1985). Public policy and the testing profession: You've never had it so good? *Educational Measurement: Issues and Practice, 4*, 5-11.

Madaus, G. F. (1985). Test scores as administrative mechanisms in educational policy. *Phi Delta Kappan, 66*(9), 611-617.

Madaus, G. F. (1988). The influence of testing on the curriculum. In L. Tanner (Ed.), *Critical issues in curriculum, Eighty-seventh yearbook of the National Society for Study of Education* (pp. 83-121). Chicago: University of Chicago Press.

Madaus, G. F. (1990). Legal and professional issues in teacher certification testing: A psychometric snark hunt. In J. V. J. Mitchell, S. L. Wise, & B. S. Plake (Eds.), *Assessment of teaching: Purposes, practices and implications for the profession* (pp. 209-259). Hillsdale, NJ: Lawrence Erlbaum.

Madaus, G. F. (1989). The Irish Study Revisited. In B. Gifford (Ed.), *Test Policy and Test Performance: Education, Language, and Culture* (pp. 63-89). Boston: Kluwer-Nijhoff.

Madaus, G. F., Airasian, P. W., & Kellaghan, T. (1980). *School effectiveness: A reassessment of the evidence.* New York: McGraw-Hill.

Madaus, G. F., & Kellaghan, T. (1991). *Student examination systems in the European Community: Lessons for the United States.* (Contractor report). Washington, DC: Office of Technology Assessment, U.S. Congress.

Madaus, G.F., & Kellaghan, T. (1992). Curriculum, evaluation and assessment. In P. W. Jackson (Ed.), *Handbook of Research on Curriculum* (pp. 119-154). Washington, DC: American Educational Research Association.

Madaus, G. F., & Pullin, D. (1987). Teacher certification tests: Do they really measure what we need to know? *Phi Delta Kappan, 69*(1), 31-38.

Malone, T. W. (1980). *What makes things fun to learn? A study of intrinsically motivating computer games* (CIS-7 (SSL-80-11)). Palo Alto, CA: Xerox Palo Alto Research Center.

Marklein, M. B. (September 16, 1992). Coaching tips off students to the tricks of the test. *USA Today,* p. 9A.

Maslow, A. P. (1983). *Staffing the public service.* Chelsea, MI: Book Crafters, Inc.

Matarazzo, J. M. (1983). Computerized psychological testing. *Science, 221,* 323.

Mayrhauser, R. T. (1987). The manager, the medic and the mediator: The clash of professional psychological styles and the wartime origins of group mental testing. In M. M. Sokal (Ed.), *Psychological Testing and American society 1890-1930* (pp. 128-157). New Brunswick, NJ: Rutgers University Press.

Mayrhauser, R. T. V. (1989). Making intelligence functional: Walter Dill Scott and applied psychological testing in World War I. *Journal of the History of the Behavioral Sciences, 25*(1), 60-72.

McClelland, M. C. (1988). Testing and reform. *Phi Delta Kappan, 69*(10), 768-771.

McLaughlin, M. W. (1975). *Evaluation and reform: The Elementary and Secondary Education Act of 1965.* Cambridge, MA: Ballinger.

Medina, N., & Neill, D. M. (1988). *Fallout from the testing explosion.* Cambridge, MA: FairTest.

Mehrens, W. A., & Kaminski, J. (1988, April). *Using commercial test preparation materials: Fruitful, fruitless, or fraudulent?* Paper presented at the Annual Meeting of the National Council for Measurement in Education, New Orleans, LA.

Messick, S. (1980). *The effectiveness of coaching for the SAT: Review and re-analysis of research from the fifties to the FTC.* Princeton, NJ: Educational Testing Service.

Messick, S. (1981). The controversy over coaching issues of effectiveness and equity. In B. F. Green (Ed.), *Issues in testing: Coaching, disclosure and ethnic bias* (pp. 21-53). San Francisco: Jossey-Bass.

Messick, S., & Jungeblut, A. (1981). Time and method in coaching for the SAT. *Psychological Bulletin, 89,* 191-216.

Messick, S. A. (1989). Validity. In R. L. Linn (Ed.), *Educational measurement.* (3rd ed.) (pp. 13-104). New York: Macmillan.

Miller, J. (1988, February 24). Regan seeks $900-million education hike. *Education Week,* pp. 1, 17.

Miller, J. (1991, April 24). Bush strategy launches 'crusade' for education. *Education Week,* pp. 1, 26.

Mitchell, J. (Ed.). (1983). *Tests In Print III.* Lincoln: University of Nebraska Press.

Mitchell, J. V. (Ed.) (1985). *The ninth mental measurements yearbook 9MMY.* Lincoln, NE: The Buros Institute of Mental Measurements, University of Nebraska-Lincoln.

Miyazaki, I. (1976). *China's examination hell.* New York: Weatherhill.

Monsaas, J. A. (1992, April). *Cheating on standardized tests: Evidence from a statewide survey of teachers.* Paper presented at the Annual Meeting of the National Council for Measurement in Education, San Francisco, CA.

Moreland, K. L. (1985a). Computer-assisted psychological assessment in 1986: A practical guide. *Computers in Human Behavior, 1,* 221-233.

Moreland, K. L. (1985b). Validation of computer-based test interpretations: Problems and prospects. *Journal of Consulting and Clinical Psychology, 53*(6), 816-825.

Moreland, K. L. (1987a). Computer-based test interpretations: Advice to the consumer. *Applied Psychology: An International Review, 36*(3-4), 385-399.

Moreland, K. L. (1987b). Computerized psychological assessment: What's available. In J. N. Butcher (Ed.), *Computerized psychological assessment: A practitioner's guide* (pp. 26-49). New York: Basic Books, Inc.

Mosteller, F., & Moynihan, D. P. (Eds.). (1972). *On equality of educational opportunity.* New York: Random House.

Murphy, J. (Ed.). (1990). *The educational reform movement of the 1980s.* Berkeley, CA: McCutchan.

Nairn, A. (1980). *The reign of ETS: The corporation that makes up minds: The Ralph Nader report.* Washington, DC: Learning Research Project.

National Commission on Excellence in Education. (1983a). *A nation at risk.* Washington, DC: U.S. Government Printing Office.

National Commission on Excellence in Education. (1983b). *Meeting the Challenge: Recent efforts to improve education across the nation.* Washington, DC: U.S. Government Printing Office.

National Commission on Testing and Public Policy. (1990). *From gatekeeper to gateway: Transforming testing in America.* Chestnut Hill, MA: Author.

National Council on Education Standards and Testing. (1992). *Raising standards for American education.* Washington, DC: U.S. Government Printing Office.

National Merit Scholarship Corporation. (1978). *Guide to the National Merit Scholarship Program.* Evanston, IL: Author.

National Register Publishing Company. (1991). *Who owns whom: Directory of corporate affiliations.* Wilmette, IL: Author.

Natriello, G., & Dornbusch, S. M. (1984). *Teacher evaluative standards and student effort.* New York: Longman.

Neuralytic Systems. (1988). *Announcing Dr. Shrink.* San Mateo, CA: Author.

New York Senate and Assembly Standing Committees on Higher Education. (1979, May 9). *Minutes of Proceedings at a Joint Public Hearing of the New York Senate and Assembly Standing Committees on Higher Education.*

Noah, H. J., & Eckstein, M. A. (1989). Forms and functions of secondary-school leaving examinations. *Oxford Review of Education, 15,*

Nolen, S. B., Haladyna, T. M., & Haas, N. S. (1992). Uses and abuses of achievement test scores. *Educational Measurement: Issues and Practice, 11*(2), 9-15.

Novick, M. (1982). Ability testing: Federal guidelines and professional standards. In A. Wigdor, & W. Garner (Eds.), *Ability testing.* (pp. 78-98). Washington, DC: National Academy Press.

Office of Technology Assessment-U.S. Congress. (1987). *State educational testing practices: Background paper.* Washington, DC: Office of Technology Assessment; Science, Education and Transportation Program.

Office of Technology Assessment-U.S. Congress. (1990). *The use of integrity tests for pre-employment screening.* Washington, DC: Author.

Office of the Assistant Secretary of Defense. (1987). *Population representation in the military services, Fiscal year 1986.* Washington, DC: Department of Defense.

Owen, D. (1985). *None of the above: Behind the myth of scholastic aptitude*. Boston, MA: Houghton-Mifflin.

Paris, S. G., Lawton, T. A., Turner, J. C., & Roth, J. L. (1991). A developmental perspective on standardized achievement testing. *Educational Researcher, 20*(5), 12-20.

Pascarella, E. T., & Terenzini, P. T. (1991). *How college affects students*. San Francisco: Jossey-Bass.

Pedulla, J. J., Airasian, P. W., & Madaus, G. F. (1980). Do teacher ratings and standardized test results of students yield the same information? *American Educational Research Journal, 17*, 303-7.

Peter Dalton v. Educational Testing Service. (1992 August 7). Supreme Court, Queens County (NY).

Peterson, J. J. (1983). *The Iowa testing programs*. Iowa City: Iowa University Press.

Phillips, G. W., & Finn, C. E. (1988). The Lake Wobegon effect: A skeleton in the testing closet? *Educational Measurement: Issues and Practice, ,* 10-12.

Pike, L. W. (1978). *Short-term instruction, testwiseness and the Scholastic Aptitude Test: A literature review with research recommendations*. Princeton, NJ: Educational Testing Service.

Plisko, V. (Ed.). (1983). *The condition of education*. Washington, DC: US Government Printing Office.

Popham, W. J. (1991). Appropriateness of teachers' test-preparation practices. *Educational Measurement: Issues and Practice, 10*(4), 12-15.

Popham, W. J. (1992). A tale of two test-specification strategies. *Educational Measurement: Issues and Practice, 11*(2), 16-17, 22.

Powell, B., & Steelman, L. C. (1984). Variations in state SAT performance: meaningful or misleading? *Harvard Educational Review, 54*, 389-412.

Psychological Corporation. (1978). *Summaries of court decisions on employment testing*. New York: Author.

Psychological Corporation. (1988). *Tests, products, and services for education: 1988 Catalog*. San Antonio, TX: Author.

Psychological Corporation. (1992). *Resources for measuring educational performance*. San Antonio, TX: Author .

Public Law 100-297 (1988). Augustus F. Hawkins-Robert T. Stafford elementary and secondary school improvement amendments of 1988. *P.L. 100-297, 102 STAT. 130.*

Qualls-Payne, A. L. (1988). SRA responds to Cannell's article. *Educational Measurement: Issues and Practice, 7*, 21-22.

R. R. Bowker Company. (1970-1987). *The Bowker annual of library and book trade information*. New York: Author.

Radwin, E. (1981). *A case study of New York City: Citywide reading testing program.* Cambridge, MA: The Huron Institute.

Raivetz, M. J. (1992, April). *Can school districts survive the politics of state testing initiatives?* Paper presented at the Annual Meeting of the American Educational Research Association, San Francisco, CA.

Ramsberger, P. F., Means, B., & Laurence, J. H. (1987). *Military performance of low aptitude recruits: A reexamination of data from Project 100,000 and the ASVAB misnorming* (Final report 87-31). Alexandria, VA: Human Resources Research Organization.

Rapple, B. A. (1991). Payment by results (1862-1897): Ensuring a good return on government expenditure. *The Journal of Educational Thought, 25*(1), 183-201.

Raudenbush, S. (1984). Magnitude of teacher expectancy effects on pupil IQ as a function of the credibility of expectancy induction. *Journal of Educational Psychology, 76*(1), 85-91.

Ray, A. (1984). *Cost-benfit analysis: Issues and methodologies.* Baltimore, MD: Johns Hopkins.

Reisner, E., Alkin, M., Boruch, R., Linn, R., & Millman, J. (1982). *Assessment of the Title I evaluation and reporting system.* Washington, DC: U.S. Department of Education.

Resnick, D. (1981). Testing in America: A supportive environment. *Phi Delta Kappan, 62,* 625-628.

Riverside Publishing Company. (1988). *Test resources catalog 1988.* Chicago: The Riverside Publishing Company.

Robb, C. (1991, April 1, 1991). Reports question validity of 'honesty' tests. *Boston Globe,* pp. 37-8.

Roberts, S. O., & Oppenheim, D. B. (1966). *The effect of special instruction upon test performance of high school students in Tennessee.* Princeton, NJ: Educational Testing Service.

Romberg, T. A., Zarinnia, E. A., & Williams, S. R. (1989). *The influence of mandated testing on mathematics instruction: Grade 8 teachers' perceptions.* Madison: National Center for Research in Mathematical Science Education, University of Wisconsin.

Ross, D. (1972). *G. Stanley Hall: The psychologist as prophet.* Chicago: University of Chicago Press.

Rothschild, M. L. (1987). *Marketing communications.* Lexington, MA: D. C. Heath.

Rudman, H. (1990). Corporate mergers in the publishing industry: Helpful or intrusive? *Educational Researcher, 19*(1), 14-20.

Rudman, H. C. (1987). The future of testing is now. *Educational Measurement: Issues and Practice, 6,* 5-11.

Rudner, L., Stonehill, R. M., Childs, R. A., & Dupree, J. (1990). *Educational measurement productivity.* ERIC Clearinghouse on Tests, Measurement and Evaluation.

Ruger, M. C. (1975). A history of the American College Testing Program (1959-1974). *Dissertation Abstracts International, 36.* (University Microfilms No. 76-00222)

Sagan, L. A. (1988, July 10). What language does your doctor speak? [Review of Medicine & Culture]. *New York Times Book Review,* p. 11.

Schoenfeld, A. H. (1988). When good teaching leads to bad results: The disasters of "well-taught" mathematics courses. *Educational Psychologist, 23*(2), 145-166.

Schramm, W., & Roberts, D. F. (Eds.). (1974). *The process and effects of mass communication.* Urbana, IL: University of Illinois Press.

Shanker, A. (1988, April 24). Exams fail the test. *New York Times,* p. 7.

Shepard, L. (1989, March). *Inflated test score gains: Is it old norms or teaching to the test?* Paper presented at the Annual Meeting of the American Educational Research Association San Francisco, CA.

Shepard, L. A. (1990). Inflated test score gains: Is the problem old norms or teaching to the test? *Educational Measurement: Issues and Practice, 9*(3), 15-22.

Shepard, L. A., & Kreitzer, A. E. (1987). The Texas teacher test. *Educational Researcher, 16*(6), 22-31.

Shepard, L. A., Kreitzer, A. E., & Graue, M. E. (1987). *A case study of the Texas teacher test: Technical report.* Los Angeles: Center for Student Testing, Evaluation, and Standards, University of California.

Shepard, L. A., & Smith, M. L. (1988). Flunking kindergarten: Escalating curriculum leaves many behind. *American Educator, 12*(2), 34-39.

Singleton, M. C. (no date). *Historical survey of issues considered by the committee on psychological tests and assessment: 1895-1976.* Washington, DC: American Council on Measurement.

Slack, W. V., & Porter, D. (1980). The Scholastic Aptitude Test: A critical appraisal. *Harvard Educational Review, 50,* 154-175.

Slavin, R. E., & Madden, N. A. (1991). Modifying Chapter 1 program improvement guidelines to reward appropriate practices. *Educational Evaluation and Policy Analysis, 13*(4), 369-379.

Smith, M. L. (1991). Meanings of test preparation. *American Educational Research Journal, 28*(3), 521-542.

Smith, M. L. (1991). Put to the test: The effects of external testing on teachers. *Educational Researcher, 20*(5), 8-11.

Snyder, T. D. (Ed.) (1987). *Digest of education statistics.* Washington, DC: U.S. Government Printing Office.

Snyder, T. D. (Ed.). (1991). *Digest of education statistics 1990.* Washington, DC: U.S. Department of Education, Office of Educational Research and Improvement.

Sokal, M. M. (1981). The origins of the Psychological Corporation. *Journal of the History of the Behavioral Sciences, 17,* 54-67.

Sokal, M. M. (Ed.).(1987a). *Psychological testing and American society 1890-1930.* New Brunswick, NJ: Rutgers University Press.

Sokal, M. M. (1987b). James McKeen Cattel and mental anthropometry: Nineteenth-century science and reform and the origins of the psychological testing. In M. M. Sokal (Ed.), *Psychological testing and American society 1890-1930* (pp. 21-45). New Brunswick, NJ: Rutgers University Press.

Stancavage, F. B., Roeber, E., & Borhnstedt, G. H. (1992). A study of the impact of reporting the results of the 1990 Trial State Assessment: First report. In *Assessing student achievement in the states: Background papers* (pp. 259-284). Stanford, CA: National Academy of Education.

Stedman, L. C., & Smith, M. (1983). Recent reform proposals for American education. *Contemporary Education Review, 27,* 85-104.

Stenner, A. J., & others (1978, March). *The standardized growth expectation: Implications for educational evaluation.* Paper presented at the Annual Conference of the American Educational Research Association, Ontario, Canada.

Sticht, T. G. (1989). *Military testing and public policy: Selected studies of lower aptitude personnel.* Paper prepared for the National Commission on Testing and Public Policy.

Stonehill, R. M. (1988). Norm-referenced test gains may be real: A response to John Jacob Cannell. *Educational Measurement: Issues and Practice, 7,* 23-24.

Strenio, A. J. (1981). *The testing trap.* New York: Rawson, Wade Publishers, Inc.

Strickland, B. R. (1986). Clinical psychology comes of age. *American Psychologist, 43*(2), 104-107.

Suhor, C. (1985). Objective tests and writing samples: How do they affect instruction in composition? *Phi Delta Kappan, 66*(9), 635-639.

Sutherland, G. (1973). *Policy-making in elementary education, 1870-1895.* London: Oxford University Press.

Tallmadge, G. K., & Wood, C. T. (1976). *User's guide: ESEA Title 1 evaluation and reporting system.* Mountain View, CA: RMC Research Corporation.

Task Force on the Prediction of Dishonesty and Theft in Employment Settings. (1991). *Questionnaires used in the prediction of trustworthiness in pre-employment selection decisions: An A.P.A. task force report.* Washington, DC: American Psychological Association.

Taylor, H. C., & Russell, J. T. (1939). The relationship of validity coefficients to the practical efffectiveness of tests in selection. *Journal of Applied Psychology, 23*, 565-578.

Tenopyr, M. L. (1981). The realities of employment testing. *American Psychologist, 36*(10), 1120-1127.

Texas Coordinating Board. (1986). A generation of failure: The case for testing and remediation in Texas higher education. Austin, TX: Author. (ERIC No. ED 278 297)

Thomas, J. (1992, January 15). Questionable excellence: Illinois principal is accused of ordering faculty to rig student tests. *Boston Globe*, p 3.

Thorndike, E. L. (1913). *Educational psychology, Vol. 1: The psychology of learning*. New York: Teachers College.

Toch, T. (1984, December 5). News firm to buy test-coaching centers. *Education Week*, pp. 1,15.

Tyler, R., & White, S. (1979). *Testing, teaching and learning: Report of a conference on research on testing*. National Institute of Education.

U.S. Bureau of the Census. (1975). *Historical statistics of the United States, colonial times to 1970: Bicentennial edition, part 1*. Washington, DC: U.S. Government Printing Office.

U.S. Department of Education. (1991). *America 2000: An education strategy: Sourcebook*. (ED/OS91-13). Washington, DC: Author.

U.S. Department of Labor. (1987). *Workforce 2000: Work and workers for the 21st century*. Washington, DC: U.S. Goverment Printing Office.

U.S. General Accounting Office. (1979). *Federal employment examinations: Do they achieve equal opportunity and merit principle goals*. Washington, DC: Comptroller General of the United States.

U.S. Office of Personnel Management-Council of State Government. (1979). *Analysis of baseline data survey on personnel practices for states, counties, cities*. Washington, DC: Author.

U.S. Office of Personnel Management. (1985). *Uniform guidelines on employment selection procedures*. (20 CFR Part 1607). Washington, DC: Equal Employment Opportunity Commission, U.S. Department of Labor.

Valentine, J. A. (1987). *The College Board and the school curriculum*. New York: College Entrance Examination Board.

Vernon, P. E. (1954). Practice and coaching effects in intelligence tests. *Educational Forum, 18*, 269-280.

Ward's Business Directory. See Gale Research.

Weiss, D. J. (Ed.). (1983). *New horizons in testing: Latent trait test theory and computerized adaptive testing.* New York: Academic Press.

Wells, P. (1991). Putting America to the test. *Agenda, 1*(Spring), 52-57.

Wigdor, A. K. (1982). Psychological testing and the law of employment discrimination. In A. Wigdor, & W. Garner (Eds.), *Ability testing.* (pp. 39-69). Washington, DC: National Academy Press.

Wigdor, A. K., & Garner, W. R. (Eds.). (1982). *Ability testing: Uses, consequences, and controversies: Part 1. Report of the committee.* Washington, D.C.: National Academy Press.

Wigdor, A. K., & Green, B. F. (Eds.). (1991). *Performance assessment for the workplace.* Washington, DC: National Academy Press.

Williams, P. L. (1988). The time-bound nature of norms: Understandings and misunderstandings. *Educational Measurement: Issues and Practice, 7,* 18-21.

Wirtz, W. (1977). *On further examination: Report of the panel on the Scholastic Aptitude Test score decline.* New York: College Entrance Examination Board.

Wise, A. E. (1979). *Legislated learning: The bureaucratization of the American classroom.* Berkeley: University of California Press.

Wolf, D. P., LeMahieu, P. G., & Eresh, J. (1992). Good measure: Assessment as a tool for reform. *Educational Leadership, 49*(8), 8-13.

Yalow, E., Collins, J., & Popham, W. J. (1986, April). *Content validity conundrums.* Paper presented at the Annual Meeting of the American Education Research Association, San Francisco, CA.

Yerkes, R. M. (Ed.). (1921). *Psychological examining in the United States Army. Memoirs of the National Academy of Sciences (Vol 15).* Washington DC: National Academy of Sciences.

Zamora, G. (1984). *Testimony before the subcommittee on elementary, secondary, and vocational education of the Committee on Education and Labor, U.S. House of Representatives, second session on H.R. 11.* U.S. Government Printing Office, Washington, DC.

Zuman, J. P. (1987). The effectiveness of special preparation for the SAT: An evaluation of a commercial coaching school. *Dissertation Abstracts International, 48.* (University Microfilms No. 87-22714)

APPENDIX 1: ESTIMATION OF NUMBER OF STUDENTS TESTED IN STATE-MANDATED TESTING PROGRAMS

Our calculations of the numbers of students tested in state mandated assessment and minimum competency testing (MCT) programs involved data from several sources. In some cases, for example, where a state only administered assessments, not MCT programs, estimates of students tested were obtained directly from a table in the Office of Technology Assessment's (OTA) 1987 report, *State Educational Testing Practices*. The report presents data collected by the Northwest Regional Educational Laboratory in 1985.

The OTA report, however, did not provide figures for the numbers of students tested in MCT programs. To obtain these latter estimates, the number of students in a grade level in a given state was derived from data in the *Digest of Education Statistics* concerning the number of K-8 and 9-12 students by state for the 1985-86 school year. The K-8 state-level figure was divided by 9 to obtain a rough estimate of number of students per grade level in that state in elementary school. The 9-12 figure was divided by four for the estimate of numbers of students per grade level in high school.

The primary source for data concerning state involvement in state mandated assessment or minimum competency testing programs was the OTA report. Other sources consulted were 1) data collected by the Education Commission of the States in 1985 and reported in table form in the *Digest of Education Statistics*, also concerning grade levels and uses of MCT programs by state and 2) John Jacob Cannell's report *Nationally Normed Elementary Achievement Testing in America's Public Schools: How All Fifty States are Above the National Average.* The Cannell report was not intended to be comprehensive coverage of the extent of state testing, and thus was used only when information from no other source was available or when Cannell's information was clearly relevant.

These various sources contained a great deal of conflicting and confusing information. This lack of clarity prompted us to consider upper and lower bounds estimates of students tested in state-mandated programs. As an example of the conflicting evidence and the way we reported the information, we take the case of North Carolina.

Source	Information Presented
OTA State Assessment Table	475,000 students tested in grades 1, 2, 3, 6,9
OTA MCT Table	Students are tested at grade 11 in MCT programs.
Digest of Education Statistics MCT Table	Students tested at grades 3, 6, 8, 10
Cannell Report	Grades 1, 2, 3, 6 are tested.

In the case of North Carolina, we assume that the number of students and grade levels provided by the state department of education for state assessment programs is true. Since in North Carolina, the state assessment and minimum competency testing programs are not the same, we must add a certain number of children for the MCT program. Here, however, we have conflicting evidence. The OTA report indicates only one grade level tested, grade 11. We estimate the enrollment for a high school grade to be 83,000, and add that to the state assessment number for our lower bounds estimate. The *Digest of Education Statistics* (1987) indicates MCT programs in place at grades 3, 6, 8, and 10. Grade 3 and 6 are already represented in the state assessment programs, so we add the estimated enrollment in grades 8 and 10 to our assessment number for our upper bounds estimate.

In general, decision rules about the estimates included that the lower bounds estimate could never be lower than the number the states themselves reported for the state assessment programs. Further, when a state reported testing in grades 4, 5, and 6, we counted testing at three grades. If, however, the testing was reported at grades 4-6, we assumed, (absent an explanatory note to the contrary, which we have not included here) that this meant that one grade level somewhere between the fourth and sixth grades was tested.

State	OTA MCT # (grades)	OTA State Assess-ment # (grades)	Digest of Educ. Stats. # (grades)	Cannell # (grades)	Upper Bounds	Lower Bounds
Alabama	217,722 (3,6,9,11)	385,000* (1,2,4,5, 7,8,10)	217,722 (3,6,9,11)	209,483 (1,2,4,5)	602,722	602,722
Alaska		15,000 (4,8)			15,000	15,000
Arizona	508,000 (K,1,2,3, 4,5,6,7,8, 9,10,11, 12)	461,000 (1,2,3,4, 5,6,7,8,9, 10,11,12)	78,250 (8,12)	260,002 (1,2,3,4, 5,6)	508,000	461,000
Arkansas	102,000 (3,6,8)	100,000* (4,7,10)	136,000 (3,4,6,8)	29,491 (4)	202,000	202,000
California	1,283,722 (4-6,7-9,10,11)	1,100,000 (3,6,8,12)	641,861 (4-11, 16yr+)	597,486 (3,6)	2,383,722	1,100,000
Colorado	43,250 (9-12)		86,500 (9,12)	76,602 (3,6)	86,500	76,602
Connect-icut	35,750 (9)	127,000 (4,6,8,11, 12)	107,334 (4,6,8)		162,750	162,750
Delaware		67,500 (1-9,11)	15,250 (1-8, 11)		67,500	67,500
D.C.	6,000 (10)	39,000* (1-6,8,9, 11)			45,000	39,000
Florida	464,917* (3,5,8,10)		464,917 (3,5,8,11)		464,917	464,917
Georgia	160,333 (3,10)	320,000 (1,3,6,8, 10)	485,665 (K,1,3,6, 8,10)	158,396 (2,4)	485,665	320,000

State						
Hawaii	38,333 (3,9,12)	88,000 (2,3,6,8,10)	15,333 (3, 9-12)	24,000 (3,6)	114,000	101,000
Idaho	16,778 (8)	11,917 (11)	14,750 (8-12)	14,072 (8)	28,695	26,667
Illinois		7,500 (4,8,11)			7,500	7,500
Indiana		63,100 (3,6)	299,334 (3,6,8,10)		299,334	63,100
Kansas		150,000* (2,4,6,8,10)	157,224 (2,4,6,8,10)		157,224	150,000
Kentucky		710,000* K,1-12	50,111 (K-12),	272,557 (1-6)	710,000	710,000
Louisiana	63,000 (2-5)	120,000 (7,10)	252,000 (2,3,4,5)		372,000	183,000
Maine		48,000 (4,8,11)		14,012 (4)	48,000	48,000
Maryland	156,000 (3,7,9)	175,000* (3,5,8)	106,000 (7,9)	75,102 (3,5)	281,000	281,000
Massach-usetts	195,472 (1-6,7-8, 9-12)				195,472	195,472
Michigan		330,000 (4,7,10)	393,112 (4,7,10)		393,112	330,000
Minne-sota		270,000 (3,4,6-11)			270,000	270,000
Missis-sippi	143,083 (3,5,8,11)	Unstated (1-4,9-12)	143,083 (3,5,8,11)	114,054 (1,4,6)	213,944	143,083
Missouri	60,222 (8)	17,000 (6,12)	60,222 (8)		77,222	77,222
Nebraska	20,667 (5)		20,667 (5)		20,667	20,667
Nevada	47,888 (3,6,9,11)		47,888 (3,6,9,11)	20,000 (3,6)	47,888	47,888
New Hamp-shire			36,362 (4,8,12)	11,381 (4)	36,362	36,362
New Jersey	93,500 (9)		93,500 (9-12)		93,500	93,500
New Mexico	19,250 (10)	55,000 (3,5,8)	19,250 (10-12)	40,001 (3,5)	64,250	64,250
New York	984,638* (3,5,6, 8 or 9,11 or 12)	unstated (3,5,6,8, 11,12)	795,416 (3,5,6,8-12)		984,638	984,638

North Carolina	83,000 (11)	475,000 (1-3, 6,9)	334,001 (3,6,8,10)	327,301 (1,2,3,6)	641,667	558,000
Ohio	426,888 1-4,5-8, 9-12)				426,888	426,888
Okla-homa				41,000 (3)	41,000	41,000
Oregon	34,000 (one grade)	25,000* (8)		4,513 (8)	34,000	25,000
Pennsyl-vania	368,667 (3,5,8)	60,000 (5,8,11)	368,667 (3,5,8)	206,288 (3,5)	388,667	388,667
Rhode Island		1,400 (3,6,8, 10)		16,691 (3,6)	16,691	16,691
South Carolina	281,555 (1,2,3,6, 8,11)	200,000 (4,5,7, 10)	281,555 (1,2,3,6,8, 11)	97,777 (4,5)	481,555	481,555
South Dakota		21,000 (4,8,11)		9,562 (4)	21,000	21,000
Tennes-see			253,251 (3,6,8-12)	120,273 (2,5)	253,251	253,251
Texas	709,084 (3,5,9)		1,639,918 (1,3,5,7,9, 11,12)	730,849 (1,3,5)	1,639,918	709,084
Utah	26,000 (8)	7,500 (5,11)		4,500 (5)	33,500	33,500
Vermont	6,889 (1 grade)		6,889 (1-8)		6,889	6,889
Virginia	147,194 (1-6, 10)	200,000 (4,8,11)	147,194 (K-6,10-12)	67,567 (4)	347,194	347,194
Washing-ton		110,000 (4,8,11)		52,779 (4)	110,000	110,000
Wiscon-sin			176,500 (1-4,5-10)	176,500	176,500	
West Virginia		115,000 (3,6,9, 11)		47,332 (3,6)	115,000	115,000
Wyom-ing		8,000 (4,8,11)			8,000	8,000
TOTAL					14,256,906	11,029,707

APPENDIX 2: CONSUMER PRICE INDEX ADJUSTMENTS FOR INFLATION

All constant dollar figures reported in this book have been adjusted for inflation using the consumer price index for all urban consumers (CPI-U). The CPI is a measure of the average change in prices over time of basic consumer goods and services. Beginning in January 1978, the U.S. Bureau of Labor Statistics began publishing CPI's for two population groups: the CPI-U for all urban consumers, covering about 80% of the national population and the CPI-W for urban wage earners and clerical workers covering about 32% of the national population. In addition to the wage earners covered by the CPI-W, the CPI-U includes professional, managerial and technical workers, the self-employed, short-term workers, the unemployed and others not in the labor force. Since the CPI-U is thus the more general of CPI indices, and the most well-known of a variety of inflation indexes, we have chosen to use the CPI-U whenever we have calculated dollar figures in constant terms. The specific data used in all such adjustments are shown on the next page. These CPI data, for the entire period, 1913 - 1991, are from two sources:

U.S. Department of Labor (Aug. 1989). *Handbook of Labor Statistics.* Washington, DC: U.S. Government Printing Office.

U.S. Bureau of the Census (1992). *Statistical Abstract of the United States 1992* (112th Edn.). Washington. DC: U.S. Government Printing Office.

CPI-U, All urban consumers, base 1982-1984 = 100

Year	CPI	Year	CPI
1913	9.9	1953	26.7
1914	10.0	1954	26.9
1915	10.1	1955	26.8
1916	10.9	1956	27.2
1917	12.8	1957	28.1
1918	15.1	1958	28.9
1919	17.3	1959	29.1
1920	20.0	1960	29.6
1921	17.9	1961	29.9
1922	16.8	1962	30.2
1923	17.1	1963	30.6
1924	17.1	1964	31.0
1925	17.5	1965	31.5
1926	17.7	1966	32.4
1927	17.4	1967	33.4
1928	17.1	1968	34.8
1929	17.1	1969	36.7
1930	16.7	1970	38.8
1931	15.2	1971	40.5
1932	13.7	1972	41.8
1933	13.0	1973	44.4
1934	13.4	1974	49.3
1935	13.7	1975	53.8
1936	13.9	1976	56.9
1937	14.4	1977	60.6
1938	14.1	1978	65.2
1939	13.9	1979	72.6
1940	14.0	1980	82.4
1941	14.7	1981	90.9
1942	16.3	1982	96.5
1943	17.3	1983	99.6
1944	17.6	1984	103.9
1945	18.0	1985	107.6
1946	19.5	1986	109.6
1947	22.3	1987	113.6
1948	24.1	1988	118.3
1949	23.8	1989	124.0
1950	24.1	1990	130.7
1951	26.0	1991	136.2
1952	26.5		

APPENDIX 3: CALCULATION OF STANDARDIZED GROWTH EXPECTATIONS (SGEs)

As explained in chapter 7, the idea of a standardized growth expectation or SGE has been adopted from Stenner et al. (1978) to mean the amount of growth (expressed in standard deviation units) that an average student must demonstrate over the course of one year in order to maintain an average or 50th percentile ranking in national norms. The basic idea for calculating SGEs from norms tables for tests is to find the standard score equivalent to the 50th percentile in national norms for grade x and then to find the percentile score that is equivalent to the same standard score in grade x+1. For example, if a standard score of 25 is equivalent to the 50th percentile in spring grade 4 norms, one need only look in spring grade 5 norms to find the next grade level's percentile equivalent for that standard score. Suppose this was the 33rd percentile. If a student received exactly the same standard score in grade 5 as in grade 4, his or her percentile ranking would have dropped 17 percentile points (from 50 in grade 4 to 33 in grade 5). Using tables for normal distributions, it is easy to see that this student would have to gain 0.44 standard deviation units in order to maintain his or her 50th percentile standing on this test (because 17% of the area under a normal curve lies between z=0 and z= -0.44).

Though the basic idea of SGEs is straightforward, several practical and theoretical problems with them should be noted. First of all, since most publishers now report test norms for both fall and spring of each grade level, it would be possible to calculate annual SGEs using fall to fall norms or spring to spring norms (or even school year SGEs using fall to spring norms). We decided to use spring norms as consistently as possible since spring norms are slightly more common across all grade levels than are fall norms.[1] Second, different publishers report their norms tables in different forms and in different ways. For their tests, CTB/McGraw-Hill and the Psychological Corporation report norms in separate norms booklets (specific ones used are listed in chapter 7). However, for the Iowa Tests of Basic Skills (ITBS), Riverside publishes norms tables as part of its *Teachers Guides* (again specific documents used are listed in chapter 7). Also, for the ITBS, norms tables are reported in a somewhat different manner than for most other major test series. Specifically, the *Teachers Guides* for the ITBS do not provide norms tables showing standard scores and corresponding national percentiles. Instead they provide tables showing national percentiles and grade equivalent scores. Therefore for the ITBS we would look up what grade equivalent score was equivalent to the 50th percentile in the spring norms of one year and then look up the percentile score corresponding to that same GE score in the norms for the next grade's spring norms. Theoretically, this should be equivalent to the procedure followed for the other major test series, and in general SGE results for the ITBS parallel those for the other major test series. However we note that for the upper elementary grades (specifically grades 5-7 for Total Reading scores and grades 4-8 for Total Math) the SGEs for the ITBS were larger than for any other test series (as shown Table 7.1). We suspect that this tendency derived not from the manner in which we had to calculate SGEs from available norms tables, but instead from differences in what content different publishers include in Total Reading and Total Math scores and different procedures and populations used in deriving national norms.

Finally we should note two theoretical issues regarding SGEs. In the text of chapter 7, we noted the similarity of the SGE to the idea of effect size now widely utilized in the meta-analysis literature. However, it should be noted that given the manner in which we calculated SGEs from test norms from grade x to grade x+1, as suggested by Stenner et al. (1978), we are in effect expressing growth in terms of the variability not of grade x, but of grade x+1. To make the SGE more directly comparable with the effect size based on the standard deviation of the control group, it might have been preferable to calculate SGE in

---

[1] The only exception to this general pattern was for the California Achievement Test (1986). For the CAT (1986) we included data derived from winter (Dec.-Feb.) norms for grades 2-12 as indicated in Table 7.1. This was done simply because we could not locate any spring norms for grades 5-12 for the 1986 CAT.

reverse, that is by finding the standard score equivalent to the 50%ile at grade x+1 and then finding the percentile score equivalent to the same standard score at grade x.

Also we note the dangers of trying to infer patterns of growth from cross-sectional as opposed to longitudinal data (e.g. cohort or period effects implicit in cross-sectional data can lead to incorrect inferences about patterns of growth). Two aspects of our work with SGEs lead us to feel that such problems are not severe in the present case. First is the simple fact that we found similar patterns of change across the grades for six major test series which were normed on somewhat different cohorts of students. Second is that preliminary work in comparing SGEs based on cross-sectional norms with SGEs calculated on longitudinal test score changes (see, for example, note 3 in chapter 7) indicates that the two approaches seem so far to yield comparable results.

INDEX

Academic Therapy Publications, 32, 34
  number of tests listed in *Tests in Print*, 30
Accountability testing, 271
Achievement test batteries, 227, 267
  federally sponsored, 144
  group administered academic, 149
  number and percentage of tests in print, 53
  preparation programs, 177
  standardized growth expectations, 232–235
  test coaching effect, 242–244
  testing cost function, 109, 112–113
Achilles, Paul, 21, 23
Acorn Publishing, number of tests listed in
  Tests in Print, 30
ACT. *See* American College Testing Program
Adaptive testing, 170–174
Addison-Wesley Publishing Company, Inc.,
  16
  number of tests listed in *Tests in Print*, 30
Adult education tests, 20
Advance Placement Test, 176
Advanced Systems in Measurement and
  Evaluation, 38, 70
Adverse impact, 213
Advertising, of tests, 196–203
Affirmative disclosure, 198, 201
Air Force Officer Qualifying Test
  (AFOOT/Air Force), 80
Air Traffic Controllers Exam, 176
Albemarle Paper Company v. Moody, 211
Alexander, Lamar, 251n
American Achievement tests, 132–133, 152,
  256
American Association of Teachers of
  German, 36
American Chemical Society, Examination
  Committee of, 35
American College Testing Program (ACT),
  17, 23–25, 29, 65–66, 70
  athletic eligibility determination, 251–255
  company sales 1987 or 1988, 13
  corporate status, 12
  disapproved use of test results for
    determining athletic eligibility, 251
  history, 12, 23–24
  major testing activities, 12

military testing for entrance into officer
  training programs, 80
  1972 ranking by Holman & Docter, 13
  1986 ranking by Fremer, 13
  no sales staff, 194
  number of tests given annually in late
    1980s, 61
  number of tests listed in *Tests in Print*, 30
  revenue decrease, 71
  revenues (annual), 25
  revenues from 1970 to 1991, 70, 71–72
  Ruger's 1975 history of, 7
  SIC classification, 78–79
  state rankings meaningless, 251
  studied in Carnegie/Boyer Report, 131
  test coaching, 183
American Council on Education, 15
American Educational Association, 135, 136,
  273
American Educational Research Association
  (AERA), 190, 273
  no sanctions for violations of ethical
    standards, 278
American Federation of Teachers (AFT), 228
American Guidance Service, Inc., 35
  number of tests listed in *Tests in Print*, 30
American Institute of Certified Public
  Accountants, 48
American Institutes for Research (AIR), 40
American Management Association, 88
American Printing House for the Blind, 34
  number of tests listed in *Tests in Print*, 30
American Psychological Association, 21–22,
  41, 135, 136, 279–283
  advertising of tests, 196
  first formal code of ethics for
    psychologists, 273
  integrity testing Task Force report, 187,
    188
  sanctions for violations of ethical
    standards, 278
  supported bill barring polygraph tests to
    screen job applications, 184–186,
    187
  Task Force report, 217–218
  validity and quality in testing, 190

American Society for Personnel
    Administrators, private sector
    employment testing, 87–88
American Society of Clinical Pathologists, 48
Americans with Disabilities Act, 142–143
American Telephone & Telegraph Company,
    computerized adaptive testing market, 173
American Testronics, 27, 29
    number of tests listed in *Tests in Print*, 30
"America 2000" strategy for educational
    reform (1991), 152, 156–157,
    255–256, 264, 266
    National Education Goals, 132–133
Amity (coaching firm), 182
*Analysis of Baseline Data Survey on
    Personnel Practices for States,
    Countries, Cities,* 83
Anastasi, Anne, 9
Anrig, Gregory, 57, 207, 209, 250,
    251n–252n
APA-AERA-NCME test *Standards*, 279–283
Aptitude tests, civilian public sector survey of
    testing methods, 84
ARCO, 176
Armed Forces Qualification Test (AFQT), 43
    composite score, 44, 45–46
    mental category ranges, 44–45
Armed Services Vocational Aptitude Battery
    (ASVAB), 43–46, 79, 80, 176, 255
    AFQT mental category ranges, 44–45
    content areas tested, 44
    scoring, 44
Army Alpha test, 38, 41–42, 127
Army Beta test, 38, 41–42, 127
Army General Classification Test (AGCT),
    42–43
Arnold, Matthew, 270
Aspen Publishers, 33
Assessment Centers, civilian public sector
    survey of testing methods, 84
Assessment Systems Corporation, 38
    microcomputer-based system to develop
    test item pools, 170
Association of American Medical
    Colleges (AAMC), 48, 287–288
ASVAB. *See* Armed Services Vocational
    Aptitude Battery (ASVAB)
Athletic eligibility, 286
    ACT and SAT test results and, 251–255
"At the margin," 93
Augustus F. Hawkins-Robert T. Stafford
    Elementary and Secondary School
    Improvement Amendments of 1988,
    140, 147
Australian Council for Educational Research,

    number of tests listed in *Tests in
    Print*, 30
Authentic assessments, 133, 260
Author-publishers, 36–37

Bangert-Drowns, R.L., 224, 228, 237
Bar code readers, 161
Barnes and Noble, 176
Barrons Educational Series Inc., 176
Basic Skills Proficiency Testing, 89, 90
Becker, B.J., 224, 228, 238, 239, 241, 243
Beta Inc., 39
Better Business Bureau, National
    Advertising Division (NAD), 198
Bienvenu, Millard, 36–38
Bilingual students (English as second
    language), testing of, 64–65, 176
Binet, Alfred, 171
Binet-type intelligence test, 171
Bingham, Walter, 21, 42
Black, John, 34
Bobbs-Merrill Company, 33
    number of tests listed in *Tests in Print*, 30
Boyer, Ernest, 131
Brigham, Carl, 14
Brown, Robert, 178
BRS/After Dark, 2n, 3, 4
Bruce (Martin, PhD) Publishers, number
    of tests listed in *Tests in Print*, 30
Bureaucratic organizations, essential features,
    153
Bureaucratization of education, 152–155
Bureau of Educational Measurement,
    KS/Emp. State U., number of tests
    listed in *Tests in Print*, 30
Bureau of Educational Research, University of
    Iowa, number of tests listed in *Tests
    in Print*, 30
Bureau of Publications, Teachers College
    Press, 32
    number of tests listed in *Tests in Print*, 30
Bureau of Tests, number of tests listed in *Tests
    in Print*, 30
Buros, Oscar, 11, 274, 275
Buros Institute, 32, 277
Buros-Mitchell MMY-TIP series, 26
Business Education tests, 22
    number and percentage of tests in print, 53

Cadet Evaluation Battery (CEB/Army), 80
California, booklet cost figures, 73
California Achievement Test (CAT), 19, 20,
    178

price data (1986), 112
standardized growth expectation, 232, 233, 234
test preparation materials, 226
California Achievement Test (CAT) Learning Materials (CTB/McGraw-Hill), 177–178, 226
California Psychological Inventory, 34, 37
California Test Bureau (later CTB), 8, 11, 18–21
California Adult Student Assessment System (CASAS), 40
Callahan, Raymond, 127
Cannell, John Jacob, 130–131, 191, 192–194, 195, 222, 224, 226, 227, 320
Cannell Report, 319–323
Career Assessment Inventory, 18
Carnegie/Boyer Report, 131
Carnegie Corporation, 136
Carnegie Foundation, 131
Carnegie Foundation for the Advancement of Teaching, 15
Cavazos, Lauro, 250–251
CASAS, 40
Casebook on Ethical Standards of Psychologists, 196, 197
CAT. *See* California Achievement Test
Cattell, James McKeen, 7, 21
Celebrezze, Anthony, 138
Center for Research on Evaluation, Standards and Student Testing (CRESST), 191
Center for the Study of Testing Evaluation and Educational Policy at Boston College, 40
Certification tests, 58
Chauncey, Henry, 15
Cheating, on standardized tests, 174, 192-193, 222, 226, 227, 275n
Childs, R.A., 25
China's Examination Hell, 221–222
Civil Rights Act of 1964 (Title VII), 135–136, 150, 155, 210, 211, 212–213
Civil Rights movement, 127–128
Civil Service Commission, 48
Guardians Association of the New York City Police Department vs. Civil Service Commission, 213–214
Civil Service testing, 81–84
survey results on testing methods, 84
Clark, Ethel, 18–19
Classification schemes, tests in print, 53, 54
Clayton, 140, 141
Cliff notes, 176

Clinical psychological testing, 34
Coaching, 174-184; *see also* Test coaching
Code of Fair Testing, 273–274, 279
Cognitive Abilities Test, 25
Coleman Report, 136, 150–151
College Admissions Testing, 60, 65–66, 71
numbers of tests given annually in late 1980s, 61
College Board. *See* College Entrance Examination Board
College Entrance Examination Board, 14–16, 23–24, 29n, 38, 48, 65–66
Computerized Placement Tests, 173
decline of SAT scores, and factors contributing, 128–129, 131
ETS revenue, 71
marketing books of old Scholastic Aptitude Tests, 227–228
number of tests given annually in late 1980s, 61
number of tests listed in *Tests in Print*, 30
sponsor of SAT, 248
TESTWISE, computer software to prepare for SAT, 175–176
"truth-in-testing" New York law, 288, 289
Valentine's 1987 history of, 7
"Commercially prepared" tests, 5
Committee on Ability Testing (NRC), 49–50
Compensatory education, 127–128
Comprehensive Adult Student Assessment System (CASAS), 40n
Comprehensive Test of Basic Skills (CTBS), 19, 20, 59
standardized growth expectation, 232, 233, 234
Compu-Psych Systems Inc., computer interpreted reports of psychological test results, 165
Computer-based test interpretation (CBTI), 163–169, 216–221, 277
Computerized adaptive testing (CAT), 170–174
Computerized Placement Management Software, 173
Computerized Placement Tests, 173
"Computers in Human Behavior," 201–202
Computer software, 20, 39, 165–176, 199, 216–221
allowing microcomputers to read and analyze optical scanners' output, 27, 208–209, 276–277
CTB, 20
Comras, Jay, 229
Conant, James Bryant, 150
The Condition of Education, 62

Consulting Psychologists Press, Inc., 34, 37
    integrity testing, 187
    number of tests listed in *Tests in Print*, 30
    psychware products, 168
Consumer price index adjustments for
        inflation, 325–326
Contract companies, 38–39
Contreras v. City of Los Angeles, 213–214
Cooperative Tests and Services, ETS, 15
    number of tests listed in *Tests in Print*, 30
Corbett, H.D., 271
Corporate and Industry Research Reports
        (CIRR), 76–78, 91
Correction Officers Exam, 176
Cost-benefit analysis, educational testing,
        96–98
Cost effectiveness analysis (CEA),
        educational testing, 97–98
Cost function for testing, 119
Courtis Arithmetic Test, 22
Cowden, P., 195
Crammers, 174, 179
"Creationist" perspective, 220–221
Credentialing exams, 20
Cremin, Lawrence, 126
Criterion-referenced tests, 292
Criticism, educational and psychological
        testing, 8
Cronbach, Lee J., 9, 214–215
Crouse, J., 65, 180
CTB/McGraw Hill (formerly California Test
        Bureau), 11, 23, 26, 29
    achievement test preparation programs, 177
    adult education tests, 20
    annual revenues, 14, 19
    catalog, 33
    CAT Learning Materials, 177–178
    company sales 1987 or 1988, 13
    computer software for school
        administration, test scoring and
        reporting, and test construction, 20
    corporate status, 12
    credentialing exams, 20
    customized test building, 39
    diagnostic tests, 20
    key historical facts, 12
    major testing activities, 12
    minority education tests, 20
    modifying national tests to meet state
        specifications, 205
    1972 ranking by Holmen & Docter, 13
    1986 ranking by Fremer, 13
    norms table reported, 328
    number of tests listed in *Tests in Print*, 30
    performance-assessment exams, 262

    sales force, 194
    special education tests, 20
CTBS. *See* Comprehensive Test of Basic
        Skills
Cubberly, Elwood, 127
Cult of efficiency, 127
Culture bias in test items, 215–216
Curran, R.G., 224
Curriculum alignment, 229
Curriculum Reference Test of Mastery, 22
Customized test development, 38–40

Daniels, Arlene Kaplan, 279
Davis, *Washington v. Davis* case, 211, 214
Debra P. v. Turlington, 214
Defense Department, 48
Defense Production Act of 1950, 144
Degrees of Reading Power (test), 64, 178
Della-Piana, G., 279–280
Delta Recognition Corporation, 39
Department of Educational Research, Ontario,
        number of tests listed in *Tests in
        Print*, 30
DerSimonian, R., 224
Descriptors, database, 2, 3, 4
Developmental tests, number and percentage
        of tests in print, 53
Diagnostic tests, 20
Dialog, 2n–3n
Digest of Education Statistics, 319–323
Direct Instruction "treatment," 243
Discount rate, in calculating value of time,
        105
District assessment programs
    breakdown of direct and indirect marginal
        costs, 117
    direct costs per student per test hour, 114
    hypothetical benefit function, 121–124
    total national cost estimates (millions of
        1988 dollars), 118
DLM Teaching Resources, number of tests
        listed in *Tests in Print*, 30
Docter, R., 11, 13, 17, 20, 21, 25, 26, 27, 37,
        135, 275
*Dr. Gary Gruber's Essential Guide for Test
        Taking for Kids* (grade 3, 4, 5),
        176–177
Dr. Shrink, 200
Documentation, 279–280
Drug testing, 89, 90
Duke Power, *Griggs v. Duke Power* case, 211
Dunbar, S.B., 192, 243, 244
Dupree, J., 25
Dyer, H.S., 192

Economic Opportunity Act of·1964, 138–139
Education, bureaucratization in America,
    152–155
EdITS/Educational and Industrial Testing
    Service, 35, 168
    number of tests listed in *Tests in Print*, 30
Educational receivership, 57
Educational Records Bureau, 15
    number of tests listed in *Tests in Print*, 30
Educational reform
    four tracks of, 132
    major cycles (five) contributing to growth
        in testing, 127
Educational Resources Information
    Clearinghouse (ERIC), database,
    2–3, 4
Educational Resources Information
    Clearinghouse on Tests,
    Measurement and Evaluation
    (ERIC/TME), 16–17, 25
The Educational Software Selector (TESS)
    catalog, 175
Educational Measurement, 280
Educational testing
    accountability, 282
    achievement test batteries, 109, 112–113, 227
    answer sheet and scoring costs in 1988
        dollars, 74
    battery test make-up, 63
    benefit function of testing, 120-124
    booklet cost figures, 73, 74
    breakdown of direct and indirect marginal
        costs for state and local testing
        programs, 117
    comparing costs and benefits at the margin,
        119–120
    computerized adaptive testing, 170–174
    costs and benefits, 96–98
    cost structure, 98–109
    direct cost function, 120–121
    direct indicators of growth, 59–66
    dollar volume of sales of standardized
        tests, 67
    Education Index listings under testing and
        curriculum (column inches), 75
    end-of-chapter review tests scanned by
        OMR machines, 162
    estimated testing cost function, 109–119
    estimation method for per hour per student
        indirect costs of testing, 115–116
    estimation method used for direct costs
        of state and local testing programs
        per student per test hour, 114
    forces contributing to phenomenal growth
        in testing marketplace, 155–158
    full cost function, 121–123
    high stakes tests, 265–267, 268, 271
    indirect indicators of growth in educational
        testing, 66
    legislation, 133–149
    legislation from 1979–1988 of U.S.
        Congress, 143-149
    marginal full cost function, 122–123
    misleading test results, 191
    motivation role, 266–267
    negative impact on students, 267
    norm-referenced testing programs, 63
    number of states authorizing minimum
        competency testing and assessment
        programs, 68
    numbers of tests given annually in late
        1980s in education sector, 61
    quality. *See* Quality in testing
    scoring services, 160–161
    social costs 6-10 times greater than direct
        costs, 253
    source of bias in tests, 260
    stand-alone scanners, 161–163
    standardized sale of tests, 67
    standardized sales of tests (1955–1990), in
        millions of 1988 dollars, 69
    test preparation and coaching, 174–184
    test validation, 276, 279–282, 291
    total national cost estimates for state and
        district testing programs (millions of
        1988 dollars), 118–119
    volume per year in U.S., 59, 60
Educational Testing Service (ETS), 7–17,
    23–24, 37–38, 57, 206
    achievement test preparation programs, 177
    bidding on teacher recertification testing
        programs, 207
    company sales 1987 or 1988, 13
    computerized adaptive testing, 173
    corporate status, 12
    criticisms, 15–16
    customized test building, 39
    develops and administers SAT, 70, 248
    disliked use of SAT scores to make state
        comparisons, 250–251, 251n-252n
    Golden Rule settlement, 209
    history, 14
    key historical facts, 12
    major testing activities, 12
    Nairn & Associates' 1980 history and
        critique of, 7
    nationwide computerized test network, 173
    1972 ranking by Holmen & Docter, 13
    1986 ranking by Fremer, 13
    no sales staff, 194

number of tests listed in *Tests in Print*, 30
Placement Research Service offered, 173
ranking as No. 1, 28–29
"research scientist" as employee title, 10
revenues from 1970 to 1991, 70–71
SIC classification, 78–79
software to prepare for Graduate Records
    Examination, 176
Standards, 274–275
"truth-in-testing" law in New York, 288, 289
validation study of NTE for use in teacher
    certification, 212–213
Educational Testing Service/College Board
    books, SAT preparation, 175–176
*Educational Testing Service Standards for
    Quality and Fairness*, 274–275
Education Computer Software Inc., 39
Education Consolidation and Improvement
    Act of 1981, 140
Education for All Handicapped Children Act
    of 1975 (P.L. 94–142), 142–143, 154
The Education for Gifted and Talented
    Children and Youth Improvement
    Act of 1984, 145
Education of test users, as mending strategy,
    272, 284–286
Education Test Bureau, number of tests listed
    in *Tests in Print*, 30
Educators'-Employers' Test Service, 35
    number of tests listed in *Tests in Print*, 30
Educators Publishing Service, Inc., number
    of tests listed in *Tests in Print*, 30
Edwards Brothers, 39
EEOC's Equal Employment Opportunity
    Guidelines, 287, 289
Effect size, 232, 237–239, 240n, 243
    SGE calculation, 328
Eighty percent rule, 213, 214
Elementary and Secondary Education Act
    (ESEA) (1965), 38, 134, 137–142
    amendments to, 146
The Emergency Jobs, Training and Family
    Assistance Act of 1983, 144
Employee Attitude Inventory, 187
Employee Reliability Index, 187
Employment testing, 285, 287
    over-weighting needing reduction, 294
    regulated by federal government through
        Uniform Guidelines, 255
    use increasing substantially after 1980, 253
Engelmann, A., 243
England, "payment-by-results" scheme and
    Revised Code, 269–271
English tests, number and percentage of tests
    in print, 53

Equal Educational Opportunity Survey, 136,
    155
Equal Employment Opportunity Commission
    (EEOC), 287, 289
    employment testing practices' legality,
        210–211
    guidelines on use of tests in employment
        selection, 135–136
Equality of Education Opportunity Report
    (EEOR), 150–151
ERIC. *See* Educational Resources Information
    Clearinghouse
Essay testing, 260, 261
ETS. *See* Educational Testing Service
Evergreen (coaching firm), 182
Examinations Committee, American
    Chemical Society, 35
    number of tests listed in *Tests in Print*,
        30
Exceptional Children, Project on the
    Classification of, 278, 287
Exploration and Assessment System, 18
Eyde, L.D., 199–200, 201–202, 218–219
Eysenck Personality Questionnaire (U.S.
    edition), 35

FairTest, 59
Family Life Publications, Inc., number of
    tests listed in *Tests in Print*, 30
Federal civil service testing, 48–49
Federal employment examinations, 94
Federal sector testing, 81–82
    number of applications requiring written
        tests, 82
Federal Trade Commission
    advertising of tests, 197–198
    test coaching inquiry, 179–180, 183
Fine Arts tests, number and percentage of
    tests in print, 53
Finn, Chester, 152, 261n, 266, 268–269
Firefighters Exam, 176
Fishburne, F.J., 218–219
Five SATs, 228
Follow Through Planned Variation
    experiment, 238
Follow Through (FT) program, 128, 138–139,
    242–243
Foreign Language tests, number and
    percentage of tests in print, 53
Four-fifths rule, 213, 214
Freedom-of-information laws, 285
Fremer, J., 7, 11, 13, 14, 17, 19, 20, 22n, 25,
    26, 27, 28, 36
Friedman, T., 49–50, 51, 88

"Friends for Education," 191
"Full cost" function, 119, 122–123

Gallup, George, 203
Gardner, John, 136
Garner, W.R., 88
Gates-MacGinitie Reading tests, 25
Gay, G.H., 229
General Aptitude Test Battery (GATB), 85–86, 255, 291, 292
General Cinema, 23
General education development (GED) testing, 144
Georgia, test-taking skills taught, 229
Georgia State University, revenues, 40
Gibson (Robert) and Sons, number of tests listed in *Tests in Print*, 30
Gilmore, M.E., 224
Ginn & Company, Ltd., number of tests listed in *Tests in Print*, 30
Ginsburg, A.L., 249
Golden Rule Insurance Company, 209
Gough (Harrison) of U. California, Berkeley, 37
number of tests listed in *Tests in Print*, 30
Government regulation, as mending strategy, 272, 286–289, 293
Government testing programs, 6
Graduate and Professional Testing, 71
Graduate Management Admissions Council (GMAC), 48, 288
"truth-in-testing" law in New York, 288
Graduate Management Admission Test (GMAT)
software test preparation, 176
test coaching, 181–182
"truth-in-lending" law in New York, 288
Graduate Management Aptitude Test, 176, 206
Graduate Record Examination, 15, 176
offered through ETS at Sylvan Centers in computerized format, 173
software for test preparation, 176
test coaching, 180, 181
Graduate Record Examination Advanced Test, 206
Graduate Records Examination Board, 48
"truth-in-testing" law in New York, 288
Graphics scanners, 161
Graue, M.E., 191–192, 235–236, 237
Gray Oral Reading Tests, 33
Green, Bert, Jr., 159–160
Gregory (C.A.) (Bobbs-Merrill), number of tests listed in *Tests in Print*, 30

Griggs v. Duke Power, 211
Gruber, Gary, 176
Grune & Stratton, Inc., number of tests listed in *Tests in Print*, 30
Guardians Association of the New York City Police Department vs. Civil Service Commission, 213–214
Guidance Centre, University of Toronto, number or tests listed in *Tests in Print*, 30
Guidelines for Computer-Based Tests and Interpretation (APA, 1986), 208–209, 276–277

Hall, G. Stanley, 7
Hall, J.L., 63n
Hamill, Don, 32–33
Haney, W.M., 74, 140
Hanus, Paul, 127
Harcourt, Brace and World, 8, 11
Harcourt Brace Jovanovich, Inc. (HBJ), 22, 23
number of tests listed in *Tests in Print*, 30
performance assessment exams, 262
Harlan, John H., Company, 26, 27, 70, 76
Scantron as a subsidiary, 76
Harrap (George G.), Ltd., number of tests listed in *Tests in Print*, 30
Hartigan & Wigdor report (1989), 291
Hawkins-Stafford Amendments of 1988, 140
Head Start Program, 128, 138–139
Heyneman, S.P., 149
The Higher Education Amendments of 1985, 146
High School: A Report on Secondary Education in America, 129, 131, 255
High school equivalency certificates, 144
High-stakes tests, magnitude of distortion in district tests results, 243–244
HIV infection testing, 89, 90
Hodder & Stoughton Educational, number of tests listed in *Tests in Print*, 30
Hoffmann, Banesh, 8–9, 11, 25, 26
Hogan Personnel Selection Series, 187
Holmen, M.G., 11, 13, 17, 20, 21, 25, 26, 27, 37, 135, 275
Holtzman, Wayne, 202–203
Home-Index, 37
"Honesty" testing, 35, 58, 89, 184–188, 202, 217, 254
paper and pencil, 90
small companies developing, 272
Horizon Research and Evaluation Affiliates, 39

Houghton Mifflin Company (HM), 25–26
    number of tests listed in *Tests in Print*, 30
House Education and Labor Committee, 292
House Rule (H.R.) 252, 144
House Rule (H.R.) 901, 145, 146
House Rule (H.R.) 1227, 145, 146
House Rule (H.R.) 2483, 144
House Rule (H.R.) 3154, 148
House Rule (H.R.) 4323, 263
House Rule (H.R.) 4949, 143–144
House Rule (H.R.) 5017, 144
House Rule (H.R.) 5461, 144
House Rule (H.R.) 5586, 145
House Rule (H.R.) 5596, 145
House Rule (H.R.) 5749, 145
Hubbard (publishing firm), 33
Human capital, 103
Human Edge Software, 166, 199
Human Sciences Research Council, number
    of tests listed in *Tests in Print*, 30
Hunter, Frank, 94

Illinois Insurance Agent License Exam, 209
Improving Test-taking Skills (Riverside Press),
    226
In-Basket Tests, civilian public sector survey
    of testing methods, 84
Independent auditing agency, as mending
    strategy, 272, 290–292, 293
Individual educational plans (IEPs), 142
Individuals with Disabilities Education Act
    (IDEA). 143, 154
Industrial Relations Center, number of tests
    listed in *Tests in Print*, 31
Inflation, consumer price index adjustments
    for, 325–326
"InfoWorld," 202
Institute for Behavior Research and Creativity,
    39
Institute for Personality and Ability Testing,
    Inc., 168
    number of tests listed in *Tests in Print*, 31
    teleprocessing, 164
Institute of Educational Research, 39
Instructionally worthy assessment, 260
Instructional Materials Laboratory, Ohio
    State University, number of tests
    listed in *Tests in Print*, 31
Instructional Objectives Exchange (IOX), 38,
    70
    number of tests listed in *Tests in Print*, 31
Integrated Professional Systems, 168
Integrity testing, 35, 184–188, 202, 217, 254
Intelligence Tests, 149

civilian public sector survey of testing
    methods, 84
Intelligence tests (& Scholastic Aptitude), 149
    number and percentage of tests in print, 53
Interest Determination, 18
International Assessment of Educational
    Achievement (IEA), 129
International Education Reauthorization Act,
    146
International Personnel Management
    Association survey results on testing
    methods, 84
Interpersonal Communication Inventory,
    36–37
Interstate Printers and Publishers, Inc., 33
Iowa, booklet cost figures, 73
Iowa series, 20
Iowa Testing Programs, Peterson's 1983
    history of, 7
Iowa Tests of Basic Skills (ITBS), 25, 26,
    160, 178
    norms table reported as part of *Teachers'
        Guides*, 328
    price data (1986), 112
    standardized growth expectation, 232, 233,
        234
Iowa Tests of Educational Development,
    23–24, 25, 26, 131
Ireland, essay examinations, 269
Item banks, 169–170
Item pools, 169–170
Item practice, 239

Jastak Associates, 33
Jensen, Arthur, 215–216
Job Competency Testing, 89, 90
Job Corps Amendments of 1983, 145
Job Knowledge tests, civilian public sector
    survey of testing methods, 84
Job proficiency testing, 89, 90
Johnson, Jim, 200
Johnson, Kathy, 200
John Sexton (coaching firm), 182
Joint Committee on Testing Practices of the
    American Psychological Association,
    273
*Joint Standards for Educational Tests and
    Manuals*, 136
Journal of Educational Measurement,
    126–127
Juku schools (Japan), 174
Jungeblut, A., 224, 238, 240

Kaminski, J., 177, 178, 225, 226, 227, 228

Kansas University, 29
Kaplan coaching chain. *See* Stanley H. Kaplan Educational Centers, LTD.
Katzman, John, 182–183
Keillor, Garrison, 190–191
Kellaghan, T., 261n
Keppel, Francis, 136, 150
Keywords, database, 2
Kleine, P.F., 63n
Kohn, S., 25–26
Koretz, D.M., 192, 243, 244
Kough, Jack, 23
Kowal, D.M., 199–200, 201–202, 218–219
Kreitzer, A.E., 225
Krug, Samuel E., 166–169, 220–221
Kulik, C.C., 224, 228, 237
Kulik, J.A., 224, 228, 237

Laird, N.M., 224
Lake Wobegon phenomenon, 189–193, 225–226, 231, 235–237, 245
    distortion of test results, 47, 130–131, 222, 255, 268
The "Lake Wobegon" Report: How Public Educators Cheat on Standardized Achievement Tests, 192
Larry P. IQ testing case (California), 284
LaValle, Kenneth, 10
LaValle Bill (S. 5200, New York), 143
Law School Admission Council, 48
Law School Admission Services, 48
Law School Admission test, test coaching, 180
Lawton, T.A., 267
Learning disability, 142
Learning problem screening tests, 22–23
Lee, C., 50–51
Legal defensibility testing problems, 210–216
Levin, H.M., 94–95
Licensing tests, 58
Licensure, 84–85, 86
Life Science Associates, 168
Lindquist, E.F., 18n, 23, 25, 135
Linn, R.L., 191–192, 235–236, 237, 243, 244
Lippmann, Walter, 8, 42
Litigation, as mending strategy, 272, 283–284, 293
Local education agencies, federal grant programs for assistance, 148
Local public sector testing, 83–84, 95
Locator tests, 171
Lomax survey, 163
London House, 76, 91
    integrity testing, 187
Lord, Frederick, 173

Los Angeles, *Contreras v. City of Los Angeles*, 213–214
LSAT, 176
    test coaching, 179, 181

McCann Associates, Inc., 35
    number or tests listed in *Tests in Print*, 31
McCarrell, Ted, 23
McCarthy Scales of Children's Abilities, 22
McGraw Hill, 19; *see also* CTB/McGraw-Hill
Machine-readable forms, 27
Machine scoring services, 39
Macmillan/McGraw Hill School Publishing Company, 19, 20, 29, 91
Madaus, G.F., 261n, 269
Mallone, 242n
Manson, Ira, 34
Marland, Sidney, 128
Massachusetts Advocacy Center, 107
Mathematics tests, 54
    number and percentage of tests in print, 53
Maxwell Communication Corporation, 19
Measurement Dimensions, 39
Measurement Inc., 39
Measurement Research Center (MRC), University of Iowa, 18, 23, 135
Medical College Admissions Test (MCAT), 40, 176, 287–288
    test coaching, 181
Medicine & Culture: Varieties of Treatment in the United States, England, West Germany, and France, 219
Meeting the Challenge, 130
Mehrens, W.A., 177, 178, 225, 226, 227, 228
Mending strategies, 271–294
    development of new kinds of tests and assessment strategies, 272, 292
    education of test users, 272, 284–286
    government regulation, 272, 286–289, 293
    greater reliance on the marketplace, 272–273
    independent auditing agency, 272, 290–292, 293
    litigation, 272, 283–284
    professional standards and peer review, 272, 273–283
    professional standards and peer review, interpretation and reliance on judgement, 279–282
    professional standards and peer review, nonadherence and lack of enforcement, 278–279
    professional standards and peer review, politicization of testing, 282–283

Mental groups, 44
Mental Measurements Yearbook (MMY)
    series, 16, 36–37, 50–51, 274, 276
    ninth, 17, 20, 22, 26, 274
Merit systems, 81, 86
    public assistance and public health
        programs, 48
Merrill (Charles E.) Publishing Company,
    number of tests listed in *Tests in*
    Print, 31
MESA Inc., 39
Messick, S., 214–215, 223, 224, 230, 238,
    239, 240, 242n, 280, 281–282
Meta-analysis, 231, 232, 237, 239
    SGE calculation, 328
METRI/TECH Inc., 39
Metropolitan achievement tests (MAT), 20,
    22, 64, 178, 243
    booklet cost figures, 73
    Follow Through (FT) program, 242–243
    price data (1988), 113
    standardized growth expectation, 232, 233,
    234
Microsystems for Education and Business,
    169
Military testing, 38, 40–47, 79–81, 287
    buttressing calls for social and educational
        reforms, 127
    number of tests, 80
    numbers tested, 80
    phases (four), 41
    SAT/ACT batteries, 80
    subtests, 80
Miller Analogies Test, 176
Million Clinical Multiaxial Inventory, 18
Million Dollar Directory, 27–28
Mind Prober, 199–200, 202
Minimum competency testing (MCT)
    programs, 62
    estimated number of students' tests in
        state-mandated programs, 319–323
Minnesota Multiphasic Personality Inventory
    (MMPI), 18
Minority education tests, 20
Mintz, P., 149
Miscalibration, 45–47
Miscellaneous tests, number and percentage
    of tests in print, 53
Misclassification rate, polygraph testing,
    185–186
Misnorming (miscalibration), 45–47
Mitchell, James V., 26, 274
Miyazaki, I., 221
MMPI. *See Minnesota Multiphasic*
    Personality Inventory

Monarch Press, 176
Monitor, number of tests listed in *Tests in*
    Print, 31
Monsaas, J.A., 229
Moody, *Albemarle Paper Company v. Moody*
    case, 211
Mosteller, Frederick, 151–152
Moreland, K.L., 218, 221
Moynihan, Daniel, 151–152
Multi-aptitude batteries, number and
    percentage of tests in print, 53
Multi-Health Systems, 168
Murphy, Linda, 32
Music Competency Test, 36

National Academy of Sciences, 264, 291
National Advertising Division (NAD) of the
    Better Business Bureau, 198
National Advertising Review Board, 198
National Assessment of Educational Progress
    (NAEP), 64, 129, 136–137, 148
    Greenbaum, Solomon and Garet's 1977
        history of, 7
    Hazlett's 1974 history of, 7
    studied in Carnegie/Boyer Report, 131
National Association of Secondary School
    Principals, 229
National Board of Medical Examiners, 48
National Bureau of Standards for
    Psychological Tests and Testing,
    proposal for establishment, 278
National Collegiate Athletic Association
    (NCAA), 286
    user of SAT and ACT results, 248,
        251–255
National Commission on Excellence in
    Education, 129
National Commission on Testing and Public
    Policy (NCTPP), 261
National Computer Systems (NCS), 11,
    17–18, 54, 76–77
    annual revenues, 17, 18
    company sales 1987 or 1988, 13
    computers linked to testing, 160, 162
    corporate status, 12
    dominant in clinical testing market, 165
    high-speed computer imaging system, 18
    history, 17
    integrity testing, 187
    Iowa City service bureau (Lindquist's
        MRC), 17–18
    key historical facts, 12
    major testing activities, 12
    1972 ranking by Holmen and Docter, 13

1986 ranking by Fremer, 13
optical mark reading technology, 135
revenues from 1970 to 1991, 70, 71
sales force marketing to school districts, 194
sales of standardized tests, 69–70
teleprocessing, 164
testing contract revenues, 39
National Computer Systems Interpretive
    Scoring Systems, 29
number of tests listed in *Tests in Print*, 31
National Computer Systems/Professional
    Assessment Services, 168
National Council Licensing Exam for
    Registered Nurses, 176
National Council of Bar Examiners, 48, 51
National Council of State Boards of Nursing,
    20, 48
National Council on Measurements Used in
    Education, 273
National Council on Education Standards and
    Testing (NCEST), 256
    Raising Standards reports, 260, 262,
        263–264, 266, 291
National Council on Measurement in
    Education (NCME), 135, 136, 273,
        284–285
    no sanctions for violations of ethical
        standards, 278
    opposed legislative proposals for
        "truth-in-testing," 287
    validity and quality in testing, 190
National Defense Education Act (NDEA) of
    1958, 127, 134–135, 140
National Defense Education Act of 1983
    (H.R. 2483), 144
National Education Association (NEA),
    284–285
"National Education Goals" (1990,
    President Bush and National
    Governors Association), 132–133,
        255, 259
National Education Goals Panel, 291
National Education Standards and
    Assessments Council (NESAC), 291
National Evaluation Systems (NES), 38, 70
National German Examination for High
    School Students, 36
National Institute for Personnel Research,
    number of tests listed in *Tests in
    Print*, 31
National Institute of Education (NIE), 146
National Merit Scholarship Corporation
    (NMSC, 1955), 134–135, 155
National Occupational Competency Testing
    Institute, 35

number of tests listed in *Tests in Print*, 31
National Parent Teacher Association, 284–285
National Research Council, 9, 41, 42, 291
National School Lunch Act (1946), 134
National standards, 257
National Teachers Examination, 15
National Test Bureau, 287
*Nationally Normed Elementary Achievement
    Testing in America's Public Schools:
    How All Fifty States are Above the
    National Average*, 319–323
A Nation at Risk, 129–131, 255
Nationwide computerized test network, 173
Native intelligence, measurement of, 41–42
NCS. *See* National Computer Systems
*The Necessary Revolution in American
    Education*, 150
Negligent-hiring lawsuits, 186
Neighborhood Schools Improvement Act
    (1992), 263
New England Evaluation Designs, 39
New England Scoring Services, 39
New York State's Standardized Testing Law
    (1979), 287–289
Neuralytic Systems, 200
Neuropsychological tests, number and
    percentage of tests in print, 53
The 1990 Riverside Test Resource Catalog,
    160
NFER (Nelson) Publishing, number of tests
    listed in *Tests in Print*, 31
NLCS, 17
Noell, J., 249
Norming, 240n
Northwest Evaluation Association, test item
    bank, 169
Northwest Regional Educational Laboratory,
    40, 319–323
Nursing, National Council of State Boards of,
    20
Nursing Boards, test coaching, 182

Office of Technology Assessment (OTA),
    319–323
    1987 report, 62
    1992 report, 260
Officer Aptitude Rating (OAR/Navy and
    Marine Corps), 80
Officer's Candidate School Exam, 176
Ohio Scholarship Tests, Ohio State
    Department of Education, 32
    number of tests listed in *Tests in Print*, 31
Oliver & Boyd Ltd., number of tests listed in
    Tests in Print, 31

Oppenheim, D.B., 224
Optical character recognition (OCR), 161
Optical mark reading (recognition) (OMR),
    160, 161–162
    equipment, 76–77
    school building-level equipment, 26–27
Optical scanning equipment, 135
Oral Exams (Structured), 261
    civilian public sector survey of testing
        methods, 84
Otis, Arthur, 22
Otis/Terman group intelligence test, 22
Owen, D., 175, 176

Paine-Webber, stand-alone scanners in school
    market, 161
Paris, S.G., 267
Payer, Lynn, 219
"Payment-by-results" scheme (England),
    269–271
Perfection Form Company, number of tests
    listed in Tests in Print, 31
Performance assessments (testing), 152, 260
    262, 268–269, 292
    civilian public sector survey of testing
        methods, 84
    Psychological Corporation, 272
Personality scales, 35
Personality Tests, 54
    civilian public sector survey of testing
        methods, 84
    number and percentage of tests in print, 53
Personal Outlook Inventory, 187
Personnel Decisions, 50–51
Personnel Management, 50
Personnel Reaction Bank, 187
Peters, Eric, 170
Pike, L.W., 225
Plisko, V., 249
Police Exam, 176
Polygraph testing, 89, 90, 184–188
    Congressional ban in 1988, 254
Porter, D., 224
Practical Nurses Licensing Exam, 176
Practicing to Take the GRE General Test
    Number 4 (ETS), 176
Precision People, 168
Pre-employment tests, 51
Prentice-Hall, 36
    annual sales, 28
    private sector employment testing, 87–88
Primary Leaving Certificate essay
    examinations (Ireland), 269, 270n
Princeton Review, 182–183

revenue growth, 183–184
Private sector employment testing, 87–90
    average investment in testing programs,
        88–89
    effectiveness of test use in employment
        selection, 94
    for job selection rather than job promotion,
        89
    larger firms testing more than smaller
        firms, 89
    literature on business testing as an indicator
        of growth, 91–92
    selection procedure, 94
    selection ratio, 94
The Productivity and Human Investment Act,
    144
PRO-ED, 54, 168
    annual revenues, 33
    catalog, 33
    history and growth, 32–33
    number of tests listed in Tests in Print, 31
    software scoring and report system offered
        for Detroit Tests of Learning
        Aptitude, 165
    special education testing, 143
Professional Development Resources Center
    Act of 1984, 145
Professional standards and peer review, 272,
    273–283
    interpretation and reliance on judgement,
        279–282
    nonadherence and lack of enforcement,
        278–279
    politicization of testing, 282–283
Proposition 48, 251–255, 286
PSAT, compliance with New York's "truth-in-
    testing" law, 288
PsychCorp. See Psychological Corporation
Psychological Assessment Resources, 168
    number of tests listed in Tests in Print, 31
Psychological Corporation (PsychCorp), 8,
        11, 21–23, 26, 29, 168
    annual revenues, 14, 22
    catalog, 33, 194
    company sales 1987 or 1988, 13
    corporate status, 12
    customized test building, 39
    history, 21–22
    key historical facts, 12
    major testing activities, 12
    military testing revenues, 41–42
    1972 ranking by Holmen & Docter, 13
    1986 ranking by Fremer, 13
    norms table reported, 328
    number of tests listed in Tests in Print, 31

performance-assessment exams, 262, 272
sales force, 194
sales of standardized tests in Elhi market,
    69
SIC classification, 79
Sokal's 1981 account of the founding of, 7
Psychological or behavior testing, 89, 90
Psychological tests and personnel decisions,
    94
Psychological Test Specialists, number of
    tests listed in *Tests in Print*, 31
Psychologists and Educators Press, 32
    number of tests listed in *Tests in Print*, 31
Psychologists, Inc., 168
"Psychology Today," 202
Psychometric Affiliates, number of tests
    listed in *Tests in Print*, 31
Psych Systems Inc., 163
    computer interpreted reports of
        psychological test results, 165
    computerized adaptive testing market
        projection, 172–173
Psychware, categories to describe products
    listed in Krug sourcebook, 166–169
Psychware Sourcebook (Samuel Krug),
    166–169
Public Law 94-142, 154
Public Law 99-498, 146
Public Law 100-297, 147–148
Public School Publishing Company
    (Bobbs-Merrill), number of tests
    listed in *Tests in Print*, 31
Public sector testing
    federal, 81–82
    local, 83–84
    overall estimate, 86–87
    state, 83–84
"Pull-out" programs, 141
Purdue University, 29

Quality Education Act of 1987, 148
Quality in testing, 189–194
    advertising, 196–203
    computer-based test interpretation,
        216–221
    contracted test building, 204–216
    diffusion of responsibilities, 208–209
    direct sales, 194–195
    job relatedness, 210–216
    Lake Wobegon phenomenon, 190–193
    norm-referenced tests, 195
    promotion of legal defensibility, 210–216
    request for proposals (RFP) process,
        204–216

test matched to existing district curriculum,
    195
test preparation and coaching, 221–230
validity, 189–190, 201, 218–221, 264
Quotas, in employment hiring, 155

R&R Evaluations, 39
Race-norming, 85
Raising Standards for American Education,
    256
Random House, 178
Ratings of Training and Experience, civilian
    public sector survey of testing
    methods, 84
Reading tests, 54
    number and percentage of tests in print, 53
Real Estate Licensing Exam, 176
Reliance on the marketplace, greater,
    272–273
Request for Proposals (RFP) process, 38, 39,
    194, 204–216
Resource Management Corporation (RMC),
    39
Revised Code (England), 269, 270
Rice, Joseph Mayer, 126–127
Richardson, Bellows, Henry & Company,
    Inc., number of tests listed in *Tests in
    Print*, 31
"Rising junior" tests, 60
Riverside Publishing, 11, 12, 25–26, 29
    annual revenues, 14, 25–26
    company sales 1987 or 1988, 13
    corporate status, 12
Iowa Tests of Basic Skills' norms table
    reported in *Teachers Guides*, 328
    key historical facts, 12
    major testing activities, 12
    1972 ranking by Holmen & Docter, 13
    1986 ranking by Fremer, 13
    number of tests listed in *Tests in Print*, 31
    performance-assessment exams, 262
    sales force, 194
    test preparation booklets marketed, 177
Roberts, S.O., 224
Romberg, T.A., 108
Rooney, Patrick, 209
Roth, J.L. 267
Roughness Discrimination Test, 34
Ruger, M.C., 23
Rudman, H.C., 20–21, 26, 33, 140, 207–208
Rudner, L., 25

Sagan, Leonard, 219
Sales aptitude test, 35

Sales Edge, 199
Sanders, N.M., 191–192, 235–236, 237
SAT. *See* Scholastic Aptitude Test
Scanning Systems, stand-alone scanners, 161
Scantron Corporation (SCNN), 14, 26–27, 29,
  54, 76
  annual revenues, 26, 27
  company sales 1987 or 1988, 13
  computers linked to testing, 160
  corporate status, 12
  first desktop scanner to read and score test
    answer sheets via microcomputer, 26
  history, 26–27
  key historical facts, 12
  major testing activities, 12
  1972 ranking by Holmen & Docter, 13
  1986 ranking by Fremer, 13
  optical mark reading technology, 135
  recent significant trends illustrated in
    testing marketplace, 27
  revenues from 1970 to 1991, 70, 71–72
  sales force marketing to school districts,
    194
  stand-alone scanners, 161, 162
Schmidt, John, 94
Scholarship awards, 24
Scholastic Aptitude Test (SAT), 14–15, 23,
  24, 65–66, 176
  athletic eligibility determination, 251–255
  compliance with New York's "truth-in-
    testing" law, 288, 289
  military testing for entrance into officer
    training programs, 80
  national decline of scores, 127, 128–129
  number of tests given annually in late
    1980s, 61
  old tests marketed by CEEB, 227–228
  score gains and SGEs, 240–241, 242
  scores used by realtors as indices of school
    quality, 290
  state rankings meaningless, 250
  studied in Carnegie/Boyer Report, 131
  test coaching effect, 179, 180–181, 183,
    223, 227–228, 238, 239
  test coaching and rates of gain, 245
  test preparation material, 175, 176–177
  used by higher education as requirement
    for application, 248
Scholastic Testing Service, Inc., 38, 70
  number of tests listed in *Tests in Print*, 31
School delivery standards, 257
  state-level, 263–264
  voluntary national, 263
School district testing programs, 60, 62–64

numbers of tests given annually in late
    1980s, 61
School environment preference survey, 35
School Improvement Act of 1987, 147
Schultz, Theodore, 103–104, 116n
Science Research Associates (SRA) tests, 8,
    11, 19–20, 23, 27, 29
  Achievement Series, standardized growth
    expectation, 232, 233, 234
  number of tests listed in *Tests in Print*, 31
  sales force, 194
Science tests, 54
  number and percentage of tests in print, 53
Scoring costs, educational testing, 109–110
Scoring High, 178
Scoring-High CAT (Random House), 226
Scoring High in Math and Reading (Random
    House), 226
Scoring services, 160–161
Scott, Walter Dill, 7
Secondary School Basic Skills Acts, 145, 146
Securities Exam, 176
Selective Service, 43
Senate (S.) 319, 145
Senate (S.) 373, 146–147
Senate (S.) 493, 144
Senate (S.) 508, 145
Senate (S.) 913, 148
Senate (S.) 1700, 148
Senate (S.) 1701, 148
Senate (S.) 1926, 146
Senate (S.) 2111, 145
Senate (S.) 2367, 145
Senate (S.) 2397, 144, 145
Senate (S.) 2422, 145
Sensory-motor tests, number and percentage
    of tests in print, 53
Sequential Tests of Educational Progress
    (STEP), 15, 19–20
Shanker, Albert, 228–229
Shareware, 170
Shepard, L.A., 98, 106, 191, 192, 195, 225,
    243, 244
Sheridan (Supply Company) Psychological
    Services, Inc., number of tests listed
    in *Tests in Print*, 31
Sienna Software, 168
Silver Burdett, 36
Silver Platter, 2n–3n
Singleton, M.C., 275
Slack, W.V., 224
Slosson Educational Associates, 33
Slosson Intelligence Test, 33
Slums and Suburbs, 150

Smith, M.L., 226–227
Social forces, 125–158
    dissatisfaction and reform, 126–133
Social investment in educational testing, 93–124
Social Studies tests, number and percentage of tests in print, 53
Sokal, M.M., 21
South Carolina, *United States v. South Carolina*, 211–213
Special Child Publications, 33
Special populations testing programs, 20, 22, 60, 64–65, 142–143, 258
    numbers of tests given annually in the late 1980s, 61
Speech and Hearing tests, number and percentage of tests in print, 53
Speech pathology problem screening, 22–23
Spencer, Lyle, 23
Stand-alone scanners, 161–163
Standard Industrial Classification Manual, 78–79
Standard Industrial Classification (SIC) system, 78–79
Standardized growth expectation (SGE), 231–240, 244
    calculation of, 327–329
Standardized testing
    costs, direct and indirect, 5
    purposes, 4
Standards for Educational and Psychological Testing, 190, 196–197, 208–209, 216–217
Standards for Education and Psychological Testing, kinds of decisions to which tests contribute, 49
Stanford Achievement Test series, 20, 22, 140, 178
    booklet cost figures, 73
    price data (1984), 112
    standardized growth expectation, 232, 233, 234
Stanford-Binet Intelligence Scale, 25
Stanford Press, 34
Stanford Test of Academic Skills, 140
Stanley H. Kaplan Educational Centers, LTD., 180–182, 183
    revenue growth, 183–184
State, Department of, 48
State assessment programs
    breakdown of direct and indirect marginal costs, 117
    costs and numbers of students tested per state (1984), 111

    direct costs per student per test hour, 114
    total national cost estimates (millions of 1988 dollars), 118
State Educational Testing Practices, 62, 319–323
State employment testing, 83–84
State High School Testing Service, Purdue University, 32
    number of tests listed in *Tests in Print*, 31
State-mandated testing programs, 60, 62, 67
    estimation of number of students tested, 319–323
    numbers of tests given annually in late 1980s, 61–79
    scoring services, 161
State public sector testing, 95
States
    comparisons of SAT test results in wall chart, 249–251
    establishment of school delivery standards, 257
    estimation of number of students tested in state-mandated programs, 319–323
State Trooper Exam, 176
Steck Company (Steck-Vaughn), number of tests listed in *Tests in Print*, 31
Stenner, A.J., 231, 327, 328
STEP. *See* Sequential Tests of Educational Progress
Sticht, T.G., 45
Stoelting Company, number of tests listed in *Tests in Print*, 31
Stonehill, R.M., 25
"Stranglehold of standardized testing," 141
Strayer, George, 127
Strenio, A.J., 66
Student Achievement and Advisement Test (SAAT), 131
Student performance standards and assessments, national, 257, 263
Summaries of Court Decisions on Employment Testing 1968–1977, 211
Sylvan Learning Centers, 173
System performance standards, 257

Teacher certification exams (state), 38
Teacher rating scale, 35
Teachers College of Columbia University, 29
Teacher testing programs, 97, 98–109
Teaching Resources Corporation, 32
    number of tests listed in *Tests in Print*, 31
Technical Recommendations for Achievement Tests (1955), 273

Technical Recommendations for
    Psychological Tests and Diagnostic
    Techniques (1954), 273
Teleometrics International, 35
    number of tests listed in *Tests in Print*, 31
Teleprocessing, 164
Ten SATs, 228
Terman, Lewis, 7, 22, 42
Test Buster Pep Rally, 178
Test coaching, 174–184, 221–230, 240,
    241–245
    effect on test results, 255
    growth in industry, 254
Testing industry, 7–55
    clinical and counseling testing, 47, 51–52
    composition of test publishers, 247–248
    domination of the industry by handfull of
        test publishers, 11
    employment-occupational testing, 35
    governmental licensing boards, 47, 51
    history and development, 7
    keeping track of who publishes what tests,
        32
    kinds of tests in print, 53
    lack of scrutiny, 7–9
    major companies, 12–13
    medium-sized test publishers, 27–35
    private admissions and licensing boards,
        47, 48–49
    private sector employment testing, 47,
        49–51
    public sector employment testing, 47
    secondary industry, 37–40
    small publishers, 36–37
    social forces contributing to the bull
        market, 125–158
    universities and research centers, 39–40
Testing organizations, 7
Test item pools, 169–170
TestMaker, shareware item bank program,
    170
Test of English as a Foreign Language,
    64–65, 176
Test of Standard Written English (TSWE),
    65–66
Test preparation
    kinds of meanings "in action," 226–227
    seven types of, 225–226
Test preparation and coaching, 174–184
Test preparation material, 176–179
Tests in Print (TIP), 53, 274
    TIP1, 19, 28–32
    TIP2, 15, 26, 28–32, 36
    TIP3, 9, 15, 19, 22, 25–36, 53
    TIP4, 15, 28–31, 33–36

Test User Qualification Working Group
    (TUQWoG), 274
Test validity, 5, 16, 190
TESTWISE, computer SAT test-preparation
    software, 175–176
Texas Examination of Current Administrators
    and Teachers (TECAT), 225
The Educational Software Selector (TESS),
    163
Thesaurus of ERIC Descriptors, 2n
Thorndike, Edward Lee, 7, 21, 127
Thoughtware, 166
Time, value of, to students in school,
    105–106, 108
Title I programs of Elementary and
    Secondary Education Act of 1965,
    128, 139–140, 141, 146, 268
Title II of the Economic Opportunity Act of
    1964, 138–139
Title VII (mandated nondiscrimination in
    employment), 135–136, 283–284;
    see also Civil Rights Act of 1964
The Transformation of the School:
    Progressivism in American
    Education 1876–1957, 126
Trial State Assessment (TSA) of the National
    Assessment of Educational Progress,
    137, 282
Trusheim, D., 65, 180
"Truth-in-testing" legislation, 143–144
"Truth-in-testing" legislative proposals,
    287–289
Turlington, *Debra P. v. Turlington*, 214
Turner, J.C., 267
Turnbull, William, 10
The Tyranny of Testing, 8

Uniform Guidelines on Employee Selection,
    213, 287, 289
    regulation of employment testing by
        federal government, 255
U.S. Citizenship Test, 176
U.S. Department of Education, 248–251, 276,
    282, 290
U.S. Employment Service (USES), 48–49
    job placement testing, 85–86
United States Government Printing Office, 32
    number of tests listed in *Tests in Print*, 31
U.S. Secretary of Education, user of SAT
    results, 248, 249–251, 276, 282, 290
United States v. South Carolina, 211–213
University Book Store, Purdue University,
    number of tests listed in *Tests in*
    Print, 31

University of Alabama, testing center revenues, 40
University of Georgia Testing Scoring, revenues, 40
University of Iowa, 23, 26, 29
University of Kansas Center for Educational Testing and Evaluation, revenues, 39
University of London Press Ltd., number of tests listed in *Tests in Print*, 31
University of Rhode Island Center for Evaluation Research, revenues, 40
U-SAIL, 39
The Use of Integrity Tests for Pre-employment Screening, 186

Validity Generalization (VG), 85–86, 94
Validity generalization theory, 85
The validity of occupational aptitude tests, 94
Variable stopping rule, 171
Vernon, P.E., 224
VG-GATB, 85–86
Vocational Instructional Materials Laboratory, Ohio State University, number of tests listed in *Tests in Print*, 31
Vocations tests, number and percentage of tests in print, 53

Wainer, Howard, 173
Wall chart, of state SAT rankings, 249–251, 276, 282, 286, 290
Ward's Business Directory, 22n, 25n, 26, 27–28
Washington Post Company, 181

Washington V. Davis, 211, 214
Watson, J.B., 203
Wechsler Intelligence Scales, 22
Weiss, D.J., 171
We Must Take Charge: Schools and Our Future, 152
Western Psychological Services (WPS), 33–34, 168
    annual revenues, 34
    number of tests listed in *Tests in Print*, 31
Westinghouse Learning Corporation, 18n
Wide Range Achievement Test (WRAT)-Revised, 33
Wigdor, A.K., 88
Wilkerson Pre-Employment Audit (WPA), 185
Williams, E.B., 49–50, 51
Williams, P.L., 88
Williams, S.R., 108
Wilson, B.L., 271
Winkler Publications, number of tests listed in *Tests in Print*, 31
Wirtz report, 129
Within-group conversion, 85
Woodworth, Robert, 21
World Book Company, 22
WRAT. *See* Wide Range Achievement Test

Yerkes, Robert M., 41, 42
Youth Education and Training for Employment Act, 145
Youth Incentive Employment Act, 144, 145

Zarinnia, E.A., 108
Zuman, J.P., 224, 228

Printed in the United States
33951LVS00002B/32

9 780792 393382